Empire and Black Images
in Popular Culture

Empire and Black Images in Popular Culture

Joshua K. Wright

McFarland & Company, Inc., Publishers
Jefferson, North Carolina

LIBRARY OF CONGRESS CATALOGUING-IN-PUBLICATION DATA

Names: Wright, Joshua K., 1978– author.
Title: Empire and black images in popular culture / Joshua K. Wright.
Description: Jefferson : McFarland & Company, Inc., Publishers, 2018. |
    Includes bibliographical references and index.
Identifiers: LCCN 2018014964 | ISBN 9781476673677 (softcover : acid
    free paper) ∞
Subjects: LCSH: Empire (Television program : 2015) | African Americans
    on television.
Classification: LCC PN1992.77.E47 W75 2018 | DDC 791.45/72—dc23
LC record available at https://lccn.loc.gov/2018014964

BRITISH LIBRARY CATALOGUING DATA ARE AVAILABLE

ISBN (print) 978-1-4766-7367-7
ISBN (ebook) 978-1-4766-3250-6

© 2018 Joshua K. Wright. All rights reserved

*No part of this book may be reproduced or transmitted in any form
or by any means, electronic or mechanical, including photocopying
or recording, or by any information storage and retrieval system,
without permission in writing from the publisher.*

Front cover image of golden microphone and New York skyline
© 2018 LeoTroyanski/video-doctor/funnybank/iStock

Printed in the United States of America

McFarland & Company, Inc., Publishers
   Box 611, Jefferson, North Carolina 28640
        www.mcfarlandpub.com

This book is dedicated to
Iris L. and Arthur S. McLaughlin
The Rev. Obie and Dr. Arthuree Wright
The Thornton and Willis Families
The Reed and Roman Families
Mrs. Frances Bethea Grant
Mrs. Marie Flood Cooper
Dr. David McLaughlin
Ms. Teya Green
The Rev. Brenda Girton-Mitchell and James Mitchell
Metropolitan Baptist Church
Howard University
Peanut

Table of Contents

Preface   1

Introduction: The Empire *State of Mind—The Birth of a Cultural Phenomenon*   11

1. The Lyon Family Hustle: A New Look at the Black Family on TV   27
2. Boom, Boom, Boom, Boom: Lucious Lyon and the Black Outlaw's American Dream   56
3. The Name's Cookie, Ask About Me: The Fierce and Flawed Feminism of Cookie Lyon   82
4. My Three Sons: Reflections on Black Masculinity in *Empire*   110
5. Lee Daniels Doesn't Care About Black People! Representation vs. Exploitation   136
6. The *Empire* Effect: The Revolution Will Be Televised!   170

Chapter Notes   197
Bibliography   216
Index   227

Preface

It is no secret that television has a vital influence on the way we see ourselves and the perceptions that others have about those individuals who look like us. As an introverted, middle class black kid and only child growing up in the Washington, D.C., metropolitan area during the 1980s and 1990s, I found solace in and took many cues from my imaginary friends on the tube. But no matter how much shows like *Leave It to Beaver* or *I Love Lucy* made me laugh, the differences between those white families and my own were pretty apparent. My family was more like the Huxtables on *The Cosby Show,* although we were not fortunate enough to reside in an upscale Brooklyn brownstone. *The Cosby Show* reinforced my parents' values and instilled in me the mindset that it is not improbable for a black family to have both biological parents living together and for them to send their children to first-rate universities, become successful professionals, and avoid criminal activity. While my parents worked at Howard University and often brought me to campus as a little boy, *The Cosby Show* spinoff, *A Different World*—about Hillman College, a fictional historically black college and university (HBCU)—had just as much of an influence on my desire to attend college. The sitcom's depiction of the erratic, sometimes tortured comedic romance of Whitley and her beau "Dwaaaaayne" taught me something about young black love. Perhaps it was *A Different World* that inspired me to complete my doctoral studies at Howard University rather than at one of the predominantly white institutions I had previously attended.

The Lyon's Roar

In 2016, I spent my Thanksgiving holiday at Yale University in New Haven, Connecticut. For four days, I had the privilege of interacting with an eclectic group of brilliant African Americans under the age of 30. The group included two educators, an architect, a film director, a psychologist/actress with familial ties to the Black Panther Party, a budding playwright, and graduate level drama students from Yale and Columbia Universities. During Thanksgiving dinner, we had an exhilarating 90-minute conversation on the state of black images in film, music, and television. Halfway through the conversation we began discussing the polarizing FOX series *Empire*. I say polarizing because most people either love or hate it. *Empire* became a worldwide phenomenon in the spring of 2015 shattering records for a new primetime television show with 15 million viewers weekly and dominating social media discussions. Often described as the hip-hop rendition of the 1980s soap opera *Dynasty*, the FOX series is at times wildly fun, outrageous, and absolutely ridiculous. At other times, its melodramatic approach to storytelling tugs at your heart and forces you to grapple with several inconvenient truths. What made *Empire* unique on scripted network primetime television during its breakthrough debut season was its dedication to what, at the time, were often ignored topics in the African American community such as LGBTQ issues, mental illness, ownership of a publicly traded enterprise, the mass incarceration of black mothers, and the emerging Black Lives Matter.

Media critics have lauded *Empire* for its unfiltered honesty regarding the complexities of the African American family and experience in the early 21st century. The *New York Post* credited the series with opening the floodgates for diversity in television. The paper points to the rise of minority actors Morris Chestnut (*Rosewood*), Priyanka Chopra (*Quantico*), and Ken Jeong (*Dr. Ken*) in leading primetime roles on the major commercial broadcast networks since *Empire*'s first season.[1] Nevertheless, *Empire* makes many blacks cringe. They view the series, which follows two former drug dealers turned hip-hop moguls with "morally" flawed sons, as a modern-day minstrel show and the rebirth of Blaxploitation Cinema. In an era of racially motivated attacks on the former first family, Black Lives Matter protests, debates about black patriotism and the national anthem, escalating gun violence in cities like Chicago, mass incarceration rates so high that they portend a new Jim Crow, and the unsettling presidency of Donald Trump, many blacks fear that FOX is promoting a toxic version of the United States' race narrative.

I must admit that I never intended to watch *Empire*. I saw a commercial promoting the series for nearly three months. If a thought bubble appeared over my head on the night of the series debut, it would have read: "A late night soap opera about drug dealers turned hip-hop moguls? Sounds cliché.... I will pass!" The only soap operas I had ever watched were *Dallas*, *Days of Our Lives*, *Another World*, and *Generations* when I spent summer vacations with my grandparents.[2] A week passed before I watched the pilot using the Video on Demand feature on my cable box. I did not want to like the series, but Terrence Howard got me hooked. Perhaps it was the awful perm he wore or when he stuffed his son in a garbage can for being gay. Taraji P. Henson got me hooked. Perhaps it was her character's diva attitude, floor length fur coat, and doorknocker earrings. The series' compelling narrative definitely got me hooked. The original music in the soundtrack was much better than I had expected. Before I knew it, I was tuning in to my Video on Demand every Saturday morning to catch up on that week's episode.

Empire is among the most interesting scripted series with a majority black cast to air on television in the 21st century. The series is at the forefront of a renaissance in black images found on television and other mediums of popular culture. Lee Daniels and Danny Strong have created a series that is didactic in nature, yet always entertaining. When I began writing this book, there were no other scholarly publications about the series. In fact, many people questioned my decision to write a book on this topic because they did not think the series had any scholarly value. Rather than praising *Empire* for breaking barriers in television or condemning it for sampling stereotypes, I wrote this book to provide an empirical, holistic study of the series. Because I completed this book in the midst of *Empire*'s fourth season, I am unable to address topics and new storylines occurring beyond that point.

My objectives are to do the following: (1) explain why *Empire* works and has been so popular; (2) offer an unbiased analysis of the multifaceted issues presented in the series from an interdisciplinary perspective that can be used for research and constructive discussion by scholars, post-secondary students, and collectives of insightful thinkers on social media; (3) assess *Empire*'s role in the evolution of the African American image in American television and other mediums of popular culture; (4) evaluate the series as a microcosm of past and present macro discussions on family, class, gender, power, authenticity, and respectability politics in the African American community; (5) assess quantitative and qualitative data collected from 100 respondents to determine how some African Americans, between the ages of 18 and 40-years-old, view the series; (6) discuss what I call the *Empire* Effect, which is the series' influence on the development of new television programming targeting primarily African American audiences between June 2015 and June 2018; and (7) use *Empire* as a case study for evaluating the effectiveness of black empowerment in Hollywood. How are these developments in Hollywood strengthening the entire African American community and influencing race relations in the country?

Empire is a chapter within the metanarrative of the African American experience. It is an invigorating topic to research because it presents a kaleidoscopic list of pertinent subject matter for anyone interested in African

American studies, gender, media, or popular culture. I base my definition of popular culture on Ray Browne's theory that it is the study of everyday life.[3] Since this series is so polarizing, I expect a myriad of strong opinions on this subject. The extant literature devoted to *Empire* is limited to a master's thesis, newspaper and magazine articles, blogs, think pieces, and social media posts. This is not surprising since the series just premiered in 2015. Hopefully this book will fill in the literary gaps and serve as a provocative analysis of the series. Four readings that were particularly useful in the early stages of my research were Christine Acham's *Revolution Televised: Prime Time and the Struggle for Black Power* (2004); Donald Bogle's *Primetime Blues: African Americans on Network Television* (2001); Herman Gray's *Watching Race: Television and the Struggle for Blackness* (2004); Darnell M. Hunt's *Channeling Blackness: Studies on Television and Race in America* (2004); and Kristal Brent Zook's *Color by Fox: The Fox Network and the Revolution in Black Television* (1999). Hunt's edited work contained interesting readings by Molefi Kete Asante and Stuart Hall pertaining to race on television. Other helpful sources included dissertations and journal articles on blackness in television and popular culture.

I have tried to write this book for an audience interested in the media's role in shaping perceptions of blackness and race relations in America. My target audience is undergraduate college students in American studies, African American studies, gender studies, and media studies courses; graduate level researchers; and Millennials and Generation Xers engaged in conversations on these topics on social media sites like (Black) Twitter. The fact that *Empire* is a primetime soap opera influenced by past series such as *Dynasty* and *Dallas* should not be ignored when evaluating the series. I use the writings of soap opera scholars Ien Ang, Charlotte Brunson, Christine Geraghty, and Tania Modleski to explain how *Empire* applies the melodramatic structure of past soap operas to draw in its target audience.

Family is the underlying theme of *Empire*. Chapter 1 discusses the series' portrayal of the African American family. The literature review for this chapter began with E. Franklin Frazier's *Negro Family in the United States;* Herbert Gutman's *The Black Family in Slavery and Freedom* and John Hope Franklin's *From Slavery to Freedom*. Since familial dysfunction is a major aspect of *Empire,* I examined Daniel P. Moynihan's controversial 1965 report, "The Negro Family," which blamed black pathologies and broken households on the effects of slavery and black mothers. Jennifer Fogel's dissertation, "A Modern Family: The Performance of 'Family' and Familialism in Contemporary Television Series," provided perspectives on the depictions of the American family on television. Much of her research focused on white families; however, Fogel acknowledged the absence of the black nuclear family from most traditional television narratives. Robin D.G. Kelley's *Yo' Mama's Disfunktional!: Fighting the Culture Wars in Urban America* (1998), Stephanie Coontz's *The Way We Never Were: American Families and the Nostalgia Trap* (1993), and academic articles on black fatherhood and motherhood were also useful.

In my preparation for analyzing *Empire*'s Lyon family in relation to other fictional television black families, I watched entire seasons of *Good Times, The Jeffersons, The Fresh Prince of Bel Air, The Bernie Mac Show, Black-ish,* and *The Carmichael Show* on Netflix and Hulu. I watched all eight seasons of *The Cosby Show* and read multiple academic reviews of the series to discuss the dichotomy between its idealized Huxtable family and that of the broken Lyon family portrayed in *Empire*. Unlike *The Cosby Show*, which has been placed on a pedestal as a model of respectability, *Empire* is stringently attacked for making black families look bad. I like to call the Lyons a hip-hop hybrid of the Jacksons (Motown's first family) and *The Sopranos* (HBO's first crime family). However, my research revealed that many of the show's representations of the black family are just as, if not more, nuanced than those found in *The Cosby Show*. Readings by Donald Bogle, Michael Eric Dyson, Henry Louis Gates, Jr., and Sut Jhally and Justin Lewis challenge the myth of the idealized black familial experience presented in *The Cosby Show*.

Empire's depiction of the elite black family deviates from traditional depictions found in E. Franklin Frazier's *Black Bourgeoisie* (1957), Lawrence Otis Graham's *Our Kind of People* (2000), and Margo Jefferson's *Negroland* (2015). Unlike these other elite blacks who arrived at their distinct social standing through inheritance, higher education, or hard work, the Lyon's wealth originated from the illegal drug trade of the ghetto. Even their association with the hip-hop industry is disruptive to the prim and proper image of the black bourgeoisie. The Lyon family's reputation puts them at odds with rival wealthy black and white families in the series. What the Lyons do have in common with other fictional elite black families on other contemporary series like Oprah's *Greenleaf* and Tyler Perry's *The Haves and the Have Nots* is an enormous amount of dysfunction. Do such depictions of the black elite simply mimic the behavior of the Ewings and the Carringtons—wealthy white families on primetime soap operas *Dallas* and *Dynasty*; or do they promote underlying messages, dating back to The Moynihan Report, about the failure of the African American family? And what does *Empire*'s high viewership in black households say about the state of the African American family?

Gender is another pivotal theme in *Empire*. The next three chapters highlight the multitude of ways the series addresses this topic. Chapter 2 places Lucious Lyon (Terrence Howard), *Empire*'s patriarch, in the historical context of the African American male outlaw. Since the late 19th century multiple black men have challenged existing power structures and law enforcement in an attempt to achieve the American dream. For these men, the American dream meant equality, power, being providers for their family, and having the freedom to carry themselves like men (not boys). For some men, the criminal underworld became an enticing alternative to civil disobedience and Black Nationalism. Success excused all wrongdoing. Jesus Christ, in St. Mark 8:36, asks the question: "What good is it for someone to gain the whole world, yet forfeit their soul?" This question is pertinent to many of these outlaws.

Cecil Brown's *Stagolee Shot Billy* (2004), William Van Deburg's *Hoodlums* (2004), John Roberts' *From Trickster to Badman* (1990), and biographies of African American outlaws shaped my understanding of the historical significance of these figures. Since the turn of the 20th century the African American male outlaw has become an anti-hero in folklore, 1970s Blaxploitation Cinema, black gangster films of the early 1990s, hip-hop albums, and more recent television dramas *The Wire* (2002–2008), *Power* (2014–), and *Empire*. Shawn "Jay Z" Carter, a crack cocaine dealer turned hip-hop mogul, has been credited as the inspiration for the *Great Gatsby*—like characterization of the nouveau riche exemplified by Lucious Lyon. Mark Anthony Neal and Miles White are among the scholars to dissect Jay-Z's rise to glory. How does Lucious Lyon compare to these past and present examples of the black outlaw? What does the celebration of, and interest in, these outlaws in black popular culture say about the constituents of heroism, success and the American dream within the African American community?

Chapter 3 delves into the fierce yet flawed feminism of *Empire* matriarch Cookie Lyon (Taraji P. Henson). Is Cookie Lyon a feminist? This is a complex question given black women's unique relationship with the term. Many black women would rather be called womanists because they associate feminism with middle-class white women. Those who call themselves feminists may recognize clear distinctions within their brand of feminism. In the eyes of several media critics, Cookie is at the forefront of a feminist movement in network and cable primetime television being led by other fictional black female characters—namely Olivia Pope (*Scandal*), Annalise Keating (*How to Get Away with Murder*), and Mary Jane Paul (*Being Mary Jane*). She rivals white female outlaws on new series like TNT's *Animal Kingdom* (2016–) and USA's *Queen of the South* (2016–). She exhibits the feminist characteristics of previous primetime soap opera icons such as Alexis Carrington (Joan Collins) and Sue Ellen Ewing (Linda Gray).

Cookie is a contemporary version of the "badass" heroines popularized by Pam Grier in the 1970s Blaxploitation Cinema era films *Coffy* (1973) and *Foxy Brown* (1974). Grier's characters, like Cookie, juxtaposed images of toughness with vulnerability and sex appeal with intelligence. Like Grier's heroines, Cookie raises debates about what constitutes a respectable example of black feminism and womanism. For some she is a caricature—too loud and "ghetto" to be an appropriate role model for young black women and girls. In my opinion, Cookie is an embodiment of the fierce and flawed values of empowerment, independence, and sexuality promoted by Pam Grier, many contemporary black female heroines, and by hip-hop stars—most notably Beyoncé.

In Chapter 4 I discuss the illegible characterizations of black masculinity in *Empire* presented by the three sons of Lucious and Cookie Lyon. Andre Lyon (Trai Byers), the eldest son, is an outlier in his own family, as well as in some corners of the black America; yet he is the media's idealized representation of black men. He is not a rapper, singer, or an athlete. He is not a thug or gangster like his daddy. Nor does he exhibit any stereotypical "black" behavior. Andre is Ivy League educated and married to a white woman for a period. His white wife, academic prowess, and lack of street smarts make him less of "a real black man" in the eyes of his father. Andre suffers from a bipolar disorder, which his parents refer to as a "white" disease. At times Andre feels cut off from "the culture." He offers a case study on upper class black men and the pitfalls they face when attempting to not just gain mainstream acceptance, but to transcend their race.

Jamal Lyon (Jussie Smollett), the middle son, embodies the struggles of gay black men to achieve acceptance within their families, the black community, and hip-hop. Jamal defines manhood on his own terms and boldly defies many of the stereotypes that have been long associated with the LGBTQ community. Robert Humphrey does an excellent job addressing homosexuality in the series and provides a useful literature review on this subject in his 2016 master's thesis, "Representing Race, Gender, and Sexuality in Empire: (Counter)Hegemonic Masculinity, Black Fatherhood, and Homosexuality in Primetime Television."

Hakeem Lyon (Bryshere Gray), the youngest son, offers a fascinating perspective on the performance of black masculinity within hip-hop today. He embodies the reckless characteristics of many of today's young artists like Chris Brown. Furthermore, Hakeem's self-identity is in a continual state of flux. He mirrors the shifting paradigms of masculine performance found in hip-hop, resulting from the recent success of Kanye West and rapper Drake. At times Hakeem presents a multidimensional image of black masculinity. However, he frequently exhibits the hyper-macho characteristics historically aligned with hip-hop and still popularized by artists like Migos when he feels the need to prove his authenticity as a "real" black man.

Empire is the most watched series for blacks 18 to 40-years-old; therefore in Chapter 5 I describe quantitative and qualitative data collected by surveying 100 respondents (via SurveyMonkey) between the ages of 18 and 40 from April to October 2016. Nearly all respondents classified themselves as black or African American. The respondents resided in Maryland, Virginia, South Carolina, Ohio, Chicago, Connecticut, and Washington, D.C. They consisted of college students from the University of Maryland Eastern Shore and Howard University; young professionals whom I met in previous work environments, church, graduate school, the gym, and the barbershop; and friends and family members from around the country. One of the deficiencies of the survey is that the majority of respondents are female, black, college educated, and middle class. It would be interesting to see how much the responses would differ with a more diverse group. Some respondents failed to answer every question or gave little thought to their written responses to the essay questions. 50 percent of the respondents thought that the series was setting black progress backward. One respondent asked, "Why does television's most successful black family have to be so flawed and dysfunctional?" When I presented a paper on my initial research at a 2015 academic conference on African American history and culture an older black female professor said that she does not watch *Empire* because she believes that FOX's promotion of the series is a part of a larger conspiracy to tarnish the black image by promoting historical stereotypes and a false sense of racial uplift.

In Chapter 5 I discuss how FOX has a history of striking gold with series like *In Living Color* and *Martin* that have catered to young "urban" blacks and suburban white kids in the MTV generation since the early 1990s. Kristal Brent Zook's *Color by Fox: The Fox Network and the Revolution in Black Television* documents much of this history. FOX was also home to *Cops*, a reality show that often depicted the arrests of scary black criminals for 25 seasons. The Fox News Channel, its sister network, is notorious for its vilification of black leaders and issues and its unabashed acceptance of divisive demagogues. Does a conspiracy really exist? How much does respectability politics play in the rejection of *Empire* by some middle-class blacks? How do black Millennials on social media sites (i.e., Black Twitter) impact the series' popularity and opinions on its depictions of blackness? Finally, does a popular television series like *Empire* have a responsibility to do more than simply entertain audiences and make money? I will address these questions in this chapter.

The book concludes with Chapter 6, a discussion of what I call "the *Empire* Effect." I believe that the evidence shows that *Empire*'s success has influenced newly scripted black programming that has appeared on network television, cable, and digital streaming services between June 2015 and June 2018. I think it is fair to give *Empire* some credit for this current revolution on television that has produced groundbreaking series such as *Atlanta, Insecure, Greenleaf, Luke Cage, Queen Sugar* and *The Carmichael Show*. Blacks are also appearing in lead roles on interracial and primarily white series such as *24: Legacy, Ballers, Claws, Lethal Weapon, Snowfall*, and *This Is Us*. Moreover, this renaissance in black programming is providing new opportunities for black directors, producers, screenwriters, showrunners, costume designers, musicians, grips, and publicists. Blacks have a level of power, not seen in previous decades, because they have control over every aspect of their series. These advancements on television come at a time when blacks are also making history in cinema with critically acclaimed films like *A Wrinkle in Time, Black Panther, Detroit, Get Out, Fences, Hidden Figures, I Am Not Your Negro, Mudbound,* and *Moonlight.* How do these new television series compare and contrast with *Empire*? How do they reflect recent trends in the portrayal of the African American community? What is their overall value to the African American community and race relations in America?

Introduction: The Empire State of Mind
The Birth of a Cultural Phenomenon

> "Hip-Hop wasn't born on Wall Street, Miss Whiteman. Where we come from, if the cops raid your house that makes you a G. If the Feds raid your house that makes you an O.G."[1]
> —Lucious Lyon

Although television, like other aggregations of popular culture, has not always been respected in academic circles, it has since its inception provided a dominant space for representations of race, class, gender and cultural politics within America. When significant numbers of African Americans began appearing on television between the 1970s and 1990s, some scholars feared that whites would set their expectations of the entire African American community based on those fictional examples of blackness and archetypes in mass media. According to sociologist Herman Gray, television has historically presented blackness within the boundaries of white, middle-class, patriarchal values and beliefs.[2] Having the power to control their image has always been a consequential facet of African Americans' long civil rights struggle for equality and respect. "We might read television treatments of blackness not just in terms of how they measure up to the empirical world beyond the small screen, but in terms of the aesthetic and formal strategies that challenge or reproduce historical treatments of blacks," says Gray.[3]

Before the introduction of television, Americans found their entertainment at the movies and on radio. The first full-length American feature film was D.W. Griffith's Civil War era romance, *Birth of a Nation* (1915). In the film corrupt northern white carpetbaggers, black politicians, and black soldiers seize control of the South during the Reconstruction, prompting the chivalrous, Christian white men of the Ku Klux Klan (KKK) to save the day.

All the film's black characters were portrayed by white actors disguised in blackface. The National Association for the Advancement of Colored People (NAACP) unsuccessfully protested the openings in New York and Los Angeles. To combat the negative stereotypes being perpetuated by the film, Emmett J. Scott, Oscar Michaeux, and the brothers Noble P. and George Johnson rose to the forefront. Emmett J. Scott, one of Booker T. Washington's closest advisors created the film *The Birth of a Race,* billed as the true story of the Negro.[4] The Johnson brothers launched The Lincoln Motion Picture Company—the nation's first company to produce race films—in 1916. Race films, popular from 1916 to the early 1950s, featured all-black casts. Oscar Michaeux produced and directed more than 44 films between 1919 and 1948.[5] Micheaux was a distiller of the black experience whose work was decades ahead of his time. Historian Gerald Butters says these race films countered the misconceptions of blackness and reshaped constructions of black masculine identity.[6]

By the 1920s Alain Locke, the chair of the Department of Philosophy at Howard University, began advocating for a "New Negro" that would counter the stigmatizing images of blackness. Locke inspired the aesthetic of the cultural movement known as the Harlem Renaissance and highlighted the promotion of the "New Negro" through the arts and black urban life in cities like New York, Chicago, and Washington, D.C.[7] He believed that blacks should use the arts and entertainment for the sole purpose of inspiring social consciousness and uplifting the race.[8] In spite of the push for respectability, Hollywood remained committed to promoting racist archetypes of blackness and derogatory depictions of the African American community. Lincoln Perry, who went by the stage name Stepin Fetchit, appeared in 54 films between 1925 and 1976, making him Hollywood's first black millionaire.[9] Perry was an educated man who wrote thoughtful articles for the *Chicago Defender,* but he was commonly associated with what scholar Donald Bogle calls cooning. Coons were black characters who were comical, lazy, illiterate, emasculated, childlike, and shuffled when they walked. Walt Disney cartoons also spread racist imagery in their children's films.

During the 1940s, musical films featuring all-black casts, such as *Cabin in the Sky* (1943) and *Stormy Weather* (1943), showcased the musical and theatrical acumen within the African American community. The 1944 World War II propaganda film, *The Negro Soldier,* offered a new image of blackness within the U.S. armed forces. By the 1950s movie stars Sidney Poitier, Harry Belafonte, and Dorothy Dandridge continued to redefine the black image. Dandridge received an Academy Award nomination in 1954 for her performance in *Carmen Jones* (1954). Ten years later Poitier became the first black man to win an Academy Award for Best Actor in the film *Lilies of the Field*. Other notable films featuring blacks in the 1950s included *Imitation of Life* (1959), a remake of a 1934 film about a light-skinned black woman passing for white.

The African American voice came to television in the early 1950s with *The Beulah Show* (1950–1952) on ABC and *The Amos 'n' Andy Show* (1951–1953) on CBS. The NAACP accused *Beulah* of glorifying the mammy image that harkened back to the Lost Cause myths found in the 1939 film *Gone with the Wind*.[10] The civil rights organization viewed *Amos 'n' Andy* as an updated minstrel show. Minstrelsy was one of the earliest examples of cultural appropriation and racial cross-dressing, in which whites and blacks interpreted and misinterpreted each other for decades. Ralph Ellison said of this art form, "The Negro is reduced to a negative sign in a comedy of the grotesque and unacceptable."[11] Beginning in 1951 the NAACP led a national boycott to ban the popular television series. The NAACP, adopting the position that art should only uplift the race, argued that the sitcom would stain the reputation of all blacks. *Amos 'n' Andy* was cancelled in 1953 but remained in syndication until it was officially banned from the air for almost 40 years beginning in 1966.[12]

Over the next 50 years the African American community remained engaged in an ongoing struggle for authentic depictions of their experience. Blacks used television to promote their socio-political agenda, but since television was controlled by whites, the image of blackness was transmitted primarily through a white perspective.[13] This was evident in interracial series with black leads such as *I Spy* (1965–1968), and *Julia* (1968–1971). The black characters on these series were often accused of being detached from the ongoing struggles within segregated black environments. Nevertheless, these series gave viewers a taste of what was to come in television and film in the ensuing decades.

Throughout the 1970s sitcoms gave white America a glimpse of black family life. In her book *Revolution Televised: Prime Time and the Struggle for Black Power* (2005), professor Christine Acham argues that the humor in these sitcoms captured the triumphs and failures of people of color coming on the heels of the social activism of the turbulent sixties.[14] For example, *Sanford and Son* (1972–1977) was about a black father and his adult son living in a post-riots Watts neighborhood.[15] *Good Times* (1974–1979), the first sitcom about a two-parent African American family, explored the topics of poverty, welfare, and social inequality in ways not seen in most of today's television programming. Both series, along with *The Jeffersons* (1975–1985), which introduced television's first middle-class black family, were created by Norman

Lear, a white progressive television writer, who made it his mission to normalize the African American family experience.[16]

The success of black television in the 1970s paved the way for *The Cosby Show* (1984–1992), which offered viewers an unprecedented celebration of black achievement in the form of an affluent, wholesome family who unapologetically embraced African American culture and history. *The Cosby Show* arrived at a time in the nation's history characterized by the villainization of the black underclass as immoral and irresponsible by conservative politicians. Herman Gray credits the sitcom's "use of Blackness and African American culture as a kind of emblematic code of difference."[17] The fictional Huxtables on the sitcom showed white viewers that black families were not different from their own. *The Cosby Show* initiated a call for new black programming that targeted crossover audiences from the mid–1980s through the mid–1990s. *A Different World* (1987–1993), *Frank's Place* (1987–1988), *The Fresh Prince of Bel-Air* (1990–1996), and *Family Matters* (1989–1997) were byproducts of its success. The growing abundance of home video devices and cable in white households led to declining viewership for network television during the 1980s. However, black families with less money and fewer entertainment options were still faithfully tuning into network television. *Newsweek* reported that blacks watched the networks' programming at a rate that was 40 percent higher than white Americans. Network executives that had initially been resistant realized that black viewers equaled money and soon began greenlighting large numbers of black programs—especially those that could be marketed to a more mainstream audience.[18]

As diversity on network television began waning in the mid–1990s, FOX and upstart mini-networks United Paramount Network (UPN) and the Warner Brothers Network (WB) produced a plethora of programming in the mid–1990s through the early 2000s specifically geared towards younger black audiences growing up on hip-hop. These networks sometimes scheduled black programming head-to-head on the same night from 8:00 p.m. until 10:00 p.m. Unlike earlier series, many of these programs were written and directed by blacks. These new networks became the primary destination for niche black programming, even though the quality of the new shows was not always good.[19] Chuck D., the lead rapper in Public Enemy, acknowledged content issues by nicknaming UPN the United Plantation of Negroes. Spike Lee, the most influential black filmmaker of the late 20th century, said that he would rather watch *Amos 'n' Andy* than many of the black programs on these networks.[20]

Cable television networks Black Entertainment Television (BET) and the Turner Broadcasting Station (TBS) would provide younger black directors Mara Brock Akil and Tyler Perry with a platform to produce new programming for black audiences beginning in the early 2000s. From 2003 until 2006 *Chappell's Show* on Comedy Central offered television's most enthralling observations of race in history and modern times. Unlike Flip Wilson, who whitewashed his jokes to appeal to the masses on his sketch series in the seventies, Chappelle did his best to make white audiences as uncomfortable as possible.

Since the year 2000 television has presented viewers with an array of black images from the nouveau riche on docu soaps to the incarcerated on melodramas. While some series, in recent years, have fed viewers weekly servings of the post-racial myth, others have manifested the modern black experience through the lens of the Black Lives Matter Movement, the dimming of Obama's inspired vision of audacious hope, and the chilling realization of Trump's America. Blacks are dominating television right now like never before yet the variety of black stories and images is still limited. For every *Insecure* there are a hundred shows about single white women. Thus, *Empire* takes on greater relevance.

The Making of an Empire, *Part I*

Empire is the creation of Lee Daniels, an African American filmmaker, and Daniel "Danny" Strong, a white Jewish American screenwriter. Daniels, who is gay, was stuffed into a trash can at the age of eight by his father for putting on his mother's high heels.[21] His father, a police officer and former bodyguard for Muhammad Ali, was murdered during an armed robbery four years later. Daniels left his hometown, Philadelphia, to attend Lindenwood College in St. Louis, Missouri. He dropped out after his junior year and, with $7 in his pocket, relocated to Los Angeles to chase stardom. Hollywood, however, was not waiting to welcome Daniels with open arms. He found himself homeless for a while, living out of his car and in local churches.[22]

He received his first big break as an assistant casting director on the Prince film *Purple Rain* (1984). Riding this wave of success, he formed his own entertainment management company in New York City. In 2001, he produced the film *Monster's Ball*, starring Halle Berry, who became the first black woman to win an Academy Award for Best Actress for her role in the film. While Berry's Oscar was a historic feat, many individuals in the African American community objected to the film's graphic nudity and sex.[23]

Precious (2009), the first major film directed by Daniels, was even more polarizing than *Monster's Ball*. White film critics in Hollywood called the film a beautiful piece of artwork. A review in *Time* magazine said the film was "too powerful for tears."[24] The film received six Academy Award nominations, including one for Best Picture and Best Adapted Screenplay. Gabourey Sidibe, now a cast member on *Empire*, received a Best Actress nomination. Comedian Mo'Nique, originally the lead candidate for the role of Cookie Lyon, won the Academy Award for Best Supporting Actress. Oprah Winfrey's production company, Harpo Films, produced the film. *Precious* grossed over $60 million at the box office, a remarkable return for a film made for only $10 million. Some blacks praised it for showcasing the often-ignored plight of the black underclass; yet others found it to be grossly offensive. Armond White, the chief film critic of the New York Press and the chairman of the New York Film Critics Circle, lambasted the mainstream news media for uplifting *Precious* while they ignored more "respectable" films like *Akeelah and the Bee* (2006), about an 11-year-old black girl who wins the Scripps National Spelling Bee.

Jada Smith, a contributor for *The Root*, charged Daniels with promoting colorism. All of the positive figures in Precious' life are biracial and light-skinned. Smith calls *Precious* the brown paper bag test all over again.[25] Brown paper bag parties, which originated with lighter-skinned free people of color in New Orleans in the 19th century, were popular during the first half of the twentieth century.[26] Blacks lighter than the paper bag could gain entrance into elite Greek organizations, universities, and churches. Accusations of colorism have followed Daniels to his current work on *Empire*. Rosalind Cummings-Yeates questions why many of his darker characters in *Empire*'s first season had menial or subservient roles. She refers to the emotionally tortured, biracial character Anika (Grace Gealey) as a representation of the tragic mulatto archetype.[27]

Most blacks favored Daniels' 2013 film *The Butler* about Cecil Gaines (Forest Whitaker), a character based on Eugene Allen, the longest tenured African American butler in the White House. A year after *The Butler*'s release, Daniels began working on *Empire*. Danny Strong, a winner of two Emmy Awards and Writers Guild of America Awards, had a far different upbringing than Daniels. While he was in high school the native of Manhattan Beach, California, befriended future Academy Award winning film director Quentin Tarantino, who worked at a local movie rental store. Tarantino provided Strong with his earliest lessons on cinema. Strong graduated from Tarantino's storefront chats to attend film school at the University of Southern California (USC). After graduating from USC Strong had a successful acting career in television series such as *Buffy the Vampire Slayer*, and *Gilmore Girls*. In 2008 the versatile Strong wrote his first script for what became the HBO film *Recount* about the controversial 2000 presidential election. Four years later he wrote the Peabody Award winning script for the film adaptation of the 2010 book *Game Change: Obama and the Clintons, McCain and Palin, and the Race of a Lifetime.*

Although most people associate *Empire* with Lee Daniels, it was Danny Strong's idea. He was listening to a story about a business deal closed by hip-hop mogul Sean "Puffy" Combs on his car radio when he was inspired to create the series.[28] Originally, he envisioned *Empire* being a film about a father based on music moguls Puffy and Jay-Z.[29] Strong thought the film should be a musical and he wanted Daniels to direct it. Daniels loved the concept; however, he thought it would work better on television. The unlikely dynamic duo based their new program on William Shakespeare's early 17th-century tragedy *King Lear,* about a British king who decides to divide his kingdom among his three daughters. The daughter that loves and flatters him the most will receive the largest portion of his kingdom.[30]

Watching Empire: *Soap Opera and the Melodramatic Imagination*

In addition to Shakespeare, Daniels and Strong used the ABC soap *Dynasty* (1981–1989) for inspiration. *Dynasty* focused on the Carringtons, a wealthy white family, living in Denver, Colorado. The Carrington's empire was headed by the family patriarch and oil tycoon Blake (John Forsythe). The first season dealt with Blake's dysfunctional relationship with his family. Blake is at odds with his younger wife and former secretary Krystle (Linda Evans) who feels unappreciated. He is at odds with his youngest son Steven (Al Corley), who has been picked to lead the dynasty once he retires. Steven objects to his father's obsession with money and immoral ways. Blake harbors hatred towards Steven's homosexual lifestyle. This storyline is reminiscent of Lucious' relationship with his son Jamal.

Dynasty had low ratings its first season; however, the insertion of Blake's devious ex-wife Alexis (Joan Collins) made it the number one show in America by 1984 and 1985, averaging 21.2 million viewers per episode. Critics called Alexis television's first female anti-hero. Alexis, with her stunning outfits, hats, makeup, jewelry, and badass attitude, was the original Cookie Lyon. African American households tuned in specifically to see Dominique Deveraux (Diahann Carroll), world-famous singer and Blake's half-sister. Dominique's debut was an event in and of itself. She arrived on the screen dressed in an audacious lynx (cat) coat, $350,000 worth of jewelry, and Cartier luggage. Cookie was also inspired by Dominique.

Since *Empire* is a primetime soap opera it is important to understand how this format shapes the series' storylines, pacing, characters, look, and popularity. A soap opera is a serial melodrama that revolves around strong emotional relationships and sensational, if not stereotypical, narratives and characters. Soaps, with their emphasis on fictional wealthy families, are drenched in fantasy and escapism. The storytelling is often based on mini-narratives that have an uneven rhythm and several cliffhangers. The earliest soap operas were radio programs in the 1930s, which advertised soap and detergents during commercial breaks. Historically the soaps have targeted women, especially housewives. In 1964 ABC's *Peyton Place*, became television's first primetime soap opera. During the late 1970s and early 1980s soap operas became a staple on late night television. Networks could spend more money on these soaps because they aired once a week as opposed to the daytime soaps. An average episode of *Dallas* cost $700,000. While daytime soaps used very minimal single camera work and sparse locations, the visual images were pivotal to the success of their evening counterparts.

Evening soaps were all about excess—characters stabbing each other in the back, being over the top, gusto, and having fun. The characters were larger than life, more evil, more cunning, more manipulative, and more gorgeous. Fans wanted to live and dress like them. The wardrobe was critical to creating the chic of these fictional characters. When the *Dynasty* range opened at Bloomingdale's, 26,000 women stormed the New York store to dress like their favorite characters. Primetime soaps targeted a wider audience, which allowed for more progressive female characters and displays of feminism. The wealthy white male patriarch may have been the protagonist; however, his authority was often challenged by outspoken women like Alexis.[31] The woman's role in the private and public sphere was heightened in these soaps due to the nature of the family's business.[32]

CBS's *Dallas* (1978–1991) is the highest rated primetime soap in American television history. *Dallas* focused on the Ewings, a wealthy yet dysfunctional white family in Parker, Texas, who controlled their own oil empire. The Ewings resided in a luxurious mansion at the 5,900-square foot Southfork Ranch. The protagonist of the series was the family's patriarch and oil tycoon J.R. Ewing. (Larry Hagman), who mastered in corruption the way a gourmet chef masters food. J.R. was shot in the final scene of season three, but the killer was unknown. For months millions of Americans were obsessed with this whodunit mystery. The query, "Who Shot J.R.?" might be the most famous pop cultural phrase in American history. Multiple attempts are made on Lucious' life on *Empire*. He is nearly shot at the end of one season and the victim of a car explosion in another season. An underlying storyline in *Dallas* was a feud between the Ewings and a rival elite family, the Barneses. *Empire* adapts a similar storyline by introducing a rival black family, the Duboises, to the Lyons' galaxy.

Ien Ang's book *Watching Dallas: Soap Opera and the Melodramatic Imagination* (1985) not only explains the reasons behind the *Dallas* phenomenon, but it also provides a rubric for assessing *Empire*. Ang found that fans of *Dallas* formed relationships with the characters, found realism in the storytelling, and were generally entertained by it. The characters in the soap opera were so convincing that they took on independent lives outside the series for devoted fans. Ang argues that this has a lot to do with the fact that soap operas have a quality like a fictional text. She says that a text can be read at two levels, the connotative and the denotative. The former level relates to recognizable features of a text to which readers, or in this case, viewers, can relate.[33] Her interviewees who expressed the most displeasure with *Dallas* stated that series was ridiculous and too unrealistic. She says they were viewing the series at the denotative level, which takes everything literally.[34]
In my conversations with *Empire* lovers and haters, I found similar reactions.

Ang believes the overly emotional display by the characters, cliffhangers, ongoing family conflict, and constant dysfunction, which resembles a Greek tragedy, is essential to a successful melodrama. While such exaggerated behavior and plots turn off some television viewers, it is what made *Dallas* and *Dynasty* lucrative in the 1980s and what drives *Empire* today. While these earlier series were condemned for being too campy and failing to address real social issues, *Empire* goes out of its way to be socially relevant. At the same time, its melodramatic structure and emphasis on entertainment do not allow for it to treat such social issues with the depth they rightfully deserve. "The most important characteristic is its economic marketability. Aiming at a very broad market means that content must be reduced to universally consumable motifs. This reduction to normal human aspects means that the content is recognizable to a wider audience, but it offers a stereotypical image of reality," says Ang.[35]

The Making of an Empire, *Part II*

Before *Empire* debuted a critic at the ATX Television Festival warned that if the series failed, network television would not invest in another drama with an all-black cast for the next 20 years. Daniels and Strong assembled an all-star lineup of producers, screenwriters, and showrunners to ensure the project's success. Brian Grazer, a producer of the 2002 Academy winner for

Best Picture, *A Beautiful Mind*, is an executive producer for *Empire*.[36] *Empire*'s production list rounds out with Ilene Chaiken, the co-creator and executive producer of the Showtime series *The L Word* (2004–2009). The remaining producers are Sanaa Hamri, Malcolm Spellman, Attica Locke, and Loucas George.

Empire, set in New York City, is filmed primarily in Chicago, Illinois. The series provides work for many of the Windy City's black actors, wardrobe production assistants, camera operators, location managers, extras, and hair and make-up stylists.[37] While Daniels and Strong have given unknown blacks job opportunities behind the camera, they have tapped several well-known black filmmakers to direct episodes. An interracial group of male and female scriptwriters is responsible for the show's storylines.

Music and fashion are essential elements to *Empire*'s success. Viewers are encouraged to stream new original music on Apple Music at the end of each new episode. Lee Daniels selected Timothy "Timbaland" Mosley, a super producer in the music industry, to serve as the show's executive producer of music. His soundtrack for *Empire*'s first season earned the number one spot on the Billboard 200 chart for top albums.[38] Original *Empire* songs "You're So Beautiful," "Drip Drop" and "Good Enough" charted well on iTunes purchases. Timbaland was replaced, after season two, by Rodney "Darkchild" Jerkins and Ester Dean.[39]

Lee Daniels admits that much of his knowledge about hip-hop and rap music is based on what he learns from his adopted children, which might explain *Empire*'s limited portrayal of the culture. Audiences are often spoon-fed the most basic version of hip-hop, characterized by minimal lyricism, mumble rap, and misogynistic lyrics. This representation of hip-hop ignores the recent success of socially conscious, nonviolent, and more lyrical rappers such as Kendrick Lamar, J. Cole, and Chance the Rapper. *Empire*'s writers have made some efforts to diversify the content of the rap music by introducing a socially conscious teenage emcee named Zeah (Ezri Walker) in season three. Jamal's music is routinely infused with politically charged and socially relevant lyrics.

Besides hip-hop and pop music *Empire* makes frequent use of the Lacrimosa movement of Mozart's *Requiem* to set the mood for some of its most melodramatic scenes. The mesmerizing music in the show's weekly soundtrack is complemented by the grandiose attire of the characters. Paulo Nieddu serves as the costume designer. He selects many of the outfits worn by *Empire*'s characters from Neiman Marcus, Barneys New York, and Saks Fifth Avenue. Nieddu does not limit his selection to high-end stores. He finds outfits in magazines, the internet, and a local consignment shop in Chicago.[40]

No detail is too minute for Nieddu. In an interview with Fashionista.com, he discusses the size of Hakeem's diamond earrings, which were downsized for season two to reflect his growing maturity. As Gabourey Sidibe's character Becky moves up the corporate ladder, Nieddu looks to the wardrobes of Oprah and Michelle Obama for ideas.[41] Costume designer Rita McGhee has also played a vital role in *Empire*'s chic, runway style. Saks Fifth Avenue launched an "Empire State of Mind" collection for men and women. Cover-Girl created a limited "Empire" cosmetics collection. Cast members Grace Byers, Gabourey Sidibe, Sereya, and Kaitlin Doubleday appeared in the commercials.[42]

Numbers Never Lie

Empire debuted with 9.90 million viewers on January 7, 2015. Each week the number of viewers increased at an unheard-of rapidity for a modern scripted series. The season one finale tallied an astonishing 17.62 million viewers.[43] With 62 percent of its primary audience being African American, *Empire* proved to networks that a series based on an African American family could still garner huge ratings and profits.[44] Each week the *Wall Street Journal's* online blog on the arts, Speakeasy, gave readers a recap of the latest episode. *Saturday Night Live, Black-ish, His & Hers, Good Morning America,* and *RuPaul's Drag Race* have parodied the series. Jimmy Fallon and the Roots created a hilarious parody called "Jimpire" on *The Tonight Show*. During a 2015 trip to Ghana, I was surprised to meet native West Africans who were so familiar with *Empire* that they could name each character. Yes, *Empire* has gone global. It airs on FOX affiliates in the United Kingdom, Finland, Canada, Germany, India, Serbia, and Africa.

Empire's historic rise during its first season was based on several factors, starting with a strategic marketing campaign. FOX promoted the series on multiple networks at 20th Century Fox movie screenings, online, on the radio, and in print. During the National Football League (NFL) season, *Empire* advertisements were shown weekly leading up to the series premiere. Cross-promotion with the network's former ratings juggernaut *American Idol* helped. Dana Walden and Gary Newman, incoming co-CEOs of the Fox Television Group, made *Empire* the network's top midseason priority. All their resources were used to develop a promotional strategy that specifically targeted blacks and members of the LGBTQ community. FOX used different commercials to appeal to a distinct subgroup within their target audience. For example, commercials that prominently featured Taraji P. Henson were used to attract black women who were fans of reality series such as *The Real Housewives of Atlanta*.[45] Golden *Empire* tote bags were distributed to black hair salons and at shopping malls on Black Friday 2014.[46]

To attract a 37 percent male audience in the first season, FOX marketed the series during the Manny Pacquaio–Chris Algieri boxing match on November 22, 2014. The network went a step further to gain male viewers by providing 450 black barbershops with *Empire* merchandise. The show's debut had a decent showing, but to ensure that the numbers would not decline, FOX increased spending on the marketing campaign heading into the second week of the season. Each week the number of viewers grew at an unexpected pace. Network executives believed that the show had potential to grow through word of mouth and video on demand, which allowed people to view the show outside of the original air date. The series debut earned 3.2 million views on Hulu, FOX Now, and video on demand services.

Empire's success has been a boon for the network's other primetime series on Wednesdays. The first season of the action series *Rosewood*, starring Morris Chestnut, aired on Wednesdays at 8:00 p.m. in 2015 and 2016. *Rosewood* recorded its best numbers during its final 15 minutes leading up to the start of *Empire*. The following fall *Rosewood* was replaced in that time slot by the television adaptation of the film franchise *Lethal Weapon*. Debuting on the same night as *Empire*'s season three premiere, *Lethal Weapon* pulled in an impressive 7.93 million viewers for its pilot episode. The series, picked up for a second season, quickly became the network's third most watched show behind *The Simpsons* and *Empire*. *Empire* moved to the 8:00 p.m. time slot to begin its fourth season to boost ratings for Daniels' new series *Star*, airing afterward. The African American centered cable network TV One, owned by Cathy Hughes, began airing *Empire* in syndication in June 2016 following a two-day marathon over Memorial Day weekend. TV One ran a three-day marathon over the 2017 Independence Day holiday weekend.[47]

Empire provides viewers with an in-depth fictional exploration into the business side of the hip-hop music industry. Fans not only get a taste of the way records are produced and business deals are closed; they are privy to the lengths that record labels will go to have chart topping music. Fans experience the initial success of brand new artists and the struggles of established artists to rebound from poor album sales and substance abuse. Much of the initial preoccupation with *Empire* stemmed from its willingness to expose uncomfortable realities in the African American community. By placing so much emphasis on issues like mental illness, homophobia, the drug trade and addiction, and mass incarceration, *Empire* defies the respectability police and dumps out all the dirty laundry in black America's proverbial hamper.

Another reason for *Empire*'s success might be the creators' decision to follow a strategy used successfully by Tyler Perry. Perry built his $400 million empire from the ticket purchases of black churchgoers who support his plays and films. Perry's success on the stage and big screen led to multi-million-dollar television deals with TBS and OWN.[48] *Empire*'s focus on Andre's evolving faith, the family's lack of church participation, Rhonda's atheism, Lucious' god complex and frequent use of biblical references is in line with Perry's formula.

Empire *Falling: The Death of a Dynasty*

How long will the Lyon Dynasty last? FOX's decision to expand *Empire*'s sophomore season to a full television season spanning September through November and March through May, as opposed to the three-month span of season one, backfired. Despite an impressive opening night that attracted 16.18 million viewers, the season finale only had 10.88 million viewers. iTunes sales of the season two soundtrack and singles also declined. "Is *Empire* in trouble?" became a frequent question asked by various media outlets throughout the sophomore season. *Complex* magazine offered the following list of reasons for the show's decline: (1) Season two had too many celebrity guest cameos that were miscast in their roles and did not advance the narrative. (2) The fast-paced storytelling never fully developed in season two. *Complex* pointed out two other FOX series targeting young audiences, *The O.C.* and *Glee*, which rose to the top quickly due to nontraditional storytelling and then faded quickly once the plots became "repetitive, hyperbolic, or melodramatic."[49] (3) *Empire* tackled far too many subjects in season two. This formula hampered the show's ability to establish a coherent arc and may have caused its youngest viewers to lose interest. (4) FOX series have a history enjoying incredible starts before plummeting in the ratings. Past examples include *American Idol, Glee, Gotham,* and *Sleepy Hollow*.[50] *Complex*'s critique missed the fact that *Empire* is a soap opera, which is the reason for the criticism raised in points two and three.

FOX built its network on the backs of black viewers in the 1980s and 1990s; nevertheless, these programs have experienced significant declines in viewership each season. Does FOX invest less money in the long-term success of its black programming? After heavy promotion for *Empire*'s first two seasons the network ran more ads for its new Wednesday night series *Lethal Weapon* than for *Empire*'s third season. NBC's seminal sitcom *The Cosby Show* experienced an increase in viewers each of its first three seasons before declining steadily over the final five seasons. *The Fresh Prince of Bel-Air*, another NBC sitcom, increased its viewers in seasons two and three before having a significant drop. Now it should be noted that Americans have far more entertainment options today than they did 20 to 30 years ago. The variety of black shows is at an all-time high giving black audiences more choices. Fans who may have faithfully tuned into *Empire*'s first season are now presently devoted to new shows like *Atlanta*, *Greenleaf*, *Insecure*, and *Queen Sugar*. ABC's hit family sitcom *Black-ish* competed with *Empire* in the same Wednesday evening time slot from 2015 to 2017. *Black-ish* also experienced consistently declining viewership every season since its premiere.

Empire's season three and four premieres pulled in 10.87 and 7.05 million viewers; however, the numbers dropped on a weekly basis. But here is the irony: even *Empire*'s least watched episode garnered 7 million viewers, which is far more than any other current black series.

Empire may have fewer viewers now, but it still dominates social media discussion. This fact provides an interesting case study on African American social media traffic and television ratings. How have black Millennials on social media sites impacted *Empire*'s popularity and opinions about its depictions of blackness? Social media has been pivotal to *Empire*'s rise and fall. FOX executives did their research on the show's target audience before its debut to learn their taste in music and fashion. The network uses social media sites Facebook, Instagram, and Tumblr, to showcase fashions worn by characters for the fans after each episode airs. During season one fans used social media to express their likes and dislikes with each episode as they were being broadcast. Taraji P. Henson now has more than 12 million combined followers on Instagram and Twitter who help to keep people talking about the series as it airs and throughout the week. Henson's fans have created their own Twitter hashtags such as #CookieMonsters and #TeamCookie. Shonda Rhimes, creator of ABC's *Scandal* and *How to Get Away with Murder*, tweeted "So now I am all about Empire. ALL ABOUT #EMPIRE, tweepies."[51] Right before the start of the season three premiere on September 21, 2016, *Empire*'s stars encouraged viewers to live tweet their thoughts about the episode during the broadcast. This trend continued throughout the season.

Empire's writers have even stressed the importance of social media in their scripts. Multiple episodes feature characters tweeting about their music or posting videos to attract more fans. After Hakeem's boys post a vine of him drunk and making disparaging remarks about President Barack Obama, his new bad boy image boosted his marketability. Another episode has Cookie convincing a star professional football player to tweet that he likes Jamal's new song "Keep Your Money" so that his Twitter followers will download and request the song in large numbers. The season two premiere began with a #freeLucious concert emphasizing the disproportionate rate of mass incarceration for men of color. The scene included cameos from civil rights activist the Rev. Al Sharpton and CNN host Don Lemon. The scriptwriters were trying to make a connection between Lucious' imprisonment and the ongoing dialogue over social media about police brutality, racial profiling, and mass incarceration. On the fourth episode of that season Cookie indirectly referenced the #SayHerName movement by making a remark about Sandra Bland, a 28-year-old incarcerated black woman found hanged to death in her cell.[52]

According to a 2016 Nielsen report, "Young, Connected and Black: African-American Millennials Are Driving Social Change and Leading Digital Advancement," black Millennials are only second to Asian Americans in smartphone ownership. Ninety-one percent of black Millennials use the Internet on their smartphones. Fifty-five percent of black Millennials spend an hour a day checking social media sites on their smartphones.[53] Black Twitter is a collective of African American Twitter users who converse, across the globe, on a variety of topics. Black Twitter has taken the lead on popular hashtag campaigns like #BlackLivesMatter, #SayHerName, #DonLemonLogic, #OscarsSoWhite, #OscarsSoBlack, and #BlackGirlMagic.[54] Meredith Clark, a professor of Journalism, divides Black Twitter into three levels of connection: Personal community—the way black people connect offline; thematic notes—the topics that black people tweet about such as politics, religion, social issues, and popular culture; and the intersection of personal community and thematic notes.[55] Bavity.com and other Internet sites post weekly updates on Black Twitter's reactions to *Empire*'s latest episodes.

Black Twitter's influence on *Empire* cannot be ignored. It was television's most tweeted series, averaging 451,270 tweets per episode. The series may have fewer viewers; however, it remains number one in Nielsen Social Content Ratings. A week before it was preempted for the final 2016 presidential debate, the latest *Empire* episode had 700,000 posts on Facebook and 200,000 tweets. One fan posted the following tweet: "@HillaryClinton is channeling #CookieLyon! YAAASSS!"[56] What this could mean for the future of television programming is that networks may take a television show's social media traffic into consideration when deciding to keep it in their lineup. It could also determine how much money a network and their sponsors choose to invest in that show. Keep in mind that black buying power grew from $995 billion to $1.3 trillion between 2010 and 2015.[57] *Empire* provides a market of consumers that sponsors want to attract during commercial breaks.

If declining ratings do not derail the Lyon dynasty, legal issues might do the trick. FOX won an $8 million lawsuit filed against it by Empire Distribution, a record label and publishing company, to discontinue using the name "Empire" for the series.[58] The network was also sued by Sophia Eggleston, a black woman from Detroit, who claimed that Lee Daniels stole her life story to create Cookie Lyon.[59] Daniels claims that Cookie was inspired by his "corrupt politician" grandmother and his "drug dealing sister."[60] When Cookie beats Hakeem with a broom on the pilot episode, Daniels says that he is recreating a beating his mother once gave him. Music mogul Damon "Dame" Dash accused Lee Daniels of stealing his biographical story to create Lucious Lyon. Daniels claims that he based Lucious on himself, his father, and powerful businessmen who have used unconventional methods to reach the top such as Berry Gordy, Jay-Z, Puffy and Joseph P. Kennedy.[61] Marvin Gaye, III, son of the late Marvin Gaye, threatened to sue Daniels because *Empire* reminded him of a series he proposed to networks in 2010 called *Diamonds & Ballads* based on the family of Motown founder Berry Gordy.

Only time will tell if *Empire* is remembered as one of television's defining series or just another intriguing episode of *Unsung Hollywood*.[62]

1

The Lyon Family Hustle
A New Look at the Black Family on TV

"We not the Brady Brunch. We not the Partridges. Hell, we not even the Jacksons. We are the Lyons."[1]
—Cookie Lyon

Music, Family, Power. These words appeared prominently, in all capital letters, on a promotional poster for *Empire*. The word "family" protrudes the most because the Lyons are unlike any African American family that has ever appeared on television. They manifest the evolution of the fictional black family in primetime since the 1970s. Music and crime have allowed them to overcome the poverty experienced by the Evans of *Good Times*, television's first black family, and move on up beyond *The Jeffersons*. The family's patriarch Lucious plays the taskmaster role of Joe Jackson, Michael Jackson's father, placing his children's musical careers high above their happiness and emotional well being. The Lyons act more like business partners and rivals than a loving unit. Their insatiable thirst for power, based on a willingness to commit crimes and endanger one another in the process, has placed the family on a perpetual road to self-destruction. The Lyon family's values are more akin to the Ewings, the Carringtons, and the Sopranos than the wholesome Huxtables.

Empire provides a picture of the elite African American family that deviates from customary depictions found in historical studies and memoirs such as Lawrence Otis Graham's *Our Kind of People: Inside America's Black Upper Class* (1999) and Margo Jefferson's *Negroland: A Memoir* (2015); or television series like *The Fresh Prince of Bel-Air*. While other elite black families achieved their social status through inheritance, higher education, or lawful hard work, the Lyon's wealth originated within the illegal drug trade and hip-hop. What the Lyons do have in common with other fictional elite black families on television today is an extraordinary amount of dysfunction. Do such characterizations simply mimic the behavior of wealthy white families on primetime soap operas, *Dallas* and *Dynasty*, or do they promote underlying messages, dating back to The Moynihan Report of 1965, about the failures of the African American family? What does *Empire*'s high viewership in black households reveal about the state of the African American family?

At its core *Empire* is a television show about family. There is the relationship that the Lyons have with one another and their extended relatives. Minor storylines focus on the relationship between the Lyons and their new rivals—the elite Dubois family. Artists, employees, and business associates such as Anika, Tiana, Nessa, Becky, Thirsty, Vernon, and Shyne form fictive kinships with the Lyons.[2] When Cookie attempts to secure the support of investors for Empire's Initial Public Offering (IPO), her speech focuses on family legacy. To correctly analyze this depiction of the Lyon family, we must look back to the earliest depictions of American families in primetime television.

Television and the American Family

In 1950 the Los Angeles community of Lakewood ran an advertisement reading: "Veterans wake up! Your dream home is here. Dreaming of the good life? Beautiful Lakewood is more than owning a home…. It is a new and better way of living."[3] Lakewood, like many new suburban communities, was promising World War II veterans home ownership and a piece of the American dream as they returned from fighting abroad. Under the Servicemen's Readjustment Act of 1944 (the GI Bill of Rights) each veteran received $2,000 in loans to purchase a new home. The Veterans Administration mortgage program allowed veterans to own a home without making a down payment. The government funded $20 billion in home loans from the Veterans Affairs and the Federal Housing Administration.[4] President Franklin Roosevelt believed that home ownership was the key component in helping the nation to transition smoothly into a postwar climate.[5] The rise of the suburbs would shape the Cold War image of the American family, television, and race relations for the next four decades.

The first example of an American suburb was Levittown, a small community in New York constructed by the building firm, Levitt and Sons. Abraham Levitt and sons, Alfred and William, completed their first 2,000 home rental community, marketed to young veteran families by the summer of 1947. As the demand for more homes grew the Levitts built over 17,000 additional communities, which offered special schools, churches, and businesses for residents. The suburban lifestyle became synonymous with the American ethos of democracy, opportunity, and prosperity. During the 1950s Madison Avenue's original mad men began targeting these new middle-class families to purchase a multitude of consumer products. The television became one of the most sought out items in these households. Early television programming consisted of variety shows and sitcoms that modeled "how families were *supposed* to live; falsely reassuring *all* viewers of the ease with which they could achieve this new way of life," says Jennifer M. Fogel.[6]

Father Knows Best (1954–1960) and *Leave It to Beaver* (1957–1963) were perfect for American Cold War propaganda. The role of these happy-go-lucky fictional families living in their comfortable suburban homes was to promote good old-fashioned American values of democracy and challenge communism. The Andersons and the Cleavers never experienced financial hardship or any real suffering. Stephanie Coontz unveils the problems with these sitcoms in her book *The Way We Never Were: American Families and the Nostalgia Trap* (2016). These *wholesome* television shows were dangerously deceptive because they cloaked a host of problems for the sake of advancing patriotism. First, they attempted to teach Americans proper values based upon 19th century Victorian Era notions of the family. The television housewife, modeled after patriarchal norms, lived to please her family. She attained a college education, not to enter a career, but to become the perfect suburban wife and mother. As protector and provider, the husband was the master of the home—the king of his castle. The children were mischievous, but not to the point that it jeopardized their futures. Sitcom domesticity romanticized an era of rigid hierarchical ordering of gender roles.

The other myth being promoted by these sitcoms was that racism was a thing of the past. *Leave It to Beaver* was post-racial 50 years before the term was in vogue. This myth would have been easy to believe given the fact that black people were nonexistent in the lily-white sitcom universe. The sitcoms reflected suburban life for many white families. Do you remember Levittown? Well, this "progressive" community was symbolic of the Jim Crow system that infected the nation's ethos like an untreatable wound. When the Myers, a black family, moved into Levittown in 1957 white residents expressed fears of crime, declining property values, loss of social status, and forced miscegenation.[7] The Federal Housing Administration and the Levittown developers made an agreement that all applications submitted by black families would be denied. The FHA redlined older urban neighborhoods leading to the growth of inner city ghettos and white flight to the suburbs.[8] Redlining was the withholding of home loans, insurance coverage, and basic services like health care and super markets from neighborhoods consisting of working class black and brown families.

"Ain't we lucky we got 'em."

Good Times (1974–1979), introduced television audiences to the African American family that was invisible in past sitcoms. Premiering on CBS on February 8, 1974, *Good Times* was a spinoff of the Norman Lear sitcom *Maude* (1972–1978), which featured a black maid named Florida Evans played by Esther Rolle. Unlike the black maids previously found in popular culture, Florida was intelligent and quite assertive. She manifested the evolving images of blackness in the post–Civil Rights Movement years. Norman Lear, a Jewish American television producer who created the 1970s hit sitcoms *All in the Family* (1971–1979) and *Sanford and Son* (1972–1977), decided to develop a comedy centering around Florida's family. The Evans family included her husband James (James Amos) and their children James Jr., (Jimmy Walker), Thelma (Bern Nadette Stanis), and Michael (Ralph Carter). The Evans clan was a poor working family struggling to make ends meet in the crime-ridden Cabrini-Green housing projects located on the Near North Side of Chicago.

James Evans was the embodiment of the strong black father archetype promoted in African American literature, folklore, black power rhetoric, and Sunday morning sermons. A Korean War veteran, possessing only a sixth-grade education, James worked 16-hour shifts at various blue-collar jobs to keep a roof over their heads. James Amos said of his character, "*Good Times* helped shatter that misconception that black fathers have had to shed, which is: one, we don't love our children; two, that most black fathers are absentee fathers."[9] As a kid watching reruns of the sitcom, James intimidated me. I could never understand why he was always so angry. He would raise his voice at Florida, her best friend and neighbor Willona Woods (Ja'net Dubois), his kids, the apartment building superintendent Nathan "Buffalo Butt" Bookman (Johnny Brown), and any other "jive turkey" that increased his level of unrelieved frustration. When his youngest son Michael was suspended from school for calling President George Washington a racist, Florida had to implore James not to beat the black off his behind. After binge watching the entire series, as an adult, I came to understand why James was so angry. Nearly every episode dealt with the hardships of ghetto life. On episode 40, "Operation Florida," James spent the family's entire savings to pay for Florida's gallbladder operation. In his book, *Making the Second Ghetto*, sociologist Arnold Hirsch explains how discriminatory government policies in Chicago created the slums that housed underprivileged minority families. The Evans family provided viewers with a visual presentation of this reality.

New York Times critic John J. O'Connor wrote that black audiences "no longer have to be content with *Father's Knows Best*, which was unreal even for many white Americans. On the other side, whites are being given glimpses of Black life that, however simplified, can't help but weaken artificial racial barriers." According to *Ebony* magazine, *Good Times* was "the tube's best effort to date at showing a real slice of ghetto Black life."[10] One of the show's lasting legacies was its use of Afro-centric artwork by Earnie Barnes. His famous painting, "The Sugar Shack," used as the cover art for Marvin Gaye's *I Want You* (1976) album, appeared during the opening and closing credits.

Good Times was not only the first television series about a two-parent African American family, but it also countered the portrayal of black households in the controversial Moynihan Report and the sitcom *Julia*. By 1965 the unemployment rate for black males, welfare enrollment, and crime in urban areas were all on a steady rise. Blacks had children at a rate 25 percent higher than whites. Furthermore, the number of black families headed by single mothers reached a disturbing rate in the eyes of the federal government. During his June 4, 1965, commencement address at Howard University President Lyndon Johnson proclaimed that "Negro" poverty resulted from the breakdown of the nuclear family.[11] President Johnson appointed sociologist Daniel Patrick Moynihan to serve as his Assistant Secretary of Labor. Moynihan was expected to devise programs that would aid President Johnson in his War on Poverty. The result was the 1965 report entitled "The Negro Family: The Case for National Action," nicknamed The Moynihan Report. Moynihan argued that the wealth gap between black and white households was due to the collapse of the nuclear black family. Moynihan used original data published by black sociologist E. Franklin Frazier in *The Negro Family in the United States* (1939) as his foundation for the report. Frazier had blamed slavery and Jim Crow for the absence of a healthy two-parent structure in most black homes. The 1940 census showed a larger proportion of black families headed by single women in the rural and urban South. In northern cities with a total population of 100,000 or more, 30 percent of the black families had single female heads. There were several causes for the absence of black fathers. In many cases, men had sired children out of wedlock. In other cases, the men deserted their families to find work.[12] Although historian Herbert Gutman refuted Frazier's claims in his 1977 study, Moynihan either missed or ignored data that Gutman found significant.[13]

The Moynihan Report popularized the myths that black families were dysfunctional, black fathers were irresponsible, and two-parent households were a rarity. Making matters worse, the report blamed single black mothers for "a tangle of black pathologies." The assumption was that the poverty, crime, violence, drug abuse, and unemployment suffered by blacks were caused by a ghetto culture resulting from female-headed households.[14] Ulf

Hannerz, a Swedish urban anthropologist, published an article stating that these lower class single mother headed households had reverted to a primitive evolutionary stage.[15] Critics like psychologist William Ryan accused Moynihan of blaming the victim.[16] Andrew Billingsley's 1968 book *Black Families in White America* charged that the Moynihan Report ignored the 75 percent of black middle-class families residing in the nation at the time.[17]

Criticism of the Moynihan Report within the African American community trickled down to sitcoms that appeared to support his assessment. NBC's *Julia* (1968–1970) starred Diahann Carroll as Julia Baker, a nurse and single mother of a six-year-old son. Julia lived in a middle-class, mixed-race apartment building. She was the only black person in her office, and her son's best friend was white. *Ebony* accused *Julia* of presenting a fictional middle-class black life to which working class blacks could not relate. Robert Lewis Shayon of *The Saturday Review* wrote that the series diluted the nation's race problem by masquerading one fortunate black woman's life as the common African American experience. Others saw a fulcrum of the Moynihan Report dramatized in the absence of a strong black male presence.

Initially, *Good Times* was viewed favorably for its groundbreaking depiction of a happily married black couple, but this praise soon faded. Although Esther Rolle and James Amos were the backbones of the series, comedian Jimmy Walker, who played the 18-year-old J.J., was the headliner. J.J. was an aspiring painter with a robust appetite for pretty ladies.[18] The wisecracks and insults heaped on his younger sister Thelma kept audiences laughing. His trademark attire consisted of floppy hats and brightly colored outfits that clung to his skinny 6'1" frame. His buffoonish mannerisms, animated facial expressions, and "Kid DY-NO-MITE" catchphrase made him a mainstream superstar for kids who purchased his T-shirts and pajamas. J.J. lacked the book smarts and black nationalistic attitude of his militant little brother Michael, who aspired to become the next Thurgood Marshall.[19] The scriptwriters' increasing emphasis on J.J. did not sit well with the other costars who saw his character as a jive talking abomination of black manhood. Esther Rolle told *Ebony*, "He's 18 and he doesn't work. He can't read and write…. I resent the imagery that says to Black kids that you can make it by standing on the corner saying 'Dyn-o-mite!'"[20]

J.J. did not sit well with James Amos either. Amos, in a 2015 interview with the American Archives of Television, claimed that he was fired from the show because he refused to succumb to minstrelsy. He questioned the producers' decision not to focus more on the other characters in the show that had a more positive image. Amos said the producers' disapproval of his attitude killed off his character in a car accident on the season four premiere.[21]

James Evans' death may have given black audiences one of the greatest lines in television history: Esther Rolle's "Damn, damn, damn!" But it also meant that another television series was playing on tropes of single black female-headed households. Throughout the 1970s other black sitcoms like *What's Happening!!* (1976–1979) continued this "Moynihanesque" trend. *What's Happening!!*, like *Julia*, was not dealing with black pathologies, but it upheld the notion that black fathers did not take care of their families. *What's Happening!!* was a crossover hit that attracted white viewers which made it even more problematic.

Norman Lear's next hit black sitcom, *The Jeffersons* (1975–1985), was television's first series about an upper middle-class African American family. George Jefferson (Sherman Hemsley), like *Empire*'s Lucious Lyon, was a proud black man from very humble beginnings who enjoyed mainstream luxuries (a maid and a dee-luxe Manhattan apartment in the sky-y-y) without ever forgetting from where he came. *Essence* magazine praised *The Jeffersons* for portraying television's first wealthy black man as a fiscally responsible entrepreneur who did not cheat and rob his way to the top or blow his riches on Cadillacs.[22] George was not a saint by any stretch of the imagination. He was a shallow bigot who tormented his neighbors Tom (Franklin Cover) and Helen Willis (Roxie Roker), television's first interracial married couple. George routinely took his wife Louise (Isabel Sanford) for granted and sought unsuccessfully to pass on his worst traits to his adult son Lionel (Mike Evans and Damon Evans), who did not follow in his footsteps. George did not patronize his black housekeeper Florence (Marla Gibbs) in the manner of the rich white men in past films. Instead, he just called her lazy and talked down to her every chance he got. And Florence always had a hilarious insult waiting for him. With all his flaws, however, George was a successful businessman, a faithful husband, and a dedicated father. *The Jeffersons* ended in 1985 opening the door for the next black family that would change popular culture forever.

Huxtable Family Values

Herman Gray says the family sitcom has been the primary vehicle for black images on television.[23] Whether it is fair or not all black family sitcoms and dramas are measured against *The Cosby Show* (1984–1992) starring Philadelphia comedian Bill Cosby. Cosby's decision to tell clean jokes that were devoid of the explicit content and racially charged political overtones found in the comedy of Redd Foxx, Richard Pryor, and Dick Gregory made him a favorite of middle class white and black audiences.²⁴ Cosby made history on NBC's *I Spy* (1965–1968) as the first black man in a lead role in a television series. He earned Emmy Awards for Outstanding Lead Actor in 1966, 1967, and 1968 for his portrayal of an undercover Pentagon agent. *Variety* magazine called him the Jackie Robinson of television. Education was crucial to Cosby, who earned both a master's degree and a doctoral degree in Education from the University of Massachusetts Amherst (UMASS) in 1972 and 1976, respectively. His 242-page doctoral dissertation was titled "An Integration of the Visual Media via Fat Albert and the Cosby Kids into the Elementary School Curriculum as a Teaching Aid and Vehicle to Achieve Increased Learning." This mouthful of a title referenced *Fat Albert and the Cosby Kids* (1972–1985), Cosby's educational cartoon for kids.

On September 20, 1984, Cosby began his career-defining role as Dr. Heathcliff "Cliff" Huxtable on *The Cosby Show*. Dr. Huxtable was an obstetrician, usually attired in colorful sweaters, married to the beautiful Clair (Phylicia Rashad), an attorney and partner at a law firm. The Huxtables lived in a Brownstone in an upper middle-class Brooklyn neighborhood with their five children: Sondra, Denise, Theo, Vanessa, and Rudy. They were unlike any black family seen on television up to that point. Cliff and Clair were happily married, seldom fought, and always made time for romance. Their marital bliss was modeled after their parents who were married for more than 50 years. Money was never a serious issue for the family. Cliff and his father Russell (Earle Hyman), a prominent jazz trombonist, had an exceptionally close relationship, which he tried to duplicate with his son Theo (Malcolm-Jamal Warner). Over the course of the series Theo, who was based on Cosby's now deceased son Ennis, matured from an immature teenager with dyslexia in danger of failing high school to a top graduate from New York University (NYU). Cliff's love for Theo, which often reminded me of my relationship with my own dad, is still one of the best father-son portrayals on television.

Education was an important theme in *The Cosby Show*. During his final years at NYU Theo gets an internship teaching math at a community center for less fortunate kids. The Huxtable's oldest child Sondra (Sabrina LeBeauf) graduated from Princeton University and eventually went to law school, despite taking a head scratching detour to open a wilderness store with her sexist husband, Elvin Tibideaux (Geoffrey Owens). Elvin eventually decided to become a medical doctor, and the couple had twins named after South African leaders Winnie and Nelson Mandela. The second oldest daughter Denise (Lisa Bonet) was the nonconformist of the family. After failing several classes during her freshman year at her parents' alma mater, Hillman College (a fictional HBCU in Virginia), she dropped out of school.²⁵ She then travelled to Africa where she met and married divorced Navy Lt. Martin Kendall (Joseph C. Phillips). Denise returned to live with her parents, now as a wife and the stepmother of a three-year-old girl named Olivia (Raven Symone). Eventually Denise would go back to school to become a teacher. The other daughters, Vanessa (Tempsett Bledsoe) and Rudy (Keshia Knight Pulliam), were both excellent students who engaged in typical sibling rivalry. When Clair's distant teenage cousin from the hood, Pam Tucker (Erika Alexander), moved in with the family in the final two seasons the Huxtables' talented tenth-like lifestyle inspired her to apply for college. Dr. Huxtable paid for her college tuition.

The Cosby Show was a first in many aspects. It presented a diverse black family in skin complexion. Sondra, Denise, and Olivia were very fair skinned in comparison to their darker family members. Cliff's father was also a fair skinned man. In previous black series this diversity in complexion was absent. Unlike series today, complexion was not an issue in the Huxtable household where everyone was treated equally. The Huxtables also provided nuanced depictions of gender. Black men were responsible fathers who did not rule with an iron fist. They were loving husbands, who were sensitive to the needs of their wives. They were scholars and athletes, but not necessarily in the mold of the "super negro" who excelled flawlessly at everything. As for the Huxtable women, they were highly educated professionals whose income either rivaled or exceeded their husbands. They were outspoken feminists without being stereotypically loud or angry. Despite their stressful careers they always found time to be active in their children's lives and keep the fire burning in their marriage. The women dressed in a conservative manner that was aligned with standards of middle-class respectability. Clair Huxtable rejected every Sapphire, mammy, or Jezebel archetype ever associated with black womanhood. *Boston Globe* columnist Renee Graham says that the Huxtables did not have to deal with controversial issues because their mere existence in primetime was a deep issue.[26]

The Cosby Show's emphasis on the nuclear family, education, and middle-class values was not coincidental. Bill Cosby was very instrumental in the show's scripts and character development. He brought in Dr. Alvin Poussaint, a black professor of psychiatry at Harvard Medical School and published author on child psychiatry for African American families, to serve as his consultant. Cosby and Poussaint intentionally set out to challenge every negative stereotype associated with the black family. In 1986 liberal pundit Bill Moyers, a former spokesman for President Lyndon Johnson, released his documentary film "The Vanishing Black Family—Crisis in Black America." The film took viewers to a Newark, New Jersey, housing project, to see how the black family actually lived. The film, which won a DuPont award for excellence in broadcast journalism, revitalized the commentary of the 1965 Moynihan Report.[27] Moyers' film coincided with the "welfare queen" mythology being promoted by the Reagan administration.[28] The "welfare queen" myth was based on a Chicago con artist named Linda Taylor who was receiving $150,000 annually in welfare checks. Reagan used Taylor to make a sweeping indictment on all single black mothers receiving federal aid. *The Cosby Show* presented a perfect and pristine image of the black family, which was aligned with Reaganism's emphasis on the "traditional family" and personal responsibility. More importantly, it proudly promoted African-American history and culture as something to be revered.[29]

Unlike *Julia*, this show did not mute the blackness of its characters nor did it exaggerate that blackness as so many of the 1970s sitcoms did. Theo did not need to walk around saying "dyno-mite" to demonstrate how *down* he was. The Huxtables exhibited black pride in many not so subtle ways, whether it was gathering around the television to reflect on attending the March on Washington and listening to Martin Luther King, Jr.'s "I Have a Dream" speech; wearing sweatshirts with HBCU logos; wearing natural Afrocentric hairstyles; reading *Black Enterprise* magazine; displaying black artwork on the wall by artists like Varnette Honeywood; displaying posters of black pop singers, including jazz and the blues in the soundtrack; or featuring cameos by black celebrities Lena Horne, B.B. King, Count Basie, Stevie Wonder, and Sammy Davis, Jr. Each season featured a new opening that often included diverse black musical themes and dance routines. Still, to this day, my favorite Huxtable moment is when the entire family gives their best lip-synch battle rendition of Ray Charles' hit song, "Night Time Is the Right Time." The closing scenes of episode 151 were filmed at the St. James Presbyterian Church in Harlem and featured a soul stirring performance by gospel music legend Mavis Staples and the church choir.

The Cosby Show was number one in the Nielsen ratings for five straight seasons, from 1985 to 1989. Only two other television shows, *All in the Family* and *American Idol*, have pulled off that historic feat. At its peak, the show was being watched in 30,502 million homes. The Huxtables possessed a quality that appealed to the black families that watched *Good Times* and the white families in love with *Family Ties* and movies by John Hughes.[30] When Cliff recited the words "I am an American, and this is my American family," during an acceptance speech as the physician of the year to a room of mostly whites dressed in black-tie attire, this was a powerful statement that resonated with mainstream audiences.[31] The series and its actors received Emmys, Golden Globes, NAACP Image, Peabody, and People's Choice awards.

The Cosby Show influenced the family's image in several future black sitcoms from *Family Matters* (1989–1997) to *My Wife and Kids* (2001–2005) and *Reed Between the Lines* (2011). Reality shows about younger black families have mimicked aspects of the *Cosby* formula. MTV's reality show *Run's House* (2005–2009), about the family of Rev. Run, a retired member of the pioneering rap group Run D.M.C., felt like hip-hop's version of *The Cosby Show*. Atlanta rapper T.I. (Clifford Harris) and his family paid homage to *The Cosby Show*'s opening dance routines with their own routine to begin each season four episode of their VH1 reality series *T.I. & Tiny: The Family Hustle*. "The Johnson Show" episode of Kenya Barris' *Black-ish* was about the father's obsession to model his family after his heroes, the Huxtables. ABC's sister network Freeform even greenlit a *Black-ish* spinoff called *Grown-ish* for 2018. The series follows the eldest daughter's college experience which is exactly what *The Cosby Show* spin-off, *A Different World*, initially tried to do thirty years ago with Denise Huxtable.

"The Huxtables Have Fallen"

During a stand-up routine in October 2014, comedian Hannibal Burress made several references to multiple rape allegations against Bill Cosby stemming back to the 1960s. In the wake of the Burress routine 60 women accused Cosby of either rape, drug facilitated sexual assault, or child sexual abuse. On December 30, 2015, three Class II Felony charges of aggravated indecent assault were filed against the comedic genius.[32] Cosby's criminal trial began on June 5, 2017. Nearly two weeks later a Pennsylvania judge declared a mistrial because the jury was "hopelessly deadlocked."[33] The allegations not only stained Cosby's reputation but they impacted his beloved sitcom. Beginning in November 2014 multiple networks including TV Land, Aspire (owned by Earvin "Magic" Johnson), and BET Centric pulled reruns of the series off the air.[34] Online subscription streaming services Amazon, Hulu, and Netflix cancelled it in 2015. Bounce TV, founded by the Rev. Martin Luther King, III, and the Rev. Andrew Young, cancelled *The Cosby Show* in July 2015; however, the series returned to network on December 19, 2016. TV One began airing it daily in the spring of 2017. When *Ebony* released its November 2015 issue with a fractured picture of the Huxtable family on the cover it set off a debate throughout the African American community. Many blacks thought it was disrespectful to tarnish what they considered Hollywood's most positive representation of authentic blackness. Goldie Taylor, a writer for *Ebony*, said in an interview that many blacks considered any criticism of the series to be blasphemous.[35]

There is a substantial amount of irony in the fact that *Empire*'s Lyon clan became television's most prominent African American family in the same year that the Huxtable dynasty had fallen. The Lyons are the antithesis of Cosby's model family. Lucious Lyon, the family patriarch, is a former drug dealer who is responsible for multiple deaths. Describing Lucious as a sociopathic narcissist would be a compliment. His ex-wife Cookie is a former convicted felon who served 17 years in a federal prison for selling crack cocaine. The seed money for the family's business, Empire Entertainment, came from their involvement in the criminal underworld. Even now, as the owners of a publicly traded entertainment enterprise, they still engage in outlaw behavior to maintain their social status as members of the 1 percent.[36]

Violence is a way of life for the Lyon family: Andre, in an attempt to drive a wedge between his two younger brothers Jamal and Hakeem, arranges a robbery during a recording session at the Ghetto Ass Studio in the hood. Andre's plans went awry when one of the stick-up boys shoots a man working in the studio. The two thugs were casual associates of Hakeem leading Jamal to blame him for the attempt on his life. Later in the series, Andre pays someone to plant explosives in his father's car. Lucious survives but is left with amnesia and a prosthetic left leg. One of Lucious' proudest moments is watching Jamal threaten to throw his rival Billy Beretti from the roof of a high-rise building unless he signs over the masters to his music. A disgruntled boyfriend of Jamal's ex-girlfriend Olivia pulls a gun on the entire family on the night that Lucious signs the paperwork for his initial public offering (IPO). On another occasion, the family comes together to celebrate the biggest night of their musical career at the American Sound Awards (ASAs). As they walk the red carpet, Jamal nearly loses his life after he jumps in front of a bullet meant to assassinate Lucious. During the wedding of the family's youngest son Hakeem, a federal agent crashes the party to serve a subpoena to Lucious' ex-fiance Anika, who also happens to be Hakeem's baby's mama. The wedding comes to a sudden halt when Shyne Johnson, a criminal ally of Lucious and Cookie from back in the day, cracks a champagne bottle on the head of a security guard. The bride's father immediately pulls her out of the wedding stating that he refuses to give away his daughter to a family of thugs. Lucious marries Anika, pregnant with Hakeem's daughter Bella, in a last ditch effort to prevent her from being subpoenaed by the FBI. When Anika goes into labor Lucious accompanies her to the delivery room. He stands near her hospital bed, dressed in scrubs, whispering death threats in her ear to make sure she keeps quiet about his criminal behavior. What makes this scene even more confounding is the fact that Anika had just pushed Andre's wife Rhonda off a rooftop, killing her instantaneously, before Anika went into labor.

If the Huxtables were a picture of respectability and happiness, the Lyons would symbolize dysfunction. Screaming and yelling are their most common forms of communication. Never was this more evident than when Lucious enticed Hakeem to go on a tirade with his brothers during a live performance on Empire Xtreme, their 24-hour streaming service. The fight publicly exposes an abundance of the family's dirty laundry. Hakeem ridicules Andre for having mental health issues. And he mocks Jamal for being gay, saying that he has been dressing like a girl since he was 10 and referring to him as a "wannabe Frank Ocean." When the cameramen begin to turn away, Lucious demands that they continue filming because he realizes that making his family look like extras on *The Jerry Springer Show* (1991–) will increase the number of subscribers to his streaming service.[37] The camera shifts to a scene of hundreds gathered in Times Square to watch this epic cacophony of screaming and shouting. As usual, Lucious puts profit and celebrity over his family's stability. He takes pleasure in watching his sons display his devilish traits just as long as they dare not cross him.

If you have ever witnessed Denzel Washington's magnificent performance of Troy Maxson in the 2016 film adaptation of August Wilson's play *Fences*, you remember him being an extremely difficult man to love. Troy never praised his sons. He made them feel worthless if they failed to meet his expectations or follow his orders. Lucious is cut from a similar cloth. Jamal and his brothers believe that they are survivors just for growing up as his children. Throughout much of his life Jamal is treated like trash by Lucious (who literally stuffed him in a garbage can when he was a child) as punishment for a display of homosexual behavior. Hours before Jamal put his life on the line for him at the ASAs, Lucious declared that he hoped he would soon die from AIDS so that he could no longer embarrass him. The shooting makes it impossible for Jamal to sing in public without being high on drugs or suffering a nervous breakdown. Rather than comfort him, Lucious uses this as an opportunity to challenge his son's manhood again. He even threatens to release him from his contract at Empire if he could no longer do live performances. While Lucious is not an absentee father in the physical sense, he is emotionally absent. Therapist Deborah Luepnitz suggests that a father's emotional absence can be just as devastating for the children.[38] This is evident in the behavior of the three sons. Jamal goes to rehab for a pill addiction, Andre attempts suicide, and Hakeem gets arrested and has a child out of wedlock with Anika. Lucious might as well be the stereotypical absentee black father.

In her book *Female Masculinity* (1989), Judith Halberstam notes that traditional versions of masculinity are often praised while alternative forms are demonized.³⁹ Lucious struggles to identify with Jamal because he is gay. The only thing that brings Lucious and Jamal together is their passion for music. But it also drives a wedge between them as Jamal's career begins to exceed Lucious' accomplishments. A striking example of this occurs when Jamieson Hinthrop (William Fichtner), a gay white marketing executive, asks Lucious if he is proud to see Jamal doing better than himself. Lucious says no, but then tries to act as if he is just flippant. On another occasion, Pepsi picks Jamal for their new commercial. Lucious is unable to veil his envy when he learns that the director does not want to include any of his music in the ad. After he and Jamal are both nominated for the ASA Song of the Year, Lucious begins spreading rumors that Jamal fabricated being a homosexual to hurt his credibility with the ASA voters. In season three he convinces Jamal to postpone the release of his album *When Cookie Met Lucious* so that his comeback album, *Inferno*, could be in the spotlight.

Lucious has inculcated his youngest son Hakeem with his values and worldview since he was a child. Hakeem's admiration for Lucious disappears after he learns that he blackmailed his former lover, Camilla, to leave town and may have killed his beloved uncle Bunkie. Hakeem breaks from Empire, establishes a competitive record label, Lyon Dynasty, impregnates his father's ex-fiance Anika, and casts the deciding vote on Empire's board of trustees to remove Lucious from his position as the company's CEO. After Hakeem replaces him as CEO, Lucious vents his wrath by meeting with him at the docks where he killed Bunkie. He hands Hakeem a gun and dares him to shoot as he walks off. When that fails to work, Lucious takes advantage of every opportunity to sabotage his son's leadership. First, he coerces the lead member of a Latina girl group that Hakeem is developing for Lyon Dynasty to sign with Empire. Next, he has Freda Gatz, a lesbian gangsta rapper signed to Empire, release a "diss" record that brutally emasculates Hakeem by referring to him as "daddy's little girl" repeatedly in the song's hook. Lucious plants drugs on the tour bus of Hakeem's girl group, Mirage a Trois. He has Andre stall the release of an app(lication) for Swiftstream, Empire's new subscription based music streaming service. Lucious highjacks a status meeting with Empire's board of trustees and investors to publicly humiliate Hakeem for all of the company's recent shortcomings under his leadership. This maneuver convinces the board members to replace Hakeem with him and Cookie as co-CEOs.

Lucious manipulates Andre to do his dirty work to keep the family business afloat. After police began investigating him in the wake of Bunkie's murder, Lucious has Andre use his magical penis to seduce Deputy Mayor Raquel Alvarez to hand over transcripts from an interview with a homeless man who witnessed the shooting. This chicanery was just the latest example of Andre breaking the law as a demonstration of love for his father. When he was a child, he hid his father's gun in a pile of his Lego toys as police officers raided their home in search of illegal firearms. Andre pays bribes to, and solicits prostitutes for, the company's investors. He even prostitutes his wife for business deals. Andre expects her to sleep with an elderly board member confined to a wheelchair. There is no such thing as unconditional love when it comes to Lucious and Andre. Lucious makes him the president of Empire's Gutter Life Records because he helped him beat a legal case. Andre becomes the president of Empire Xtreme after he uncovers a computer hacker targeting Empire.

Andre earned a Master of Business Administration (MBA) from the Wharton School to become Empire's chief financial officer (CFO). He traveled home during his final exams to tend to his father's business. It was his idea to take the company public. Andre, perhaps more than any of the sons, has gone out of his way to gain his father's love. So why does Lucious routinely shame him and treat him with contempt? Lucious' feelings towards Andre stem from multiple factors. First, he is the only family member that does not possess musical talent. Cookie may not perform, but she has a gifted ear for music, arranging and producing songs, and developing artists. Andre often feels excluded when his family shares musical moments together. While they happily perform Lucious' hit "You're So Beautiful" at Lucious' nightclub, before adoring fans, Andre is back at Empire headquarters having a mental breakdown.

The series premiere of *The Cosby Show* revolved around Cliff's concerns about Theo's poor report card. Cliff tries to warn his son of the dangers of being a slacker in school. On the series finale, Cliff is overcome with joy as he attends Theo's graduation from NYU. But on *Empire,* rather than celebrate Andre for his academic achievements, Lucious berates him for lacking "street" smarts.[40] Patricia Hill Collins notes that this lack of appreciation for formal learning has become a perceived component of black masculinity.[41] It brings to mind stories that my father shared with me of family members telling him not to read so many books because excessive reading might cause an ulcer. Lucious views Andre as a sellout for not only assuming that he deserves to inherit Empire, but believing his Ivy League degree and his lovely, blond-haired white wife allows him to transcend race.

Making matters worse, Andre suffers from the same bipolar disorder that drove Lucious' mother, Leah Walker (Leslie Uggams), to nearly drown him as a child. Child protective services separated Lucious from his mother, who would end up homeless. When Lucious became famous, he found her on the street and hid her away in a group home for the mentally ill. He told the public a false story that she had taken her life 20 years ago playing Russian roulette because he was ashamed of her condition. Lucious projects his feelings for his mother onto Andre: "The truth is, you've got mental issues. I sent you to all those fancy schools, let you marry Rhonda … my mom was a nut job. I was embarrassed by her. Same way I'm embarrassed by you."[42] Andre gets baptized in an attempt to cure his psychological ailments and find a greater purpose for his life. Rather than support him, Lucious mocks his spiritual awakening. Lucious sees Andre's baptism as a sign of weakness. "You're asking me to watch someone dunk you in tap water. There is no God, you just need to man the hell up," Lucious tells him.[43]

Then there is Lucious' capricious relationship with Cookie. She accepts her prison sentence for the sake of her family. She never admits to Lucious' involvement in the illegal drug operation, but he divorces her and begins dating other women. He refuses to give her co-ownership of Empire when she returns from prison. He kicks her out of business meetings with little regard for her feelings. Lucious shoots her cousin Bunkie to death. When she learns the truth about Bunkie's death, she tries to suffocate Lucious in his sleep. Lucious flaunts his flings with other women, Anika, Harper Scott, and Giuliana Green, in her face. He marries Anika to avoid potential prison time; however, he is so possessive of Cookie that he refuses to allow her to date other men. When he takes from the shares promised to his sons to give Cookie stock in the company, Rhonda accuses him of trying to buy her loyalty. He eventually fires her from Empire causing her to start her own record label. Rather than allow Cookie to shine he purchases APEX Satellite Radio, granting him the power to keep her artists off the radio. The former couple's drama is always one insult away from boiling over into a full blown fight as was manifested during the middle of a visit to see Jamal while he is staying at a drug rehabilitation center.

On rare moments Lucious does act like a loving father. He may hurt his family, but he would die before anyone else laid a finger on them. The best example of this is when tells a crazed gunman that he was responsible for getting his girlfriend pregnant to make the gunman shoot him instead of Jamal or Cookie. He orders the death of the ruthless gangster Frank Gathers (Chris Rock) to protect Cookie and his family. Lucious asks his mother if she thinks that he is a good father. She responds that he will never be a good father until he learns to be a good person. She blames his sins on the guilt that he has carried since witnessing his father's murder as a child. When I polled 100 respondents about *Empire* only 24.32 percent of them associated the word "father" with Lucious, in comparison to words like gangster (51.35 percent) and entrepreneur (59.46 percent).

If his parenting skills fail to meet the Huxtable's standards, the same can be said of Cookie's maternal image. Do not get me wrong. I am aware that Cookie loves her sons unconditionally, refuses to let them make the same mistakes that put her in prison, and would risk her life for their safety. Her 17-year incarceration could be looked upon as the ultimate sacrifice. These facts notwithstanding, she knowingly plays a part in her ex-husband's egotistical ploy to make their sons nearly battle to the death for his *conditional* love. Cookie supports the lifestyles of Jamal and Andre; however, by referring to Jamal as a "faggot," a "stupid sissy," and a "queen," she plays a role in queer bashing. Likewise she playfully refers to his Latin ex-boyfriend Michael as Michelle. Cookie tells Andre that he is crazy and questions his marriage to Rhonda. And then there is her strained relation with Hakeem. Since she was incarcerated when he was just a baby, their mother-son relationship has been nonexistent. During their first encounter, he calls her a bitch. Cookie responds by beating him with a broom, leaving a bruise by his eye and cut on his lower lip. On episodes of *The Cosby Show* Clair responded to her children's misbehavior with maternal displeasure. She often told Cliff to deal with it before she had to kill someone. But for all of her talk, viewers never saw Clair or Cliff Huxtable use any physical force to discipline their children.

Sibling rivalry is an underlying theme in the series. The Lyon boys love each other, yet bicker on a regular basis. Cookie and her sisters have issues dating back to their father's death. The relationship between Lucious and his half-brother Tariq represents a modern day example of Cain and Abel. Tariq has been envious of his older brother since childhood. His mother did her best to prevent the two siblings from developing a close relationship. Their father, a police officer named Joe Walker, was murdered because he was having an affair with Tariq's mother. Tariq's hatred and envy of Lucious stem from the fact that he was robbed of developing a close relationship with their father because he was viewed as the bastard child. Tariq, now an FBI agent, uses that hatred of his brother to launch an investigation to destroy the Lyon Empire and put Lucious behind bars. As fate would have it, just as the brothers attempt to reconcile with each other Tariq is murdered by Lucious' mother. The deranged old woman stabs Tariq in the neck with a letter opener as revenge for his mother sleeping with her husband. She stands by watching the blood gush out of his neck as he gasps for his final breaths.

Music is the unifying factor in the Lyon family. Whenever they are experiencing dark moments music is the healing source of their strength to break every chain of despair. When Cookie was locked away to rot in prison for nearly two decades it was the sounds of Lucious' music stored in her memory that got her through it. Jamal and Hakeem sing the lyrics of Bill Whithers' inspiring anthem "Lean on Me" to help calm Andre after he experiences a manic moment while the three are trapped in an elevator. The brothers use music to console Andre after Rhonda suffers a miscarriage after being pushed down a flight of stairs by Anika. Music allows Lucious and Jamal to establish some semblance of a father-son relationship. Lucious is partially persuaded to name Jamal his successor after he helps him to develop a new song, "Nothing to Lose." The family communicates with each other and reveals their secrets and problems through the music. Jamal tries to use his music to heal his family's wounds. The business of music has made this family wealthy for generations to come, but it is also what ultimately tears them apart.

When the Lyons Met the Huxtables

It would be too facile to categorize the representation of the African American family on *Empire* as bad and *The Cosby Show* as a good. I view these two series as the Ying and the Yang of black television. They are contrary images of the African American family that complement each other. *The Cosby Show* was knocked off its lofty pedestal of respectability more than two decades before the contentious *Ebony* cover. Henry Louis Gates, Jr., accused *The Cosby Show* of reassuring whites that racism was a relic of the past. Conservative whites and blacks could use the Huxtables to support their argument that the black underclass was the result of laziness and personal flaws.[44] *The Village Voice* accused Bill Cosby of not being black enough to be considered an Uncle Tom. A writer for *The New York Times* described the sitcom as *Leave It to Beaver* in blackface.[45]

In 1992 professors Sut Jhally and Justin Lewis published a damning book titled *Enlightened Racism: The Cosby Show, Audiences and the Myth of the American Dream.* Jhally and Lewis interviewed 52 focus groups about the images depicted in the series. They concluded that while viewers appreciated the show's avoidance of stereotypes, its upper middle-class presentation of the African American experience distorted the experience of most blacks, relieving white viewers of responsibility and concern about race relations.[46] Michael Eric Dyson, author of *Is Bill Cosby Right? Or Has the Black Middle Class Lost Its Mind?* (2005), took Cosby to task for what he believed was his indifference to the problems of the black poor. Dyson says this was reflected in his sitcom's refusal to address social issues impacting thousands of less fortunate blacks. Ironically, NBC aired *The Cosby Show*'s series finale the week of the infamous 1992 Los Angeles Riots. On NBC, the Huxtables were celebrating Theo's college graduation. On the other networks poor blacks in

South Central, Los Angeles, were shouting burn baby burn in protest of the Rodney King trial verdict.

The Cosby Show ignored local racially charged incidents at the time such as the Central Park Five or the murder of Michael Griffith at Howard Beach in Queens.[47] The series ignored the crack cocaine epidemic, which has left an indelible mark on the black community until this day. Mothers became junkies willing to become prostitutes and sell their children's belongings for a fix.[48] Grandmothers were left as the legal guardians of "crack" babies. Drug related gang violence turned neighborhood sidewalks into killing zones in which anyone could become a target. President Ronald Reagan and the U.S. Congress responded to the crack epidemic with a continuation of Richard Nixon's 1971 War on Drugs.[49] A first-time offender caught with crack cocaine, even if there was no evidence of intent to sell, received a minimum five-year prison sentence. Michelle Alexander, the author of *The New Jim Crow* (2010), describes the war on drugs as a government approved demonization of African American and Latino men and women.[50] Essentially, it was a pass to reinstate convict leasing or slavery by another name.[51] By 1991, 25 percent of black males were behind bars serving time for non-violent drug offenses. President Bill Clinton's 1994 crime bill and three strikes rule increased funding to build a prison industrial complex system nationwide.

According to economist Derek Neal, the likelihood of a black person going to prison for drug trafficking tripled between 1985 and 2000.[52] Black fathers were removed from households making it the greatest separation of black families since slavery. The Southern Coalition for Social Justice reports that black women became three times more likely of being incarcerated as white women.[53] Drug offenses have been responsible for 29 percent of the state prison sentences for women. By 2015, one in every 14 black children had a parent in prison.[54] Lucious and Cookie Lyon are byproducts of the crack generation, the war on drugs, and the new Jim Crow. Cookie struggles to rebuild relationships with her sons and Lucious after being separated from them for nearly two decades while she was incarcerated. Cookie's younger sister Carol is a recovering junkie. In one episode Cookie has to travel to Philadelphia to search for Carol in a crack house. Crack has severed the Lyon family; however, paradoxically, crack is partly responsible for the family's exit from poverty.

Empire addresses several issues within the black family that *The Cosby Show* sidestepped to eliminate degrading black images and controversial topics from the program. These issues include drug abuse, mass incarceration, welfare, infidelity, divorce, and interracial marriage. *Empire* has been both praised and judged severely for its emphasis on the LGBTQ community, but these nonconformist individuals did not exist in the Huxtable's "perfect" conservative version of America. (Chapter 4 delves further into *Empire*'s LGBTQ emphasis.) "While unintentional, *The Cosby Show* enabled some of the ugliest Reagan-era fantasies," says Chauncey DeVega.[55] Cookie's abusive treatment of Hakeem raises attention to the larger issue of corporal punishment in black households. If black parents spared the rod, would they spoil the child? Are spankings an extension of the violent beatings and scars of slavery?[56] This question had become a hot take for talk radio, think pieces, social media, debate-oriented television shows, and black sitcoms like *Black-ish* because of NFL football star Adrian Peterson's child abuse scandal.[57] The Huxtables disciplined their children without the use of corporal punishment. While that is an accurate depiction of some black families, there are many black households in which spankings are a rite of passage for the children.

One of *Empire*'s best contributions to television is tackling the issue of mental illness in black families and the overall African American community. Andre and his paternal grandmother suffer from bipolar disorder, a mental illness characterized by depression and elevated mood swings called mania. The disorder can drive individuals to commit suicide. In season one Andre puts a loaded gun to his head in an unsuccessful attempt to take his life in his father's recording studio. His grandmother had a similar experience nearly 40 years earlier. Lucious and Cookie have a difficult time accepting their son's condition. Lucious blows a fuse when a medical doctor first tells him of Andre's condition. Cookie mocks his condition as a white person's disease. Her attitude reflects popular opinions about mental illness held by many people in the African American community. Episode 14 of the NBC sitcom *The Carmichael Show* (aptly titled "The Blues") depicts the matriarch Cynthia's (Loretta Devine) shame of undergoing therapy due to the stigma of mental illness. She and her family initially dismiss her feelings of depression as just something with which black people deal. Her husband Joe (David Allen Grier) sarcastically implies that all the best black music comes from pain. In his 2016 action-comedy film *Central Intelligence* comedian Kevin Hart says black families do not seek professional therapy, they simply go to the barbershop. And one of the characters on *Black-ish* said talking to a therapist just feels too much like snitching.

Mental illness is no joking matter for black families. University of Texas at Austin professor King Davis is leading a groundbreaking research project on the history of mental illness in the African American community. In his 2016 paper, "Central Lunatic Asylum for Colored Insane 1865–1900: the First 50,000 Admissions," he presents an overview of the earliest recorded cases of blacks with mental illness. According to Davis, the common belief in colonial era medical schools was that only wealthy whites experienced mental illness. Due to their property ownership, their lives were more stressful. However, in the 1840s hospitals in Virginia began admitting free blacks as patients diagnosed with mental problems. On June 7, 1870, the Central Lunatic Asylum was opened to treat blacks labeled mentally insane. This was the first hospital of its kind in the world. A similar hospital was opened in Crownsville, Maryland, in 1911. The black patients in Crownsville were forced to participate in "industrial therapy," which meant working in the tobacco fields, basket weaving, and other forms of agricultural labor. They were also given "hydrotherapy," a practice of placing patients in ice-cold tubs. The black doctors, who began working at the hospital after the 1940s, believed that this treatment was not only therapeutic but also helped to uplift the race.[58]

Racist attitudes tainted the diagnoses of black patients. In addition to manic episodes and depression, blacks were admitted for the some of the following causes: religious excitement, unhappy marriages, idiocy, masturbation, talking back to white superiors, criminal deviance, and *freedom*.[59] Racist white physician Samuel A. Cartwright coined the Greek derived phrase "Drapetomania," in 1851, to refer to a mental illness that caused slaves to run away from their plantations or seek freedom.[60] In his book *Sick from Freedom: African American Illness and Suffering during the Civil War and Reconstruction* (2012), Jim Downs documents the number of diagnosed cases of newly freed blacks who experienced a host of sicknesses.[61] Black families developed a distrust of psychiatrists causing mental health to become a stigmatized topic.

Historically black parents have taught their sons and daughters to be emotionally strong. The past experiences of the ancestors during slavery and Jim Crow serve as examples of the innate fortitude that all blacks are supposed to possess. Far too many black parents or their children are still living with mental illness in silence.[62] "With black Americans leading the country in unemployment, child abuse, domestic violence, all of which can exacerbate stress, it is not surprising that the community leads the country in mental health struggles," writes Keli Goff in a 2013 article for *The Root*. Goff reports that many blacks do not seek professional medical attention due to a stigma, lack of insurance, and a belief that the church and prayer will solve their problems. *Psychology Today* notes that black men are less likely to seek treatment because it makes them look weak.[63] Between 1993 and 2012 the suicide rate for black boys increased from 1.78 to 3.47 per million.[64] Hip-Hop executives Shakir Stewart and Chris Lighty, assumed to be suffering from mental illness, both died from self-inflicted gunshots.[65] Such tragic news makes the scenes of Andre taking his medication even more poignant.

Elaine Flores, a contributor for *The Root* living with bipolar disorder, says *Empire* exaggerates Andre's condition in the first season by having his moods constantly fluctuating from extreme highs to extreme lows. Andre is the worst-case example of the condition, in her opinion. She says that having him take a shower in his business suit or play Russian roulette in his father's studio is more stereotypical than educational. Flores admits that his reckless spending during manic fits, such as buying a new Lamborghini on the company credit card or bags of Christmas gifts in July, is realistic but needs to be placed in a better context. Despite her criticism, she still credits *Empire* for at least trying to tackle a sensitive subject for black families.[66] Viewers watch his wife Rhonda routinely remind him to take his daily medication and see the tragic consequences if he forgets to do so.

King Davis says that there is a great deal of truth in Andre's refusal to use his medication once he joined the church. A large number of black Christians believe that prayer is all they need to cure their mental ailments.[67] Davis tells a story of a black pastor in Texas who was encouraging his members to bring all their prescription drugs to the front of the church and give them over to the Lord.[68] I had the privilege of interviewing the Rev. Danielle Graham, an associate black pastor in her early thirties at Metropolitan Baptist Church in Largo, Maryland. The Reverend Graham was diagnosed with depression and anxiety in 2008. After a suicide attempt, while in seminary, she went to her pastor in Pittsburgh, Pennsylvania, for counseling. She was saddened by the lack of support and understanding from a few church leaders whose best advice was: "Pray about it." Her family members gave her similar advice based on their understanding of Paul's epistle to the Philippians, chapter four, verses six through seven, which says, "Be anxious for nothing, but in everything by prayer and supplication, with thanksgiving, let your requests be made to God; and the peace of God, which surpasses all understanding will guard your hearts and minds through Jesus Christ."[69] The Reverend Graham appreciates *Empire* for shining light on this issue. When a music therapist, played by Jennifer Hudson, prayed with Andre it reminded her of her own therapy. When Andre stopped taking his medication because his pastor said he did not need it, she thought of her own experience. Graham, who started a Facebook group called "Depressed in the community of faith," was moved to organize a faith-based *Empire* watch party to discuss the show's presentation of mental illness with attendees.[70]

Black family sitcoms in the 1970s made viewers believe that the black characters were depressed or angry because they were poor. The sitcoms of the 1980s made everyone appear to be happy much of the time. *Empire* tells families that it is okay to acknowledge mental illness and encourages them to seek treatment for it. I would not be surprised to learn that Lucious suffers from narcissistic personality disorder. This mental disorder is characterized by an unusually inflated ego, insatiable need for admiration, and a lack of empathy for anyone else. Individuals diagnosed with this disorder shield their fragile self-esteem with an outward confidence that makes them feel superior to others.

The Rich and the Dysfunctional

The Lyons clan is not the first upper class black family to rule primetime television ratings. The success of *The Cosby Show* paved the way for NBC's next hit sitcom, *The Fresh Prince of Bel-Air* (1990–1996). *Fresh Prince* was inspired by the true story of Benny Medina, a 32-year-old music executive responsible for launching the career of Jennifer Lopez. Following his mother's death, Medina became a wayward adolescent who was in and out of juvenile detention centers. His life changed forever when he was given the opportunity to move into the Beverly Hills, California, home of Motown Records founder Berry Gordy. Quincy Jones, the legendary music producer, took Medina's story to NBC with the intention of creating a new sitcom. NBC loved the pitch and assigned Andy and Susan Borowitz, upper middle-class Harvard educated white scriptwriters and producers, to develop the series.

Will Smith, at the time a member of the rap duo DJ Jazzy Jeff & the Fresh Prince, was selected to play Will, a teenager, from West Philadelphia, born and raised, sent to live with his wealthy Uncle Phil(lip) and Aunt Viv(ian) Banks in Beverly Hills. The Banks lived next door to former President Ronald Reagan in a mansion located in the predominantly white Brentwood neighborhood. Uncle Phil (James Avery) was a Princeton University and Harvard Law School educated judge. Aunt Viv (Janet Hubert-Whitten and Daphene Maxwell Reid) was a former Alvin Ailey dancer turned college professor with a Ph.D. Season one revolved around Will's culture shock trying to assimilate into this elite world while maintaining what he believed was authentic blackness. On the series premiere, Uncle Phil was disgusted with Will's urban, hip-hop attire and slang. Uncle Phil wanted Will to behave more like his son Carlton (Alfonso Ribeiro). The early episodes contrasted the "cool" street smart Will with his preppy cousin Carlton, who was obsessed with gaining admission into Princeton University. Carlton's older sister Hillary (Karyn Parsons) came across as a "valley girl" possessing no trace of black self-identity or cultural awareness. Only Ashley (Tatyana Ali), the youngest of the family's children, was interested in learning about life outside of her bubble of opulence. While Aunt Viv outwardly embodied black culture, Uncle

Phil came across as an out-of-touch, zealously opportunistic republican obsessed with meeting standards of respectability. He held a weekly high tea in the living room where the family sat together drinking tea and listening to Bach's Brandenburg Concertos. There is nothing wrong with Bach, but Phillip intentionally chose not to expose the kids to any of the black music that he grew up listening to as a teenager. Whenever Will questioned Uncle Phil's blackness, he lectured him on his past involvement in black power protests and the Civil Rights Movement.

Despite the writers' attempts to humanize the Banks as a multi-dimensional family, they upheld countless myths about the black elite. Historically this social group has not been viewed favorably outside of their confined communities. E. Franklin Frazier's book, *Black Bourgeoisie* (1957), criticized upper middle-class blacks for being more preoccupied with their conspicuous consumption and leisure than they were with weightier matters. Kevin Gaines states in *Uplifting the Race: Black Leadership, Politics and Culture in the Twentieth Century* (1996), that black elites developed a middle-class ideology of racial uplift to defeat racism with material and moral progress. During the 19th, century this racial uplift ideology evolved as part of a "liberation theology" centered on the collective advancement of the race. However, by the dawn of the 20th century, black elites began focusing more on advancing themselves and drawing distinct divisions from other blacks based on class.[71]

Many elite black families were descendants of the privileged house slaves and free black families. Margo Jefferson's *Negroland: A Memoir* (2015) and Lawrence Otis Graham's *Our Kind of People: Inside America's Black Upper Class* (1999) provide primary accounts of elitism within privileged black communities.[72] Elite families defined themselves by placing their children in special social programs like Jack and Jill of America. Jack and Jill was established in 1938 to provide wealthy black children with proper educational, cultural, and civic opportunities. Wealthy black parents could shield their children from riding segregated buses to substandard public schools because they had the means to drive their own cars to private schools. Elite blacks attended Ivy League universities and what were considered the most prestigious HBCUs: Howard University, Morehouse College, Spelman College, and Fisk University. They joined "the right" collegiate Greek chapters: Alpha Phi Alpha, Delta Sigma Theta, Omega Psi Phi, Alpha Kappa Alpha, and Kappa Alpha Psi.[73] Professional adults sought admission into social clubs like Sigma Pi Phi Boule and The Links. Their social outings included debutante cotillions and vacationing at the village of Oak Bluffs, Martha's Vineyard.[74]

Colorism was an issue in many of the institutions and organizations that the elite joined. Individuals, at times, gained admission based on the brown paper bag test, which measured the lightness of one's skin complexion.[75] If you were too dark, your admission would be denied. Lawrence Otis Graham recalls his grandmother telling him not to stay out in the sun too long because it would darken his skin. Graham reflects on her other prejudices in his book. She called the civil rights protestors "a bunch of nappy-headed Negroes screaming and marching." She could not stand Marvin Gaye or Aretha Franklin because they sang "low-class, Baptist, spiritual-sounding rock and roll music." Although she was proud of Sidney Poitier for winning an Academy Award in 1964, she hated the fact that his skin was so black.[76] Many elites at the turn of the 20th century espoused notions of racial uplift and viewed themselves as members of the talented tenth. In her dissertation "In Search of Purity: Popular Eugenics & Racial Uplift Among New Negroes 1915–1935," Shantella Sherman argues that elites and intellectuals such as Howard University professors Ernest E. Just and Kelly Miller promoted Social Darwinism. They believed that certain blacks were genetically inclined to be superior. It was up to these blacks to uplift race with their respectability. The elites who accepted these ideas of Darwinism and popular eugenics feared that the less educated, unattractive, and uncivilized dark skinned blacks were reproducing too much.

The Lyon family exhibits an obsession with material items, money, and power. Lucious perms his hair, Cookie spends thousands on hair weaves and wigs, and Lucious' mother uses skin-lightening creams. Nevertheless, the Lyons' affiliation with the streets and hip-hop makes them outliers among this elite class. Cookie's uppity older sister Candace (Vivica A. Fox), is married to a rich white man. Candace's children attend the best private schools and are involved in social activities traditionally associated with the well-to-do. Candace views Cookie as an imposter and looks down on her for the way she attained her social status. "If 17 years of prison taught you anything it's definitely how to dress like a monkey and talk like a pimp," she tells Cookie.[77] The Lyons are not supposed to be here. The Lyons were on welfare in the 1980s. They sold drugs and undervalued education. Except for Andre and Rhonda, there is never any mention of schooling for any of the other family members during the first two seasons. They are not members of any dignified groups or social organizations. They are disconnected from the church, politics, and civil rights.

Empire further highlights these class differences with the introduction of the Dubois family in season three. Cookie begins dating a black city councilman, Angelo Dubois (Taye Diggs). Dubois, a product of Jack and Jill and cotillions, is running to become New York's first black mayor since David Dinkins. Angelo hails from one the city's oldest elite black families. This family has produced governors, senators, and presidential cabinet members. Angelo's mother is the illustrious Diana Dubois, played by *The Cosby Show*'s leading lady Phylicia Rashad. You cannot imagine how tickled I was to see Mrs. Huxtable join *Empire*'s cast. Mrs. Dubois, however, is as cold as she is prim and proper. She throws more shade towards the Lyons than a palm tree.[78] "I read books, not graffiti," she tells Lucious. She worries about her son's association with the Lyon family as he runs for office. She calls the Lyons, with their thuggish behavior and rap music, a setback to the entire (black) race.

Cookie attempts to gain the favor of Mrs. Dubois by hosting family dinner at her home. There is a quite a bit of irony in seeing *Empire*'s matriarch going out of her way to earn the favor of *Mrs. Huxtable*. Although Cookie's goal was to put on airs for Mrs. Dubois, the dinner ends up further highlighting the differences between their two families. Jamal is sky high on the prescription pills that he has been abusing. Hakeem shows up with his baby crying unceasingly. Andre skips the dinner. Lucious and Anika make an unannounced visit causing a scene. Lucious takes delight in spilling all of the family's "shameful" secrets to sabotage Cookie's chances of having a new relationship. Mrs. Dubois eventually accepts Cookie, but with major reservations. She cannot afford to have her family's name sullied by the Lyons. After Cookie publicly rejects Angelo's marriage proposal and ruins his mayoral campaign, Mrs. Dubois' swears that she will ruin the Lyon family; going as far as to have child protective services take Cookie's grandbaby Bella. Mrs. Dubois then takes the baby for herself. Cookie's best quote so far might be her dismissal of Rashad's character: "I don't trust that fake-ass Clair Huxtable."[79] Mrs. Dubois' desire for power ultimately leads to her arrest and Angelo's death.

The Lyons and the Dubois become a modern day version of the Hatfields and the McCoys.[80] The feud is reminiscent of those found in the popular 1980s primetime soap opera *Dallas*. *Empire* provides just one example of upper-class African American families on primetime television today. The Oprah Winfrey Network (OWN) has two successful primetime soap operas depicting these elite families. Tyler Perry's *The Haves and the Have Nots* (2013–) features the fictional Harrington family in Savannah, Georgia. David Harrington (Peter Parros) is a corrupt, wealthy judge and lieutenant gubernatorial contender married to Veronica (Angela Robinson), a snobbish, treacherous Ivy League educated attorney. Veronica displays much of her wickedness towards her gay adult son Jeffery (Gavin Houston) whom she views as a punishment from God for a past abortion. Her contempt for Jeffrey is far worse than Lucious' treatment of Jamal. Veronica blames Jeffrey for David's infidelity and later tries to burn David to death by pouring a flammable liquid around his bed. David survives and asks for a divorce. Jeffrey stabs Veronica, but the blade gets lodged in her breast implants, saving her life. The real star of the soap opera is an upscale escort named Candace Young (Tika Sumpter) who hails from a working class family. Then there is OWN's series *Greenleaf* (2016–), about a fictional first family of a megachurch in Memphis, Tennessee. Bishop James Greenleaf (Keith David) is the founder, senior pastor, and CEO of Calvary Fellowship World Ministries. Over the past 40 years, the bishop grew Calvary from a tiny storefront to a multimillion dollar empire. The Greenleafs live in a luxurious mansion equipped with black servants. Every member of the Greenleaf family is involved in the ministry. Sadly, there is much to abhor, little to admire. Adultery, financial corruption, secret homosexual relationships, pedophilia, rape, violence, and murder threaten to destroy the family and the church.

The sophisticated Dubois family on *Empire* has their host of shameful secrets, too. The family's fortune originated from bootlegging during prohibition. When Mrs. Dubois learns that a reporter plans to publish an article, on the eve of the mayoral election, revealing a scandalous secret about Angelo she looks to Lucious for assistance. It turns out that when Angelo was 17-years-old, he was arrested for drunk driving. His car crashed into a lake. He escaped while an unidentified young woman drowned. The Dubois family had his record expunged, and all memory of the incident disappeared. His mother, realizing that Lucious is a gangster, asks him to do whatever it takes to prevent that article from being published. She promises to ruin her son's relationship with Cookie in exchange for Lucious' support.

Friends have asked me why these prominent black families have to carry themselves shamefully to be viewed as "real" and relatable to the masses. Why can't they be more like the Obamas or the Currys, the NBA's first family, who are held up in the media as models of perfection?[81] Why can't the Lyons reflect the more positive traits of the black family found in *Black-ish* or *The Carmichael Show*? Those Norman Lear inspired sitcoms address the uncomfortable issues ignored by *The Cosby Show* without using any of the stereotypes found in *Empire*. *Black-ish*, in particular, makes it a priority to present the black family in a positive light without appearing too idealistic. The patriarch Dre has an extremely close relationship with his five children. His parents are divorced, but they both play pivotal roles in his life. Dre, an advertising executive and Howard University graduate, is happily married to the beautiful Rainbow (Tracee Ellis Ross). Bow is a bi-racial anesthesiologist who graduated from Brown University. The Johnsons are this generation's version of the Huxtables. For the record *Black-ish* creator Kenya Barris finds *Empire* to be distasteful and the opposite of what he is doing.[82]

Does Hollywood have a hidden agenda to tarnish the black family? The answer is complicated and cannot be answered with a terse response. *Blackish* is a favorite of the critics every awards season. Most blacks praise it for its willingness to tackle interracial and intraracial topics with blunt honesty. Surprisingly, only a quarter of its audience is black. Based on these facts the answer is no. However, *The Carmichael Show*, despite positive reviews and its depiction of a more universally relatable middle class family, was cancelled by NBC after only three seasons due to low viewership. Since Empire has the highest ratings of the three series will Hollywood executives be more likely to duplicate the Lyons or the Johnson/Carmichaels? Will there be more family programming like the solemn Oprah Winfrey Network drama *Queen Sugar* or the campy Empire? Will networks follow the lead of NBC's award winning drama, *This Is Us*, which presents a unique look at a black family on a predominantly white series? As previously stated *Empire* is based on primetime white soaps from the 1980s, *Dynasty* and *Dallas*. The Carringtons and the Ewings were television's original dysfunctional families. As Ien Ang reiterates in her book *Watching Dallas,* perpetual family drama and tragedy is the overwhelming characteristic of all successful melodramatic soap operas. The feuds between married and divorced couples, parents and children, siblings, lovers, and the ex-wives and the mistresses are what drive ratings. You had the homophobic father who opposed his gay son. Furthermore, the series in which the family and the family business overlap is always a source of disunity between the husband and the wife or the patriarch and the children who eventually are expected to inherit his fortune.[83] The overbearing patriarch, for example Blake Carrington in *Dynasty*, often excused his own bad behavior and emotional absence by saying that his actions were for the good of the family business. How many times have *Empire* fans heard Lucious use this same excuse?

But since we are not living in a post-racial society and given the historic depiction of the black family dating back to the Moynihan Report, such representations cross the line between realism and stereotypical behavior. Moynihan and Moyers said the black family was decaying due to the absence of a male figure. The paradox lies in the fact that on *Empire* you have an example of a nuclear family unit, not living in poverty, still plagued by a host of pathologies. This complexity certainly muddies the waters through which to think about family life in black communities. Does the popularity of this series reflect experiences that many black families can relate to such as divorce, jealousy, the incarceration of a parent, and broken relationships? Although *Empire* greatly exaggerates these problems they are indeed issues faced by many families, regardless of race. Until recently these issues in the black family were either ignored or given minimal attention on sitcoms. *Empire* reveals how much the image of the black family in primetime television has changed over the last 40 years. When I began writing this book there was a profusion of television programming about the black family. *Black-ish, Braxton Family Values, Greenleaf, Marlon, Queen Sugar, Black Lightning, Survivor's Remorse, The Carmichael Show,* and *Welcome to Sweetie Pie's* are just a few examples. Black families have other viewing options than *Empire*. Nevertheless, *Empire* has the largest platform in America and overseas which adds more significance to its portrayal of the family.

2

Boom, Boom, Boom, Boom
Lucious Lyon and the Black Outlaw's American Dream

> "*You can fool this country you legit, but I know you ain't nothing but a punk ass gangster.*"[1]
>
> —Bunkie

Lucious Lyon is a father, a musician, a gangster, a businessman, and most definitively a dreamer. The opening scene of *Empire*'s series premiere finds him in the studio trying to get a young artist to pour more of her emotions into a ballad. His passion for turning her song into a platinum hit is manifested in his tireless efforts to make her get it right. It is this passion that has fueled his rise to the top of the music industry. But his story is not that of the standard New York City executive. "I started selling drugs when I was nine years old in Philadelphia. I did it to feed myself. But it was the music that played in my head that kept me alive when I thought I was gonna get shot," he tells his company's board of directors.[2] Music gave him the opportunity to abandon the corners and move on up to a Madison Avenue corner address. His endeavors to make Empire a publicly traded enterprise, in season one, symbolize his desire to achieve not only power and riches but, most importantly, acceptance from those who have always treated him as an outcast. When Cookie's cousin Bunkie reminds him that he is nothing more than a gangster, Lucious puts a bullet in his forehead. He exhibits no remorse and has the nerve to stand before a packed church delivering a tearful eulogy for his dear childhood friend. On the surface, Bunkie's murder was provoked by his ill-planned threat to extort $3 million from Lucious. However, Bunkie's death symbolized something much deeper. Lucious was eliminating an impediment to his pursuit of the American dream.

Lucious Lyon is the latest version of the African American outlaw. As far back as the late 19th century, black men have been challenging existing authoritative institutions and law enforcement in an attempt to empower themselves. For these men, the American dream meant equality, power, being providers for their family, and having the freedom to carry themselves like men (not boys). While some men chose to protest, march, or attend school for this dream, others took alternative routes in the criminal underworld. Since the turn of the 20th century, the African American male outlaw has become a folk hero in black neighborhoods and popular culture. The black outlaw's quest for the American dream, by any means necessary, has been acclaimed in folklore, cinema, television, and rap music. How does Lucious Lyon compare to these fictional and nonfictional anti-heroes of the past and present day? What does the celebration of, and interest in, these outlaws in black popular culture manifest about what constitutes heroism, success and the American dream within the African American community?

Dreams and Nightmares

The phrase "the American Dream" first appeared in the 1912 novel *Susan Lenox: Her Fall and Rise* by David Graham Phillips. This dream was a fantasy not a reality or promise of prosperity. The phrase "American Dream" appeared for a second time in a 1923 *Vanity Fair* article by Walter Lippmann. The *Vanity Fair* article focused on the failure of the dream due to a lack of white-collar jobs for all college educated Americans. James Truslow Adams, in his 1931 book *The Epic of America*, defined the dream as "a better, richer and happier life for all citizens."[3] Two years later Adams declared in a *New York Times* article that the American dream had been hijacked. The dream became a failure; it was a broken promise of happiness. Moneymaking and power had become the end goal for Americans at the expense of social responsibility. Adams' critique was proffered by W.E.B. DuBois in his 1903 criticism of Booker T. Washington's philosophy on uplift. "If we make money the object of man-training, we shall develop money-makers but not necessarily men," said DuBois.[4]

Despite this intellectual criticism, politicians sold the American dream ideology to their constituents. Over time the dream became rooted in the founding fathers' promise of life, liberty, and the pursuit of happiness. For African Americans, the American Dream is a complicated subject. The dominant feature in African American life is un-freedom.[5] Reverend Martin Luther King, Jr., preached that the dream was an unfulfilled promise. America had given the Negro people a bad check that came back marked insufficient funds. Black men, living in the 1960s, found themselves fighting for the same rights they won in the 1860s. That is, black men were elected at nearly every level of political authority across the South during the Reconstruction (1865–1877). Sixteen black men served in the U.S. Congress between 1870 and 1877.[6] At the Reconstruction's zenith, it would have been inconceivable to imagine black men carrying placards that read "I Am a Man" 100 years later. Approximately a century after the dawn of Reconstruction, African American social critic James Baldwin and conservative intellectual William F. Buckley were debating if the American dream came at the expense of "the Negro." More than a half-century later, today's literary progeny of Baldwin, Ta-Nehisi Coates, argues that the dream is an exclusionary fantasy based on white privilege, an ignorance of history, and black suppression.[7] It is not coincidental that King's most recognized speech is titled "I Have a Dream."

King's Christian-centered, nonviolent struggle for voting rights, jobs, and justice was rooted in an American Dream ethos. Theologian James Cone points out that while King was dreaming about love and equality coming on that great gettin' up mornin,' Nation of Islam spokesman Malcolm X was having a nightmare.[8] To borrow a quote from Malcolm's 1964 "The Ballot or the Bullet" speech, "I see America through the eyes of the victim. I don't see any American dream; I see an American nightmare."[9] Malcolm's nightmares were about segregation, Ku Klux Klansmen terror, and the threat of incarceration for black southerners simply for registering to vote. For decades black men and women could be imprisoned for six months for as little as vagrancy or stealing a pig worth $1. Malcolm's nightmares included unrelenting visions of lynch mobs terrorizing black bodies hanging from the poplar trees.[10] According to the Tuskegee Institute archives, at least 4,730 blacks were lynched between 1882 and 1951. Victims were tortured, burned alive, dragged behind vehicles and, in several cases, their bodies were dismembered. Ida B. Wells, a black investigative reporter and co-founder of the NAACP, discovered that many of these victims were black men falsely accused of raping white women. The most gruesome lynching in the state of Maryland occurred just five minutes away from the university where I teach. On October 16, 1933, in Princess Anne, Maryland, Mary Denston, a 71-year-old white woman was robbed by a 23-year-old black man named George Armwood and a white man named John Richardson. Ms. Denston told authorities that Armwood raped her. A crowd of 2,000 whites used two 15-foot timbers as battering rams to break into the Princess Anne jail and kidnap Armwood. The mob placed a noose around his neck, dragged him out of jail, stabbed him, and tied him to the back of a truck. Then they cut an ear off and removed his gold tooth. His body was taken to the town courthouse, hung from a telephone line, and set on fire.

The black men (and women) who escaped this racial violence in the South during the Great Migration were met with housing discrimination, unemployment, crime, police brutality, and drugs in northern ghettoes. They were made to feel like outcasts and exotic others. Such conditions created a breeding ground for what Cornel West calls nihilism or a lack of hope. Out such conditions emerged outlaws (numbers runners, pimps, drug dealers, and gangsters) who refused to be broken. In his 1965, autobiography Malcolm reflects on his time working for West Indian Archie, a numbers runner in Harlem, New York. Malcolm said that Archie's ability to remember large combinations of numbers should have garnered him a career in mathematics or science. Instead, the color of Archie's skin reduced him to a life of crime.[11]

West Indian Archie was among a growing number of early 20th-century black men, like Caspar Holstein, who relied on the underground economy to transform their nightmares into dreams. Caspar Holstein, an immigrant of African and Danish descent from St. Croix, and a First World War veteran was Harlem's most notorious numbers runner in the 1920s. Holstein was introduced to this illegal lottery system through his employment as a janitor and doorman for a rich white Wall Street banker. The numbers game that he devised was a simplified version of the New York Stock Exchange. The three-digit winning number was selected as a combination of the last two digits of the New York Stock Exchange total for the day and a third digit from the last number of the "balances total." Black Harlemites would place their bets with Holstein, serving as their bookie, in grocery stores, barbershops, beauty parlors, and nightclubs. One lucky individual could earn $60 from a ten-cent bet. Holstein, nicknamed "Bolita King," earned $12,000 a day and amassed a net worth over two million dollars from running numbers.[12]

Holstein used his platform to become a powerbroker in Harlem's African American community, a political activist, and even a philanthropist, building a school in Liberia. He owned a social club called the Turf Club and Liberty Hall, a building which housed the headquarters for Marcus Garvey's Universal Negro Improvement Association (UNIA). He sponsored beauty contests for the black middle class and was a benefactor for literary contests organized by *Opportunity: A Journal of Negro Life*. He financed dormitories at historically black colleges and universities (HBCUs) throughout the South. During the Harlem Renaissance, he sponsored artists and wrote articles for the *Crisis*, the official publication of the NAACP. Sociologist E. Franklin Frazier dedicated a small section of his 1957 book *Black Bourgeoisie* to Holstein. Frazier noted that these bad men gained access to, and acknowledgment from, the black bourgeoisie because of their financial status. After becoming the president of the Virgin Islands Congressional Council of New York, a lobbying group of West Indian nationalists, in 1923, Holstein traveled to Washington, D.C., to lobby on behalf of the citizenship rights of the Virgin Islands. He took out a full-page ad in the *Washington Post* and published articles in the *Negro World* and *Opportunity* to promote his political agenda.

On September 21, 1928, white men disguised as police officers abducted Holstein as he was departing the Turf Club. The men blindfolded him, bound his hands and feet with wire, and robbed him of his $3,000 diamond ring. Rumors spread throughout Harlem that their Bolita King was kidnapped as ransom for a $30,000 debt incurred at the Belmont horseracing track. Three days later "Harlem's favorite hero," as he was dubbed by *The New York Times*, returned home, but the end of his empire was imminent. Police raided the Turf Club days before Thanksgiving in 1935. He was found guilty in the justice system of running an illegal numbers racket.

Caspar Holstein's successor was Ellsworth Johnson, who was known on the streets of Harlem as Bumpy. Bumpy Johnson got his start as a bodyguard for Harlem's numbers queen Stephanie "Queenie" St. Clair, an immigrant from Marseilles who was earning an astonishing $250,000 a year. Bumpy left Queenie to work for Charles "Lucky" Luciano, head of the Mafia's Genovese Crime Family. Bumpy worked out a deal with the Mafia that allowed Harlem's black racketeers to stay in business and operate independently if they paid a tax. His temerity to stand up to the Mafia earned him respect and legendary folk status. Boxing champion Sugar Ray Robinson and music legends Billie Holiday and Lena Horne could be found in his company. *Jet* magazine and the *Amsterdam News* ran stories on this Robin Hood of the ghetto who delivered turkeys to the poor on Thanksgiving. Bumpy's service to the community did not erase his wrongdoings, but it allowed some to see him as more than a gangster.

After Bumpy Johnson suffered a fatal heart attack in 1968 hundreds of black Harlemites braved cold temperatures to pay their respects at St. Martin's Episcopal Church. Scholar Boyce Watkins says the African American community tends to believe that as long as an individual is financially successful, that justifies all of his behavior.[13] We see this played out several times in *Empire* whenever Lucious is in the presence of working class blacks who admire him. When he returns to Philadelphia for Bunkie's funeral, he is treated like royalty as he enters the church. He pays a visit to a local jail to sign a recently incarcerated rapper named Titan. A black police guard on duty can hardly contain his exuberance when sees Lucious enter the building. When Lucious ends up in prison for Bunkie's murder, the other inmates look up to him and allow him to run the facility.

Bumpy Johnson was replaced on the streets by his protégé Frank Lucas, who earned his street cred(ibiity) by killing a local hoodlum named Tango, who stood 6'5" and weighed 270 pounds. "I shot him," said Lucas in a 2000 interview with *New York* magazine. "Four times: *bam, bam, bam, bam*.... This was my initiation fee into taking over completely down here because I killed the baddest motherfucker, not just in Harlem but in the world."[14] Frank Lucas moved his five brothers from Greensboro, North Carolina, to Harlem to form The Country Boys crime syndicate. The brothers used American Air Force planes to transport heroin from Southeast Asia to the United States stashed in the cadavers of American soldiers killed in the Vietnam War. Denzel Washington portrayed Frank Lucas in the 2007 blockbuster film *American Gangster,* produced by *Empire*'s producer Brian Grazer. One of the most memorable scenes in the film takes place in a diner shortly after Frank's brothers' arrival. He tells them that while his mentor Bumpy had money, he was not "white man rich." Bumpy did not own anything; he simply leased the property that the white man (the Mafia) allowed him to use. Frank's mission in life was to be his own self-made man. Frank and his wife, the former Miss Puerto Rico, were decked out in full-length chinchilla coats as they attended the "Fight of the Century" between Ali and Joe Frazier at Madison Square Garden on March 8, 1971. Frank's $100,000 coat and his matching $25,000 hat were manifestations of his $1 million-a-day heroin empire.[15] For some blacks, Frank Lucas was a super hero, and that gaudy chinchilla was his cape. When I saw *American Gangster* at a majority black theater, the audience applauded at the film's conclusion. The film earned $266.5 million at the box office, demonstrating the public's insatiable appetite for compelling stories about black outlaws.

The popularity of Frank Lucas in 2007 and Lucious Lyon today stems from the ballad of Stagolee. Born Lee Shelton on March 16, 1865, in Texas, Stagolee was a dark-skinned man with a crossed left eye, which had resulted from a fight as a boy. Stagolee, also spelled Stagger Lee and Stack O' Lee, was a part-time pimp who owned the Modern Horseshoe Club in St. Louis where gambling, prostitution, and interracial mixing were common features. On Christmas night in 1895, he got into an argument with another man, William "Billy" Lyons, at the club. During the argument, Billy Lyons snatched Stagolee's beloved Stetson hat from the top of his head. The confrontation ended with Stagolee pulling out his .44 Smith & Wesson and killing Lyons. His first trial for murder ended in a hung jury, but his second trial earned him 25 years in prison. Legend has it that he responded to his punishment by telling the judge that his sentence was nothing when compared to his father who was already doing a 299-year-bid at the Sing Sing prison.[16]

In the 1920s and 1930s, the Library of Congress and Works Progress

Administration sent white folklorists into the South and Southwest to record the songs of black blues singers. Because of their efforts Stagolee's tale spread throughout mainstream popular culture. Lloyd Price's 1959 song "Stagger Lee" climbed to the top of the pop charts. The song was so popular that he was invited to perform it on Dick Clark's *American Bandstand*. White folk singers began recording multiple versions of Stagolee's tale throughout the 1950s and 1960s. Black Panthers' co-founder Bobby Seale recruited new members to his organization by sharing the outlaw's narrative. Although he was a villain, Stagolee was the lesser of two evils, for many blacks, when compared to white racists who intentionally kept blacks disenfranchised. H.C. Brearley writes that the black outlaw's deviant behavior is treated with admiration rather than contempt.

Cecil Brown, a novelist and screenwriter for Richard Pryor's film, *Which Way is Up?* (1977), published multiple books on the public's first celebrated black villain. Brown's research while on the faculty at the University of California, Berkeley resulted in a book, *Stagolee Shot Billy*, which was published by Harvard University Press in 2008. Brown attributes the fascination with outlaws within the African American community to historic circumstances:

> *Generally, the African-American hero in popular culture is a crystalized attempt of blacks trying to tell their story about a figure trying to escape the harsh circumstances into which he has been forced. Neither Stagolee nor a Frank Lucas emerges from an ideal situation. From the moment you have slavery you will have a Stagolee or a Frank Lucas. From the beginning this black man can never be the traditional hero because he has been cast in the light of the captive or the villain. As a result, he is forced to defend himself, but in doing so, he will be seen as the anti-hero.*[17]

Brown's comments about Lucas ring out when considering uncomfortable truths. For example, Southern politicians and the FBI often associated Martin Luther King, Jr., and his peaceful followers with deviance. They were blamed for a rising crime rate and riots taking place across the nation in the 1960s. In 1971 President Richard Nixon called for a War on Drugs which planted the seeds of mass incarceration.[18] John Ehrlichman, President Nixon's domestic policy chief, admitted in a 1968 interview with *Harper's* magazine that the president used his war on drugs as a political tool for his Southern Strategy to gain votes from previously democratic white southern voters. Nixon told his aides to publicly associate African-Americans with heroin abuse more than any other racial group.[19] Such outright attacks on the image of the African-American community coming from the White House made it possible for black anti-heroes to become heroes.

Mr. Untouchable

Following Bunkie's death, a local black police detective places Lucious Lyon on his short list of possible suspects. Lucious uses his charm and mendacity to talk his way out of every confrontation with the detective. He coerces Andre to have sex with the Deputy Mayor to get her to turn over the details about the detective's investigation. He gets Vernon, his best friend and Empire chairman, to pay off a local thug to take the rap for Bunkie's murder. Despite his efforts, Lucious is hauled off to the Brooklyn Correctional Prison on the day that Empire goes public on the Wall Street Stock Exchange. While incarcerated Lucious meets Ms. Roxanne Ford, a black prosecutor hell-bent on seeing that he spends the rest of his life behind bars. Ford orders the prison guards and doctors to withhold the medication used to treat his myasthenia gravis as means of coercing him to admit his guilt. Next, she tries to persuade the judge at his bail hearing to reject his plea. Lucious outsmarts Ms. Ford, whom he refers to as a "black bitch in cheap shoes," with the aid of his shady lawyer Thirsty (Andre Royo), who uses embarrassing photos of the judge involved in lewd sexual acts to entice him to free Lucious on $1 million bail.

A large group of supporters cheers Lucious upon his release from prison, as he raises a fist in the air like John Carlos and Tommie Smith.[20] Ms. Ford arrests Cookie on falsified charges in a failed attempt to trick her into turning against Lucious. She also has the FBI raid his home and the offices of Empire. When Ms. Ford and her federal agents arrive at Lucious' mansion, he greets them in his bedroom standing butt naked with a devilish grin on his face. Lucious rids himself of Ms. Ford for good when he has Thirsty leave the gruesomely decaying corpse of his murdered best friend Vernon on the front passenger seat of her car. Ms. Ford had been searching for Vernon, who was missing for months, to testify against Lucious in court. Law enforcement's inability to capture Empire's Teflon don only heightens his reputation as the scariest man in the music industry and the new Mr. Untouchable.

One of the black outlaw's defining traits is his ability to elude the authorities and all rivals. *American Gangster* focused on New Jersey detective Richie Roberts' ongoing efforts to build a case against Frank Lucas solid enough to bring his empire down. The film featured the Academy Award winning actor Cuba Gooding, Jr., in the role of Frank's archrival Leroy "Nicky" Barnes. Nicky Barnes organized an illegal business reaping annual earnings of $10 million from heroin. After the New York Yankees' All-Star fielder, Reggie Jackson, hit three home runs in game six of the 1977 World Series against the Los Angeles Dodgers, New York *Daily News* sportswriter Jimmy Breslin asked a nine-year-old black boy if Jackson was his hero. The boy replied, "Nicky

Barnes is my hero." The authorities experienced so much difficulty apprehending this outlaw that he graced the cover of the June 5, 1977, issue of *New York Times* magazine wearing a dapper grey suit and red, white, and blue tie.[21] Nicky looked more like a sophisticated businessman than a street hustler from the ghetto. The magazine's cover read, "'Mr. Untouchable.' This is Nicky Barnes. The Police Say He May Be Harlem's Biggest Drug Dealer. But Can They Prove It?"[22] The magazine cover demonstrated the paradox of the American dream. The dream promised that anyone could make something of himself if he worked hard and bought into capitalism. So, on the one hand, Nicky was a walking billboard for the dream; however, on the other hand, he represented the tragic effects of capitalism run amok and the pursuit of the dream at all costs.

What makes these black outlaws so elusive is the salient fact that they are tricksters. The trickster is a figure that uses cunning and deception as a means of fun, mischief, and survival. In 1885 the term "trickster" was first used to describe mythic figures in Native American culture. Several countries and cultures have their own versions of the trickster. The trickster can be found in West African folklore in the form of a man, a woman, or an animal such as the hare, hyena, coyote, or spider. A famous West African tale involves the trickster Ananse meeting with a man named Hate-to-be-contradicted. Throughout the story, Hate-to-be-contradicted kills anyone who dares to contradict him. Ananse outsmarts the man by tricking him into contradicting another individual. Ananse orders Hate-to-be-contradicted's children to kill him for contradicting someone else.[23] Lawrence Levine acknowledges the influence of these West African tricksters on African American storytelling and folklore during slavery.[24] Roger Abrahams sees a link as he explains the role of the trickster in African American slave societies: "In the guise of the small (childlike) animal, the Negro is fulfilling the role in which he has been cast by his white 'masters.' At the same time, in this role he is able to show superiority over those larger and more important than himself through his tricks."[25] The Br'er Rabbit tales portrayed the American slave in the form of a rabbit who used ingenuity to reclaim autonomy by outsmarting cruel plantation owners.

John Roberts' *From Trickster to Badman: The Black Folk Hero in Slavery and Freedom* (1990) examines the evolution of the West African trickster to the African American outlaw. Roberts observes that Africans often experienced severe shortages of food and other vital resources. In several animal tales, the trickster outsmarted his adversaries to secure food for himself and others in the community.[26] While these trickster tales served as forms of entertainment for slaves on the plantations, they may also have transmitted subliminal instructions about dealing with adversity. Historian John Hope

Franklin notes that slaves frequently relied on trickery as a subtle form of resistance. Some slaves worked slowly or pretended to be sick to get out of doing their work. Others ran away from the plantations to reunite with family members or escape to freedom.[27]

While the 19th-century version of the trickster often represented a godly, moral hero concerned with helping the collective group and outsmarting whites, this was not the case moving into the 20th and 21st centuries. African American works such as Lorraine Hansberry's 1959 play *A Raisin in the Sun* portrayed tricksters as con artists and thieves. Scott Leonard and Michael McClure call tricksters greedy, vain and impulsive. "They can be seen as agents of chaos."[28] Trickster stories are often morally ambiguous. John Roberts argues that the term hero is defined in the eyes of the beholder. Thus, a trickster, in the form of the bad man who breaks laws for his own selfish reasons, can still be viewed in a positive light by some individuals. *Deep Down in the Jungle: Negro Narrative Folklore from the Streets of Philadelphia* (1970) by Roger D. Abrahams told stories of these deviant tricksters popular among Philadelphia's black urban dwellers.

Lucious Lyon is a trickster whose duplicitous methods and devilish grin mask his treacherous disposition. An example is found in season three when his old flame Giuliana Green (Nia Long) comes to New York. Giuliana is a wealthy businesswoman from Las Vegas; she was Lucious' first true love interest while Cookie was incarcerated. Lucious sleeps with her and pretends to choose her over Cookie in an attempt to close a business deal allowing him to open a chain of his Leviticus nightclub in Las Vegas. Giuliana thought that she was a co-owner of the club, but it turns out that Lucious had his lawyers write up the contracts in such a manner that she unknowingly signed over full ownership rights to him. He then bans her from *his* club. Lucious tricked her because years earlier she and her abusive husband Rafael duped him out of $10 million. Lucious not only gets his revenge, but also gains a stake in Sin City and wins back Cookie in the process. As Bunkie reminds Lucious, just before he meets his demise, his greatest achievement is tricking the American public into seeing him as a legitimate entrepreneur worthy of running a publicly traded enterprise.

He's a Baaaaad Man!

A noteworthy storyline is the relationship between Lucious and his half-brother Tariq, an FBI agent trying to succeed where Roxanne Ford failed. Tariq is motivated by a personal vendetta, related to their father's murder, as much as he is to uphold the law. This example of a strained relationship between two siblings on opposite sides of the law is not new in Hollywood. The 1973 film *The Mack* focused on brothers, John (Max Julien) and Olinga (Roger G. Mosley), living in Oakland, California. Olinga was a community organizer dedicated to Black Nationalism and saving one black life at a time. His younger brother John, nicknamed Goldie, was an ex-convict who became the biggest pimp in Oakland. He would drive through town in his pimpmobile handing out money, like the piped piper, to admiring schoolboys. Goldie's lifestyle put him at odds with Olinga:

> *Goldie:* Being rich and black means something. When you and I were kids there were no heroes. There all sorts of heroes now. There are kids who even look up to me.
> *Olinga:* That's just teaching black kids to exploit their own kind. And that's sick.
> *Goldie:* It's sick when you have a chance to get out of a rat-infested ghetto and don't.[29]

Goldie's statement about a lack of heroes raises some interesting points. Not all blacks growing up poor viewed their activists, politicians, and preachers as heroes. This was partly due to the hypocrisy displayed by some of these figures. In other cases, there was just simply a lack of communication between these groups. As a result, you get young men who grew up admiring the hustler and pimp with money, who did not hide his sins, instead of the figures traditionally viewed as more acceptable. Goldie's character was based on Oakland gangster Frank Ward who controlled Oakland's black criminal underworld with his brothers. *The Mack* was a dramatization of the struggle between outlaws like the Ward brothers and socially conscious groups like the Black Panthers for the hearts and minds of the underclass. William Van Deburg's *Hoodlums: Black Villians and Social Bandits in American Life* (2004) identified two versions of the black outlaw: the bad man and the baaad man. The former is a social bandit dedicated to fighting corruption in society, such as portrayed by Olinga and, to a lesser extent, Tariq. Ironically, law enforcement was more concerned with groups like the Panthers than they were with the real troublemakers selling dope and sex. FBI director J. Edgar Hoover released a report detailing the agency's Counterintelligence Program (COINTELPRO) to expose, disrupt, discredit and neutralize the activities of black activists.[30] On September 8, 1968, Hoover told the *New York Times* that the Black Panthers were the greatest threat to national security. Over the next four years, 253 of the 295 COINTELPRO black hate group operations were directed towards the Panthers.[31]

The antithesis of Van Deburg's "bad man" is the "baaad man." The numbers runners, gangsters, hustlers, and pimps belong to this latter category. Historian Robin D.G. Kelley says some black men, not benefiting from the activism of the sixties, saw criminal activity such as hustling an alternative to being poor.[32] The baaad men were wealthy, respected, and away from Hoover's watchful eye. The baaad men did not have to live by any moral compass, other than the code of the streets. As a result, they were more relatable to the masses and anyone looking to make quick money to support their families. Melvin Williams, Baltimore's most notorious drug kingpin and the inspiration for the HBO series *The Wire*, was so respected that police and municipal leaders sought him out to end the riots after the assassination of Martin Luther King, Jr.[33] Then there was Oakland hustler Felix "The Cat" Mitchell whose 1986 funeral included a procession of horse drawn carriages conveying his $6,000 bronze coffin, 14 Rolls Royce limousines, and Ferraris before thousands of mourners. Black residents mourned King Felix's home going as if he had been an African monarch.[34] Hollywood recreated these black gangsters in the form of figures like *The Mack*'s Goldie. Goldie did not find any value in marching or protesting. Eventually, his brother Olinga joins the dark side when the pair works together to kill the crooked white police officers responsible for their mother's death. Likewise, Lucious chose to reject social activist groups or to work with law enforcement unlike Tariq or their deceased father, Joe Walker.

The Return of Super Fly

The Blaxploitation era, 1971 and 1976, reflected Hollywood's recognition of life in poor black neighborhoods in the immediate years after the decline of the Black Power Movement. The outlaw became one of many archetypes that defined this controversial period in cinematic history. Junius Griffin, the president of the Beverly Hills-Hollywood branch of the NAACP, coined the term Blaxploitation Cinema to describe this new genre of films produced and written by white men to make a profit from black moviegoers. The writers and directors of these films were accused of misappropriating blackness and glorifying historic stereotypes. African American film scholars Donald Bogle and Ed Guerrero offer contrasting viewpoints on the significance of this genre. Bogle brands these films as glamorizing the ghetto and incorrectly depicting the underclass as the dominant representation of authentic blackness. Guerrero attributes the rise of Blaxploitation to the growing militancy among young blacks inspired by the activism of the Black Power Movement.

Guerrero finds an interrelationship between the growing popularity of the badass black militants of the late 1960s and the rise of Blaxploitation era antiheroes. Older conservative black actors like Bill Cosby, Sidney Poitier, and Harry Belafonte, who were admired by adults for their respectable characters, did not appeal to younger blacks who preferred Malcolm over Martin. Younger blacks disliked the fact that Cosby's and Poitier's characters were always so perfect, nonaggressive and sexless. Even if the Blaxploitation characters were anti-establishment, they were seen as a lesser evil when compared to the racist white cops and crooked white politicians.

The success of Blaxploitation cinema also highlighted the growing popularity of African American pulp fiction about pimps and hustlers by novelists Donald Goines and Iceberg Slim. This street literature provided some of the original narratives about black gangsters coming from nothing. Although these books were overlooked in mainstream stores and classrooms, they were popular in tiny black owned bookstores, barbershops, beauty parlors, and the corner. *The Mack* was influenced by Iceberg Slim's autobiography *Pimp* (1967). The release of Melvin Van Peebles' independent film *Sweet Sweetback's Baadasssss Song* on April 23, 1971, launched the Blaxploitation era. Hollywood studios saw a profit in mimicking Van Peebles' blueprint for *Sweetback*. These new films provided work for black actors, photographers, stylists, and soul singers like Marvin Gaye, Isaac Hayes, James Brown, and Earth Wind and Fire. At their best, these films addressed social problems plaguing the black underclass. They turned black men and women into never before seen heroes and heroines on the big screen. But at their worst these films were white male fantasies of blackness. Boyce Watkins has criticized *Empire* by referring to it as modern-day Blaxploitation cinema.

Media scholar Todd Boyd refers to *Super Fly* (1972) as the magnum opus of the Blaxploitation era.[35] *Super Fly* was an American dream narrative that paved the way for all future representations of the black outlaw. The film's fictional protagonist, Youngblood Priest (Ron O'Neal), sells powder cocaine to New York City's elite. Cocaine has provided Priest with a luxurious Manhattan apartment, expensive clothes, a pimpmobile, a beautiful black girlfriend, and a rich white mistress. He is committed to making one "final score" so that he can retire from hustling and live a legitimate life. Priest has had a Damascus Road experience that puts him on an inevitable path to becoming a good man.[36] To accomplish his goal, he receives a loan of 30 keys (kilos) of cocaine from his mentor Scatter (Julius Harris), who is a father-like figure to him. Scatter is an older black man who used his drug money to open a popular restaurant and nightclub. Deputy Commissioner Reardon, a corrupt white police officer, is Scatter's connect (drug supplier). Reardon learns of Priest's plan and promises Priest and his partner, Eddie, that he will provide them protection from law enforcement. All they must do is pay him $10,000 for every key they sell.

One of *Super Fly*'s memorable scenes involves Priest and his girlfriend Georgia (Shelia Frazier) standing behind a fence overlooking a beautiful, snow-covered park where white parents watch their children play. As they stand there, Priest shares his dream of getting out of "the life" with Georgia. August Wilson's play *Fences*, about a working class black family in Pittsburgh, Pennsylvania, during the 1950s, used the fence as an allegory for various themes within his plot. The fence kept the play's protagonists safe from harm. Simultaneously, the fence was a barrier to their experiencing the rest of the world and life to the fullest extent. In *Super Fly*, the fence symbolizes the feelings of melancholy and alienation shared by black urban dwellers who saw their dreams deferred and dried up like raisins in the sun.[37] The fence also allows for Priest's existential ruminations of a better life that allows him to live free from fear of arrest or violent death. He desires to be a good man and live happily ever after with Georgia. But not everyone shares his goals, especially his best friend and crime partner Eddie (Carl Lee). Let Eddie tell it, an eight-track stereo, color TV, and enough cocaine to snort daily is the American dream.[38]

A hip-hop influenced remake of the film was released in theaters, June 2018. *Super Fly*'s themes of escapism and tearing down fences to seize the American Dream runs throughout the outlaw narratives in the following television series: *The Wire, Power,* and *Empire. The Wire* (2002–2008), an HBO melodrama about Baltimore city's war on drugs at the turn of the millennium, introduced some of television's most memorable villains. Russell "Stringer" Bell (Idris Elba) is second-in-command to Avon Barksdale (Wood Harris), West Baltimore's most powerful drug lord. While Avon was obsessed with maintaining command over his corners, Stringer's goal was to focus on developing luxury condominiums and other legitimate business ventures for his company B&B Enterprises. Stringer enrolled in economics courses at Baltimore City Community College and studied *The Wealth of Nations* (1776) by Scottish economist Adam Smith to prepare for his new career path. The creators of *The Wire* based Stringer's character on Kenneth A. Jackson, a former drug dealer turned legitimate public figure. Jackson left the corners to earn a degree in business from American InterContinental University in Atlanta, Georgia. He established a political action committee (PAC), which donated $8,000 to the campaigns of Baltimore's black mayors Kurt Schmoke and Shelia Dixon. Jackson's PAC also fought for voting rights to be given to prisoners.

Sociologist Alford A. Young, Jr., in his book, *The Minds of Marginalized*

Black Men: Making Sense of Mobility, Opportunity, and Future Life Chances, observed black men in disenfranchised environments who did not allow their social condition to limit their worldview.[39] In his article "For Whom the BELL Tolls," Ernest L. Gibson, III, states that Stringer Bell was too black for the discriminatory white-capitalist world from which he so desperately craved recognition.[40] However, his worldview had grown too big for the short-sided expectations of the corners. Stringer learns that he is beyond his scope of competence as he begins associating with a crooked black state Senator, Clay Davis (Isiah Whitlock, Jr.), to help him advance in the upscale real estate industry. When Davis cheats Stringer out his money, his first inclination is to have Avon's thugs settle the score. Stringer is startled to learn that his threats do not scare a government official. He is also surprised to learn that he no longer has the support in the streets to carry out his attack. Mark Anthony Neal calls Stringer a man without a country.[41]

Gibson's assessment of Stringer Bell's worldview can also apply to James "Ghost" St. Patrick, the anti-hero of the STARZ series *Power* (2014–) created by drug dealer turned music mogul Curtis "50 Cent" Jackson and Courtney Kemp Agboh, a Brown University educated African American female television writer. Omari Hardwick describes his character Ghost as an individual trying to break good from bad. Despite being a gangster whose past sins haunt him like ghosts, he is on the precipice of reforming his life.[42] The astute Ghost believes that his trendy Manhattan nightclub, Truth (which he calls "the dream"), and an affair with his high school love Angela Valdez (Lela Loren), a prosecutor for the federal government, will allow him to atone for his sins as he becomes a good man. It is funny that his source of escape is a club called 'Truth,' given that his entire existence is soaked in deception and fantasy. Ghost, a father of three who is always impeccably attired in well-tailored conservative Tom Ford business suits with colorful ties and pocket squares, is much too urbane to be a gangster. While most of his childhood cronies are either dead or in jail, he lives on the top floor of a luxurious Manhattan penthouse, which is home to the city's investment bankers, lawyers, and doctors. His two oldest children attend an elite private school on the Upper East Side.

50 Cent admits that he was influenced to create *Power* after re-watching *Super Fly*. Ghost's best friend Tommy (Joseph Sikora) is an updated version of Eddie. Tommy is a redheaded white male in love with the streets, who does not share his *brother's* ambition to do more with his life. Ghost's wife Tasha (Naturi Naughton), who has always been his most loyal ally and ride-or-die chick, can only picture her husband being "the biggest goddamn drug dealer" in New York City. Ghost turns to his mistress because she always envisioned more for his purpose in life. The theologian Howard Thurman

once said, "Never reduce your life to the event you are facing right now."[43] If you reduce your life to your current state, you will never be able to see what is ahead of you. Lucious once told Cookie that he loved her because she could see, upon their first encounter, that his destiny was bigger than his reality. This sentiment is a feeling to which black males from all walks of life can relate—the kid who survives poverty and gang violence to earn a college degree, the storefront preacher who grows his congregation into a megachurch, the fatherless black teenager who becomes the 44th president.

Ghost is routinely transforming himself and code switching to meet the expectations of others. Around Tasha, Tommy, and his street associates he is Ghost. The professional world knows him as Mr. James St. Patrick. Angie affectionately calls him Jamie. The kids call him dad. He must navigate between white racism in corporate America and the unceasing violence of the criminal underworld. Ghost, like Lucious, tries to mold his *sons* into his vision of black excellence and manhood. He sends his teenage son Tariq (Michael Rainey, Jr.) to that private school to prepare him for college. He grooms two young men who could be described as surrogate sons, Shawn (Sinqua Walls) and Dre (Rotimi), to succeed in corporate America. Ghost gives Shawn a job as his chauffeur. He makes Dre his executive assistant at Truth. He requires Shawn and Dre to wear tailor-made suits and teaches them how to speak in a professional setting. His efforts fail because he is unable to distance his criminal ties from his profession and personal life. Dre uses Truth as a place to sell drugs and become a kingpin, Tariq joins a gang led by Ghost's former mentor Kanan (50 Cent), and Shawn is murdered by his father, Kanan. Ghost's inability to keep Tariq out of trouble results in the untimely murder of his oldest daughter Raina (Donshea Hopkins).

A commonality between Ghost and Lucious is their nonadherence to code. Not only do they view themselves as being above the law, but they also are amoral figures who dishonor the code of the streets. Lucious does not blink an eye when close friends, Bunkie and Vernon, die. Ghost is willing to cooperate with the same police officers trying to arrest him if it helps to defeat his adversaries like Kanan. Ghost and Tasha were culpable for plotting behind Kanan's back years ago to send him away to prison for 15 years. Each season of *Power* finds Ghost habitually resorting to crime to maintain credibility as a "good man" in society's eyes and his own mind. I will say that one of the most notable differences between these two fictional outlaws is the fact that Ghost naively believes that he can separate himself from his wrongdoings. Ghost is the gangster; James St. Patrick is the entrepreneur and a loving father. Whenever Ghost commits a murder, he changes out of James' suits into a dark hoodie and dark ski cap. The wardrobe alteration not only reflects the bipolar nature of Ghost's persona, but it is also a subtle hint about how black men are perceived based on their attire.

Ghost's attempts to separate his underground persona from his new mainstream one become a liability when he goes to prison. Both he and Lucious are arrested for murder, but they handle their incarceration differently. Although Lucious is harassed by a sadistic prison guard, Officer McKnight (Chris "Ludacris" Bridges), he turns the prison into his sanctuary. His reputation in the streets and in music make him a god to his fellow inmates. He even finds time to record his first hit song in years from behind bars. Ghost, on the other hand, struggles to adjust to having his freedom taken. While Lucious is cool and calm, Ghost initially appears to be weak and timid. He meets an evil guard, Marshal Williams (Charlie Murphy), who finds pleasure in harassing and beating him unceasingly. Officer McKnight attempts to dehumanize Lucious by only referring to him as inmate; however, Marshal Williams' abuse is worse. The other inmates harass him as well due to the fact they know him only as James St. Patrick not Ghost. The men see the rich, articulate Mr. St. Patrick as soft and unintimidating.

Despite all of Ghost's past wrongdoings, this is his first time in prison. He is facing the death penalty for one of the few crimes that he did not commit, the murder of a federal agent. For so long he has thought of himself as being above the other men in the streets, like Kanan and Tommy, who were in and out of the penal system. His shackles and orange jumpsuit force him to reconsider his entire identity. Perhaps he really is the monster and menace that society always said he could only be. This is manifested when Ghost is forced to kill Williams by smashing his head with a 45-pound cast iron plate in the prison's weight room. Ghost, in the role of Mr. Untouchable, is eventually freed and exonerated. Upon his release, he attempts to rebrand himself by getting involved in upscale real estate. He begins working with a young black city councilman, Rashad Tate (Larenz Tate), to rid the city of drug dealers and clean up the crime infested neighborhoods that molded him. Unfortunately, Ghost finds himself in a similar predicament as Stringer. Councilman Tate and the legitimate white businessman that Ghost partners with end up being as corrupt as the hardened criminals he left behind.

Lucious' change in lifestyle, from hustler to legitimate entrepreneur, has nothing to do with becoming a good man. He has too much of a god-complex to find fault or a lack of morality in anything that he does. If anything, success has made him rotten to the core. He does not need a wardrobe change to murder because he is so sinister that his victims' blood bounces off his exterior. While Ghost would rather avoid using violence to solve his problems, Lucious delights in reverting to his thuggish disposition whenever necessary to prove that he has not been softened by sleeping on expensive silk sheets. To say that Lucious blurs the lines between a respected businessman and a gangster would be a blatant understatement. Bunkie's murder was only an appetizer for his seven-course meal of deadly sins. (1) For example, when a beautiful young reporter named Harper Scott threatens to leak a story that will ruin his reputation, Lucious orders his goons to kidnap her. I presume that her lifeless body is somewhere in the Hudson River. (2) After a cocky white businessman named Jargo hikes up the price of the streaming service Swiftstream, that Lucious is attempting to purchase, Lucious punches him out in a boxing ring. Later he visits Jago in the hospital and drugs him with high dosages of morphine to trick him into selling the company. (3) He watches, gleefully, as Jamal nearly throws his arch nemesis Billy Beretti off the roof of a high-rise building. (4) When an irate manager for his former artist, V. Boseman, gets loud with him Lucious calms him down by using a strategy from Suge Knight's rules of conflict resolution: he beats him to a pulp with a golf club.[44] (5) He deposits an exhumed decomposed corpse in district attorney Roxanne Ford's car as a warning of what will happen to her if she does not cease her investigation of him. (6) Lucious forces Camilla (Naomi Campbell), the culprit responsible for his temporary ouster as Empire's CEO, to drink a lethal poison at gunpoint. (7) He whispers threats into Anika's ear while she is having her baby in the hospital delivery bed. (8) In another instance, he learns that Gram, the ex-boyfriend of his artist Tiana, has hacked into Empire's database and leaked private information online. Lucious and his goons pay a surprise visit to the young man's apartment. The last time we see Gram, he is being carried out to the balcony against his will. Lucious sits back and laughs. (9) There is the incident with his former boss Frank Gathers. He and Gathers find themselves in the same federal prison. After Lucious learns that Gathers has ordered a contract to harm his family, he has Frank murdered in prison. Once again Lucious laughs as he hears the screams of imminent death. (10) And lastly, when his company is snatched from him he hires the gangsters he met in prison to get it back by targeting board members and candidates daring to replace him as CEO. Their tactics include assault, car explosions, and killing pets. A board member comes home to find her cat hanging from the ceiling.

Even with all his death-dealing malice, Lucious appears to have achieved what Ghost covets the most: the American dream. Ghost is unable to do interviews, take publicity photos, or have a social media page to promote Truth for over a year because he is so concerned about the authorities investigating his past. He literally is a ghost to most people in the legitimate business world. There is a scene in season one in which Ghost and Tasha visit the home of Simon Stern (Victor Garber), a racist white billionaire. Ghost comes to the meeting expecting to be brought in as a partner for future business. However, Stern's offer to buy Truth and make Ghost his employee is a reminder that he is still not seen as Stern's equal. Stern's attempts to make Ghost his servant continue to be an underlying theme throughout the series. Lucious, on the other hand, no longer has as far to climb because his success has afforded him that coveted seat at the table.

Great Gatsbys, Young Jovas and the Roaring Lyons

An African American drug dealer, who raps, becomes a celebrated figure in the mainstream, a CEO, and hero for the black middle class. He befriends the president and the wealthiest black businesswoman in America. Hollywood might have rejected this script 20 years ago for being too improbable. Sometimes truth is stranger than fiction. The Lucious Lyon story is loosely based on hip-hop mogul Jay-Z. Born Shawn Carter in 1969, Jay-Z grew up in Brooklyn's Marcy City Housing Projects. The youngest of Gloria Carter's four children, his father Adnis Reeves abandoned the family when he was 12-years-old. As a fatherless teenager growing up in the 1980s, Jay became another statistic in the crack generation. If you were coming of age in this crack generation President Reagan was the boogeyman, cops were villains, your mantra was "the world is yours," and your heroes were Tony Montana and Nino Brown. Charisse L'Pree Corsbie-Massay, a professor of communications and media studies at Syracuse University, says many rappers are products of the "Scarface Effect."[45] The 1983 gangster film *Scarface* told the fictional story of Antonio "Tony" Montana (Al Pacino), a Cuban refugee who became one of the richest men in Miami Beach by distributing powder cocaine for his international connect. Corsbie-Massay says black men, looking to *Scarface* for guidance, love the American dream with a vengeance.[46] Nino Brown (Wesley Snipes), the fictional hustler in the black gangster film *New Jack City* (1991), was another role model for these young street entrepreneurs. Nino truly believed Tony Montana's famous mantra that the world was his. "You have to rob to get rich in Reagan's America…. This is the American way," Nino told his crew, the Cash Money Brothers.[47]

An episode of *Empire* shows Lucious as a teenager rapping about how he wants to "run the world." On another episode, he reminds his former boss, Frank Gathers, that while Gathers wanted to run the streets, he desired to rule the world. In the 1980s my father pastored a church in Ivy City, then one of the poorer Washington, D.C., communities, bearing the scars of long-term political neglect. One Wednesday afternoon about the time a session of the church's weekly afterschool program was scheduled to begin, a young black male was fatally gunned down, in a car chase, near the church's entrance. According to rumor, D.C. crack kingpin Rayful Edmond, III, the successor to legendary drug kingpin Cornell Jones, was the instigator.[48] For a while, Rayful thought that he ruled the world. He shopped at the finest boutiques in the city, hung out with the star basketball players at Georgetown University, and drove Mercedes Benzes when it was an anomaly for most black men to own anything finer than a Cadillac or a Buick.[49] He was still earning millions, thanks to a partnership with the son of Columbian drug lord Griselda "Godmother" Blanco from the Medellin Cartel, even after he was incarcerated.

Professor James Peterson refers to this hustler's mentality as the "come up narrative." The "come up" means doing whatever is necessary to improve one's lot in life.[50] Rappers have taken the monikers of famous domestic and foreign drug lords to define themselves. Rap music has always been aspirational. It is no coincidence that many rappers wear Air Jordan sneakers with their iconic logo of a man literally jumping out of his circumstances to attain unfathomable heights of greatness.[51] No rapper symbolizes the aspirational "come up" worldview better than Jay-Z. From age 13 to 26 he sold drugs to make it out of the projects. "I've never had an inferior complex. I was defiant to the system. That's how you end up hustling. You felt like you were dealt an unfair hand, so you have to live on the other side of the law," says Jay-Z.[52] He was introduced to hustling by a drug dealer that he refers to pseudonymously, in his autobiography *Decoded* (2010), as Hill. Jay-Z, along with his friend De-Haven Irby and cousin Emory Jones, sold crack in New York City; Trenton, New Jersey; parts of Virginia; and in Maryland's Eastern Shore. In their book *Freakonomics* Steven Levitt and Stephen Dubner estimate that the average corner boy just entering the drug game earns three dollars and thirty cents an hour. Although working at McDonalds for $7.25 an hour makes more sense, the corner boy devalues working long hours for low wages and takes a shot at being the next Scarface. Jason Read says, "The illegal drug trade acts as a sustained allegory for capitalism. It is at once outside of the world of legitimate business, governed by different rules and principles of loyalty, and the dark mirror of business, revealing the effects of a relentless pursuit of profit on the lives of those caught in its grip."[53] Rather than challenge or attempt to reform the economic system that has historically displaced them and their peers, these hustlers try adapting, unsuccessfully, to the system.

Jay-Z was still on the streets selling crack when DJ Clark Kent introduced him to a cocky, young manager from Harlem named Damon Dash. After being rejected by countless record labels, Jay combined the money he made hustling with additional funds raised by Dash and another hustler, Kareem "Biggs" Burke, to launch his own record label, Roc-A-Fella Records.[54] On June 25, 1996, at the age of 26, Jay released his debut album, *Reasonable Doubt*. He appeared on the album cover dressed like a gangster from the roaring twenties donning a black suit with a white scarf, white tie, and a black hat while holding a cigar in his right hand. The album cover art is intriguing given the state of America during the 1920s. Some immigrants overcame poverty through bootlegging, the illegal sale of alcohol. In 1926 the *New Yorker* published the article, "A Bootlegger's Story. How I Got Started." The young immigrant being interviewed said that within six years he had an office on Wall Street and was earning $10,000 annually, just from one of his many clients, due to his illegal enterprise.[55] Several bootleggers were involved with the mob, but they desired to be accepted as legitimate entrepreneurs. Al Capone, Chicago's iconic Italian American mobster and bootlegger, refused to view himself as a criminal. Capone's attire could have come from the closet of the CEO of a large department store.

The music on *Reasonable Doubt* reflected Jay-Z's experiences in the criminal underworld. It was supposed to give a voice to the voiceless young men in the streets hustling to survive. Jay's lyrics could be considered an explicit and profane interpretation of sociologist William Julius Wilson's theories of the self-destructive effects of poverty on the urban poor.[56] The earliest years of his music career appeared to have been predestined for failure. He was arrested in December 1999 for stabbing Lance "Un" Rivera, a record executive, because he leaked copies of Jay's *Vol. 3... Life and Times of S. Carter* (1999) album before the release date. He faced 15 years in prison before pleading guilty and receiving probation. Four months later he was arrested again for possession of an unlicensed Glock 9-mm semiautomatic.[57] Fast forward to the present and Jay-Z is watching life from atop a throne that no one could have imagined 20 years ago. He has broken Elvis Presley's record for number one albums as a solo artist. Only The Beatles surpass his record for number one albums. His records have sold over 100 million worldwide and earned him 21 Grammy awards. He became the first and only rapper to be inducted into the Songwriters Hall of Fame.[58]

Jay-Z's business acumen is even more impressive than his musical accolades. He served as a minority owner of the Brooklyn Nets basketball franchise from 2004 to 2013. His current empire includes chains of the 40/40 Club, a $20 million deal with Samsung, Roc Nation, and Roc Nation Sports, which represents NBA superstar Kevin Durant. Roc Nation (the *real* Empire Entertainment) not only employs music artists, publishers, and songwriters, but it also develops concerts and tours. He has a deal with an upscale champagne brand, Armand de Brignac (or Ace of Spades), which retails between $400 and $1,000 a bottle.[59] In 2012 Budweiser became the sponsor for his annual "Made in America" musical festival in Philadelphia. Jay-Z purchased Tidal, a music streaming service, from the Swedish company Aspiro in 2015 for $56 million.[60] Sprint purchased one-third of Tidal for $200 million in January 2017.[61] The release of his 13th studio album, *4:44*, served as a comeback after a four-year absence and a brilliant marketing strategy for Tidal's new multi-million-dollar partnership with Sprint. Jay also signed a deal with the Academy Award winning group The Weinstein Company (TWC) in 2016 to develop television and film projects such as Spike TV's *TIME: The Kalief Browder Story* and a forthcoming six-part docuseries on the killing of Trayvon Martin.[62] His net worth as of 2018 was $900 million.[63] Business analysts predict that the partnership with Sprint is a steppingstone to a larger business deal down the road which could make him a billionaire.[64]

Duke University Professor Mark Anthony Neal refers to Jay-Z as the embodiment of a hip-hop cosmopolitan; a figure who is comfortable in a multiplicity of cultural and geographic settings. Neal observes that Jay, who goes by various monikers (Jehovah, J-Hova, Young Hov, S. Carter, Iceberg Slim, and Jigga), can navigate successfully between his new mainstream CEO identity and his former "thug n_gga" identity.[65] Whether it is performing at the prestigious Carnegie Hall (with tickets going for $500 to $2,500), attending the exclusive Met Gala in a plush white Tuxedo jacket, vacationing abroad with wife Beyoncé and their three children, discussing business strategies with billionaires Warren Buffet and Oprah Winfrey, campaigning for the Obamas and Clintons, or rapping in performance art music videos about owning paintings by Pablo Picasso, Jay-Z has mastered the art of fitting in with the elite. *Esquire* magazine writer Miles Raymer says, "Jay's now saying money cannot only buy happiness, but it can buy aesthetic refinement as well, something he sees as essential to real acceptance by the rest of his tax bracket. Money alone will get you a spot in the ruling class, but good taste is what separates legitimate or authentic one percenters from the nouveau riche."[66]

Lucious Lyon is the fictional version of Jay-Z. Lucious, whose birth name is Dwight Walker, goes from homelessness, welfare, and selling crack on the streets of Philadelphia to becoming an internationally known pop star. Drug money allows him to launch his own enterprise. Over the next decade, his empire expands to include over 30 artists, a professional sports management division, a fashion line, premium alcohol, electronic gaming, chains of his Leviticus nightclub in New York and Las Vegas, concert tour management, and an endorsement deal with Pepsi. In 2015 Empire Entertainment became a publicly traded enterprise on the Wall Street Stock Exchange.[67] Later that year Lucious purchased Swiftstream, a music streaming company modeled after Tidal. Swiftstream would be relaunched under a new banner called Empire XStream. Lucious marries up, settling down with an Ivy League educated debutante. He has rubbed shoulders with Oprah Winfrey and President Barack Obama. Like his nonfictional muse Mr. Carter, Lucious continues to record new music to remain relevant on the Billboard charts. His comeback album, *Inferno*, unintentionally mirrors *4:44* from a business standpoint. *Inferno* officially launches Empire's new business partnership in Las Vegas.

Lucious may not be as smooth as Jay-Z, but he is learning to live the cosmopolitan's lifestyle as he navigates his way around Madison Avenue. He frequently engages in the code switching that Mark Anthony Neal discusses. Before a televised interview with a cable news network, Lucious has Andre help him practice speaking in a nonthreatening manner that will not scare white people. Cookie scornfully rebukes Lucious for what she thinks is "selling out" because he now speaks *proper* English, has a live-in older black maid named Juanita (Claudette Burchett), receives monthly manicures, and hangs rare Gustav Klimt paintings on the walls of his multi-million-dollar estate.[68]

Fashion is also essential to creating Lucious' public image as a CEO. Robin Givhan, the Pulitzer Prize winning fashion editor for *The Washington Post*, makes an interesting point when she refers to Lucious' style as mid-evolution Jay-Z. The Lucious Lyon wardrobe includes bold $2,000 floral suits by Gucci, $250 Tom Ford neckties, and $500 velvet slippers by Stubbs & Wootton. His fedoras and full-length overcoats keep him warm in the winter. On the pilot, he is introduced wearing a permed hairstyle. Costume designer Rita McGhee is one of the creative geniuses behind Lucious' style. "His look is gangster, it's revolution—that's the inspiration with those ascots, with the scarves, with his different pocket squares."[69] She dresses him in regal colors that are out of the reach of commoners.[70]

Lucious' wardrobe expresses the notion of black excellence promoted by music moguls Puffy and Jay-Z. His wardrobe distances him from other men in his past such as Bunkie and Shyne who lacked his foresight to do more with themselves. Case in point, there is a scene in the pilot episode in which we see Lucious with Bunkie. Bunkie is wearing a valor sweat suit, nice sneakers, and a "phat gold Dookie Rope chain" (a large gold necklace popular in the 1980s). Bunkie dresses like a guy in the hood trying to flaunt his perceived wealth and what he hopes to achieve. Lucious, attired in a suit and fitted overcoat, looks like a man who does not need loud jewelry to attract the world's attention. Monica L. Miller discusses the importance of fashion for black men in her book *Slaves to Fashion: Black Dandyism and the Styling of*

Black Diasporic Identity (2009). Miller says fashion was originally used to turn black men into luxury servants for their white masters in 18th century England and later in the American colonies. During the twentieth century, black men became arbiters of style in an attempt to redefine and empower themselves.[71] Therefore, clothes are more than mere accessories for men like Lucious.

Even though on the surface Lucious appears to be far removed from men like Bunkie and Shyne, looks can be deceiving. F. Scott Fitzgerald published his seminal novel *The Great Gatsby* in 1925. *Gatsby* characterized the American dream as a rags-to-riches fantasy that is little more than a reckless exercise in futility. The novel tells the narrative of James Gatz, a prohibition era bootlegger, who transfigures himself into this mythic figure the Great Jay Gatsby. He surrounds himself with opulence as a sign of his success. Gatsby's Achilles heel, according to scholar Stephany Rose, "rests upon a false sense of inclusion, the illusion that he has become the quintessential American when, in actuality, he is merely imitating the lives of those who are." Lucious Lyon, in many ways, is a modern-day version of Gatsby. As mentioned earlier, he attempts to assimilate into the white mainstream by dressing a certain way, altering his speech, code switching, marrying Anika, and hanging elaborate artwork on the walls of his mansion.

On episode 38, "The Unkindest Cut," we witness a hair stylist applying "process" to his perm. He has to run off to the bathroom to wash the chemicals out of his hair before they burn him. The scene is reminiscent of Denzel Washington, as a young Malcolm Little in the 1992 Spike Lee biopic *Malcolm X*, nearly burning his scalp from the conk being applied to straighten out his nappy hair and rushing to dunk his head in a toilet bowl. Black men used conk (short for congolene) to make their hair look like that of a white man, in the 1920s through the1960s, because a permed hairstyle was more acceptable by mainstream standards.[72] James Brown and other mainstream celebrities wore this hairstyle. *Empire*'s conk scene is relevant because it contradicts some of Lucious' previous statements and his disapproval of his son Andre. "They will accept your money, Dre, but they will never accept your black ass. I don't give a damn how many white women you marry. They will never accept you."[73] Lucious is a hypocrite because he chastises Andre's interracial marriage, yet he has gone from wearing cornrows to straightening his hair.

In her 2011 book chapter "Black Marketing Whiteness: From Hustler to HNIC," Stephany Rose classifies Jay-Z as a modern-day Gatsby. She argues that the mogul, much like the fictional Jay Gatsby, demonstrates the possibility of rising from rags to riches by any means necessary. Ironically, Jay-Z was the executive producer for the soundtrack to the 2013 film adaptation of *The Great Gatsby* starring Leonardo DiCaprio. Jay-Z and his wife Beyoncé had better seats at Barack Obama's first inauguration than the esteemed civil rights activist, the Rev. Jesse Jackson, Sr. But, unlike Gatsby, he is not pretending to be something that he is not. His more recent albums have focused on themes of black excellence juxtaposed with inequality, racism, and poverty. In the 2017 music video for "The Story of O.J." he delivers a Suze Orman-styled wealth building lesson as we witness blacks on slave auction blocks. In a 2011 video, "Otis," he raps in front of a large American flag and fireworks. The video opens with Jay and Kanye West deconstructing a $350,000 Mercedes Maybach. Fredrick Douglass, in 1852, spoke of Fourth of July holiday being a time of mourning for descendants of slaves. In "Otis" Jay-Z is recreating symbols of American independence and exceptionalism on his terms. Although, I would argue that Jay-Z is clearly aware of his existence as a black man, he does not behave disingenuously because he has money. Jay-Z is on the precipice of joining the billionaire boys club. His evolution as a businessman, husband, father, activist, and more spiritual being has helped some to excuse his past.

Nevertheless, he has several detractors. Bill Adler, a music journalist and former director of publicity at Def Jam Recordings, believes that there is no difference between the current version of Mr. Carter and the outlaw who sold crack and shot his own brother. Conservative talk show host Tomi Lahren felt the need to remind the public that Jay-Z sold drugs for 14 years.[74] Perhaps the creators of *Empire* saw Gatsby in Jay-Z as well, which may have shaped their portrayal of Lucious. Lucious has a seat at the table, yet detractors still remind him that he does not belong there. Anika's father, a white medical doctor, tells him that he never approved of their engagement because he saw Lucious as a thug. Cookie's new lover Angelo Dubois, the product of an elite family, reminds Lucious that his wealth did not come from selling drugs or hip-hop.

The underground economy has provided Lucious and Jay-Z with an entrance into the music industry, Madison Avenue, and the mainstream. The underground economy has turned Lucious and Jay-Z into one percenters who may have 99 problems, but wealth ain't one. Therein lies the question: have these men, and anyone else they represent, really achieved the American dream? Well, they have certainly reached summits about which the other previously mentioned real and imagined black outlaws could only dream. Traditionally, the black outlaw's story ends in one of two destinations: prison or the grave. Earlier I mentioned Rayful Edmond, III, the Washington, D.C., drug kingpin. Since 1990 he has been serving a life prison sentence without parole. Lucious and Jay-Z survived and proved that they did not need a high school diploma or white skin to dine with the 1 percent. So, if the American dream is based solely upon financial success and power, I would say, yes, they have achieved it.

If the dream is about more than money, especially as it relates to black people, I would resoundingly say no to the previous question. First, the number of blacks who have attained such wealth is minuscule. As a result, their wealth can never completely separate them from the stain of racial injustice. "The goal is not to be successful and famous … we have a responsibility to push the conversation forward until we're all equal," says Jay-Z.[75] *Empire*'s writers certainly realized this as well. Episode 33, "What Remains is Bestial," reveals that despite his conked hair and silk ascots Lucious has not completely lost his self-awareness. As he drives his sons through his old neighborhood, he reminds them, that as black males, they are always one catastrophic misstep away from finding themselves fenced in a state of hopelessness. His message to his sons is that their wealth only gives them a temporary pass, it does not allow them to transcend their race. Academy Award winning actor Mahershala Ali says black men are taught to walk around always playing defense out of fear of having their bodies violated by a country that still struggles to see them as equals.[76] The men who choose to live their lives playing offense become the way makers. Perhaps this self-awareness is what not only motivates men like Lucious, but it may also explain why so many blacks are fascinated with these men's relentless determination to scale the heights of an alluring fantasy, called the American dream, and turn it into a reality defined in their own terms. The dominant issue that must be addressed is if the African American community is content with clinging to these *heroes*. Racism may never die, so when do we decide that we longer need these outlaws and their concept of the American Dream to define us? Priest and Stringer Bell eventually recognized how futile their criminality was. James has tried to kill off Ghost. Shawn Carter recorded a song titled "Kill Jay-Z" and violently killed off his former self in his "99 Problems" music video. Maybe it is time that the heroic image of the outlaw dies too and becomes a thing of the past.

3

The Name's Cookie, Ask About Me

The Fierce and Flawed Feminism of Cookie Lyon

> "The streets ain't made for everybody. That's why they made sidewalks."[1]
>
> —Cookie Lyon

The 2016 Golden Globe Awards belonged to Taraji P. Henson. The vibrant 46-year-old Washington, D.C., native stole the show at the prestigious awards ceremony for the Hollywood Foreign Press Association. Henson won the award for Best Actress in a Dramatic Television Series. As she walked from her seat towards the stage to receive her award Henson passed out cookies to audience members. Her hilarious reaction to winning the award was only trumped by a memorable acceptance speech: "Who knew that playing an ex-convict would take me all around the globe? Haaa Haaaa! It just goes to show, I thought it would be Queenie ... but it's Cookie who spent 17 years in jail for selling crack."[2] Since 2015 *Empire* has turned Taraji P. Henson into a household name around the world. In addition to her Golden Globe Award, she took home a Critics' Choice Award in 2015. If she had not lost a primetime Emmy nomination for Outstanding Lead Actress in a Drama Series, Henson would have become the first African American woman to win the award. Besides the awards and accolades, *Empire* has earned Ms. Henson numerous guest spots on popular talk shows, the BET Awards, her own Christmas special on FOX, and a hosting opportunity on *Saturday Night Live* (*SNL*). Henson's appearance on *SNL* featured a skit with her as Cookie on the popular PBS children's series *Sesame Street*. Cookie joined the lovable *Sesame Street* characters Bert, Ernie and, of course, the Cookie Monster. She even dropped some words of wisdom on Snuffaluffagus: "Snuffy you need to stop rapping like you from the streets, 'cause you not about that life."[3]

Cookie has turned Taraji P. Henson into a social media phenomenon. #CookieMonsters has a million Instagram followers and over four million Twitter followers. Dressing up like Cookie was among the hottest Halloween trends in 2015. Robin Roberts and Michael Strahan appeared on ABC's *Good Morning America* Halloween special dressed like *Empire*'s first lady. Cookie's popularity extends beyond the African American community. White women and girls are walking around reciting popular "Cookisms" and quotes. Cookie's head-turning wardrobe has been promoted in *Vogue* magazine. Saks Fifth Avenue created a new fashion line for women wanting to dress like their idol. *Empire*'s Wednesday evening competitor *Black-ish* even paid homage to Cookie on an episode by having its star, Jenifer Lewis, refer to her as one "baaaaad bitch."[4]

Cookie Lyon is a loving mother, an astute businesswoman, tortured ex-wife, and television's most intriguing diva. But is she a feminist? Cookie Lyon is at the forefront of a golden age in television for women. Digital streaming networks, Netflix and Hulu, give viewers glimpses of women behind bars (*Orange is the New Black*) and in dystopian fantasies that appropriate the experiences of black slave women (*The Handmaid's Tale*).[5] Cable TV has wealthy housewives behaving badly and ruthless anti-heroes such as Teresa Mendoza (*Queen of the South*) and Janine "Smurf" Cody (*Animal Kingdom*).[6] Concurrently, network television has women cast in every role imaginable. Feminist tropes and themes are present in much of this programming. African American women play important roles in this revolution. Cookie Lyon, along with other fictional black female characters, namely, Olivia Pope, Annalise Keating, and Mary Jane Paul, paved the way for the nuanced portrayals of black women found on newer series like *Greenleaf, Insecure, Queen Sugar,* and *Claws*.[7]

Cookie is a contemporary version of the bad ass heroines popularized by Pam Grier during the 1970s Blaxploitation Cinema era. Pam Grier's characters in films *Coffy* (1973) and *Foxy Brown* (1974) juxtaposed images of toughness with vulnerability, sex appeal with intelligence. Similar to Grier's heroines, Cookie raises debates over what constitutes "respectable" forms of black feminism and womanism. For some individuals she is too loud, too "ghetto," and too "ratchet" to be an appropriate role model for young black women and girls.[8] In my opinion, whether you like Cookie or not, she is representative of the values of empowerment, independence, and sexuality promoted by Pam Grier in the 1970s; the African American heroines currently on network television; and by trailblazing hip-hop stars like Beyoncé. According to proponents of hip-hop feminism, 21st century African American women can be both fierce and flawed in their performances of womanhood.

Being a Black Woman on Television

The Cookie Lyon phenomenon did not happen in a vacuum. Historical events in society and popular culture have led to this moment. In 1939 NBC aired a one-night special called *The Ethel Waters Show*. The success of this one-night special starring legendary blues singer Ethel Waters contributed to the development of television as a medium for home entertainment. Beginning on July 3, 1950, *The Hazel Scott Show*, a 15-minute musical program debuted on Monday, Wednesday, and Friday evenings at 7:45 on the now defunct Dumont Television Network.[9] Hazel Scott, a Julliard School trained classical pianist and jazz singer from Trinidad, would perform songs in chic gowns during her show. Scott was the wife of the U.S. Congressman from Harlem, the Rev. Adam Clayton Powell, Jr., arguably the most influential African American leader in the 1940s and 1950s.[10] After Hazel Scott was accused of being a Communist Party sympathizer by *Red Channels*, a popular anti-communist publication, Dumont, cancelled her program. Scott's absence from television signaled the end of the sophisticated portrayals of black womanhood.

Around the time of Scott's cancellation, ABC debuted *The Beulah Show* (1950–1952). This weekly Tuesday evening series, originally a CBS radio program (1945–1954) featuring Hattie McDaniel, was the first sitcom to cast a black woman in the lead. The televised adaptation starred Ethel Waters as Beulah, the faithful maid of a white middle-class family named the Hendersons. The sitcom played on archetypes of black womanhood that most white Americans had been conditioned to accept. The black woman's place was in the kitchen. Beulah was so busy frying chicken and tending to her white folks that she did not have time for civil rights protests against the indignities other blacks faced daily. Furthermore, Beulah was so content raising Miss Anne's babies that she did not need a family of her own. "Don't let nobody tell you I'm in the market for a husband. Of course, I would be, but they don't sell husbands at the market," she stated jovially at the start of an episode. Ethel Waters, a year removed from her Academy Award nomination for Best Supporting Actress in *Pinky*, did her best to humanize the southern maid. But Waters grew tired of playing the role after just one season of *Beulah*. ABC replaced Waters with Hattie McDaniel. After cancer took McDaniel's life, ABC hired Louise Beavers as the new Beulah.

The NAACP chose to police television as one of their campaigns in the 1950s. The nation's oldest civil rights organization argued that Beulah's character was a throwback to the mammies glorified in Lost Cause mythology and Margaret Mitchell's novel *Gone with the Wind*. The NAACP organized a national boycott of *Beulah* and *The Amos 'n' Andy Show* (1951–1953). In August 1951, the organization published "Why the *Amos 'n' Andy* TV Show Should be Taken Off the Air." Among its grievances the NAACP accused *Amos 'n' Andy*, television's first black series, of reducing their female characters Sapphire (Earnestine Wade) and her mama (Amanda Randolph) to nothing more than a bunch of "cackling screaming shrews," who were unattractive, loud, abrasive, and angry.[11] Feminist scholar bell hooks, in her discussion of what she calls the *oppositional gaze*, remembers witnessing Sapphire during her childhood. In her eyes Sapphire constructed the black woman's image in an ugly and undesirable way.[12]

The turbulence of the 1960s brought much needed societal changes, which were reflected in primetime television. The most notable examples were *Star Trek* and *Julia*. Gene Roddenberry's *Star Trek* (1966–1969) was a groundbreaking science fiction series that combined the Cold War era's fascination with outer space and Martin Luther King's dream of an equal society. Nichelle Nichols played communications officer Lieutenant Uhura aboard the USS Enterprise. Her role was a breath of fresh air for the African American community. King applauded Nichols' work on *Star Trek*, which inspired a young Mae Jemison to become the first black astronaut to travel into outer space.[13] Nichols and her co-star William Shatner made history in the 1968 episode "Plato's Stepchildren" by engaging in television's first interracial kiss. The episode, airing nearly a year after the U.S. Supreme Court decision in *Loving v. Virginia* which struck down anti-miscegenation laws across the nation, was a watershed moment in television history.[14] The kiss was so controversial that the episode was banned in almost every southern state.

Julia, the first sitcom about a single middle class black woman, debuted on September 17, 1968. Diahann Carroll played the widowed mother of a young son and a nurse in a white doctor's office. Julia was a great mom who provided a comfortable middle-class upbringing for her son Corey. Racism was not a huge problem for her, but she did not shield Corey from learning about prejudice and issues of race. *Julia* aired on NBC for three seasons; however, it faced constant scrutiny from black male critics who disliked the show's absence of a black father figure. *Julia* was accused of perpetuating the Moynihan Report's claims that the majority of black households were headed by single mothers. Of course, it should be noted that Julia's husband had been killed in the Vietnam War. Other critics were flabbergasted with the thought of a black series which ignored problems in America's ghettos. Diane Carroll experienced so much stress-induced sickness that she declined to renew her contract with NBC. ABC's *Get Christie Love!* (1974–1975), starring Teresa Graves, was the last primetime series on a major network to cast a black woman in a lead role until 2012. The series was a spin-off of a made-for-television film about an unmarried police detective modeled after the action heroines popularized by Pam Grier films.

Good Times, The Jeffersons, and *The Cosby Show* countered the media's trend of highlighting single black women and fatherless black households. The women on these series were mothers, happily married to strong and loving black men. Unfortunately, except for *The Cosby Show,* these women were devoid of agency and voice. A good example of this was found in *Good Times.* The matriarch Florida Evans attempted to reenroll in school but had to drop out because her husband James was opposed. Her decision to go back to school was only justified when her husband decided to enroll, too. By the dawn of the 1990s, black women were stepping out on their own without a man or children to define them. The FOX sitcom *Living Single* (1993–1998) starring Queen Latifah presented four successful, professional black women living happily single in New York City. Queen Latifah's character, Khadijah James, was the editor and founder of the fictional *Flavor* magazine. *Living Single* was written and produced by Yvette Denise Lee Bowser, the first African American woman to create her own primetime television series.

Living Single was a trailblazer that planted the seeds for Mara Brock Akil's series, *Girlfriends* (2000–2008) on UPN and The CW. The women on *Girlfriends* were highly accomplished, multidimensional characters who broke popular stereotypes associated with black womanhood. Tracee Ellis Ross played the protagonist Joan Clayton, Esq., on *Girlfriends.* One of the women on the sitcom, Lynn Searcy (Persia White), held five post-graduate degrees. Another character, Antoinette "Toni" Childs (Jill Marie Jones), was a real estate agent who started her own brokerage. Despite their professional accomplishments, these women were still down to earth and not too educated to speak in Ebonics at times.[15] The success of *Girlfriends* led to a spin-off, *The Game* (2006–2015), about the mothers, wives, and girlfriends of professional athletes. Since the year 2000, we have seen black women cast as CEOs, pastors, attorneys, doctors, baseball players, sports agents, vampires, Gotham City villains, and even the president of the United States.

Gladiators in Animal Print Suits and Fur

How does Cookie Lyon compare to her African American counterparts on primetime television today? To answer this question, I want to focus on Oliva Pope, Annalise Keating, and to a lesser extent Mary Jane Paul. In 2012 *Scandal* became the first series since *Get Christie Love!* to have a black woman in a lead role. Olivia Pope is the fictional CEO of Washington, D.C.'s, most successful crisis management firm, Pope & Associates. Olivia and her band of merry misfits, referred to as "gladiators in suits," fix the problems of the nation's most powerful figures, occasionally solving murders and averting catastrophes that threaten national security. Over the course of the series, we see Oliva serve as the manager for the presidential campaigns of both President Fitzgerald "Fitz" Thomas Grant, III (Tony Goldwyn) and his wife Melody "Mellie" Grant (Bellamy Young).

Scandal is the brainchild of Shonda Rhimes, arguably Hollywood's hottest African American television screenwriter, director, and producer.[16] *Scandal* was an instant hit with women between 18 and 40-years-old. Olivia Pope became a fashion icon and a feminist heroine for millions of women and girls. The media declared Olivia to be primetime's first black female anti-hero.[17] Oliva is the epitome of a black woman who has known a privileged existence in high society her entire life. As a child, her father sent her overseas to attend a prestigious boarding school. She graduated from Princeton University and Georgetown University Law School. After school, she worked as a lawyer, a campaign manager, served as the White House Director of Communications, and finally started her own firm. Olivia lives alone in an upscale Washington, D.C., neighborhood. Her sophisticated designer wardrobe only enhances her regal mystique. Fashion conscious fans obsess over her astounding overcoats, fitted blazers, silk blouses, business suits, tailored trousers, and pencil skirts.[18] Olivia's style is classy by traditional standards and understated by neutral shades of gray, black, white, and camel except for a bold cherry-red leather trench coat that has a $5,900 price tag. Robin Givhan, *The Washington Post* fashion editor, says Olivia's neutral colors represent the metaphorical white hat that she and her gladiators wear as they swoop in to save the day.[19]

In *Scandal's* final season, Olivia serves as Chief of Staff for President Mellie Grant and the new command of B613.

The 40-year-old Ms. Pope is an attractive, light brown-skinned woman with a slim build and long straightened hair. Despite a short-lived engagement to a black Democratic senator named Edison Davis (Norm Lewis), who unsuccessfully ran for president, her most serious relationships have primarily been with white men. She dated Jake Ballard (Scott Foley), who had worked at the Pentagon in the Intelligence Department for the Joint Chiefs of Staff and served under her father in B-613, before running for vice president alongside Mellie Grant. *Scandal* revolves around Olivia's on again off again affair with the Republican President Fitzgerald Grant.

Olivia Pope is primetime television's first post-racial black heroine. Unlike previous black heroines, in cinema and television, race is never a roadblock for her. On many occasions, she could easily be replaced by a white actress due to her lack of cultural indicators. Thus, her romantic relationships with powerful white men are not a big deal. When it was leaked to the press that she was Fitz's mistress no one appeared to bat an eye over the color of her skin. University of Michigan professor Tiya Miles disputes the show's premise that interracial relationships, especially between black women and white men, are so easily acceptable regardless of class. Miles points out an interesting statistic found in data released by the popular online dating site OukCupid. While black women respond to more initial overtures than other women, their initial contacts are the most ignored.[20] The majority of Americans still marry within their race, and black women are more likely to remain single than women of other races.

Scandal is 'must watch' television for many of my female friends and the women at my church. The series has a strong following on black Twitter and other social media sites. While some black women admire Oliva Pope, her experience is not a common one. Her father Rowan (Joe Morton) is one of the most powerful men in the government. Her lifestyle isolates her from most individuals within the African American community. A glaring example occurs when she finds herself at the center of a public demonstration resulting from the fatal shooting of a black teenager by a white police officer. After being called out by a local civil rights activist named Marcus (Cornelius Smith, Jr.) for her disconnect with the local black community she decides to support the boy's father, who sits near his dead body in a lawn chair holding a gun in his lap. She and her gladiators discover that the police officer racially profiled the victim and the department tried to falsify the details surrounding the shooting. The episode ends with Olivia taking the boy's father to visit the White House. *Slate*'s Aisha Harris expressed disappointment with *Scandal*'s fairytale depiction and happy ending of Olivia's encounter with racial injustice in poor black environments.[21] In actuality, Olivia's encounter reflects the way that *some, not all,* privileged African Americans experience race. They are bystanders who can support African American struggles from afar and even attend protests if they choose to. But at the end of the day, they are free to return to their islands of exclusivity miles away from the rest of black America. Katrina McDonald discusses Oprah's connection with the black community in *Embracing Sisterhood: Class, Identity, and Contemporary Black Women* (2011). McDonald says Oprah often came across as the "sister outsider" because her talk show catered so much to a majority upper-class, suburban white female audience. Tickets to attend her live tapings cost up to $1,000 which excluded many black women. Some black women admired her success, but viewed her as a mammy.

Shonda Rhimes followed up the success of *Scandal* with her next breakout hit *How to Get Away with Murder* (2014–). *HTGAWM*, premiering slightly more than three months before *Empire*, introduced viewers to Annalise Keating, played by 2010 Tony Award winner and 2017 Academy Award winner Viola Davis. Annalise is a cutthroat defense attorney and a demanding professor of law at the fictional Middleton University in Philadelphia. Annalise is just as complicated as Olivia. A Harvard University Law School graduate, she has her own law firm which hires her brightest students from Middleton University. She was married to Dr. Sam Keating (Tom Verica), a white therapist, for a decade. The couple lost their only child after Annalise suffered a miscarriage following a nearly fatal car accident. Before their marriage, she had a romantic relationship with a white female classmate in her law school. Much like Olivia, fashion plays a major role in her public persona. Her courtroom attire is form fitting to show off her curves and shapely figure. She accessorizes her outfits with chunky necklaces, bracelets, and earrings. Annalise's attire matches her belligerent persona in the courtroom and the classroom.

Annalise did not grow up wealthy; she came from a poor family in the South. Back home they call her by her given name Anna Mae. Her fancy degrees and big city success make her an idol for her family and close friends. Unlike Olivia who is painfully stiff and buttoned up, Annalise is not too sadiddy to "back that thang up" on the dance floor with her relatives. In addition to overcoming poverty, she has dealt with problems faced by millions of black women throughout American history. She was molested by her Uncle Clyde repeatedly as a child. Rather than report her brother to the authorities, Annalise's mother Ophelia (Cecily Tyson) told her to pretend that it never happened. Her mother's complicit silence provides a lesson that black women have been hearing for centuries dating back to slavery. It is the notion that they must be physically and emotionally strong, at all times, in the face of tragedy.

One thing that I find interesting about Annalise is that she is constantly aware of her perceived place in the world as a black woman. Olivia does have some self-awareness thanks to her father who routinely reminds her that she must be twice as good as her white counterparts, but for the most part she lives in a colorblind bubble. Perhaps Annalise's background forces her to view the world differently. Annalise is a much darker woman than Olivia Pope. A powerful scene in the first season shows her in front of her mirror at night removing her makeup and permed wig to reveal a natural hairstyle. The makeup and wig are symbolic of the armor that she must wear to be considered beautiful, tolerable, and nonthreatening in the wealthy white world in which she now resides. Her armor is in step with the mask that poet Paul Laurence Dunbar said African Americans are forced to wear to survive.

Both Olivia and Annalise walk a fine line between good and evil. They both treat their employees and mentees as fictive kin. Olivia puts her cape on for the Republican Party and the American republic at all times.[22] She turns morally flawed politicians into celebrated heroes in the eyes of voters. Annalise is training some of the nation's most promising future legal experts to lie, cheat, commit perjury, and get away with murder when it benefits their personal interests. She willingly engaged in an affair with a married police officer whose wife was dying from cancer. The web of the deception to which Annalise has contributed leads to her wrongful incarceration. Both women, notwithstanding their education and high-powered careers, are susceptible to intense personal strife and moral rot. Similar qualities can be found in Mary Jane Paul (Gabrielle Union), the protagonist of Mara Brock Akil's BET drama *Being Mary Jane* (2013–2017). The highly driven, socially conscious, pro-black news anchor rebounds from a firing from CNN to work her way up from an Atlanta talk news series to being a news correspondent in New York City for the nation's highest rated morning show. Mary Jane, a product of a relatively affluent Jack and Jill family, has not committed any crimes like the other ladies or rigged elections, yet she battles personal demons. Most notably her unchecked alcoholism leads to a bad car accident and almost costs her job.

While Mary Jane is the prototypical career woman, she still clings desperately to patriarchal standards of marriage and motherhood to achieve self-fulfillment. At the beginning of the series, she is dating a married father of young children, sleeping with a younger NFL player, and secretly freezes the sperm of a lover in another relationship, in case she decides to get pregnant. In the third season, she tries her luck with a white man. By the start of the fourth season, she is a few months shy of turning 40 years old and is willing to pay $20,000 to a professional matchmaker. When it comes to friends and family, she is dealing with her mother's lupus, parents' separation, brother's drug addiction, niece's poor decision making when it comes to having children out of wedlock, and her best friend's depression-related suicide.

Mary Jane, unlike her Shondaland counterparts, has an easier time code switching. In fact, one of her faults at work is the failure to switch back to a demeanor that comforts her white guests and viewers. She keeps it "too real" at times for the white producers and jealous black men in her networks. For example, she tells a white guest that she has an "ugly black woman" inside of her. She publicly shames a younger, conservative colleague for political views and "white privilege." Mary Jane channels her inner Cookie Lyon during a televised interview with Mercedes Wilkerson (Cardi B.), a rude reality star. Mercedes accuses Mary Jane of "acting white" and being out of touch with the African American community for which she claims to speak. Mary Jane responds by insinuating that Mercedes is nothing more than a low-class gold digger with multiple kids out of wedlock. Ironically, Cookie probably has more in common with the rags to riches reality star Mercedes, minus the kids out of wedlock, than with Mary Jane and the Shondaland's gladiators.

Cookie did not grow up with a silver spoon in her mouth nor did she attend elite boarding schools as a teenager. Nevertheless, she did not grow up poor as one might assume from watching *Empire*'s inaugural season. Cookie was born Loretha Holloway in Philadelphia. The middle child in the family, she attended Catholic schools with her sisters Candace (Vivica A. Fox) and Carol (Tasha Smith). She was on track to attend Howard University and then medical school, but she gave that up to pursue a career in music. She dumped her overachieving, square boyfriend, Barry to date Lucious, who gave her the nickname Cookie when they were teens. After her father, a hardworking plumber, discovered drug money and Lucious' gun under her bedroom mattress, he banished her from his home. Weeks later he suffered a fatal heart attack. Her older sister Candace blamed her for placing too much stress on their father's heart. Cookie married Lucious and had three sons. Their first child would have been a girl, but she died during a miscarriage. Cookie soon found herself selling drugs with Lucious to support their sons and his dreams of becoming an accomplished singer. As for her dreams, they were put on hold.

Cookie did not attend an Ivy League university. She received a degree in hard knocks from behind prison bars and worked her way up the ladder in the music industry. Cookie is not as subtle around "mixed" company. She is politically incorrect, loud, and refreshingly outspoken. When Cookie walks into the middle of board meetings at Empire Entertainment, she greets the lone black woman sitting at the table with a "Hey sista girl!" The woman looks away, rolling her eyes in disgust. Basketball fans may remember Allen

Iverson's colorful mom, Ann. Well, that is Cookie with a fancier wardrobe. Cookie proudly wears her blackness on her sleeve at all times. She is what Mara Brock Akil says of her characters: "black on purpose."[23] Solange's unequivocally pro-black theme song "F.U.B.U." (For Us, By Us) could be her ringtone. Thus far Cookie has dated only black and brown men. She was a proud supporter of the Obamas during their period in the White House. She could never be ostracized for selling out at a Black Lives Matter rally.

Cookie's lower social status and perceived lack of class are underlying themes in *Empire*. Initially, she is compared to her rival Anika Calhoun. Anika always holds her debutante background over Cookie's head. Cookie's disgust boils over into a memorable knock out, drag down fight. In season three she begins dating Angelo Dubois, a black mayoral candidate from an upper crust New York family. Angelo allows Cookie to live out a fantasy of what her life could have been if she never allowed Lucious to get her involved in crime. But she discovers that dating Angelo is not easy. When he invites her to attend a public function, she is caught off guard as she arrives wearing a short, tight red dress, better suited for a nightclub, to a black-tie affair. Angelo introduces her to a pair of black women, attired in ballroom gowns, whom he has known since he was a child in Jack and Jill. When the women ask Cookie if she also vacations at Martha's Vineyard, she bluntly tells them that many of her summers were spent at the Danbury Federal Correctional Institute for Women in Connecticut. The night grows worse for Cookie when Angelo takes her to listen to an opera singer. Unfamiliar with the proper etiquette for the opera, Cookie has a black church moment and embarrasses herself by jumping out of her seat, clapping, and shouting out "you better sing that gurl." Everyone in the concert hall is shocked. After the concert Cookie overhears the two uppity women she met earlier talking in the bathroom and wondering aloud why Angelo brought that "hood rat" to the affair. They make jokes about her being an ex-convict. Cookie confronts them and warns them that she is not the one to be toyed with. She then leaves the event without saying a word to Angelo.

Cookie's relationship with Angelo highlights her curtailed education and the fact that the Lyon family's social status was not achieved by traditional means. When she invites Angelo's mother, Diana Dubois, over for dinner to impress her, Cookie finds herself going out of the way to gain Mrs. Dubois' acceptance. She recruits Candace to give her a crash course in high society etiquette 101 and redecorates her home so that it meets her potential mother-in-law's lofty standards. Candace teaches her Maya Angelou quotes and advises her to "Melania Trump the hell" out of them as if they were her own.[24] Although the dinner turns out to be a disaster, Mrs. Dubois is impressed by

Cookie's efforts. She reveals to her that her family's money came from bootlegging, so she knows how it feels not to grow up elite. Once Mrs. Dubois learns that her son's poll numbers have risen dramatically from being associated with someone as relatable to the masses as Cookie Lyon, she values Cookie exponentially. This encounter with Mrs. Dubois is also symbolic because the character is played by the captivating Phylicia Rashad, who is treated like royalty in black America because of her role as Clair Huxtable on *The Cosby Show*. Clair was pop culture's first example of a multidimensional, highly educated, middle-class black woman who was married, a mother, and had a lucrative career. Clair was the epitome of "a respectable" lady.

Cookie, on the other hand, might be characterized as the face of "ratchet" respectability. Alexander Cooper Hawley studies the representations of *nouveau riche* black women on *The Real Housewives of Atlanta*. Alexander says these women flaunt their money as a signifier of their new social status.[25] At the same time their performance of class and black womanhood (filled with eye rolling, attitude, and violent aggression) often comes across as being low class. "Ratchet replaces the term ghetto, which is synonymous with Blacks."[26] In "Brains, Booty, and All Bizness": Identity Poltics, Ratchet Respectability, and *The Real Housewives of Atlanta*," Robin Boylorn explains how "ratchet" behavior can be empowering. "Brittney Cooper argues the ratchetness can be seen as a dismissal of respectability, what she calls "disrepectability politics" ... an act of transgression that black women can use to push back against rigid expectations of acceptable womanhood. Disrepectability politics urges black women to have more agency in their race and gender performances while offering critique of whitewashed identity politics... Similiarly, Heidi Renee Lewis believes that respectability and ratchetness are capable of coexisting in the same woman at the time."[27]

Cookie's wardrobe is by far the most audacious when compared with the previously discussed heroines. Robin Givhan says Cookie's attire represents "ghetto fabulous." When she is introduced leaving prison after 17 years, she walks out wearing a tight leopard-print dress, big hoop earrings, and a white fur coat.[28] Talk about a subtle introduction! Rita McGhee, an *Empire* costume designer, says that she was trying to show viewers how fly and fabulous Cookie was back in her hustling days. "It's a combination of '80s Mary J. Blige, but it's also this grandness of 'I deserve it, and I'm going to wear it now.'"[29] Cookie's wardrobe is full of vivid colors that jump off the screen. As she transitions from hustler to an emerging music mogul, her fashion becomes even more spectacular. In one instance, she might wear an Alexander McQueen dress with a Balenciaga clutch. In another moment, she might wear a rhinestone tiger-stripe dress with a long slit up the leg. She uses big Chanel gold pendants, Cavalli necklaces, and Gucci python bags to accessorize her leopard jumpsuits. Her boldest look might be the brown sable coat she wore over skimpy lingerie when she showed up at a restaurant to see Lucious, only to learn that she was coming to his and Anika's engagement party. The stunned look on Jamal's face is priceless. The scene is made even more outrageous when she grabs her left butt cheek and shouts out "Oh, and Anika, this is an ass," as she walks out of the room filled with the entire family.[30]

What Cookie has in common with the women of Shondaland and Mary Jane is an ability to own every room she walks into, solve the problems of others, and do whatever is necessary to protect her loved ones. She is a gladiator in fur coats and animal print body suits who has all the makings of a super woman. "I gotta deal with feds, hitmen, and studio drama," she says while driving back and forth between the Bronx and Philadelphia to protect her family from gangsters and helping Jamal to record his first hit song, "Keep Your Money."[31] In 2013 CeShawn Thompson coined the phrase "Black Girl Magic," which has now become a popular hashtag on social media, to celebrate the beauty, power, and resilience of black women.[32] #BlackGirlMagic should be the motto for Cookie and these other women. But while these shows promote the black super woman archetype, they also show these women to be vulnerable and capable of experiencing hurt and sadness like the rest of us. Cookie is continually sacrificing her own happiness and health for the insecure men in her life. She loves Lucious and wants to be with him, but his selfish tendencies push her away and rob her of the respect she deserves. She suffers a heart attack and is arranging songs for Empire artists from her bed days later.

Do White Women Really Want These Cookies?

Taraji P. Henson's acceptance speech at the Golden Globes expressed surprise at the public's embrace of her *Empire* character which leads me to a deeper question: why are white women in love with Cookie Lyon? Perhaps they love her partly because she possesses the same qualities that made Alexis (Joan Collins) on *Dynasty* the most beloved woman on primetime television in the 1980s. Alexis, the ex-wife of oil tycoon Blake Carrington, was just as much of a diva as Cookie. "You can't even run your own family, let alone Colorado," she told her ex-husband. Just like Cookie, she engaged in catfights with her former beau's new love interest. Alexis, like Cookie, often challenged Blake for control of the family and the family business. "Alexis was the first woman to assert herself as the business rival to Blake. She takes on the masculine attribute of the hero. She is as brutal, as single-minded and daring as he can ever be with the additional advantage of a woman's expertise in handling emotional issues," writes Christine Geraghty.[33] Other soap opera female anti-heroes like *All My Children's* Erica Kane (Susan Lucci) captivated audiences for years. The unavoidable difference between Alexis and Cookie is their skin color.

Do white women love the *idea* of Cookie Lyon, but not the nonfictional women she represents? Kristal Brent Zook, a white journalist, published a 2015 article in *The Nation* praising Cookie for representing black women as multidimensional figures.[34] In her article for *The Feminist Wire* Desiree Adaway, a black woman, discusses *Bloomberg* magazine's "How to Dress Like Cookie From 'Empire' at Work, Every Day of the Week," and *Glamour* magazine's dress like Cookie for Halloween section. The problem as she sees it is that many of these same white women who love "the fantasy of" Cookie ignore the plight of women like her in real life. Queer feminist Moya Bailey coined the phrase *misogynoir* which describes white women receiving praise for appropriating the behavior and physical attributes of black women labeled "ghetto."[35] I view most of these white women dressing up like Cookie and quoting her as examples of *misogynoir*.

Do these white women realize that Cookie's story is a fantasy? She comes out of prison and ends up living in an upscale apartment in New York City weeks later. She has a $3 million annual salary and a job at one of the most successful record labels, designer labels in her closet, a funny assistant named Porsha (Ta'Rhonda Jones), and a perfect hair weave. Unless you are Lil' Kim or Remy Ma, formerly incarcerated female rappers who had platinum records and reality shows soon after they returned home, this type of life is not awaiting most ex-convicts. Yes, she did lose 17 years in prison and still must urinate in a cup on monthly visits to her parole officer, but she has a good life now. The writers of the series highlight the difference between Cookie's life and her former cellmates when she returns to the women's prison to host a concert for them. She is a hero to those women still trapped behind bars. *Empire*, along with the Emmy winning Netflix comedic series *Orange is the New Black* (2013–), and the third season of *How to Get Away with Murder*, are a few of the television shows to address the issue of black women and mass incarceration.[36]

Discussion of incarceration rates should not be limited to black men. Historian Talitha LeFlouria highlights the number of black female inmates used in post–Civil War chain gangs in *Chained in Silence: Black Women and Convict Labor in the New South* (2016). In recent years black women have accounted for more than 30 percent of the women's prison population and are three times as likely as white women to go to jail or prison.[37] The majority of these women serving time are there for nonviolent drug crimes. Sheranda Jones, a single mother, received life without parole for conspiracy to distribute crack. One in fourteen black kids is growing up with a parent that has been institutionalized. According to the Bureau of Justice in 2017 there were more than 120,000 incarcerated mothers with children under 18. Once these women finally gain their freedom they not only have to rekindle normal relationships with family and friends, but they also have to find work. The nonfictional Cookie Lyons are ostracized by white Middle America and Madison Avenue.[38] Michelle Alexander describes the challenges black female ex-convicts face when seeking permanent employment that pays well and housing.[39] In the digital age, it is impossible for these women to hide their pasts from potential employers. They certainly do not have luxury apartments and white billionaire investors waiting for them when they come home.

There is also the issue of the treatment of black women by law enforcement and while in police custody. On episode 14, "Without a Country," Cookie gets arrested to be questioned in a case against Lucious. As she is placed into the back seat of the police car against her will, she shouts out that if she does not return home, her death was not a suicide. Her protest was an allusion to the tragic death of Sandra Bland, a 28-year-old black woman found dead in her Texas jail cell. Bland's death was classified as a suicide; however, many suspect that foul play was involved.[40] Cookie was lucky that the police officers did not harm her when she initially tried to evade them. Nonfictional stories of black women such as Rekia Boyd (22-years-old), fatally shot in the head by an off-duty police detective in Chicago for talking too loud, and Tanisha Anderson (37-years-old), who died from being physically restrained in a prone position by Cleveland police officers, are evidence that what white viewers see on *Empire* is barely scratching the surface.[41] A flashback to Cookie's time in prison shows her repeating to herself that she just wants to die. It is unclear if this is in reaction to the mental stress of her confinement or because of abuse from an officer who beat her and raped her inmates. Even now as a free woman, Cookie is required to visit her parole officer every three months.

White privilege has historically allowed most whites to treat the African American experience and culture like a smorgasbord buffet. They can pick and choose what aspects they want to embrace. During a 1994 interview Henry Louis Gates, Jr., spoke of a gap between popular culture and reality in which some whites used these fictional television characters as substitutes for contact with real black people.[42] I would say that if white women really love Cookie Lyon, they must also respect the existence and struggles of women like her in the real world whose lives cannot be turned off after an hour of television each Wednesday.

She's a Whole Lotta Woman

Pam Grier runs all through the DNA of Cookie Lyon. Readers too young to remember just how *baaad* Pam Grier was should watch her 1974 film, *Foxy Brown*. Grier played Foxy Brown, a single black woman whose boyfriend, a federal agent, is murdered by the henchmen of Miss Kathryn Wall (Kathryn Loder). To avenge Carter's death, Foxy disguises herself as a prostitute to infiltrate Miss Wall's phony modeling agency, which serves as a cover for prostitution and heroin distribution. After Miss Wall and her boyfriend, Steve Elias (Peter Brown) uncover Foxy's real identity they send her to a heroin farm maintained by two racist white rednecks. The men chain Foxy to a bed half naked, shoot her up with heroin, and rape her. Foxy manages to untie herself, slashes the eyes of one man, pours gasoline on the other, and leaves them to burn to death. Next, she makes a plea to the men of a local Black Panther–like civic organization to help her bring down Wall. Foxy, with the help of these activists, captures Steve and delivers his severed penis in a pickle jar to Wall. Rather than kill Wall, Foxy shoots her in the arm and tells her, "Death is too easy for you bitch! I want you to suffer."[43]

Born in Winston-Salem, North Carolina, in 1949, Pamela Suzette Grier is a fair skinned woman of African American, Cheyenne Indian, Filipino, Chinese, and Hispanic descent.[44] Early in her career, white directors cast the beautiful 5'8" actress as the exotic amazon in films focused primarily on titillating, scantily clad women trying to escape from their prison cells. Her success in these B movies propelled her to become Hollywood's first black action heroine and the Queen of Blaxploitation Cinema. Grier appeared in nine Blaxploitation films, but she is best known for her leading roles as vigilantes in *Coffy* (1973) and *Foxy Brown* (1974). In *Coffy* she goes undercover as a high-class Caribbean prostitute for the pimp King George (Robert DoQui) to shut down the drug cartel that is responsible for getting her baby sister LuBelle hooked on smack (heroin) and nearly killing a former boyfriend, police detective Carter (William Elliot).

Pam Grier's ascendance in Hollywood coincided with a remarkable turning point in women's history. The legalization of birth control in 1960, Helen Gurley Brown's 1962 book *Sex and the Single Girl,* and Betty Friedan's 1963 book *The Feminine Mystique* sparked the Second-wave of the Feminist Movement. The National Organization for Women (NOW) pushed for equal pay, an Equal Rights Amendment to the U.S. Constitution, and abortion rights. More radical female activists sought an end to patriarchy and capitalism. *The Mary Tyler Moore Show* (1970–1977) used the sitcom to capture this revolutionary moment. Moore's character was the opposite of the discontented fictional housewife Lucy Ricardo who received an allowance from her husband Ricky whom she called sir.[45]

The leaders of the Feminist Movement were more concerned with problems facing middle-class white women.[46] Black women, in response to this lack of intersectionality, formed their own brand of feminism.[47] Frances Beale published her groundbreaking pamphlet, "Double Jeopardy: To Be Black and Female," which was later included in Toni Cade Bambara's anthology *Sisterhood is Powerful* (1970). Twin sisters Barbara and Beverly Smith were prominent leaders in the Black Feminist Movement, speaking on behalf of queer women. Patricia Hill Collins defines black feminism in her book *Black Feminist Thought*.[48] By the late 20th century black feminism evolved to include womanism, Africana Womanism, and Hip-Hop Feminism. Novelist Alice Walker coined the term womanism in 1983 to describe bonds formed between black women who embrace culture, spirituality, and femininity together.[49] Womanism recognizes that black women are not a monolithic group. Therefore, a single narrative is obsolete. Clenora Hudson-Weems introduced the concept of Africana Womanism in her 1993 book *Africana Womanism: Reclaiming Ourselves*. According to Hudson-Weems, the phrase distinguished itself from feminism and womanism by its emphasis on African culture, Afrocentrism, and the experience of black women in the African Diaspora.[50] Womanists and Africana Womanists reject feminism because of its intrinsic association with solely white women's issues. Finally, Joan Morgan, author of *When Chickenheads Come Home to Roost: A Hip Hop Feminist Breaks It Down*, introduced Hip-Hop Feminism to address the experiences of black women born after 1965 and raised on hip-hop culture. Morgan says hip-hop feminism allows young women of color to live within the gray as opposed to the traditional black or white terms of how a woman should behave. And then there are many black women today who refuse to be categorized by any of these labels. "So, am I a Black feminist? Yes and no. Am I a Womanist? Yes and no," writes Ashley Daniels in *For Harriet*.[51] Cardi B., hip-hop's most popular female rapper entering 2018, told *New York Magazine* that she refuses to be boxed into the traditional feminist archetype. According to Cardi feminism has nothing to do with college degrees, long skirts, or respectability politics.[52]

A precursor of the Feminist Movement was underway in the nonviolent Civil Rights Movement in the South and the more militant Black Power Movement in other regions of the country during the 1960s and 1970s. Women like Ella Baker, Diane Nash, Fannie Lou Hamer, and Dorothy Height were pivotal in the Freedom Rides, marches, sit-ins, and boycotts. Sexism in the Civil Rights Movement caused them to become hidden figures as the male leaders stood in the spotlight. Women assumed more public leadership roles in the black power organizations, most notably The Black Panther Party. Elaine Brown organized the party's first Free Breakfast program in Los Angeles and assumed leadership of the male dominated organization in 1974. Ericka Huggins was a founding member of the party's Los Angeles and New Haven chapters. After party co-founder Huey P. Newton was jailed in 1967 for the alleged murder of a white police officer, Kathleen Cleaver organized the "Free Huey" campaign, which contributed to his acquittal two years later. The artwork of Tarika Lewis in *The Black Panther* newspaper portrayed black women in strong, powerful poses brandishing firearms.[53] The Black Power Movement also saw the rise of Angela Davis and Assata Shakur to national prominence.[54]

Pam Grier's heroines reflected the spirit of feminism and Black Nationalism. In August 1975 Gloria Steinem, a national spokeswoman for white feminists, selected her to be the first woman of color to grace the cover of *Ms. Magazine*. Yvonne D. Sims, author of *Women of Blaxploitation: How the Black Action Film Heroine Changed Popular Culture* (2006), describes Grier as a heroine for women like herself because she proved that black women could be beautiful, independent, strong, and powerful.[55] Grier's characters surpassed limitations imposed on women, without denying their sensuality."[56] She kicked ass and looked gorgeous doing it. Grier's large afro, possibly modeled after Angela Davis's natural hairstyle, was iconic. Her wardrobes, including floral-print midriff tops with fitted denim bellbottoms and thigh-high split Maxi dresses with leather go-go boots, could have easily appeared in a fashion spread for *Ebony* or *Essence*.[57] When Foxy kicked in the apartment door of her dope-dealing brother Link (Antonia Fargas), she was holding a "Saturday Night Special" handgun and dressed in a glamorous silk blouse and matching silk head scarf with large hoop earrings.

Pam Grier's characters influenced other Blaxploitation era heroines, Cleopatra Jones, Christie Love, and T.N.T. Jackson. And, if you ask me, they probably inspired Lee Daniels and Taraji P. Henson. On episode 45, "Civil Unclean Hands," Cookie marches into a laundromat in a poor black neighborhood in Philadelphia attired in a floor length fur coat and sunshades. As she makes her grand entrance the funky sounds of Isaac Hayes' hit song "Do Your Thing" from the Blaxploitation era film, *Shaft* (1971), accompany her. Cookie resembles Pam Grier's protagonists in various ways that extend beyond fashion:

(1) The effects of drugs are hugely burdensome on her life. *Coffy* begins with Grier's character visiting her sister LuBelle at a drug rehabilitation center. In season two of *Empire* Cookie drives from New York to Philadelphia in search of her younger sister Carol (Tasha Smith) who is strung out in a crack house. Cookie offers Carol a job working for her at Empire Entertainment on the condition that she enter rehab. Cookie also tries to help Empire's first platinum selling artist Elle Dallas (Courtney Love) get clean and make a successful musical comeback. After Jamal becomes addicted to painkillers prescribed after he was shot, Cookie comes to his rescue. She comes to his apartment and pours all the pills down the kitchen sink. When she finds Jamal on his couch sweating profusely and unable to perform before a live audience without his pills she must make a crucial decision. Does she enable her son's addiction so that he can save his career or does she put his life ahead of fame? She decides to make a compromise. Cookie, dressed in a sparkling evening gown, grabs a wrench and gets down on the floor to retrieve the pills from the pipes under the sink. She allows Jamal to get high so that he can have a successful comeback performance at Angelo's campaign event. As Jamal happily walks off the stage he finds a Cookie-organized friends and family intervention. Everyone, even Lucious, tells Jamal that he cannot sing again until he completes rehab and gets clean.

(2) Family and close loved ones come first for Cookie just as they do for Grier's characters. Cookie puts family ahead of everything, including the music business and making money. She sold drugs, risked her life in the streets, and ultimately sacrificed her freedom, marriage, and motherhood to help Lucious accomplish his musical dreams and break her family's cycle of poverty. Cookie makes it her mission to defend her sons like a lioness defending her cubs. After Cookie's family is threatened on the streets by her former employer, Frank Gathers, she reaches out to Lucious, who orders Frank's murder. When Lucious demeans Andre for having a bipolar disorder and Jamal for being gay, Cookie stands up for Andre and supports his decision to go public about his mental illness. When Lucious thrusts Jamal into a garbage can headfirst as a little child, she comes to his rescue. Although Cookie went to prison, she promised Jamal that she would always have his back and she kept her word. Cookie tackled a thug named Reggie who pulled a gun on Jamal. When Jamal was shot by Freda Gatz during an assassination attempt on Lucious, Cookie accompanied Jamal to the hospital and prayed fervently to keep him alive. Although she has an estranged relationship with Hakeem, Cookie still looks out for him, too, and goes out of her way to bond with him. After Laz Delgado (Adam Rodriguez), a Latino concert promoter that she dates for a brief period, puts his hands on Hakeem, she slaps Delgado

and threatens to physically hurt him if he ever disrespects her son again. As much as she despises Anika, Cookie agrees to take care of her daughter Bella should harm ever come her way.

(3) Cookie, like Grier's Foxy, is intolerant of abuse from men. When she was a teenager she shot a boy in the leg for trying to rape her. She does not have any problem putting Lucious in his place or taking a broom to Hakeem's head when he disrespects her. When Kidd Fo-Fo, an overly sexist former Empire artist, threatens her on an elevator she mocks him. "You gonna Ray Rice me? I've faced bigger in prison," says Cookie.[58] She challenges a wannabe thug rapper and his "posse" to a drinking contest in exchange for getting the rapper to stay with Empire rather than signing with their rival label, Creedmore.[59] The drink of choice was promethazine mixed with codeine and Sprite soda, known on the streets as lean or sizzurp. Of course, she was the last (wo)man left standing as the men are passed out sleeping on the floor with their mouths wide open.

(4) In *Foxy Brown*, Grier addresses a room of black male community activists to gain their support. These men put aside their macho feelings to listen to her and go along with her plan. In *Empire*'s third season Cookie convinces a room full of black ex-convicts and hoodlums from the streets of North Philadelphia not to kill Lucious.

(5) Cookie makes a statement about justice like the one Foxy makes before the Black Nationalist group. Foxy appealed to them by stressing the need to fight dope pushers, pimps, and crooked law officials destroying the black community. Cookie was the keynote speaker at a star-studded concert to demand Lucious' release from prison and highlight racial inequality in policing and the judicial system.

(6) Grier's characters were tricksters who used cunning and sex appeal to outwit others. They were always able to think their way out of a tight jam. Although Cookie does not use sex and does not objectify her body as a source of power, she does use other forms of trickery. For example, she pretends to be a Muslim to persuade a black mother belonging to The Nation of Islam to help her sign her son Titan (James Washington) to Empire. In another instance, she is arrested when her assistant Porsha falsely uses her name after she is caught jumping a subway turnstile. Roxanne Ford, the prosecutor in the state's case against Lucious for the murder of Cookie's cousin Bunkie, uses Cookie's arrest as an opportunity to get her to turn on Lucious. After insulting Ford's expensive hair weave Cookie fabricates a story about Lucious killing Bunkie over control of a new business venture called Apex Radio. Ford believes Cookie and sets her free.

(7) If Grier's characters were original gangstas, Cookie can be best described

as a new school gangsta. Cookie is quick to point out her 17-year-prison stint to anyone who dares doubt her street cred(ibility). But she takes it a step further than just bragging about her past. Cookie paid her cousin Jermel (DeRay Davis) a $5,000 contract to kill Frank Gathers' goon Teddy McNally. She orders Shyne and his henchmen to beat Angelo to a bloody pulp because she suspects his mother of kidnapping her infant granddaughter Bella. She beat down Anika, aka Boo Boo Kitty, like a cast member on VH1's *Basketball Wives*, for trying to steal Lucious from her. After Hakeem is kidnapped by a Latino gang in a snatch-and-grab for a $40,000 ransom, Cookie has the misfortune of being coerced to conduct business for her music label Lyon Dynasty with his abductors. She allows Hakeem to accompany her on the meeting with the gangbangers, but her plans go awry when Hakeem pulls a gun on the men. She pleads with him to put the gun away. If he did not obey her orders she would have stepped in front of the bullet to prevent him from throwing his life away. After Hakeem gives her the gun she turns it on the men, placing it against the gang leader's forehead and leaves him with this message for threatening her family: "Welcome to my streets, bitch."[60]

Despite the many similarities, Cookie differs significantly from Grier's characters. She does not have to disguise herself as a prostitute or sleep with men to get what she wants. Cookie is more than an older sibling, a girlfriend, or a lover. She is a former wife, a mother, and a grandmother. Cookie is not a nurse living from paycheck to paycheck like Coffy. She is a powerful CEO in Manhattan overseeing the careers of the nation's biggest pop stars. Grier's characters were not allowed the opportunity to be as fabulous, multi-dimensional, and dignified as Cookie, which is a testament to the progress made since the 1970s.

Cookies and Lemonade

Is Cookie Lyon a feminist? When I posed this question to 100 people in a survey conducted between April and October 2016, only 17.57 percent of the respondents said yes. According to the dictionary a feminist is "a person who believes in the social, political, and economic equality of the sexes."[61] Zeba Blay, a writer for *The Huffington Post*, warned about oversimplifying the concept of feminism by rushing to label someone as feminist or anti-feminist. Cookie does not appear to be the type of woman who likes to be defined by labels. Nevertheless, Blay does believe that the complexities of Cookie's character make her an imperfect feminist hero. Cookie's flaws are what make her human and adored by millions of black women.[62] When she takes a baseball bat to all the awards hanging up on Lucious' walls at Empire's headquarters, one can imagine women all across America, who have been scorned by their lovers, slapping high fives. Blay states that Cookie's ordeal to regain control of Empire Entertainment represents more than just an attempt to take back what she deserves as an entrepreneur. The company Empire is synonymous with family for Cookie, who believes that music will ultimately reunite the Lyon clan. Whether she is dining with family at Lucious' mansion or attending a meeting at Empire's headquarters Cookie makes it a habit to sit at the head of the table. This is to remind everyone, Anika and Empire's staff, that the queen has returned to reclaim her throne.

Cookie has fans in very high places. During a 2015 interview with Ricky Smiley President Barack Obama revealed that Mrs. Obama was on team Cookie.[63] Barbara Smith, one of the founding mothers of the Black Feminist Movement, admitted during an MSNBC interview with transgender rights activist Janet Mock that she, too, loves the Cookie monster. Smith tells her highly educated black friends that they should all love Cookie because they all know someone like her.[64] Smith gets a kick out of hearing Cookie refer to her rival Anika as a "fake ass Lena Horne." The reference makes her laugh, but it also reminds her of the struggles that Lena Horne faced trying to break barriers as a woman of color in Hollywood. Smith especially appreciates the fact that Cookie did not attend elite schools like Olivia Pope and Annalise Keating, but she is just as smart and runs her own business. After Cookie is fired by Lucious following her failed attempt at a hostile takeover of Empire, she rents office space to launch a rival record label called Lyon Dynasty. Although Lyon Dynasty ultimately failed, her attempts to build this company demonstrated Cookie's fortitude and resilience. Cookie's setback at Lyon Dynasty set her up for a comeback. Empire's board of trustees voted her in as the company's co-CEO along with Lucious.

The literary giant Toni Morrison refused to be classified as a feminist because she did not want to marginalize herself or her work.[65] Nevertheless, many women still categorized her literature within the feminist canon. Cookie may not walk around with a t-shirt reading FEMINIST, but she is representative of the same values of empowerment, independence, motherhood, and sexuality promoted by pop icon Beyoncé Knowles-Carter, one of the leading black female voices for Millennials and the Hip-Hop Feminist Movement. When I hear Beyoncé shout "this is my shit, bow down bitches" on her 2014 hit single "Flawless," I cannot help but think of Cookie "slaying" Anika and anyone else trying to get in her way.[66] There is a lot of Queen Bey in the Cookie monster. Both women are independent bosses who define womanhood and success on their own terms. Cookie built both Empire and Lyon Dynasty from the ground up, eventually earning a place on the *Forbes* 100 most powerful women in business list. Beyoncé's $465 million net worth includes her companies Parkwood Entertainment, House of Dereon, and Ivy Park.[67] Both women are "ride-or-die chicks" linked to former outlaws turned legitimate CEOs. They are mothers over the age of 35, yet still sexy enough to give all the younger single ladies a run for their money. Beyoncé tells women that they can still be supremely confident in their sexuality as wives and mothers.[68] Cookie is a mother of three grown sons and a grandmother. Yet, she still attracts the affection of younger men like Empire's head of security Malcolm DeVeaux (Derek Luke) and concert promotor Laz Delgado (Adam Rodriguez). When topless photos she sent to her new beau Angelo's cell phone are leaked online, her response to the embarrassment of her sons and Empire employees is, "What? They perky!"

Beyoncé has proudly carried the feminist flag for years. Her Super Bowl halftime show appearance in 2013 featured a collective of 120 women dancers, a 10-piece all-women band, and all women back-up singers. The following year Beyoncé won the Video Vanguard Award at the MTV Video Music Awards (VMAs). She delivered a 16-minute performance in a front a giant banner reading FEMINIST while dressed in a sequined leotard and fishnet stockings. Her mini-concert featured the song "Flawless" which contains excerpts from Nigerian novelist Chimamanda Ngozi Adichie's April 12, 2013, TEDx talk, "We should all be feminists." Beyoncé has leveraged her authority as the world's greatest entertainer on behalf of black womanhood. In February 2016, Queen Bey returned for another Super Bowl halftime performance to introduce "Formation," her most controversial song to date. This time she performed in middle of the field surrounded by 50 black women dancers dressed in black leather outfits and donning black berets on top of their large Afros. She then led her ladies into an X formation to honor the slain civil rights leader Malcolm X. The ladies concluded their performance with raised gloved fists reminiscent of John Carlos and Tommie Smith's famous black power salute at the 1968 Summer Olympics. The performance was used to commemorate the legacy of the women in the Black Panther Party and raise awareness for the Black Lives Matter Movement, founded by three queer women.

Beyoncé's 2016 Super Bowl Halftime Show was a prelude to a year of strong images of feminism and womanism within hip-hop best manifested by noteworthy albums: Beyoncé's *Lemonade,* Solange's *A Seat at the Table,* Rihanna's *Anti,* and Alicia Keys's *Here.* Cookie Lyon may be an old soul who prefers the soulful sounds of yesteryear, but if there is one modern album that I would expect to appear in her iPod, it would be *Lemonade.* Syreeta

McFadden, a writer for the British newspaper *The Guardian*, called the 2016 album #blackgirlmagic, its most potent and a meditation on African American womanhood.[69] The album inspired Candice Benbow to create #LemonadeSyllabus on social media, an online resource of over scholarly 250 works dedicated to black women. *Lemonade*, an open letter to Beyoncé's husband Jay-Z for his rumored infidelity, takes women on a journey of heartbreak, pain from a broken marriage, healing, forgiveness, and self-love. Cookie definitely knows what it feels like to have a lover drive her to lookin' jealous and crazy as Beyoncé sings on the album's second track "Hold Up." Cookie was the one who helped Lucious pen his first platinum albums by critiquing his music during his visits to the women's prison. Cookie has had to watch their marriage crumble and Lucious share his love with Anika, Harper, Giuliana, and other "Beckys with the good hair."[70] In the midst of all his jaundiced disrespect Cookie, like Beyoncé's heroines in *Lemonade*, still finds the inner strength to reconcile with her former lover. She loves Angelo; however, her love for Lucious still burns deep inside her heart. When Lucious is crippled by a car bomb she chooses to love him stronger than ever and keep the company thriving. When he is kidnapped by a crazed nurse (Demi Moore) she comes to his rescue.

Beyoncé's *Lemonade* release was accompanied by an hour-long film, inspired by Julie Dash's 1991 independent film *Daughters of the Dust*, which aired on HBO and her online streaming service Tidal.[71] The film sampled an audio excerpt from a 1962 Malcolm X speech, "Who Taught You To Hate Yourself," in which Malcolm called black women the most disrespected persons in America.[72] Malcolm delivered this speech at a funeral for Ronald Stokes, a 29-year-old black man, fatally shot by white Los Angeles police officers while holding his hands up. Malcolm's speech foreshadows a moving scene later in the film highlighted by Beyoncé singing her song "Freedom" a cappella to the mothers of Trayvon Martin, Michael Brown, and Eric Garner. Cookie has not lost a son to police violence like these mothers of the Black Lives Matter Movement. Jamal survived his gun wounds and Andre was only harassed by the police. However, like Beyoncé, Cookie has a message of hope to deliver to other women experiencing grief. She lost her three sons and her own "Freedom" to a prison cell for 17 years of a 30-year-sentence. Her entire post-prison experience has been a journey toward healing, self-fulfillment and turning lemons into lemonade. Cookie's fictional micro story is representative of the macro experiences of black women who have lost their children, spouses, lovers, and siblings to violence or incarceration.

One of the best examples that can be used to juxtapose Cookie with Beyoncé is a scene from *Empire*'s season three spring premiere episode and

Lemonade's music video for the song "Hold Up." Cookie, attired in a stunning emerald green dress, is a one woman wrecking crew as she takes a baseball bat to Lucious, causing his head to bleed, and damaging all his platinum plaques hanging on the walls of Empire headquarters. "I gave you three sons, bitch. I had a miscarriage. I went to jail for 17 years so you could build this empire!"[73] Cookie's rage is comparable to that of Beyoncé, dressed in a stunning yellow dress, as she walks down the street shattering the windows of parked cars with her baseball bat nicknamed Hot Sauce and setting fire to everything in her path. Both women symbolize the Yoruba Deity Oshun, characterized in Nigerian folktales by her "malevolent temper and sinister smile" when she has been done wrong.[74] What these two women also have in common is a willingness to forgive their lovers. *Lemonade* concludes with a theme of reconciliation. Beyoncé and Jay-Z are shown in the film sharing tender moments. Likewise, Cookie rejects Angelo's marriage proposal and reunites with Lucious.

Empire's creators have attempted on different occasions to put Cookie on the feminist stage. The season two premiere begins with Cookie being brought on stage inside a cage wearing a guerrilla costume at a concert/rally on mass incarceration. She removes the costume revealing her face and fabulous green Gucci spring dress. "How much longer?" asks Cookie emphatically before the onlookers. How much longer will the scales of justice continue to be imbalanced?

Certainly, there are millions of women who want nothing to do with the type of "bad feminism" being promoted by Cookie.[75] Let us not ignore the fact that she was incarcerated for selling crack and has been indirectly responsible for multiple murders since gaining her freedom. Some women dislike her short dresses or how the camera lingers a second too long on her butt as she walks out of a room. Hair is an issue for many black feminists and womanists who are weary of having to conform to white beauty standards. Cookie prefers perms, weaves, and wigs to her natural hairstyle. Her hair was dyed blond when she went off to prison. Cookie engages in petty catfights and discourteous name calling with other women rather than attempting to uplift them. She publicly speaks out against the mass incarceration of black men at the #FreeLucious benefit concert, but fails to mention all the incarcerated women with whom she did time during the Lucious event. Jezz (Da Brat), a woman she befriended while incarcerated, calls Cookie out for this omission when she visits the prison.

Cookie routinely demeans her faithful younger assistant Porsha (Ta'Rhonda Jones). She sees Becky (Gabourey Sidibe) working hard to advance at the company, but allows Xavier Rosen (Samuel Hunt), an arrogant young white male, to take credit for her ideas. Xavier is promoted over Becky. Cookie makes amends by promoting Becky to head of A&R and giving her a 30 percent pay raise. Cookie fails to stand up for her favorite artist Tiana (Serayah) when a famous but racist white fashion designer refuses to allow Tiana to perform in her upscale fashion show unless she straightens her natural hairstyle and wears a dress that hides her curves. Although the fashion show ends up using another Empire artist accompanied by an ensemble of dark skinned models with natural hairstyles performing to a song titled "Black Girl Magic," Cookie had nothing to do with the racist designer's change of heart. She disrespects and violently slaps Andre's girlfriend Nessa with the back of her open hand, covered in diamond rings, because the young woman simply raised her voice. She forces Anika to sleep with a lesbian venture capitalist for the sake of Empire. Cookie and Mrs. Dubois are archenemies. Kellee Terrell writes in *Vogue* about the lack of positive female friendships in *Empire* compared to shows like *Insecure*.[76]

Cookie advises Hakeem's girl group to shake their butts. Advice completely out of line with the current "Me Too" protest. Cookie uses homophobic slurs faggot, homo, to describe Jamal, behind closed doors, even though she supports his lifestyle. As Cookie has moved up the corporate ladder she has yet to speak out on issues facing professional women such as equal pay. Others may also question Cookie for profiting from a system of capitalism that has historically been based on patriarchy and oppression of the poor. She stands idly by as her sons perform on stage, at a function for potential investors, in front of scantily clad female dancers with faux televisions over their heads. Does the fact that she works in a music culture plagued by rampant misogyny, homophobia, and hyper-macho behavior make her anti-feminist or a *bad* womanist?

I have had conversations with college educated, middle-class black women who are embarrassed by Cookie's popularity in pop culture. The underlying message I see in this criticism is an age-old debate about the appropriate image for black women. This debate did not begin with Ayesha Curry's Twitter rant on how young women should dress and conduct themselves.[77] The National Association of Colored Women Clubs (NACWC), founded in 1896, preached that black women could uplift their race through education, civic responsibility, social welfare, political initiatives, and respectability.[78] These well-educated, churchgoing, middle-class women did their best to dismantle the belief that all black women were either sassy maids or promiscuous whores. Anthropologist Leith Mullings says the jezebel myth was created during slavery to excuse the rapes.[79] Sociologist Patricia Hill Collins suggests that this myth was used to excuse further discrimination and sexual exploitation after emancipation.[80] When the NAACP led a national boycott in the early

1950s to remove *Amos 'n' Andy* from television, one of their complaints was that the series made black women appear to be "cackling, screaming shrews using street slang, just short of vulgarity."[81] In a May 1975 issue of *Sepia* magazine Tamara Dobson, star of the Blaxploitation action heroine film *Cleopatra Jones* (1973), said that she refused to be seen publicly with Pam Grier because she was giving movie audiences, what she described as, a "$3.50 peep show" by appearing nude in her movies.[82] Stephane Dunn begins the first chapter of her book, *"Baad Bitches" and Sassy Supermamas: Black Power Action Films* (2008), by discussing how she and a group of college educated black women, ages 30 to 45, cringed in their seats as they watched all of the camera's close ups on Grier's 36 D cup breasts and butt in *Coffy* and *Foxy Brown*. Grier, in their opinion, was anything but a heroine for feminism or womanism.[83]

Beyoncé has been called out for presenting contradictory messages of empowerment over the years. Kat George points out the hypocrisy of Beyoncé's anthem "Flawless" appearing on an album that condones domestic violence in Jay-Z's guest verse on the song "Drunk in Love."[84] Annie Lennox, a white Scottish soul singer and political activist, said real feminists do not twerk on stage and perform overly sexualized "exploitative" music.[85] During a 2014 panel discussion at the New School for Social Research in New York City called "Are You Still A Slave: Liberating the Black Female Body," noted 64-year-old scholar bell hooks accused Beyoncé of being a terrorist who was detrimental to the progress of black women. Her criticism was based upon the singer's scantily clad image on the cover of *Time* magazine. hooks believed that Beyoncé was sending a message to women and girls around the world that they can only be celebrated by allowing themselves to be eroticized in the male's public gaze.[86]

A year prior to hooks' criticism, University of Albany professor Janell Hobson published an article for *The Feminist Wire* comparing Beyoncé to Lauryn Hill. It is not coincidental that Hopson used Lauryn Hill as the anti–Beyoncé. Lauryn was held up as a model for the way young black women and girls should behave. Consequently, artists who rejected Lauryn's standards of respectability faced scrutiny. Kimberly Jones, better known as the Brooklyn rapper Lil' Kim, is a prime example. Promotion posters for her debut album *Hardcore* (1996) pictured her in animal print lingerie with her legs spread open. Kim's raps boasted of her ability to use sex to trick her male suitors into giving her whatever she wanted—keys to the Benz, Chanel bags, and penthouse suites. Kim proudly rapped about holding guns and selling drugs for her man. She favored hair weaves and blond, pink, and purple wigs to a natural hairstyle. Her image sold albums while stirring up controversy. Her first television interview was in 1997 on *Rolonda* (1994–1997). Kim and her mother sat on a stage as a panel discussed if her music was "sexualizing our children." As Elaine Richardson points out in her article, "Lil' Kim, Hip-Hop Womanhood and the Naked Truuf," Kim's reputation led to her being treated like a jezebel by state prosecutors when she was sentenced to a year in prison for conspiracy and perjury.[87]

Perceptions of Lil' Kim, similar to those of Cookie, are influenced by age and class. Prolific blogger Feminista Jones describes Kim as rap's Bessie Smith and a heroine for young black women like herself. Feminista Jones admires Kim as a woman who owned her sexuality and defied societal double standards based on gender. Much of Cookie's swagger is a reflection of Kim's persona twenty years ago. When Cookie leaves prison on the pilot episode wearing a fur coat and animal print dress she looks like an extra in one of Kim's videos. Today black women, under the age of 40, who love hip-hop are often forced to choose between the Solanges, Erykah Badus, Janelle Monaes, and Jill Scotts considered *good* feminists and womanists over the Rihannas, Cardi B.s and Nicki Minajes.[88] Hip-Hop feminists believe that there should be seats at the table for different voices. Scholar Evette Dionne says Rihanna's twerking on stage and in music videos should not make her any less of an impactful voice for women's rights.[89]

Joan Morgan says hip-hop feminism allows for shades of grey. Hip-Hop feminism allows black women to be messy, flawed and imperfect, without condemning them. They are allowed to engage in activity that at times appears to be out of step with the traditional tenets of feminism.[90] Cookie Lyon proudly lives life in the grey. She is in step with these other hip-hop feminists and hip-hop womanists. African American women are not a monolithic collective. One woman's idea of feminism and respectability looks different from that of another. Behavior that some women may regard as "ratchet" or "bad and boujee" is described by others as challenging hegemonic norms.[91] Cookie, flaws and all, can serve as a powerful voice for a generation of black women and girls. Cookie does not have to be Clair Huxtable to be a good mother. She may not be as educated or polished as Olivia Pope, Annalise Keating, or Mary Jane Paul; yet, she is just as fierce a professional woman. She owns late night soap operas just as *Dynasty*'s Alexis thirty years ago. Cookie kicks butt like Pam Grier without having to discard her clothes or use sex to defeat her enemies. She is not as pristine as Michelle Obama or as socially conscious as Angela Davis; however, her feminism (or womanism) should not be marginalized by these two examples. Television viewers are left with the power to determine for themselves Cookie's proper place in discussions on women's empowerment.

4

My Three Sons

Reflections on Black Masculinity in Empire

"*We already beat the odds as the children of Lucious and Cookie Lyon.*"[1]

—Jamal Lyon

On *Empire*'s ninth episode, "Unto the Breach," the Lyon brothers get stuck in an elevator. Andre has been spiraling out of control for weeks because of a failure to take his medication for bipolar disorder. Distressed by the likelihood of hours-long isolation in a compact space with little or no air, he becomes hysterical. Hakeem's face is frozen with trepidation as he witnesses his brother. Jamal attempts to regain control of the situation by reflecting on past stories when Andre cared for them as children. Jamal reminds Andre of the way he would sing Bill Withers' 1972 hit "Lean on Me" to them whenever they were frightened by the sounds of gunshots or their aunt Carol getting high on crack. Suddenly the three young men begin singing "we all need somebody to lean on." They come together in a warm embrace. The beauty of this scene is more than just brotherly love. It is the vulnerability that these men can show one another in spite of their unique differences in personality and lifestyle.

Empire presents the most nuanced portrayal of black masculinity on network television. Andre Lyon, the eldest son, is Ivy League educated and married to a white woman when the series begins. Andre is an overachiever who refuses to allow society, mental disorder, or his family to marginalize him. Andre offers a case study on the pitfalls upper-class black men face when simultaneously attempting to gain mainstream acceptance and transcend their race. Jamal Lyon, the middle son, embodies the struggles of gay black men to achieve acceptance within their families, the African American community, hip-hop, and mainstream America. Jamal defines manhood on his own terms and boldly defies stereotypes associated with the LGBTQ community. He becomes a superhero of sorts. Hakeem Lyon, the youngest son, offers a fascinating perspective on the performance of black masculinity within hip-hop. Hakeem's self-identity is in a continual state of flux. He mirrors the shifting paradigms of masculine performance found in hip-hop resulting from the recent success of rappers Kanye West and Drake. At times Hakeem presents a mature image of masculinity that is in touch with emotions, love, and romance. However, he frequently reverts to the hyper-macho performances historically aligned with hip-hop when he feels the need to prove his authenticity as a "real" black man.

Shut Up, Andre! You Ain't Black!

The dominant storyline in *Empire*'s first season is Lucious' attempt to name one of his sons to succeed him at the helm of the family business, upon the false diagnosis that he is dying from Amyotrophic Lateral Sclerosis (ALS). Although Jamal and Hakeem are musicians like their father, Andre believes that he is the most deserving because his entire existence has been based on his devotion to the business since his teenage years. After graduating from the prestigious all-male Roman Catholic High School of Philadelphia, Andre received an Ivy League education from The Wharton School of the University of Pennsylvania to groom himself to become Empire's chief financial officer (CFO). It was his idea to have Empire apply for an initial public offering (IPO). From the outset of the series, Andre is far more confident than his insecure brother Jamal, and he has the discipline and fantastic work ethic that his baby brother Hakeem lacks. In the eyes of mainstream America Andre is the ideal black man: educated, articulate, handsome, nonthreatening, and docile. So why does Lucious favor his brothers?

Certainly, you can point to the stigma of mental illness in the African American community. As I discussed extensively in chapter 1, blacks have a troubling history with mental health issues. A disproportionate number of blacks view mental illness as a sign of shame and weakness.[2] Lucious sends Andre to the best schools that his money could buy in a hidden attempt to cure him and make him "normal." Andre attempts to convince Empire's board members to vote him in as the interim CEO because of his father's declining health; however, Lucious vehemently refuses to grant the favorable deciding vote. Ultimately, this decision is based on much more than Andre's mental health problems. Lucious rejects his son because he is not the man that he raised him to be. In his eyes, Andre is a sellout who lacks self-awareness.

Lucious is a proud black man who is old enough to know something about the Civil Rights Movement. He had a bird's-eye view of black America's struggles in the age of Reagan and George H.W. Bush. He and Cookie sold crack due to these challenges. Andre has a different perspective on the world and his blackness that harkens back to the idealism of Sidney Poitier's character Dr. John Prentice in the 1967 film *Guess Who's Coming Dinner*. Prentice, who is engaged to a younger white woman, tells his father that he needs to stop seeing himself as "a colored man," and simply view himself as a man. While the elder Mr. Prentice heeds his son's advice, Lucious bluntly reminds his son of his place in America: "They will accept your money, Dre, but they will never accept your black ass. I don't give a damn how many white women you marry. They will never accept you."[3] This attitude is a manifestation of the distrust that some blacks have of others who climb up America's social ladder by distancing themselves from the African American community as far as possible.[4]

Andre Lyon is an arrogant, uptight elitist whose education and wealth have removed him from many of the experiences of less privileged black men. He turned his back on his mother Cookie while she was in prison, and never visited her during her 17-year confinement. He lacks his family's love of music and artistic talent. Hip-Hop is nothing more than a commodity for him rather than a lifestyle or a medium for socio-political protest. In the words of hip-hop enthusiasts, he is out of touch with "the culture." Andre's character follows a trend in primetime television's portrayal of well educated, upper-class black males. The popular 1990s sitcom *The Fresh Prince of Bel-Air* featured one of television's earliest depictions of this elite black man. Carlton Banks was the pretentious overachieving cousin of the show's wisecracking protagonist from the hood, Will Smith. Whether it was Carlton's obsession with attending Princeton University, his allegiance to the Republican Party, his preppy attire, or the fact that he came across as Alex P. Keaton in blackface, he always appeared to be disconnected from the souls of other black folk.[5] Will's hero was Malcolm X. Carlton's hero was Reagan. When the cousins are unfairly arrested by a white police officer on suspicion of stealing a Mercedes Benz, Carlton is oblivious to the reality of racial profiling. He is quick to accept culpability for their encounter with the law; even though their only crime was driving while black in a nice neighborhood. After they are freed, Will tries to teach him that his social status will never change how others will prejudge him solely because he is black. Keep in mind that this was the same era as the infamous Rodney King beating, Latasha Harlins' shooting, and the L.A. Riots. How could Carlton not be cognizant of the existence of implicit racial bias?

The writers of the series were obsessed with questioning Carlton's blackness and making jokes about it. When the cousins pledge a black college fraternity, the frat brothers reject Carlton because he is not "black enough" for their standards. In episode 23, "72 Hours," of season one, Carlton makes a bet with Will that he could survive three days in Compton, which at the time was considered to be the worst part of Los Angeles. Carlton adapts to his surroundings by donning loud clothing, multiple gold chains, dark sunglasses, a bandana, and nicknaming himself "C Note." He begins speaking in Ebonics and acting with an exaggerated amount of machismo. The underlying message is that Carlton must be tough and act like a gangbanger if he wants to be accepted by the other black men in this community.

The writers of *The Fresh Prince of Bel-Air* tried a different tactic in their attempt at humanizing Carlton's father, Judge Philip Banks. Uncle Phil overcame poverty in North Carolina to receive scholarships to attend Princeton and Harvard University Law School. As he climbed the social ladder, Uncle Phil's lifestyle became increasingly secluded from most of the blacks in Los Angeles. He was a Republican living next door to Ronald and Nancy Reagan. His family resided in an opulent mansion equipped with a cynical black butler from London named Geoffrey (Joseph Marcell) whose staid demeanor was constantly being tested. Uncle Phil lied about his upbringing for years because he was ashamed. He did his best to shield his children from the hardships he had faced growing up poor in the Jim Crow South. As a result, his kids lacked any comprehension of African American history and culture. His oldest daughter Hillary acted like a snobbish white girl from "the Valley" found in 1990s television shows and films, *Beverly Hills 90210* (1990–2000) and *Clueless* (1995). Phil forced his youngest daughter Ashley to take weekly violin and tennis lessons because that was a rite of passage for all the privileged white children in her private school. Whenever Will dared to question his blackness Uncle Phil, always on cue, began sharing stories of the days he marched at Selma, attended Malcolm's speeches, survived the Watts Riots, went to jail with the black power activists, danced on *Soul Train,* and worked as a civil right attorney in the ghetto. In other words, Uncle Phil was the black Forrest Gump of the African American experience who abruptly just happened to become a Republican.

Although *The Fresh Prince of Bel-Air* was fictional, it addressed problems faced by some black men. In 2014 *The Huffington Post* published interviews with black men attending Princeton. Multiple interviewees expressed feelings of not being accepted by their affluent white counterparts who often assumed they were athletes. Dating was an important aspect of the men's experience. Some interviewees admitted that they were intimidated by the black women on campus and in the surrounding community. One student revealed that he often felt like the black women did not find him to be "black enough" when compared to the "brothas" on the athletic teams. Rather than face constant rejection he chose to date white girls on campus.[6] This student found himself in social gatherings with few blacks. Andre finds himself in a similar predicament on *Empire*. He marries Rhonda, a beautiful blond whom he met at Wharton. It is unclear how much of his decision to marry Rhonda was based on unconditional love, rejection from the "sistas," convenience, or a desire for mainstream acceptance. "Why you marry that white girl?" Cookie asks him upon her release from prison.[7] Cookie is skeptical of the marriage because she has seen countless successful black men marry women outside of their race to serve as status symbols. Don Cheadle's character Marty Kaan on Showtime's dark comedic series *House of Lies* (2012–2016) provides a stellar example of such behavior. Marty, a management consultant in Los Angeles with a seven-figure salary, has a white ex-wife, a white baby mama at the office, and an ample bevy of white women in and out of his bedroom.

Empire's Wednesday night competitor *Black-ish* uses comedy to tackle race relations. The lead character, ironically named Andre (Anthony Anderson), frets that his spoiled, rich kids who are growing up in a predominantly white environment are being robbed of their cultural identity. Sheltered as they are in fabulous suburbia from the sight of the adversity multiple generations of blacks have fought to overcome, Andre worries that his children will come of age unaware of the "struggle." Andre believes that he must "keep it real" at all times to ensure they do not lose touch with their "blackness." He is especially concerned about his oldest son Andre, Jr. (Marcus Scribner) who wants to have a bar mitzvah for his thirteenth birthday. Junior, a fair skinned kid with curly hair, prefers field hockey to basketball and allows his white friends to call him Andy because it is less threatening. Andre takes Junior to the basketball court in hopes of teaching him how to act like a real "brotha." While I watched this episode of *Blackish*, it took me back to a passage from Barack Obama's 1995 memoir *Dreams from My Father*. To master the performance of black masculinity a teenage Obama, then living in Hawaii, routinely played basketball with older black males.[8]

As silly as Andre's attempts to awaken his son Junior's black sensibilities may appear, he does have a valid point. In this day and age, it is hazardous for black males to forget that there are large segments of the American populace that do not judge them solely on the content of their character. History is full of black men who met fates worthy of a Shakespearian tragedy because they failed to heed this warning. On *Black-ish*'s pilot episode Andre confides to his wife Rainbow (Tracee Ellis Ross) that his biggest fear is that one day

Junior will be on the news running from the police in a white Bronco.⁹ Andre is referring to the infamous police chase of professional football Hall of Famer Orenthal James "O.J." Simpson along Interstate 405 in Los Angeles on June 17, 1994. O.J. went from being the most beloved to the most hated black man in American history for suspicion of murdering his ex-wife Nicole and her friend Ron Goldman.

ESPN's Academy Award winning documentary *O.J.: Made in America* (2016) paints a picture of O.J. Simpson as a fallen hero whose tragic Horatio Alger story was based on the myth of transcending race to gain white approval. As a Heisman trophy winning running back at the University of Southern California, he was the most famous collegiate athlete in the nation. Harry Edwards, an adjunct professor at nearby San Jose State University, invited O.J. to take part in a boycott of the 1968 Olympics. Notable black athletes like Muhammad Ali and Bill Russell were at the forefront of the Black Power Movement in the 1960s. O.J.'s response to joining the movement was "I'm not black, I'm O.J."¹⁰

O.J. solely wanted to be judged by the content of his character and the caliber of his competence. His counterrevolutionary attitude made him a godsend for white sports fans and white businesses looking for an African American to pitch their products. During the mid–1970s O.J. became America's first great black pitchman appearing in memorable commercials for Chevrolet and Hertz. The white directors went out of their way to remove any hint of blackness, aside from his skin, in these commercials. They taught him to speak like a white man. "For us, O.J. was colorless. None of the people that we associated with looked at him as a black man," says Frank Olson who recruited O.J. for his famous 1978 Hertz commercial.¹¹ Joe Bell, O.J.s' childhood friend, believes his buddy was "seduced" by white society. After O.J. divorced his black wife to marry a white woman, he moved into the upscale Brentwood neighborhood where he was one of only three black residents.

"Success is still a synonym for white," says South African comedian Trevor Noah in the 2017 mini-documentary *Footnotes to "The Story of O.J."* "Once you attach success to the black man there is a little key that has been given to you, that gives you access to the white world. The key can be taken away—Cosby, Tiger, etc.—but at least you have a key for the time being."¹² O.J. Simpson became a victim of what blogger Jessica Ann Mitchel refers to as the Frantz Fanon complex. Mitchel points to Afro-Caribbean psychiatrist Fanon's 1961 work, *Wretched of the Earth*, which identifies the colonized man who lusted after his colonizer's most coveted possessions. This individual was willing to do anything to have a seat at the colonizer's table and even lie in his bed.¹³ O.J. wanted to sit at the colonizer's table so bad that he turned his back on the African American community. Fans of the film *Get Out* might say he fell into the "sunken place." Ironically, it was that same community that helped keep him out of prison when he was accused of murder. When Lucious decries Andre's desire to be accepted he is criticizing him for having what he believes is a colonized mind. He fears that Andre believes that he can transcend his race.

While it is easy to follow Lucious' lead in categorizing his son Andre as a sellout, that is a simplistic way of defining blackness. In his 2011 book, *Who's Afraid of Post-Blackness? What It Means to Be Black Now*, culture critic Toure argues that blackness can no longer be defined by marginal categories. Michael Eric Dyson, author of Toure's book foreword, defines three dimensions of blackness: accidental, incidental, and intentional. The accidental blacks are black only by birth. I would place Clarence Thomas and Eldrick "Tiger" Woods in this category because of their disconnection from the black masses. The incidental blacks believe that their race is important, but it does not define them or dominate their personalities. Michael Jordan could fall into this category. The intentional black person is an individual that loves their race and is extroverted in their embrace of blackness. Michelle Obama, LeBron James, and Serena Williams are examples of this mindset. According to this logic, Andre Lyon falls somewhere between the accidental or incidental category.[14]

Zadie Smith, a black novelist and professor born in London, offers an alternative perspective that I believe is useful in assessing nonfictional black men who are reminiscent of Andre. Smith, in a 2008 essay, "Speaking in Tongues," declares that an individual's blackness should not be determined by any specific parameters because it is fluid and evolving.[15] *Empire*'s third season begins with Anika accidentally pushing Rhonda off a balcony during a fight. Andre reaches the balcony in time to see his wife fall to her death. After weeks of mourning, he attempts to move on with his life by moving his belongings out of their home. As he walks out of the building with boxes in his hands, dressed in a hoodie and sweatpants, a police car pulls up. Andre tries to explain to the two white officers that he lives in that affluent neighborhood, but they tackle him to the ground, call him a boy, and put a gun to his head. This scene subtly harkens back to the 2012 murder of Trayvon Martin murder in a predominantly white neighborhood in Sanford, Florida. The 17-year-old Trayvon, dressed in a hoodie, was wrongfully accosted for fabricated mischief and killed by George Zimmerman, a neighborhood watchman. The scene also brings back memories of retired African American tennis champion James Blake being tackled to the ground and arrested outside of a Manhattan Hotel on September 9, 2015. Blake, a victim of mistaken identity, was falsely accused of being part of a cellphone fraud scheme.[16]

Andre, just like the fictional Carlton Banks, is satisfied with accepting culpability for the cops' injurious misconduct. Lucious and Cookie encourage him to file a lawsuit on the grounds of racial discrimination, but he opts to follow the advice of his white lawyer who tells him not to "go all Black Lives Matter."[17] Andre believes that his degree from Wharton and his CFO position at Empire will guarantee him a fair court hearing. He is rudely awakened when he learns that he is being charged with aggravated battery and assaulting a police officer. Andre must stand trial to avoid prison time. His lawyer advises him to cut a plea deal and accept the probation, but he finally smartens up and decides to fight for his justice. This scene in *Empire* reminds me of the catastrophic story of Kalief Browder, highlighted in Ava DuVernay's Academy Award nominated 2016 Netflix documentary *13th* and the 2017 Spike TV miniseries, *TIME: The Kalief Browder Story*. In 2010 Browder, a 16-year-old black New York City high school student was accused of stealing a backpack. Browder was given the option to plead guilty in exchange for a reduced sentence or go to trial with the possibility of a 15-year sentence. He refused to take a plea and was sent to Rikers Island while he awaited trial. His wait ended up being over 1,000 days. According to Browder, the correctional officers placed him in solitary confinement for 800 days and intentionally starved him during his stay.[18] He was beaten by guards and inmates alike. After 31 hearings, the case was dismissed and he was freed in 2013. The dehumanizing experience triggered mental health problems that led him to commit suicide by hanging himself two years later.[19]

The Lyon family's wealth and prominence prevent Andre from suffering a similar fate as Browder. Nevertheless, his family's money does not shield him from racial profiling or becoming another statistic in the correctional system. The Bureau of Justice reported in 2003 that one in three black males would go to jail or prison in their lifetime.[20] In the words of sociologist Devah Pager, prison for black males has become "a normal and anticipated marker in the transition to adulthood."[21] After the judge delivers the verdict, Lucious takes all three of his sons on a road trip to their former home in the hood. He uses this field trip to give them a sermonette on race. Lucious makes the point that their problems do not stem from mental illness, homosexuality, or being spoiled. The root of the problem is a lack of consciousness about what it means to be a black man in America. After LeBron James made a public statement about racism following the vandalism of his home with racist graffiti, Jason Whitlock, a conservative black sports journalist, remarked that wealthy black men are immune to racism because of their privilege. I am sure that Jackie Robinson, Hank Aaron, Adam Clayton Powell, Jr., Bill Russell, Prince, Oprah Winfrey, Henry Louis Gates, Jr., and the Williams sisters would all beg to differ. Lucious, in his own unique way, is imparting the same message of survival as a black man that authors James Baldwin and Ta-Nehisi Coates gave their nephew and son, respectively, in *The Fire Next Time* and *Between the World and Me*. This is a message that any black man in America can become a target regardless of his social status.

Rhonda's calamitous demise sends Andre on a downward spiral. He stops taking his medication, attending church, and reading his Bible. He begins having hallucinatory visions of Rhonda whenever his need for encouragement or instruction torments him. Andre's juvenile dependency on Rhonda's ghost for validation confirms his elusive possession of manhood. Soon Andre begins dating Nessa Parker (Sierra McClain), a younger black singer from the hood, who was recently signed on at Empire. Andre's new relationship with Nessa provides an interesting plot twist. Apparently Rhonda's death and the arrest have forced him to become more in touch with his blackness and the plight of others who have his same hue. Andre appears to run back to the black community when times get hard. After suffering a mental breakdown in season one, he turned to a black church and a beautiful black Christian music therapist to end his suffering. At the time, he contemplated leaving Empire to dedicate his life to the Lord. He found a spiritual connection with the therapist missing from his marriage. He lived with his pastor for a brief period after Rhonda left him because she was unhappy with his new lifestyle. He was becoming a better man. But this time, in season three, Andre's new outlook on life comes with dire consequences. He finally agrees to stop running from the world's expectations of him as nothing more than a gangster's son in tailored suits. It is a disgusting irony that Andre's decision to embrace his family's dark side coincides with his increasing awareness of his identity as a black man. This parallels the point that I made earlier about O.J. Simpson. Once he was ostracized by white America, O.J. resorted to the violent black buck archetype dominant in popular culture. He was paroled in 2017 after serving nine years of a 33-year prison sentence.[22]

Rhonda's ghost tells Andre that without her he could be nothing more than a Philly thug with mental problems. He begins going down the same route as O.J. On episode 38, "The Unkindest Cut," Empire artist Tiana is scheduled to perform in the fashion show for Ms. Helene Bon Wyeth (Gina Gerson), a racist fashion designer. Ms. Wyeth demands that Tiana straighten her hair because her relaxed curly Afro hairstyle is not mainstream enough for the elite audience. Andre arranges to get Tiana removed from the show by secretly recording her making disparaging remarks about Wyeth's racist past behavior such as casting only white models for a fashion collection titled "Out of Africa." With Tiana out of the way, Andre visits Ms. Wyeth's home to convince her to use Nessa, a more urban woman in tune with the black experience, for the show. Wyeth makes several racist comments, including the use of the incendiary phrase "you people," before refusing Andre's offer. As he leaves her home, he puts on a black fedora and comments on her young daughter's beautiful hair. Wyeth had been combing her long straight hair throughout the meeting. The next morning her daughter wakes up screaming to find her cut hair all over her bed. Fans of *The Godfather* (1972) will probably find amusement in this scene.[23] Nevertheless, it manifests a disturbing trend in Andre's behavior. This black fedora is symbolic of Andre choosing to wear the proverbial black hat that represents evil. In future episodes he often wears a black or tan fedora when he is up to no good.

Andre becomes strange bedfellows with his father's former lover Giuliana Green and Charlotte Frost (Eva Longoria), a married Mormon gaming commissioner in Las Vegas, to further plot his takeover of Empire. He goes behind Nessa's back to mix his business with these women with sexual pleasure. He barges into Anika's home, puts his hands around her neck, and nearly strangles her to death as retribution for Rhonda's death. Andre's downward spiral culminates with him making a secret deal with Shyne Johnson to kill Lucious. One of Shyne's goons plants a bomb in Lucious' car which leaves him a coma for three months and decapitates his leg. Cookie suffers a heart attack after she learns of Andre's act.

No Sissies Allowed

Jamal Lyon, the middle son of Lucious and Cookie Lyon, is the most talented musician in his family. Jamal's singing voice resembles musical icons Marvin Gaye, Prince, and Usher. He plays multiple instruments and arranges and composes music. In fact, he develops several songs for his younger brother Hakeem. After years of living in anonymity, he emerges as one of pop music's brightest stars garnering seven nominations at the fictional American Sound Awards (ASA) annual ceremony. Jamal's signature song "Heavy" battles his father's song "Boom, Boom, Boom" for the Song of the Year award at the ASAs.[24] In spite of his superior talent Jamal is introduced on the series premiere as an artist who can do little more than perform in small venues, coffee houses, and compose hit songs for others. Jamal, like his brother Andre, fails to meet Lucious' standards of manhood. Jamal's flaw, in his father's eyes, has nothing to do with his mental health or his education. But it does have everything to do with whom he chooses to love. A flashback from his childhood shows him at the prison with Cookie, during visitation hours, sharing stories of being bullied at school by his classmates. Cookie counsels Jamal that life will be harder for him than that of his brothers because he is "different," but no matter what she will always have his back. "I got you," she tells a young Jamal visiting her at the prison. At the time Jamal is too young to understand that she is referring to his sexual orientation. While Cookie loves him unconditionally the same cannot be said of Lucious. The most disturbing scene in *Empire*'s first three seasons involved a flashback to a Christmas party at the Lyons' home when Jamal was a six-year-old boy. Jamal comes strutting into the living room wearing Cookie's scarf and red heels. The cheerful celebration stops in an abrupt hush. Before any words are spoken, Lucious snatches Jamal up, storms out of their apartment, and dumps him into a garbage can. From this moment forward Jamal and his father have a strained relationship.

Jamal lives a closeted life as a gay man to appease Lucious, who provides for all of his expenses. Lucious forces him to marry an aspiring Empire artist named Olivia (Raven Symone) when he is only 18-years-old, in an attempt to promote him to the world as a straight rhythm and blues singer. The marriage is short-lived; however, Olivia reappears years later falsely accusing Jamal of being the father of her daughter Lola. Jamal's growth as an artist and a man is stunted because Lucious ingrains in him a belief that he is not good enough to carry the Lyon name. He grows up believing that black America is too homophobic to accept a "sissy." When Cookie returns home from prison, she finds Jamal wallowing in self-pity and living with an insecure Latino boyfriend, Michael Sanchez, in a $1 million apartment. Cookie becomes Jamal's manager in an attempt to help him beat out his brothers in the competition to succeed their father. "I want to show you a faggot really can run this company," she tells Lucious.[25] Following a big fight with Lucious over his relationship with Michael, Jamal decides to move out of his father's apartment and become financially independent. Jamal's emancipation results in his first hit song "Keep Your Money." Once he finds the courage to come out of the closet, publicly, his career skyrockets and he becomes a hero for the LGBTQ community.

For a short period, Lucious appears to come around and accept Jamal as a man. He makes Jamal Empire's vice chairman and his successor at the end of season one. Jamal is a logical choice given his loyalty and strong desire to do anything to please his dad. When Lucious goes away to prison for three months on a murder charge, Jamal is left to run the company. Jamal blocks a hostile takeover, preventing Cookie and his siblings from removing Lucious as the CEO of Empire. After Lucious receives an early release from prison, Jamal steps down from his leadership role at Empire to resume recording new music. Throughout much of season two, Lucious and Jamal appear to have a cordial relationship. Lucious even agrees to produce Jamal's sophomore album, *The Black and White Album*. (The album would be shelved.) But their rivalry for the Song of the Year at the ASAs reveals that old wounds have yet to heal.

Jamal has a brief fling with pop singer Skye Summers (Alicia Keys). Once Lucious finds out he is quick to say that she "fixed him," insinuating that he was no longer gay because he slept with a woman. After rumors of their relationship spread, members of the gay community began demanding that Jamal publicly reaffirm that he was still on "their team." Cookie urges him to "get his gay back," or risk losing fans. Jamal tries his best to argue that sexuality is fluid, but his proclamation falls on deaf ears and is swiftly repudiated. Lucious' hatred for Jamal's lifestyle reaches a crescendo when he catches him in Empire's recording studio kissing Derek "D-Major," Major (Tobias Truvillion), a closeted gay black man who serves as the musical director for the ASA ceremony. According to Lucious, D-Major is an opportunist who preys on naïve gay artists. In what was his vilest moment, Lucious promises Jamal that he will celebrate the day that he dies from AIDS. Rather than turn his back on Lucious, Jamal risks his life to prevent an assassin's bullets from taking his father's life.

Many of *Empire*'s critics within the African American community highlight the show's overt emphasis on LGBTQ characters and issues. Hip-Hop mogul 50 Cent, the executive producer of *Empire*'s rival series *Power*, blames *Empire*'s declining viewership since the season two premiere on "too much gay stuff."[26] A meme posted on the social media site Tumblr back in 2015 had a picture of the Lyon family under the caption "Black Propaganda." The caption that appears in front of Jamal's image is "Homosexual. The Only Logical Rational Character." At the bottom of the meme were the words "Destruction disguised as entertainment.... Very clever."[27] A common response I received from the people that I surveyed for this study was that the series turned them off because of its queer narratives. Some respondents said they stopped watching *Empire* because the homosexual depictions infringed upon their religious values. During a 2016 interview on *The Breakfast Club,* Nation of Islam leader Minister Louis Farrakhan, Sr., said that since the white man could not kill the black man he chose to feminize him.[28] Boyce Watkins has accused Lee Daniels of advocating a gay agenda for Hollywood aimed at further emasculating the black male image.

Sheena C. Howard, author of *Black Queer Identity Matrix: Towards An Integrated Queer of Color Framework*, argues that Watkins' critique is incredibly problematic because it ignores the media's dominant image of hegemonic black masculinity, which is rooted in the hyper-macho behavior and misogyny of heterosexual black men.[29] Lee Daniels and Danny Strong have publicly admitted that they are using their series to expose the debilitating homophobia that exists within the African American community and counter horrific stereotypes associated with the LGBTQ community. *Empire*'s storylines are timely given the 2015 Supreme Court ruling on gay marriage and the mass shooting at Pulse, a gay nightclub in Orlando, Florida.[30] Daniels, who spoke out against violence towards the LGBTQ community during the 2016 Democratic National Convention, based Jamal's storyline upon his own experiences as a gay black man. When Daniels was eight-years-old, his father threw him in the trash for wearing his mother's red high heels and scarf.[31]

The homophobia and promotion of gay rights depicted on *Empire* are a microcosm of the larger society. Since the turn of the 20th century, homosexuals have been characterized as "instigators" of their preference and embodiments of grotesque contradictions of masculinity. Justin Edwards and Rune Graulund say that queerness is equated with monstrosity.[32] As early as World War II gay men, regardless of their race, throughout the country faced arrest, the loss of employment, public humiliation, and violence if their sexual orientation was discovered. Schools showed students public service announcements portraying gays as sexual predators and pedophiles. Families subjected homosexual relatives to shock therapy to "cure" them. CBS News reported in 1967 that Americans considered homosexuality more harmful than adultery, abortion, and prostitution. Until 1973, the American Psychiatric Association defined homosexuality as a mental illness. Gay black men found themselves carrying a double burden of racism and homophobia on their shoulders. James Baldwin, one of the first authors to chronicle the experiences of gay black men in his novels *Go Tell It on the Mountain* (1953) and *Giovanni's Room* (1956), was investigated by the FBI director, J. Edgar Hoover, who equated Baldwin's homosexuality with communism.

Homophobia was rampant within the Civil Rights Movement. Bayard Rustin served as Martin Luther King's adviser in the early days of the Montgomery Bus Boycott and helped King deepen his understanding of the potency of the Gandhian method of nonviolent resistance to oppression. Rustin was forced to leave the boycott when rumors began circulating about his relations with men. In 1953, he was arrested in Pasadena, California, for committing a sex act in the back seat of a car with two men. Rustin's homosexuality became an issue again when he planned a massive demonstration on the Democratic Party's 1960 national convention. Senators Lyndon Johnson (Texas) and Sam Rayburn (Texas) persuaded Harlem's fiery black congressman, the Rev. Adam Clayton Powell, Jr., to stop the demonstration.

Powell threatened to provide a fabrication to the press accusing King and Rustin of being clandestine lovers. King dissociated himself from Rustin for the next three years.[33] The invisible man of the Civil Rights Movement finally received his overdue recognition when labor leader A. Phillip Randolph selected him to organize the famed 1963 March on Washington.

A powerfully determining factor in Bayard Rustin's anonymity was the moral revulsion of the black church against same-sex attraction. Within the black church, Rustin's orientation would have been baffling and condemned as the mark of an imperiously governing self-will. Homosexuality was viewed as a God-resistant choice to walk a deviant and punitive path. The third chapter of E. Patrick Johnson's book *Sweet Tea: Black Gay Men of the South* (2011) titled "Church Sissies" summarizes interviews with southern gay black men about their relationship with the church. While some were accepted by their congregations and found leadership roles in music ministries, others felt alienated by their pastors. Still, others survived by living on the down low, a slang term popularized in the 1990s to describe the act of pretending to be heterosexual.[34] Jeffrey McCune, Jr.'s *Sexual Discretion: Black Masculinity and the Politics of Passing* (2014) is the most in depth study on the down low lifestyle. Perhaps these problems in the black church are best identified in the 2015 film *Blackbird*, the ministry of Bishop Eddie Long, a viral video from the Church of God in Christ's (COGIC) 107th Holy Convocation in 2014, and the Lee Daniels' dramatic series *Star* (2017–).

Blackbird tells the fictional story of Randy (Julian Walker), a Memphis church choirboy, struggling with his sexual identity. He refrains from most teenage vices such as sex, drinking, smoking, and cursing. But he has erotic dreams about a male classmate. Ashamed and fearful of hurting his devoutly religious mother Claire (Mo'Nique), he prays to the picture of Jesus on his bedroom wall to make those "sinful" desires go away. If Randy were a real person who attended New Birth Baptist Church years ago, he would have been treated as an outcast. New Birth is a megachurch in DeKalb County, Georgia, formerly led by the late senior pastor Bishop Eddie Long.[35] On December 11, 2004, he led a march called "Stop the Silence" in support of an amendment to the state constitution that would ban same sex marriage. Long viewed gay marriage as the greatest civil rights violation of modern times.[36] "Homosexuality and lesbianism are spiritual abortions," said Long. In 2007 New Birth was sponsoring an "Out of the Wilderness" ministry to "cure" homosexuals of their "disease."[37] The OWN series *Greenleaf* addresses this issue.

The 107th Holy Convocation of the Church of God in Christ provided yet another instance of the black church's condemnation of queer lifestyles.

The highly scrutinized video featured a 21-year-old black man named Andrew Caldwell claiming to be "delivered" by God from his sinful lifestyle. "I'm not gay no more. I am delivereeeed! I don't like mensss no more. I said I like women. Women, women, women, women. I will NOT carry a purse! I will NOT put on makeup!"[38] The church erupted in joyous applause and a total praise. Deacons began doing a sanctified dance. Lee Daniels was criticized for taking jabs at renowned gospel singer Donnie McClurkin, who also claimed to have been "delivered" from homosexuality. The first season of *Star*, the Lee Daniels' follow up series to *Empire*, has a scene in which a pastor, played by Tyrese Gibson, is invited to a member's home to perform a conversion ceremony on her son who is transitioning into womanhood. The *Empire* season two premiere featured Lawrence Washington, better known as Miss Lawrence of *Real Housewives of Atlanta*, singing atop a piano. Miss Lawrence is a cross dressing Atlanta hairstylist turned host of Bravo's television series *Fashion Queens*. Miss Lawrence tells Jamal and Becky, with a smirk on his face, that Donnie McClurkin will be attending an LGBTQ awards show. Becky responds by shouting out "Shondo!" and throwing her hands in the air as if she were being slain by the Holy Ghost.[39] *Empire*'s distasteful joke was meant to "throw shade" on McClurkin for treating his feelings for men as a sin.[40]

The Donnie McClurkin insult was not the first time that *Empire* delivered underlying criticism of the black church as it relates to intolerance of the LGBTQ community. Season one's confrontation between Lucious and Jamal, which precedes Jamal's decision to move out on his own, is cloaked in religious symbolism. As Lucious shames him with a hurtful tirade, he stands in front of an electric cross that hangs on the wall behind him. The lights in Jamal's apartment are dim which accentuates the cross lit up in a blue electric light. The camera does not linger on the cross so it is possible that most viewers fail to notice what could be a subtle signifier. Another interesting aspect of this scene is Lucious' attire. He is wearing a colorful stole over his suit that resembles stoles worn by Christian clergy. Jamal comes out publicly during a live performance at an Empire event called the White Party held at Lucious' club Leviticus. The choice of the club's name might be an allusion to the third book of the Bible. In the Book of Leviticus 18:22 and 20:13, homosexual intercourse is condemned as an abomination, punishable by execution. Everyone at the party is dressed in splendid heavenly white outfits. Lucious and Jamal both wear long white robes with gold trim that make them look like pastors of an African American mega church. Jamal removes the robe just before he begins his rendition of his father's hit song "You're So Beautiful." During his performance, he publicly comes out of the closet. Undaunted, Jamal astoundingly has converted his father's club into a venue for emancipated self-avowed homosexuality. Lucious, still wearing his pearly white robe, is evocative of a minister clinging to a belief he professes as non-negotiable, while same-sex attraction is fast receding (throughout western culture) as a magnet of revulsion.

Lee Daniels and Danny Strong paint a damning picture of intolerant black fathers who have gay sons. Jamal has a brief fling with a gay photographer, named Ryan (Eka Darville), who laments with him about his struggles as the "son of a black man." Before *Empire*, the Showtime series *House of Lies* featured a similar father-son storyline. Don Cheadle's character Marty Kaan had a gay son, Roscoe (Donis Leonard, Jr.), who enjoyed wearing lipstick, women's jewelry, and purses. Marty tried much harder than Lucious to embrace his son's lifestyle, but it always remained a source of derision. Recently, I had a student in my freshman seminar course who shared a very poignant story with the class. As a high school senior, he would post videos on YouTube dressed as his alter ego, a young woman modeled after rapper Nicki Minaj. He managed to attract 2,000 followers to his YouTube page. When his parents learned of his secret acting career, his father banned all his access to electronic devices and made him write a letter promising to stop being gay. After that failed to *fix* him, they beat him and banished him from their home. Homophobia is no minor matter for black people. When I was an undergraduate student my roommates and I attended a mandatory dorm discussion on tolerance. One of the speakers talked about life as a 20-year-old gay man. My roommate, a native of the Caribbean island Montserrat, told the speaker, in his thick accent, the following: "No disrespect my brotha. But in my country, you can't be gay. You would either be killed, or you would kill yourself."

Empire does not confine its grievances to the church and black fathers for their treatment of gay sons. The series points a finger of rebuke at rap music and the hip-hop industry. In the season one finale Jamal squares off with an overly macho rapper named Black Rambo (Charles Hamilton) on Empire's roster. Jamal challenges Rambo to an impromptu freestyle battle to prove that he is just as masculine as he. Jamal's victory not only proves his point, but also exposes Rambo's ignorance. Homophobia has always been synonymous with hip-hop and rap music. The first hit rap song on the radio, Sugarhill Gang's "Rapper's Delight" (1979), used the epithet "fairy" to put down a man. During their days as emcee in the Philadelphia rap duo DJ Jazzy Jeff & the Fresh Prince, Will Smith made some very disparaging remarks about gays. A live performance of their album *He's the DJ, I'm the Rapper* at New York's Madison Square Garden in 1988 featured Will instructing all the "homeboys that got AIDS" and "all the girls that don't like guys" to be quiet. Gangsta rap pioneers N.W.A. (Niggaz Wit Attitudes) referred to lesbians as dykes on their single "Gangsta Gangsta" from their seminal album *Straight Outta Compton* (1988). Even rappers, labeled as socially conscious, have contributed to this diatribe in the music. Byron Hurt interviewed conscious rappers Mos Def and Talib Kweli in his 2006 PBS Independent Lens documentary, *Hip Hop: Beyond Beats and Rhymes*. The fellow Black Star members refused to discuss the possibility of befriending a homosexual out of fear of having their man card rejected.[41] Timbaland, *Empire*'s former head of music, admitted that he originally refused to let his children watch any scenes in the series showing gay men kissing.[42]

Until recently being queer equaled career suicide in the hip-hop industry. Big Daddy Kane was one of the first rappers to distance himself from the hyper-macho image in rap by making songs for female audiences. His reputation took a major hit when he was falsely rumored to have contracted HIV from sleeping with men. He used every opportunity to prove that he was heterosexual and not infected with the disease. Kane's longtime DJ, Mr. Cee, had to resign from his job at New York City's popular radio station WQHT 97.1 (Hot 97) after he was outed years later. In his article "Scared Straight" Marc Lamont Hill writes about the prevalence of "outing" ostensibly straight rappers in hip-hop.[43] To be labeled a "punk" is the ultimate "diss" in hip-hop circles.

In the late 1990s, there was something called the homo-thug in hip-hop circles; a gay man who appropriates the hyper-violent and hyper-sexual cool masculine performance popularized in rap music in order to avoid being outed. *The Village Voice* featured an article with interviews of gay black men who embraced this lifestyle. One of the men said the following: "Straight-up homies, n_ggaz, and thugz can do whatever they want. You can walk through the projects and be gay. But you can't walk through the projects and be a faggot."[44] This piece of advice was repeated in the Academy Award winner for Best Picture, *Moonlight* (2016), about Chiron (Alex Hibbert/Ashton Sanders/Trevante Rhodes), a painfully introverted, gay black male growing up in the projects of Liberty City, Miami. As a routinely bullied child, Chiron befriends a drug dealer named Juan (Mahershala Ali) and his girlfriend Teresa (Janelle Monet). Juan sees the inner beauty in Chiron and makes him feel like his life matters despite the minutia causing others to hate him. Chiron continues to be bullied as a teenager and is nearly beaten to death one day at school. After he goes to jail for breaking a desk on the head of the ruffian in his class who kept harassing him, we find him living in Atlanta 10 years later. While in Atlanta the frail teenager has matured into as a muscular drug dealer nicknamed Black, who has a mouth full of gold teeth. The 25-year-old version of Chiron survives by appropriating an image of masculinity that he learned as a child from watching Juan. It is unclear if anyone in Atlanta knows that he is gay. When he returns to Miami he reunites with his friend and former love interest Kevin (Andre Holland) who is also passing for a straight man.

Empire addresses this issue of "passing" and homo thugs with the character D-Major. In public, he is seen with multiple women, while in private he is sleeping with Jamal. D-Major eventually announces that he is gay on Facebook Live in an attempt to prove his love for Jamal. His announcement causes him to lose work and become the target of ridicule on social media. The condemnation that Jamal receives from Lucious and Black Rambo at the end of season one is indicative of this phobia within hip-hop. But his success also shows hip-hop's growing tolerance for LGBTQ issues in recent years. Frank Ocean's admission of being bisexual on the social media site Tumblr days before the release of his debut album *Channel Orange* (2012) was a watershed moment.[45] Ocean is an R&B singer from New Orleans associated with the hip-hop collective Odd Future. *Channel Orange*, released on hip-hop's most esteemed label Def Jam Recordings, received nonstop critical acclaim including a Grammy Award nomination for Album of the year. Ocean makes multiple references to his male lovers throughout the album. Clover Hope compares Jamal's decision to come out during his performance of "You're So Beautiful" to Ocean's revelation in the lyrics to his hit song "Thinkin Bout You."[46] In the summer of 2017 Frank Ocean's Odd Future associate, rapper Tyler The Creator, revealed that he had a boyfriend when he was 15-years-old and is attracted to white guys.

In my opinion Jamal is a hybrid of Frank Ocean and Omar Little, the fictional gay stick-up man on HBO's award winning television series *The Wire* (2002–2008). Omar, famous for robbing the city's most violent drug dealers and a trademark scar on his face, might be the scariest gangster in television history. "Yeah, he's gay, but that's not the thing you're gonna remember him for if you meet him down an alley. It's that shotgun that will have you worried, not his gayness," says actor Michael K. Williams of his groundbreaking character.[47] This image of a gay black man had never been seen before in Hollywood. For years, gay black men were not allowed to be fully developed characters in Hollywood. Jamal, like Omar, is not stereotypically effeminate or flamboyant. Jamal looks down on gay men that exhibit those traits. Omar frequently survived shootouts with rival gangsters Avon Barksdale, Stringer Bell, and Marlo Stanfield on *The Wire*. Jamal may not be a gangster like Omar, but do not test his manhood. When a couple of thugs commit an armed robbery at Ghetto Ass Studios during Jamal's recording session he dares one of the hoodlums to shoot him. On another episode Jamal dares his ex-wife's armed boyfriend to shoot him. Jamal takes a bullet for Lucious when Empire rapper Freda Gatz attempts to murder him at the ASAs. He saves an ex-lover, Warren, from a gunman. Jamal is the closest figure to television's first gay black superhero. Clearly, Lee Daniels is using his heroic image to shatter all of the taboos about gay black men. Daniels also goes out of his way to make Jamal the most empathizing and likable character in the series, not named Cookie. Whether viewers agree or disagree with *Empire*'s agenda to promote tolerance, Jamal's impact on television's depiction of gay black men cannot be ignored.

Worst Behavior

On the surface Hakeem Lyon has the least interesting story of the three brothers. He does not have to deal with mental health issues, racial identity, homophobia, the death of a wife, or spiritual warfare. He is the apple of his father's eye and has been spoiled rotten his entire life. "Much like his father, they both perform and value the same style of music, both are full of bravado and, perhaps most notably, Hakeem can exude hyper-heterosexuality in the form of excessive womanizing," says Robert Humphrey.[48] Hakeem is introduced to viewers at a party on his father's multi-million-dollar yacht adorned in multiple large gold chains, ostentatious platinum diamond earrings in both ears, a $30,000 gold watch, and designer skinny jeans and sneakers. Beautiful girls in bikinis stuff his mouth with shrimp as he sips champagne. Hakeem is the walking embodiment of the effects of hip-hop's bling era of the late 1990s, characterized by extreme materialism and misogyny, on today's young male rappers. He could easily fit in with Lil Yachty, Migos, Rae Sremmurd, 21 Savage, and other popular young artists on today's Billboard charts who promote this lifestyle in their music. Lucious expects Hakeem to follow in his footsteps at Empire, even though his son's musical career is based more on nepotism than genuine talent.

Hakeem's narrative is rooted in his struggles to define his identity and manhood on his own terms. Cookie's absence has contributed to his sexist attitudes regarding women and inability to have stable romantic relationships. As the son of former gangsters and drug dealers, he feels the need to conduct himself in a manner that belies his privileged upbringing. On episode two, "The Outspoken King," Hakeem and his entourage cause a scene at an upscale restaurant. Hakeem, wearing a black varsity jacket that has "WEALTH" blazoned across the back in large gold letters, urinates on the floor. He then begins mocking the white patrons in the restaurant and spewing contempt for then President Barack Obama. When the police arrive Hakeem ignorantly laughs it off as if he is unsusceptible to the fates of Walter Scott, Alton Sterling and Philando Castile.[49] After TMZ helps the incident to go viral his Q-Rating as hip-hop's new bad boy soars. This image attracts the attention of fellow Empire artist Tiana who initially rejected him, but now wants to have sex in his dressing room. In Hakeem's recklessness viewers can see glimpses of music's real-life bad boy Chris Brown, whose struggles handling fame at a young age are well documented in the Netflix film *Welcome to My Life* (2017). It takes the accidental birth of his daughter out of wedlock to help Brown mature. A similar storyline plays out in *Empire*.

Hakeem is stuck in a perennial state of immaturity throughout much of the series. His brief fling with Tiana ends once she caught him taking a bath with his mistress Camilla, a 46-year-old black fashion designer from London that he oddly refers to as his "mama." Hakeem has an affinity for older women who both nurture him and stimulate him sexually. This is the case with both Camilla and later Anika. The show's writers never explore his potential Oedipus Complex.[50] Some of his attraction to these maternal figures is due to the fact that his biological mother was absent for the first 20 years of his life. Hakeem, finding his thirst for the opposite sex unquenchable sleeps with a Latina singer named Valentina (Becky G) that he was recruiting for his short-lived record label, Lyon Dynasty. After a fallout with Lucious, he begins sleeping with his father's ex-fiancé, Anika.

Sex is one of the things that Hakeem uses to prove that he is a man. As a result, his interactions with the ladies become a dominant feature of his limited musical content. The Oxford English Dictionary defines masculinity as "the possession of the qualities traditionally associated with men." Synonyms for the term include virility, machismo, and strength.[51] From its genesis in the early 1970s hip-hop has allowed marginalized black males a space for the performance of what is perceived to be acceptable displays of masculinity. In the late 1980s the gruesome effects of the war on drugs inspired the rise of gangsta rap, a subgenre of hip-hop characterized by graphic depictions of poverty, crime, violence, drug abuse, and explicit sex. Black males, who felt powerless in the larger society, began using violent lyrics to intimidate one another. Rap battles went from friendly banter between rival artists to the murders of Biggie and 2Pac.[52] 50 Cent's 2003 debut album, *Get Rich or Die Tryin,'* was filled with more machismo, murder, and mayhem than any commercially successful rap album up to that period. Historian William Jelani Cobb described the representations of manhood exhibited in 50's album as updates of the hyper-violent portrayals of black men found in D.W. Griffith's *The Birth of a Nation* (1915).[53]

Social scientists Richard Majors and Janet Mancini Billson addressed hip-hop's exaggerated and ritualized masculinity in their 1992 book *Cool Pose: The Dilemmas of Black Manhood in America*. Majors and Billson argued that black males adopt a cool pose (a set of aloof attitudes, language, truculent mannerisms, swagger, and bodily movements) to mask fear and feelings of powerlessness. Fashion symbols from gaudy gold chains to sagging pants are also examples of this cool pose.[54] Black males are taught to show little emotion or empathy. bell hooks writes in her study of masculinity, *We Real Cool* (2003), that black males are taught to embrace violent and sexist behavior.[55] It was standard for music videos to display rappers either with guns, looking tough, or waking up with no less than three women lying in their beds.

Throughout the late 1990s and early 2000s exceptions could be found to these trivialized versions of manliness ranging from L.L. Cool J, Nas and Common to Outkast and The Roots. The paradigm of this black macho posturing underwent a momentous shift with the release of Kanye West's albums *The College Dropout* (2004), *Late Registration* (2005), *Graduation* (2007), and *808s & Heartbreak* (2008). The Chicago producer turned emcee challenged rap's cool pose by talking about Jesus Christ and feelings of self-consciousness. When his third album, *Graduation*, outsold 50 Cent's third album, *Curtis*, on the same release date (September 11, 2007) it signaled a shift from gangsta rap. At a time when standard hip-hop attire was oversized white t-shirts, throwback sports jerseys, and baggy jeans, Kanye's form fitting pink Ralph Lauren Polo shirts and high-end fashion dared to challenge the public's perception of how a *real* black man should dress. With *808s & Heartbreak*, an album inspired by the tragic death of his mother, Dr. Donda West, and the end of his 18-month engagement to fiancé Alexis Phifer, he created a new lane for rappers to openly emote about self-doubt, love, heartbreak, spirituality, and vulnerability in their music.[56] Andre 3000 initially did this with his *Love Below* (2003) album. Kanye's success paved the way for newer artists who were also breaking the mold of marginalized black masculinity such as Chance The Rapper, Childish Gambino, Kid Cudi, Travis Scott, The Weeknd, Vic Mensa, and most notably Drake, the world's most successful rapper since 2011. Even more established artists like Jay-Z on his *4:44* album have chosen to completely let down their cool pose and reveal their most vulnerable side.

Although their music differs, Drake and Hakeem Lyon have several similarities that reveal the complicated state of masculine performance in hip-hop today. For a brief period Hakeem matures enough to distance himself from his juvenile tendencies. He makes amends with Cookie, which allows him to have his first serious romantic relationship. Hakeem falls in love with Laura Calleros (Jamila Velazquez), the lead singer of a new Latin American girl group, Mirage a Trois, signed to Lyon Dynasty. Laura makes him a faithful boyfriend who prefers family dinners with her parents to drunken, sexual escapades with random groupies. He proposes to Laura and plans a lavish wedding. In the midst of his engagement he learns that Anika is pregnant with his baby. Rather than running from his responsibilities, Hakeem makes preparations to be a devoted husband to Laura and father to his unborn child. His music and public image also begin to reflect his personal growth.

Hakeem's newfound sensitivity is in line with Drake's public persona. Drake has been praised by scholars and music critics for undermining stereotypical tropes of black masculinity. He has been labeled as hip-hop's "everyman" who makes music that speaks to every aspect of the human experience.[57] Professor Melissa Harris-Perry says that by dancing in a non-aggressive manner in the music video for his hit song "Hotline Bling," Drake expands the boundaries for acceptable manly behavior. Perry points out the fact that he is alone in this video, dancing in a blank space without his crew or his boys at his side to affirm his manhood.[58] The majority of Drake's albums are devoted to love songs and melancholy ballads full of vulnerability, insecurity, loneliness, and angst. His hybrid style of aggressive rapping and melodic singing (originally popularized by Lauryn Hill, Nelly, DMX, and Ja Rule) has allowed him to cross genres of hip-hop, R&B, pop, Afrobeat, and reggae with groundbreaking success. Drake's *Views* (2016) was number one on the Billboard 100 for 12 straight weeks and competed with Adele's *25* and Beyonce's *Lemonade* at the 59th Grammys.[59] His video "Nice for What" is a celebration of strong women.

A prominent commonality between Drake and Hakeem is their willingness to revert to hyper-macho posturing, despite their efforts to offer more nuanced images of masculinity, whenever their manhood or street cred is publicly challenged. Drake, whose real name is Aubrey Drake Graham, was born in Toronto, Canada, in 1986 to a white Jewish mother and an African American father. His father, a musician from Memphis, abandoned the family when Drake was five-years-old leaving his mother to rear him in a middle class Jewish neighborhood. A year after his Bar Mitzvah Drake joined the cast of the Canadian teen drama, *Degrassi: The Next Generation*. From his role on *Degrassi* as wheelchair-bound Jimmy Brooks he went on to record successful mixtapes *Room for Improvement* (2006), *Comeback Season* (2007), and *So Far Gone* (2009) before signing with Lil Wayne's Young Money Entertainment. With the help his producer Noah "40" Shebib, he built his own empire with their label OVO Sound.

Although Drake is the product of a middle class Jewish upbringing he raps about how he started from the bottom. Michael P. Jeffries, a writer for *The*

Atlantic, argues that Drake legitimized his authenticity as a *real* black man early in his career by associating closely with Lil' Wayne, who grew up in the drug-infested projects of New Orleans' Hollygrove neighborhood. Wayne gave Drake an unofficial "hood" pass that helped his music ring out on the streets. In 2016 Drake released a collaborative mixtape produced by Metro Boomin, *What a Time to Be Alive,* and went on tour with Future, the South's most popular Trap Music artist.[60] In his article, Jefferies points out Drake's frequent usage of the word "n_gga," stereotypical black slang, and the sexual objectification of women in his music as other means of proving his authenticity.[61] For every one in five ballads that Drake sings there are his uber misogynistic cameos on strip club anthems like "For Free," "Pop That," and "Round of Applause." Kanye West contributed to the blueprint for such behavior. His close relationship with mentor Jay-Z gave him a hood pass. They released a collaborative album *Watch the Throne* (2011) and toured together. Kanye put hardcore rappers like 2 Chainz, Rick Ross, Pusha T, and Young Jeezy on his albums. He followed up his most emotional album, *808s & Heartbreak,* with his most misogynistic albums, *My Beautiful Dark Twisted Fantasy* (2010) and *Yeezus* (2013).

Drake's willingness to challenge tropes has led critics (or "haters") to mock him on social media with memes and gifs. Some believe that his goofy dancing in "Hotline Bling" was his way of trolling critics. Rembert Brown said during a panel discussion with MSNBC host Joy Reid, Mychal Denzel Smith, and Melissa Harris-Perry that "Hotline Blng" only works because Drake's vulnerability in that song countered several examples of hyper-masculinity such as his Meek Mill diss record "Back to Back." Drake talks tough all over that record and questions Meek's manhood. In addition to hanging out with Wayne, Drake surrounds himself with black men who symbolize the things he is praised for rejecting. The music video "Energy" juxtaposes scenes of Drake disguised as various celebrities from Justin Bieber to Miley Cyrus with scenes of himself surrounded by several intimidating black men. Drake's rivalry with R&B bad boy Chris Brown over ex-girlfriend Rihanna resulted in violence in 2013. San Antonio Spurs point guard Tony Parker suffered a scratched retina after becoming an innocent bystander in a nightclub brawl between the crews of these two artists over Rihanna.[62]

Hakeem is also guilty of appropriating this phony "hood n_gga" persona on several occasions. For example, he is invited to perform a duet with Tiana at the Teen Choice Awards. While his parents tell him to tone down his performance for the kid-friendly event, he overexerts his machismo. Cookie offers him some much needed motherly advice: "You need to stop rapping like you from the streets, 'cause you not about that life."[63] Hakeem's confused self-identity can be attributed to the pernicious model being set by his father as much as by popular culture. When Hakeem expresses concern as his producer Shyne chokes Nessa, Lucious questions if he is getting soft. Rather than continue to express his genuine feelings, Hakeem acts as if he does not care about this episode of blatant domestic violence just to impress Lucious. A decade earlier HBO's *The Wire* dealt with a similar father-son issue. Namond Brice (Julito McCullum), the 13-year-old son of a fictional gangster named Wee-Bey (Hassan Johnson), tries to impress his incarcerated father by unsuccessfully selling dope on the corner. Another relevant example is found in season two of STARZ's *Power*. A young black man named Shawn feels pressure to become a gangster and a hustler like his incarcerated father Kanan (50 Cent) to prove his self-worth. When Shawn fails to meet his father's expectations, Kanan kills him. Hakeem, along with these other fictional sons, faces a predicament experienced by countless young black males searching for proper guidance from a father figure.

On numerous occasions *Empire*'s scriptwriters poke fun at Hakeem's failed attempts to act like a thug. Although his interracial entourage consists of corny suburban males and a cross-dressing lesbian deejay named Chicken (AzMarie Livingston), he has local hoodlums, strapped with guns, hanging out on the set of his sex-fueled music video "Drip Drop." When a rival music label begins stealing artists from Empire's roster Hakeem tells Lucious that his boy can get some C-4 explosives to handle the situation. Lucious looks at him with disgust and orders him to stop making an ass of himself. On another episode Lucious shoots down Hakeem's request to talk with a prominent rapper from the hood named Titan about signing a contract with Empire. He knows that his suburban son is too soft to deal with Titan, who is serving time in jail for shooting a rival gang member. In another instance Lucious queers Hakeem by referring to his new lesbian rapper Freda Gatz as the son he never had. Freda makes matters worse by releasing a diss record calling him "daddy's little girl."

Hakeem, like Drake, reverts to dysfunctional hyper-macho behavior whenever his manhood is tested. (1) He responds to Freda's attack by arranging a rap battle with her, hosted by HOT 97 celebrity deejay Funkmaster Flex in front of a live audience, to defend his reputation. Ironically, Flex was indirectly involved in the battle between Drake and Meek Mill. After he wins the battle Hakeem goes to celebrate with Jamal and Cookie at his father's nightclub Leviticus as Drake's hit song "Worst Behavior," plays in the background. (2) Hakeem's relationship with Tiana ended because she caught him bathing with his mistress Camilla. Although he was satisfied when she forgave him he lashed out at Tiana when a video of her sensuously kissing a young white woman was leaked on Instagram. Hakeem recorded a spiteful anti-woman anthem,

"Can't Truss 'Em." (3) After Tiana's new boyfriend Gram (Romeo Miller) calls him out in her new song, Hakeem's solution is to record a song bragging that he could still "hit that" (i.e., have sex with her). (4) Hakeem throws a public tantrum on the Internet, mocking Andre's illness and Jamal's sexual orientation, because he feels betrayed by them after learning that Andre was romantically involved with his latest love interest, Nessa. (5) In season two Hakeem is kidnapped and held for a $40,000 ransom by a Latino gang. Hakeem, trying to act hard as usual, calls his abductors a bunch of cowboys. They respond to his jeers by using homophobic slurs, pistol whipping him in the head, cutting his lip and eye, and leaving bruises on his back. When he returns home Lucious advises him to man up, grow a sack and stop wallowing in "bitchassness." Lucious tells him that if "you gonna use my name put a man behind it" or to paraphrase hip-hop mogul The Birdman, put some "respek" on the Lyon family name.[64] Hakeem admits to his brothers that he was ashamed of not being able to defend himself against his abductors. Like the elevator scene during Andre's anxiety attack, the brothers console Hakeem telling him that real men get scared, too, and are smart enough to know when to fight their battles. *Empire* showrunner Ilene Chaiken told *Variety* that the writers used this storyline to begin a dialogue on black males' feelings of emasculation.[65]

Hakeem tries to counteract these threats to his masculinity at the hands of the kidnappers in a number of ways. Upon his release from his captors he goes straight to Anika's apartment to have sex with her, resulting in an accidental pregnancy. When he returns to Lucious' mansion he refuses to allow the family's doctor to examine him to determine if he was raped. When he goes along with Cookie to confront his captors he pulls a gun on them, shouting aloud "who's a little bitch now?"[66] The camera zooms in on his finger twitching uncontrollably on the trigger. He is able to give the gun to Cookie. It is interesting that the men noticeably appeared to be more intimidated by Cookie than by a gun-packing Hakeem. Perhaps they realized that he lacked the courage to pull the trigger.

Hakeem's manhood is the underlying theme of episode 42 "Strange Bedfellows." He celebrates his 21st birthday by live streaming himself partying and club hopping for 21 straight hours. At his first club stop the party promoter attempts to cheat him out his money because his family members are not there to protect him. He has to rely on a group of gun strapped thugs who come to his aid in attempt to make a quick buck. Rather than show weakness he readily accepts their help and then tries to embarrass the promoter by throwing money in his face and forcing him to hand over his watch. Later that night at Leviticus one of Hakeem's new friends punches a young woman, who refuses to dance with him, causing his birthday party to end in a melee. The incident leads to a $50 million lawsuit against Empire Entertainment and accusations that Hakeem promotes domestic violence.

In spite of his efforts to be the perfect boyfriend with Laura in season two, Hakeem's overall treatment of women fails to fully evolve. Once Laura learns of Anika's pregnancy Hakeem assumes that their engagement is over. He decides to drown his sorrows at a strip club, posting videos of himself "making it rain" and pouring champagne on lingerie-clad exotic dancers.[67] Laura takes him back before leaving him at the altar during their wedding. He commiserates by getting drunk and going to Tiana's apartment expecting sex. Only a few episodes pass before Hakeem is trying to work his way into Nessa's pants. Upon learning that she is dating Andre, he decides to repair his relationship with Tiana. Over the course of season three Hakeem's maturation is in a constant state of flux. He is slowly learning to be a father to his newborn daughter Bella. Yet, in one instance he is publicly professing his love to Tiana and engaging in an exclusive relationship. At the next moment he is having a three-some in a bubble bath with Tiana and her newest girlfriend. Will he ever grow up? Only time will reveal the answer to this question. Furthermore, the same question can be asked of hip-hop as it relates to the black masculine performance. While some artists demonstrate alternative forms of black masculinity, the thug and the pimp image still make millions for the hip-hop industry.

Outro

Empire provides viewers with a multidimensional assessment of black men and discourse on illegible masculinities. Masculinity is not monolithic in the African American community. What the Lyon sons have in common is that each finds himself engaged in an ongoing struggle to develop his own self-identify by rejecting presumptions about his masculinity that marginalize him. Andre is fighting to prove that he can gain acceptance into mainstream America without being labeled an "Uncle Tom" or a "Sellout." He must prove to Lucious that his Ivy League education, white wife, and bipolar disorder do not make him any less black or less qualified to run Empire Entertainment. Jamal must stand up to the bigots in his own family and society attempting to emasculate him because he is gay. Hakeem experiences the most difficulty with this struggle as he learns that being a man is more than an appropriation of hyper-macho caricatures of black men. While *Empire*'s storylines are far from perfect, what should not be denied is the show's efforts to present these diverse representations of black men for viewers to discuss and critique.

5

Lee Daniels Doesn't Care About Black People!
Representation vs. Exploitation

> "*Empire has been accused of perpetuating violence. Do you think that the misogyny and celebration of gang warfare that's so prevalent in hip-hop music is healthy for our nation?*"[1]
> —Kelly McGann

If you ask television junkies to name the hottest show on television in 2015, they will probably say *The Walking Dead, The Bachelor, The Voice,* or *Game of Thrones*. However, *Empire* was television's top series for a three-month period that year. The Debbie Allen-directed final episode, "Who I Am," with its 17.62 million viewers, was the most watched finale of a new series since *Grey's Anatomy* in 2005. Multiple restaurants and nightclubs in the Washington metropolitan area (DMV) held viewing parties for fans who wanted to share the experience of the season finale. The cable news primetime series *CNN Tonight* hosted by Don Lemon dedicated a panel discussion to the finale. Lemon's guest panelists included Boyce Watkins, *Entertainment Tonight* correspondent Nischelle Turner, and *theGrio* editor Chris Witherspoon. Boyce Watkins, unlike Lemon and his other guests, was not impressed with *Empire*. He described *Empire* as being 21st-century Blaxploitation Cinema and a "coonish ghetto" drama. Nischelle Turner was highly offended by his scathing characterization. However, Watkins is not alone in his denouncement of the popular hip-hop soap opera. Tavis Smiley, an influential black television host and political commentator, made the following statement during an interview with Larry King: "*Empire* advances the worst of every pathology that black people have—crime and drug dealing."[2] Dwayne Bryant, a motivational speaker and CEO of Inner Vision International, told Howard University professor Wilmer Leon, on an episode of the SiriusXM Urban

View radio show *Inside the Issues*, that black parents need to turn off *Empire* and teach their kids black history if they want them to succeed.[3] The Rev. H. Beecher Hicks, Jr., the legendary pastor emeritus of Metropolitan Baptist Church in Maryland, told the attendees at a 2015 Black Youth Matter Symposium at the historic Shiloh Baptist Church in Washington, D.C., "We do not need *Empire* because shows like that only worsen conditions for the African-American community."[4]

The 1987 Robert Townsend film *Hollywood Shuffle* satirized Hollywood's commodification of stereotypical black images from pimps to break dancers, which equated to modern day minstrelsy. Stanley Crouch, a conservative black culture critic, once said that there is always a paycheck for black entertainers who are willing to coon.[5] Is the FOX Network breaking barriers with its depictions of blackness on *Empire* or profiting from the perpetuation of redundant stereotypes? To answer this question, I started by delving into FOX's long history of achieving high ratings with edgy programming targeting the African American community. Some older blacks question FOX's motives due to its affiliation with the controversial Fox News Channel. One of the things that I am attempting to do is determine if there is any merit in such accusations. Secondly, I assessed selected viewers' opinions of *Empire* using data collected from an online survey of 100 respondents between the ages of 18 and 40, from April through October 2016. Respondents resided in Maryland, Virginia, South Carolina, Ohio, New Jersey, Illinois, Connecticut, and Washington, D.C. How well do these respondents think *Empire* presents social issues and individuals within the black community? What do the respondents think about *Empire*'s impact on white Americans' perceptions of blackness? What role does respectability politics play in their assessment? Finally, does a popular television series like *Empire* have a responsibility to do more than simply entertain audiences and make money?

FOX and the New Look of Black Television

By the mid–1980s the growing popularity of cable television and the new videocassette industry contributed to declining viewership on the three major television networks. In 1985 Australian billionaire Rupert Murdoch and Barry Diller founded The FOX Network. Murdoch had built his own empire through the newspaper industry in Australia, television in Great Britain, and News Corporation in the United States which oversees *The Wall Street Journal*, HarperCollins, Twentieth Century–Fox Film Corporation, and 21st Century Fox. American business insiders thought Murdoch was crazy to assume that he could compete with the big three commercial broadcast networks: ABC, CBS, and NBC. Not since the defunct DuMont Television Network (1946–1956) had there been a successful fourth network. FOX (also known as Fox) started off with only two primetime shows per week. The network grew by taking risks on less traditional, more irreverent series like *The Simpsons* (1989–) and *Married… with Children* (1987–1997). *The Simpsons*, which started off as a comic strip short on *The Tracy Ullman Show* (1987–1990), was going head-to-head with NBC's number one hit sitcom, *The Cosby Show* (1984–1992), by the early 1990s. FOX's family sitcoms presented a counter to NBC's pristine Huxtable family. *The Simpsons* featured an animated version of the dysfunctional white "upper-lower-middle class" family. *Married… with Children*, modeled after Norman Lear's *All in the Family*, focused on a dysfunctional white working-class family in Chicago. The family's patriarch Al Bundy (Ed O'Neill) was a sexist women's shoe salesman who sat around his house with his hand down the front of his pants. Al's nagging wife Peggy (Katey Sagal) and his ditsy, underachieving son and daughter were caricatures.

FOX made policing and law and order the overarching theme in much of its early programming. *21 Jump Street* (1987–1991), starring Johnny Depp and Holly Robinson, was a teen drama about young cops who go undercover as high school and college students to investigate crimes. *America's Most Wanted* (1988–2011), a series about the search and seizure of the nation's worst criminals, became the network's second longest running series behind *The Simpsons*. As the crack cocaine epidemic ravaged poor black neighborhoods across the country and mass incarceration was on the rise, FOX benefited from its creation of television's first reality series, *Cops* (1989–2014). Police officers raided a crack house on the series premiere. *Cops* was so popular that the network began airing back-to-back episodes on Saturday evenings. Law enforcement represented good; the criminals represented evil.

By the mid-1990s the network's lineup expanded to include groundbreaking primetime dramas *Beverly Hills, 90210* (1990–2000) and *Party of Five* (1994–2000) targeting suburban middle-class white teenagers.[6] *The X-Files* (1993–2002) became one of the network's most memorable series and a cult classic for individuals interested in paranormal activity. In 1993 FOX signed a lucrative multi-year deal with the National Football League (NFL) to air games every Sunday. Since then FOX has emerged as arguably the leading non-cable network for sports airing multiple Super Bowls, The World Series, NASCAR races, NCAA college bowl games, The Professional Golfers Association's U.S. Open, and Ultimate Fighting Championship matches.

FOX owes a substantial amount of its success to African American talent and audiences starting with *The Arsenio Hall Show* (1989–1994), which was FOX's response to NBC's *The Tonight Show* (1954–) with Johnny Carson. Unlike the older Carson who appealed mainly to an older, white audience in Middle America, Arsenio catered to younger, urban America. Arsenio wanted his viewers, predominantly hailing from the MTV and hip-hop generations, to feel like they were at a nightclub when they tuned in each night. On one episode, 2 Live Crew performed their banned song "Me So Horny." Snoop Dogg appeared weeks after his debut album *Doggystyle* (1993) topped the Billboard 200 charts. At the time Snoop was under investigation for murder. The late rapper Tupac Shakur sat on Arsenio's couch several times. His most memorable appearance came while he was facing criminal charges for raping a young woman, for which he would serve 11 months in prison. Maya Angelou recited poetry on one episode. Bill Clinton, then a candidate in the 1992 presidential election, played his saxophone while wearing sunglasses. While the show had mass appeal, it remained unapologetically black. Arsenio's nearly hour-long interview with the polarizing Nation of Islam leader Louis Farrakhan offended many whites and is thought to be one of the reasons for the show's massive rating drop.[7] Unable to compete with new late-night shows hosted by David Letterman and Jon Stewart, FOX cancelled its late-night talk show four months after the interview with Farrakhan.

A year after *The Arsenio Hall Show* debuted, FOX premiered *In Living Color* (1990–1994), a hip-hop version of NBC's sketch comedy series *Saturday Night Live* with a predominantly black cast. *In Living Color*, created by Keenan Ivory Wayans, was the first American television series to be written, directed, and produced by a person of color. It satirized current events, white racism, black politicians, effeminate gays, and black women. The series launched the careers of Jim Carey, Jamie Foxx, David Alan Grier, and several members of the Wayans' family. Jamie Foxx resurrected Flip Wilson's routine of cross-dressing as a woman. He wore a blond wig, fake large breasts and buttocks, and a ridiculous amount of lipstick, highlighting his poked out big lips, to play Wanda. The series capitalized on hip-hop's growing acceptance in mainstream media and popular culture. Keenan's younger brother Shawn spun the latest hit rap records for his dance crew, The Fly Girls, which included an unknown Latina dancer named Jennifer Lopez. Rosie Perez choreographed the crew's dance routines. At its peak *In Living Color* reached the top 15 of the Nielsen ratings. Keenan saw his show as a way of using humor to counter stereotypes. Older middle and upper-class black professionals and scholars were not as impressed. Alvin Poussaint, a black psychologist at the Harvard Medical School and a consultant to the *Cosby Show*, blasted the series for satirizing myths of black incompetence during an appearance on ABC's *20/20*.

Others compared it to *Amos 'n' Andy* (1951–1953). Television scholar Herman Gray says the series' ambivalence towards its representations of blackness often came at the expense of the African American under-class.[8] "If you have a black point of view, you're damned if you show the bad side and you're damned if you don't. We have the same diversity as any other show. We don't dwell on homeboys for 30 minutes. We also have black professionals, people in suits," said Wayans in defense of the program.[9]

FOX's earliest black sitcoms were *True Colors* (1990–1992) and *Roc* (1991–1994). The former sitcom starred Frankie Faison as a widowed dentist who married a white divorced mom of a teenage daughter. Faison's character had two teenage sons from his previous marriage. *Roc* starred Charles S. Dutton as a garbage collector, in inner city Baltimore, who was married to a registered nurse. Roc's father was a retired Pullman Porter and his younger brother was a womanizing professional jazz musician.[10] Dutton received a NAACP Image Award for his commanding performance in the series. Critical acclaim in the African American community did not translate into high Nielsen ratings for *Roc* or *True Colors*. Neither series attracted a large viewership in the 18 to 40-year old African American demographic or shared in the crossover success of the more mainstream black sitcoms on ABC and NBC. Despite these early setbacks FOX rebounded to become television's leader in scripted black programming by the mid–1990s. The network's Thursday night lineup offered black viewers a much-welcomed alternative to *Friends* (1994–2004) and *Seinfeld* (1989–1998), on NBC. While the NBC Thursday night lineup was funny, finding a black person on these shows at times felt like searching for a unicorn. How could you have two series in New York City with so little color? Whites found themselves in the minority on FOX Thursdays, which started at 8:00 p.m. with *Martin* (1992–1997), an edgy sitcom about a fictional black DJ on Detroit's radio station WZUP. *Martin's* protagonist, Martin Payne, was played by Martin Lawrence who was the hottest young black stand-up comedian in urban America and the original host of Russell Simmons' *Def Comedy Jam* (1992–1997) on HBO. Episodes of *Martin* revolved around his relationship with his girlfriend Gina (Tisha Campbell) and his buddies Tommy (Thomas Ford) and Cole (Carl Anthony Payne II).

Martin ranked in the top five among black viewers between the ages of 12 and 17 and 18 to 49. The sitcom appealed most to the type of audience that made *The Arsenio Hall Show* and *In Living Color* hits years earlier. *Martin* was plagued by the same negative reviews as *In Living Color*. Bill Cosby publicly disapproved of its lowbrow humor. Martin's friend Tommy was compared to the lazy trickster George "Kingfish" Stevens from *Amos 'n' Andy* because no one knew what he did for work. "You ain't got no job man" was the running punch line on the series. Cole was a childlike simpleton who still lived at home with his "moms" and mooched off his overweight girlfriend, Big Shirley. Critics complained about the hip hugging outfits worn by Gina's best friend Pam (Tichina Arnold) that often drew the camera's gaze to her backside. The darker skinned Pam was the frequent butt of Martin's jokes due to her appearance and loud, sassy demeanor, while the light skinned Gina was placed on a pedestal. Recurring characters were the corrupt preacher Rev. Leon Lonnie Love (David Alan Grier), who ripped off his church's members and tried to sleep with his female members, and Martin's odd neighbor Bruh-Man from the "fifth flo," who always held up four fingers to explain where he lived in the apartment building. Bruh-Man (Reginald Ballard) was a large, inarticulate dark-skinned man whose small clothes never appropriately fit his massive frame. "Nuttin" and "just chillin" were his favorite phrases. Bruh-Man was reminiscent of the coon-like characters of Stepin Fetchit and *Amos 'n' Andy*'s stammering dim-witted janitor Lightnin.' Martin's other neighbor Sha Nay Nay was portrayed by Martin Lawrence in drag. Sha Nay Nay typically wore tight clothing, a tacky, long braided wig, and gaudy jewelry. Her character poked fun at the "hood rat" archetype of black women that was becoming popular in rap music videos and films like *Friday* (1995) in the early 1990s.[11]

Martin preceded *Living Single* (1993–1998) at 8:30 p.m. and *New York Undercover* (1994–1998) from 9:00 to 10:00 p.m. *Living Single* starred rapper Queen Latifah as Khadijah James, the editor of her own magazine, *Flava*. Her best friends were a lawyer named Maxine (Erika Alexander), a snobbish boutique buyer named Regine (Kim Fields), and her goofy cousin Sinclaire (Kim Coles). *Living Single* was television's first series about single, independent black women with lucrative white-collar careers. Thursday evenings concluded with *New York Undercover*, the first cop drama in television history to have an African American and Latino American in leading roles. Malik Yoba and Michael DeLorenzo played Detectives J.C. Williams and Eddie Torres, respectively. Detectives Williams and Torres were loosely based on a trio of real life black police officers from Chicago's Cabrini Green Housing Projects known as the Slick Boys who could easily blend in with the brothas on the block.

Malik Yoba played Lucious' best friend and business partner Vernon Turner in *Empire*'s first season. During a 2016 interview for the TV One documentary series *Unsung Hollywood*, Yoba credited *New York Undercover* with planting seeds that grew into *Empire*.[12] *New York Undercover* was the brainchild of Andre Harrell, founder of the now defunct Uptown record label. Harrell's Uptown Records, among the most influential music labels in the 1980s and 1990s, was responsible for two new musical genres: New Jack Swing and hip-hop soul. Uptown's celebrated roster included a very young Sean "Puffy" Combs, Mary J. Blige, Al B. Sure, Heavy D, and Jodeci. In 1992 Harrell signed a deal with Universal Pictures to develop film and television projects that infused hip-hop. *New York Undercover* was the first byproduct of Harrell's television deal. Universal hired Dick Wolfe, the producer of NBC's groundbreaking dramas *Miami Vice* (1984–1989) and *Law & Order* (1990–2010), to produce the series. Each episode opened with a distinctive scene featuring the latest rap song. The Notorious B.I.G. was among the many emcees to make a cameo. Ice-T had a recurring role as a ruthless gangster Danny Cort. The Thursday night drama's largely black writers did a remarkable job capturing the subtle nuances of urban black life at the time. The fashion reflected the attire worn in hip-hop videos and on the streets of Brooklyn and Harlem.

By *New York Undercover*'s third season the executives at FOX began complaining that it was "too black" to attract white viewers domestically and overseas or compete with *Seinfeld* in the same time slot. The increasing violence in hip-hop, the East v. West Coast feud, and murders of 2Pac and Biggie frightened FOX's white executives. Attempts were made, unsuccessfully, to change the show's image by bringing on more white characters and diversifying the soundtrack. The series was cancelled halfway through its fourth season. Kristal Brent Zook writes in her book, *Color by Fox: The Fox Network and the Revolution in Black Television,* that while many regarded FOX's black programming in the 1980s and 1990s as trivial or buffoonish, it sparked a renaissance in Hollywood resulting in more African American script writers, directors, producers, and actors. African Americans made up 25 percent of FOX's viewership by the late 1990s. According to Zook, these diverse series grew out of the black storytelling and humor of past decades and a collective struggle to achieve the American Dream.[13] Zook's argument is similar to Christine Acham's defense of the black sitcoms of the 1970s labeled as "coonery" and new age "minstrelsy" by sophisticated middle-class and elite black social critics.[14]

The rise of mini-networks UPN and the WB in the late 1990s led to an absence of black programming on FOX and the other three major networks by the turn of the century. UPN and WB copied FOX's blueprint for appealing to the 18 to 40 urban black demographic. The black creators of these series were given freedom to do and say almost anything they wanted as long as their shows pulled in viewers and financial sponsors. Steve Harvey, Cedric the Entertainer, Brandy, Jamie Foxx, Mo'Nique, and Robert Townsend each had their first signature series on these networks. UPN and the WB were successful, but polarizing in the African American community. Chuck D., the leader of the rap group Public Enemy, nicknamed UPN the United Plantation of Negroes. Spike Lee said that he would rather watch *Amos 'n' Andy* than many of the black programs on these mini-networks.[15]

Over time the networks moved away from black programming because they realized that black households had less income to purchase the items that sponsors wanted to market to viewers. *The Bernie Mac Show* (2001–2006) was FOX's lone black series from 2001 until 2006. Chicago comedian Bernie Mac turned a joke, from his routine in *The Original Kings of Comedy* tour (1999), about his experiences raising his sister's three children while she was in rehab for drug addiction into the show's premise. Bernie Mac, a staunch believer in old-fashioned discipline (bordering on abuse), had to adjust to parenting in the 21st century. He often told his wife that he would "bust the children's heads till the white meat showed," when they misbehaved.[16] *The Bernie Mac Show* was a hit in the Nielsen ratings and praised by the critics. It won a Peabody Award, The Humanitas Prize, and three NAACP Image Awards. FOX's next black program was *The Cleveland Show* (2009–2013), an adult animated spin-off of the network's hit animated sitcom *Family Guy*, created by white television producer and filmmaker Seth MacFarlane. It followed the experiences of Cleveland Brown and his dysfunctional, blended family in the fictional town of Stoolbend, Virginia. Cleveland's biological teenage son Cleveland, Jr., was obese, lazy, sloppily attired, and socially awkward despite earning good grades in school. Cleveland's adopted daughter Roberta was an attractive, popular high school student who dated an ignorant white boy, Federline Jones, who tried his best to speak and act stereotypically black. Cleveland's youngest adopted child was Rallo, a five-year-old prodigy with a huge 1960s AFRO hairstyle. *The Cleveland Show* did not fare as well as *The Bernie Mac Show*. John McWhorter, an Ivy League black professor and writer for *The New Republic* labeled it *Family Guy* in blackface.

Before he achieved stardom on ABC's *Live! With Kelly and Michael*, retired NFL star Michael Strahan had a short-lived black family sitcom called *Brothers* on FOX Sunday nights from September through December 2009. Paraplegic comedian Daryl "Chill" Mitchell and Carl Weathers (best known as Apollo Creed in the *Rocky* films) co-starred in the series. FOX cancelled *Brothers* after 13 episodes due to disappointing Nielsen ratings and critical reviews. *Empire* became the first non-animated series with an all-black cast to air on FOX since *Brothers*. FX, FOX's sister network on cable television, has also created successful programs that specifically target black audiences such as Donald Glover's uber hit comedy *Atlanta* (2016–), the Golden Globe and Emmy Award winning miniseries *American Crime Story: The People versus O.J. Simpson* (2016), and *Snowfall* (2017), a new program created by John

Singleton about the Central Intelligence Agency's role in the origins of the crack cocaine epidemic.

Fair and Balanced

In September 2015, I gave my first public presentation about *Empire* at the Annual Meeting of the Association for the Study of African American Life and History (ASALH) in Atlanta. An older black woman who was the chair of an English department at an HBCU sat in the audience. As soon as the word *Empire* rolled off my tongue, she crossed her arms and gave me a look of skepticism. Surprisingly, she was the most active participant in the question and answer session. The professor enjoyed my presentation, but she admitted that she would never watch *Empire* because of its association with FOX! The professor asked me the following questions: "Do you believe that it is just a coincidence or a conspiracy that *Empire* headlines a network that is on the same family tree as the controversial Fox News Channel? Why is a hip-hop soap opera about a drug dealing, gun toting African American family television's most watched at a time of so much racial unrest in America?" Concurrently, the legacy of the beloved *The Cosby Show* was being tarnished due to Cosby's rape scandal. Initially, I dismissed the professor's comments as a generational difference of opinion. *Empire* was not made for her so of course, she would not like it, right? As I flew home from the conference, I gave more thought to her questions. After months of research here is what I found.

FOX and the Fox News Channel are two different networks, but they are connected as subsidiaries of Rupert Murdoch's 21st Century Fox. Local FOX affiliates occasionally broadcast national reports from the Fox News Channel. The 21st Century Fox television family also includes The Fox Business Network, Fox Family Channel, Fox Sports 1 and II, FX, FXX, FX Movie Channel, and the streaming service Hulu. Fox Sports 1 is home to staunch conservative black sports personality Jason Whitlock, who is well known for offending large segments of the African American community with his social commentary. While FOX has a long history of broadcasting black programs that the other three big networks would have ignored, its 24-hour cable news sister network has an unfavorable relationship with the African American community. Fox News, launched on October 7, 1996, by Murdoch and Roger Ailes, has been the leading cable news network among viewers between the ages of 25 and 54 since 2010. Fox News, which earns $2 billion in annual profits, was the most watched network on cable television in 2016.

5. Lee Daniels Doesn't Care About Black People!   145

Critics have accused Fox News of falsifying information to support the Republican Party's agenda and ultra conservative viewpoints. Throughout Barack Obama's tenure in the White House, animus-driven criticism consistently came from the network. Media Matters for America, a George Soros funded non-profit progressive research center, uncovered multiple examples of the network's bias against President Obama.[17] Jonathan Alter's *The Center Holds: Obama and his Enemies* devoted a chapter to Fox's contentious relationship with the president. Alter pointed out repeated attempts by the network to turn every misstep in the Obama administration into a scandal. Fox News' contentious relationship with Obama dated back to his first presidential campaign when Fox personality Sean Hannity labeled him a racist. In 2009 Fox host Glenn Beck, while appearing on *Fox & Friends*, said that President Obama's defense of Henry Louis Gates, following his unlawful arrest for entering his own home, revealed his true nature. "This president has exposed himself as a guy who has a deep-seated hatred for white people or the white culture."[18]

During an August 3, 2016, interview on *The Breakfast Club* Power 105.1 professor Marc Lamont Hill shared his experiences working as a liberal black contributor for Fox News between 2007 and 2009. Hill revealed that on the night Obama won the election the demeanor of the staff resembled that of funeral attendees. He overheard Hannity and others express disbelief that their efforts to hurt Obama's chances with various roadblocks did not wreck his campaign. Hill said that his co-workers pledged to make Obama's next four years in office a living hell. This promise was upheld from the very start of Obama's tenure. The night before his first inauguration Jay-Z performed the song "My President" with rapper Young Jeezy at LOVE nightclub in Washington, D.C. The rappers took turns uplifting the nation's first black president while making explicit remarks about the outgoing Republican President George W. Bush. Megyn Kelly, the former host of Fox's top rated *The Kelly File*, and guest Michelle Malkin, expressed outrage over the hip-hop company Obama was keeping. Malkin used the rappers' lyrics as an example of how Obama deceived the public that he would usher in a post-racial era. Megyn Kelly would be a thorn in the president's side over the course of his administration. In 2010, she and other Fox hosts devoted 45 segments over a two-week period to a false story linking Obama and his attorney general Eric Holder to a radical fringe group called the New Black Panther Party that was accused of intimidating white voters in Philadelphia two years earlier. *The Atlantic*'s Dave Weigel referred to the network's coverage as a "minstrel show meant to inflame and exploit racial tensions."[19]

Frank Luntz, a conservative public opinion guru and Fox News consultant, organized a group of Republican leaders in Congress at a Washington, D.C., hotel the night of Obama's inauguration. The goal of the secret meeting was to develop a plan to win back the White House by ensuring Obama's failure. Luntz admits that Fox News played an active role in that agenda by supporting opposition groups, most notably the Tea Party Movement.[20] A faction of Tea Party members were active participants in the Birther Movement which emphatically argued that the President was unqualified to serve because they did not believe he was an American-born citizen. Donald Trump, the billionaire real estate tycoon who won the 2016 presidential election, became the loudest proponent of birtherism. Obama, annoyed with Trump's slanderous accusations, agreed to make his birth certificate public. On April 28, 2011, *Follow the Money with Eric Bolling* on Fox News held a lively panel discussion on the president's birth certificate. Eric Bolling and guest Pamela Gellar carefully dissected a blown-up version of the birth certificate that the White House released. Gellar accused the White House of releasing a certification of live birth rather than an actual birth certificate. Gellar questioned why it took the president three years to provide this information to the public. She said the White House provided a document that needed to be further examined by completing a digital forensic analysis. Gellar also stated that the American public deserved access to Obama's academic records at Columbia University and Harvard Law School and proof of the articles he published as a law student. The underlying theme of this discussion, weighted with racially coded language, was that Obama was a trickster who falsified his identity to steal the presidency.

In addition to its anti–Obama stance, the Fox News Channel has done its best to lambast the activists and protests within the Black Lives Matter Movement. Fox's hosts and special contributors such as Milwaukee County Sheriff David Clarke labeled the movement a collection of racists who despise law enforcement. The network's coverage of the Obama presidency and the Black Lives Matter Movement contributed to a climate that welcomed Donald Trump's "Make America Great Again" rhetoric and slewing of alternative facts.[21] Roger Ailes, the late co-founder and disgraced CEO of Fox News, was an adviser to Donald Trump's presidential campaign which was notorious for its use of race baiting rhetoric and dog whistles to attract disgruntled white voters who feared losing *their* country.[22]

Eleven current and former Fox News employees filed a class-action lawsuit in April 2017 accusing the network of "unlawful and hostile racial discrimination."[23] As a result of everything said thus far, I find myself scratching my head when I look at the television lineup on the Fox News Channel's sister network. Over the years the FOX network has given blacks opportunities far greater than NBC and CBS. According to a 2016 *USA Today* report FOX only trails ABC in terms of diversity on broadcast network television.[24] FOX's commitment to diversity includes two programs created by Lee Daniels (*Empire* and *Star*); *Rosewood* staring Morris Chestnut; *Pitch* starring African American actress Kylie Bunbury as Major League Baseball's first female pitcher; Damon Wayans as the co-star in *Lethal Weapon*; Keke Palmer and Niecy Nash in *Scream Queens,* and Corey Hawkins and Anna Diop in *24: Legacy*. Meagan Good, Michael Ealy, and Nicole Beharie headlined series on the network for a brief period. Jada Pinkett Smith had a recurring role in *Gotham*. In 2007 FOX's fall lineup included *K-Ville* (an abbreviation for Katrinaville), starring Anthony Anderson, about the role of the police in post–Hurricane Katrina New Orleans. FOX has also portrayed the LGBTQ community in a positive light and placed Latinos in lead roles. When asked about the network's commitment to diversity Tess Sanchez, FOX's executive Vice President of casting said, "It's built into the fabric of the network and the history of the network.... It follows a reflection of our world."[25] FOX is also associated with Rupert Murdoch's Fox Searchlight Pictures, which distributed riveting slave narrative films—*Twelve Years a Slave* (2013) and *The Birth of a Nation* (2016). Both films offered damning critiques of white racism in the nation's history. *Atlanta*, on FX, has been universally praised for its representations of black masculinity.

From March 22 until May 24, 2017, FOX aired a new ten-part drama called *Shots Fired*, written and directed by African Americans Gina Prince-Bythewood (*Love & Basketball* (2000) and *Beyond the Lights* (2014)*)* and Reggie Rock Bythewood *(Notorious* (2009). *Empire* producers Brian Grazer and Francie Calfo were also behind this program. The mini-series starred Sanaa Latham and Stephan James as investigators searching for the truth behind recent police shootings in a fictional North Carolina town. In the series, the police officer under investigation was black; the victim was a white man. The officer was the only African American on the force. He became a pariah in the police department and the community. The investigation into the shooting coincidentally brought the neglected murder of a black teenager and police corruption to light. The miniseries delved into issues of race, policing, privatized prisons, the media, race riots, and the Black Lives Matter Movement. Law enforcement is portrayed in both a positive and negative light. Fox News contributor Amy Holmes made a cameo on an episode. *Shots Fired* is the second drama that FOX has aired dealing with race relations and law enforcement.

What type of message is FOX sending viewers with liberal leaning programming like *Shots Fired* and its commitment to diversity? Are these programs challenging the anti-black rhetoric propagated by the Fox News Channel or subtly masking Rupert Murdoch's true feelings about the minorities who make him millions? I do not have enough evidence to give a definitive answer to these questions. I believe Fox News reflects the political leanings of Murdoch. However, I also believe that Murdoch is a businessman who is most concerned with his bottom line. Fox News beats out CNN and MSNBC because it presents the news in a manner that reaches the largest audience. As is the case with television dramas, sitcoms, and variety shows, the programs, in this case, the news reports that have content based on easily consumable motifs, which consist of recognizable images or stereotypes, and play on people's emotions, tend to be the most marketable. I think Murdoch applies this same strategy with the type of programming appearing on FOX and his other networks. While he may not agree with the socio-political viewpoints expressed on *Empire* and *Shots Fired*, he and his advisors are smart enough to realize what is good for business and profits. They realize that minorities and diversity equal more viewers and sponsors. While it is easy to condemn black directors, producers, and actors for lying down with strange bedfellows, we do not know if these series would have found as much support on the other networks. CBS, in my opinion, has never been great with diversity. NBC, until recently, had slacked off quite a bit when compared to the 1980s and 1990s. HBO had a problem with diversity, since *The Wire* ended, until the debuts of *Ballers* and *Insecure*. Hopefully, these blacks on FOX realize that they have an even greater responsibility not to fall into the trap of promoting stereotypes.

The People v. Empire

Does Lee Daniels hate black people? A friend of mine raised this question as I was beginning this book. My friend wondered if the negative images found in *Empire* were a revelation into what Daniels thought of black people or an indication that he was willing to do anything for profit. I decided to query as many people as possible to see how others felt about the series. Do they share the opinions of my friend, the "haters" found on social media, or the professor at my conference presentation in Atlanta? Do they enjoy watching *Empire* as purely entertainment or do they think the show has a deeper impact? To collect data for this section, I surveyed 100 respondents (via SurveyMonkey) residing in Maryland, Virginia, South Carolina, Ohio, Illinois, Connecticut, and Washington, D.C., between April and October 2016. Respondents were between the ages of 18 and 40. Most respondents classified themselves as black or African American and were middle-class college students or graduates. Below I have included sample questions and responses from my polling.

What is your highest level of education?

Table 1. Educational Level of Survey Respondents

Education Completed	Number
Doctorate (Ph.D., J.D., MD)	5
Master of Arts	12
Master of Business Administration	3
Some Graduate School	7
Bachelor's Degree	30
Associate Degree	4
Some College	31
Technical/Vocational Degree or License	6
High School Diploma	2
	100

What is your gender?

Table 2. Gender of Survey Respondents

Gender	Number
Male	32
Female	68

What is your age?

Table 3. Age of Survey Respondents

Age Range	Percent
18 to 21 years old	45.65%
22 to 35 years old	33.7%
36 to 40 years old	20.65%

What is your race?

Table 4. Race of Survey Respondents

Race (Multiple Responses Allowed)	Percent
Black or African American	96.74%
White	4.35%
Hispanic or Latino	0.00%
Asian	2.17%
Native American	1.09%
Other	2.17%

Are you a fan of *Empire*?

Table 5. Survey Respondents Who Are Fans of *Empire*

Yes, I am an *Empire* fan	61.96%
No, I am not an *Empire* fan	38.04%

How many episodes of *Empire* have you watched in the past year?

Table 6. Episodes Watched by Fans of *Empire*

Empire Episodes Watched	*Percent*
10 or More	55.91%
5 to 9	13.98%
1 to 4	19.35%
0	10.75%

Empire provides a realistic depiction of some African American families.

Table 7. Respondents Who Consider *Empire* a Realistic Depiction of African American Families

Empire is Realistic.	*Percent*
Strongly Agree	2.6%
Agree	33.33%
Disagree	36.00%
Strongly Disagree	16.00%
No Opinion	12.00%

How does *Empire* compare to past and present television series about the African American family?

The lesson that I take away from *Empire* is that African American families fight for one another and work just as hard as anyone else to make it in this world. (October 2016)

Empire depicts a strong and wealthy, high class black family while most other depictions show a middle or low class black family trying to get by in life. (September 2016)

It is the same stereotypical show about starting from the bottom and making it with obstacles along the way. It is similar to other black shows with some modern twists. (September 2016)

Empire exposed the harsher realities of many African American families ... dealing with drugs, money, and family feuds. Although this may be true in many families, it is over-dramatized in the series for entertainment. (August 2016)

It's a more modern image of how black families from the hood try to make it out. Music is a way out rather than college. (June 2016)

It was okay but I lost interest in it. I personally do not think is gives African American families a good outlook overall, but I do understand the message that it gives about how some families live. (June 2016)

I think *Empire* looks at many of the darker issues that tend to be overlooked. For example, I don't recall mental illness or sexuality being such a big part of any storyline. (June 2016)

Empire shows the various nuances a family goes through. There are of course artistic liberties taken and some extremes. But many African American families encounter dysfunction, broken relationships, deep hurt, mental illness, sexuality battles and the like. (June 2016)

I think it's a different depiction of African American families than we've seen before. Compared to our "traditional" television series like *Good Times*, *Fresh Prince*, *The Cosby Show*, etc., the dynamics of the family are different. (May 2016)

It is much more overt and explicit in its approach containing micro societal issues such as homosexuality, mass incarceration, black wealth, stereotypes, police brutality, etc. Black shows have traditionally not touched these conundrums so formidably, vividly and unremittingly. I've actually heard people complain of the intensity of *Empire*'s approach, especially about the homosexuality in it. Honestly, that aspect turned me off from the show because I felt as if it was too intense. (May 2016)

Empire seems to talk about topics that otherwise would never be mentioned such as being homosexual. It talks about drugs and shows a lot of sexual content. By contrast shows like *Good Times* would only talk about job hardships and family life. (May 2016)

I don't really consider it a series about an African American family, I consider it a series about a family in the entertainment business. There hasn't really been a show similar to it in the past. (May 2016)

In comparison to past black families on television *Empire* is much more raw, gritty and violent. But it's a show based on modern day and an industry that is notorious for it's over the top personalities and wealth. The show is trying to depict that lifestyle. In comparison to present TV black families, it is still much more graphic, violent and over the top with adult content. Other shows based on black families are more wholesome and attempt to depict the black family in a more respectable, relatable portrayal. (May 2016)

Empire is trashy; older black sitcoms showed black parents or families in a benevolent matter. Well at least after the reign of *Good Times*. (May 2016)

Empire does not compare to any of the past shows. I mean that in the most insulting way possible. Sure, *Empire* has a few socially conscious moments; however, they are outweighed by the negative and contrived efforts to force homosexuality on people. (May 2016)

Different from the past but is right on point with how most inner city black families are and interact. (May 2016)

It's stepped outside of past so-called "respectable" images of African American families. (April 2016)

Empire highlights some negative aspects of African American families that we don't like to see. (April 2016)

The Lyons are a more realistic family than the Huxtables, though neither truly captures the essence of growing up black. (April 2016)

Empire has zero substance. I believe it's an inaccurate depiction of how African American families are run. Compared to past African American shows *Empire* isn't mind stimulating, impactful, or motivational for the African American culture as a whole. (April 2016)

It is more of a type of Hollywood fictional family than an everyday type of family. But the things they go through, a lot of people can relate to. I think they care about each other, but there is a line between your job and the love of your family in this show. Some can't decide which is more important. (April 2016)

Dysfunctional families and conflict. There is no bond or typical "family" because of parental disputes that have personal effects on the children's development and perceptions as they grow. (April 2016)

While it is more modern, it overemphasizes the broken black family epidemic for the purposes of humor. (April 2016)

Past TV shows depicted families as strong with a solid foundation. *Empire* does not. (April 2016)

Shows like *Good Times* and *The Cosby Show* placed high value on morality whereas *Empire* places an emphasis on competition and endeavors to be successful. (April 2016)

Empire brings fresh insight into how some hip-hop artists become rich and famous. While the show may show how fame is achieved (assuming this is a long-standing spin off of Terrance Howard's earlier film *Hustle & Flow*), it is not a realistic depiction of black families. It does try to show some struggle with lifestyle choices and immaturity that comes with being the youngest and most talented, but it does not address the stereotypes that result. (April 2016)

Empire provides an accurate depiction of the current state of hip-hop and pop music.

Table 8. Respondents Who Consider *Empire* a Realistic Depiction of Hip-Hop

Empire Accurately Depicts Hip-Hop	Percent
Strongly Agree	11.84%
Agree	59.21%
Disagree	10.53%
Strongly Disagree	1.32%
No Opinion	17.11%

Who is your favorite character on *Empire*?

Table 9. Favorite *Empire* Character

Favorite Character	Percent
Lucious	9.33%
Cookie	57.33%
Andre	4.00%
Jamal	13.33%
Hakeem	1.33%
Anika	1.33%
Other	13.33%

Which three words best describe *Empire* patriarch Lucious Lyon?

Table 10. Three Words That Best Describe *Empire*'s Patriarch

Best description of Lucious	Percent
Entrepreneur	58.46%
Gangster	51.35%
Musician	43.24%
Homophobe	25.68%
Father	24.32%
Anti-Hero	22.97%
Misogynist	18.92%
Wannabe Jay-Z	14.86%

Which three words best describe *Empire* matriarch Cookie Lyon?

Table 11. Three Words That Best Describe *Empire*'s Matriarch

Best description of Cookie	Percent
Mother	67.57%
Survivor	67.57%
Diva	51.35%
Entrepreneur	43.24%
Gangster	18.92%
Feminist	17.57%
Ratchet Trap Queen	13.51%
Anti-Hero	2.70%

Which fictional leading lady reminds you most of the women in your life?

Table 12. A Fictional Leading Lady Who Mirrors Most Real Women

Realistic Leading Lady	Percent
Cookie Lyon	31.08%
Olivia Pope	13.51%
Annalise Keating	2.70%
None of the above	52.70%

Which fictional leading lady do you respect the most?

Table 13. Most Respected Fictional Leading Lady in a Current Series

Realistic Leading Lady	Percent
Cookie Lyon	38.67%
Olivia Pope	18.67%
Annalise Keating	14.67%
None of the above	28.00%

List the three most important issues addressed on *Empire*.

Table 14. Three Most Important Issues Addressed on Empire

Important Issues	Percent
Family	73.61%
Commercialization of hip-hop	69.44%

Important Issues	Percent
LGBTQ Issues	61.11%
Class	20.83%
Race	18.06%
Drug Abuse	13.89%
Interracial Relationships	9.72%
Mental Illness	7.67%
Religion	5.56%
Mass Incarceration	4.17%
Black Lives Matter	4.00%

Dr. Boyce Watkins calls *Empire* modern day Blaxploitation Cinema, coonery, and ghetto entertainment. Do you agree with him?

Table 15. *Empire* Is Modern Day Blaxploitation Cinema

Yes	50.00%
No	50.00%

An anonymous English Department chairwoman at a historically black university in the South refuses to watch *Empire* because it airs on a network that is associated with the controversial Fox News Channel. Do you believe *Empire*'s success is a part of a conspiracy, being carried out by the supporters of Fox News, to shame blacks with negative stereotypes?

Table 16. *Empire* Is Part of a Conspiracy to Shame Blacks

Yes	35.53%
No	64.47%

Much of the criticism of *Empire* is rooted in respectability politics.

Table 17. *Empire* Is Rooted in Respectability Politics

Yes	56.42%
No	43.48%

What is your overall opinion of *Empire*?

I think *Empire* is a really good show. I watch it every week. I think it has all different types of views on life. Everyone wants to be successful while taking other people down along the way if they have to, which isn't the right way. It shows how the hip-hop business goes with everybody fighting for that attention to have a hit record. Family may not be able to see eye to eye all the time. It's just a lot of different things that make it interesting to me. (October 2016)

I watched the first season, then only a few episodes of the second. Too much singing. I am not really into musicals. (October 2016)

The first season was good. In the second season, there was too much going on. (October 2016)

I believe *Empire* shows black people in a negative light without portraying a realistic story. It is not something that most black people and families can relate to. It pointlessly shamed black people. (October 2016)

I enjoy watching *Empire*. Although it is not a show that every culture can grasp, I have no problem with it. (September 2016)

I love it! (September 2016)

I don't think I'll ever watch it because it shows the same stereotypes of black families we've seen for years I am tired of it. (September 2016)

I think *Empire* is an okay show. I think it is good entertainment. Yes, it has buffoonery. But buffoonery is ok when we have another show depicting the black experience realistically. (August 2016)

Empire is very entertaining and I will watch the new season, but it does not present black culture in a positive light. (August 2016)

Can't compare it to any Tyler Perry productions. My brothers and sisters on *Empire*, you are being exploited and bought for the "Almighty Dollar." (July 2016)

I do not like the negative portrayal of the black family and black people in general. We have fought so hard to be treated as equals. I think the show sets us back about 50 years. (July 2016)

Overall, I enjoy the show for sheer entertainment. I do not agree with everything that is represented on the show and all of the "extra-ness," but the show is entertaining. (July 2016)

Don't watch—feel that Lee Daniels' perspective is skewed and he is celebrated because he consistently exaggerates images that depict the worst of the black community. (July 2016)

It's a good show that has both real and fictional depictions. (July 2016)

It's about black people and their issues when they have too much power. (July 2016)

I enjoy it and take it for what it's worth. (July 2016)

I think we can do without another negative show. It might be realistic; however, it's not tasteful to me. (June 2016)

I don't care for *Empire*. My biggest issue with the show is its depiction of the black family. This is a family that has somehow managed to grow a business from the ground up, but they are in-fighting with each other over who's going to run it. I mean, why not give everyone a job and keep the money in the family? It just didn't make any sense. There were just too many issues with the family. On the other hand, I actually think the idea of merging music with a television show was genius. It's a great way to promote the music, the show, and new artists. That was an excellent idea. (June 2016)

I'm not a fan of the show. I've watched it. I think the acting is good, the music is fair, and the issues raised about sexuality and mental illness are a good thing. (June 2016)

I like the show. I don't agree with all the images portrayed in the show, but there are moments they address some hard issues in the black community. Not all of them are handled and addressed well, but many of them shed light on things to an audience that may not otherwise talk about them. (June 2016)

If you give monkeys a stage, they will perform. *Empire* has had the opportunity to reach the masses. Due to its high-profile cast, director/writer, music, and celebrity cast, the viewing audience grows. *Empire* does not teach lessons on black family values nor does it realistically depict what the average black family endures. Yes, that may be the life of Puffy, but even he doesn't display it in the distasteful way *Empire* does. (June 2016)

I believe it is a good show, but its approach is too intense, and it should be paced so there are not so many plot twists happening. (May 2016)

I personally like *Empire*. It is for entertainment, not to learn from. I think some people get reality and fiction mixed up. I think that is why *Empire* is looked down upon. People forget that it is just entertainment. (May 2016)

It is a show that uses stereotypes of African Americans to sell an image to viewers. Although it is fiction, it still paints a picture of who wealthy African Americans are and how they conduct business. People who do not have any interaction with African Americans in this capacity could possibly assume this is how the majority of African Americans behave. (May 2016)

The show is cool, I guess. I personally like music and find interest in the whole music business. So it's intriguing to watch a show that gives you an inside look at how the business side of the music industry works. The characters are fresh and hip and the production is appealing. I feel like some topics are forced on viewers (homosexuality, black lives matter) in an attempt to keep the show relevant. But in all I feel like the show is a good look for the black community because just like *The Cosby Show*, it shows a black family in a social class that's better than what most black families live in reality. They paint the picture of what could be achieved as a black family in America and spread inspiration to all who watch. (May 2016)

I think *Empire* is trash, and it's a ploy to distract blacks from real issues surrounding their reality. (April 2016)

TRASH! Though, I recognize television is just for entertainment, *Empire* is very toxic. (April 2016)

I hate it! (April 2016)

Good entertainment and music but the show lacks a true focus. Is it a fashion show? Celebrity cameo show? Music show, LGBT, black lives matter, hustle show? It needs focus. (April 2016)

Good show, I'm more of a *Power* fan, because I can relate to that TV show more. (April 2016)

I think they deal with a lot of controversial topics that some people are not ready to deal with or discuss which makes some people uncomfortable. At the same time, it's a drama and has the shock value added for a reason which some people also can't deal with. (April 2016)

It is a television program for entertainment. These issues or depictions will go on whether the show existed or not. If the show disgusts a person that much, don't watch. (April 2016)

How much of an impact will *Empire* have on the depiction of blacks in popular culture and the public's perception of the African American community?

I think *Empire* will encourage people who have dreams to fight for them no matter where they come from. Believe it or not, *Empire* does have some good views for helping people that want to be successful. (October 2016)

None, it's just TV. (October 2016)

I just like this drama. As an Asian, I have always admired the influence blacks have on pop culture. (October 2016)

It could have a huge impact on the youth. (October 2016)

This show will have a great impact on public perceptions of blacks. It's a highly rated show, millions of people watch it, and many will watch it with ignorance. (September 2016)

Not that much. *Empire* is the new show that blacks are watching and talking about in the salons/barbershops across America. The show does not have that much of an impact on the depiction of blacks in America. (August 2016)

If other races besides blacks watch it, then it will make others think that all black families are like that. (August 2016)

If the world is ignorant enough to believe that a majority of blacks act and think the ways of the *Empire* cast in this series of the "show," they need to come out of their shells and have a real discussion with God-fearing, hard-working family men, and women, and make a sound decision on the "perception of blacks." (July 2016)

I think media, unfortunately, plays a major role in the perception of blacks. Perception is real and real in its consequences. We are the ones who feel the effects of the consequences, not TV stars. (July 2016)

It has a huge impact. I am an educator and students discuss the show amongst themselves. They watch faithfully even though they may be too young to understand all of the concepts. It plays a big role in their lives, and it is important that we try to represent African Americans in a positive light instead of a negative way. (July 2016)

Not sure because I refuse to watch, but seems that it perpetuates ideas that the dominant culture wants to believe. (July 2016)

Empire will probably support the negative thoughts held by some. I don't know that one television show changes that because one television show didn't start it. Television can show a broad range of white characters without being stereotyped as "representatives" of white culture. But, again, I think *Empire* will certainly reinforce negative stereotypes. (June 2016)

I don't think it will have too much of an impact because I think the characters are being depicted in a fashion in which America already sees blacks in pop culture. (June 2016)

It has a huge impact on the depiction of blacks in pop culture and hip hop. Money, greed, murder, a "by any means" attitude. It represents a depiction of the black culture. We are constantly perpetuating the notion that money rules all things and loyalty is our first virtue. One could assume that being able to obtain wealth and keeping the family together and loyal is a resolve of slavery. *Empire*'s lavish lifestyles, back-stabbing, "corporate rape of the black artist," and continued failed attempts in the current social and political climate of blacks in the United States continues to be disappointing week after week. (June 2016)

I think it has a strong, deep, profound effect on the depiction of blacks. Does it offer them an opportunity to break out of the traditional roles that they are given to play or does it reinforce the stereotype that has played out for decades? (May 2016)

Empire, UNFORTUNATELY, WILL HAVE A PRETTY SIGNIFICANT IMPACT! It is a likeable image to most of the population in America. The LOUD, GHETTO, MAD BLACK WOMAN, who is abusive to her son. The father who is a drug dealer. The majority of the population will take this and generalize to the whole entire ethnic group. (May 2016)

A tremendous amount because Cookie Lyon has become a symbol for black women, either good or bad. The show's overall magnitude is still unknown, but it certainly is real and can't be ignored. (April 2016)

White privilege has always filtered black entertainment through its lenses of respectability. Empire does no more damage than reality TV shows and social media. (April 2016)

Get Woke or Die Tryin': Commerce v. Conscious

A popular phrase being used by Millennials is "stay woke." Generation Xers may remember Lawrence Fishburne's character Dap in the 1988 Spike Lee film *School Daze* shouting "WAKE UP" in the film's dramatic closing scene. Dap was calling on the film's characters and the viewing public to awaken their eyes to the larger world around them and become socially and politically conscious. Dap's message challenged blacks who were more concerned with commerce than conscious; trivial entertainment than responsibility; and acceptance in white America than respect in the African American community. In the aftermath of the Obama presidency, the Black Lives Matter Movement, and the election of President Donald Trump, a growing number of Millennials have awakened. The same can be said of Generation Xers who may have become complacent during the prosperous Clinton years of the 1990s. I mention this because the responses to the survey reflect this growing consciousness. The responses that stood out to me were the following:

"My brothers and sisters of *Empire*, you are being exploited for the "Almighty Dollar."

"*Empire* has zero substance. *Empire* isn't mind stimulating, impactful, or motivational for the African-American culture as a whole."

"TRASH! Though, I recognize television is just for entertainment, *Empire* is very toxic."

"If you give monkeys a stage they will perform."

"Lee Daniels … is celebrated because he consistently exaggerates images that depict the worst of the black community."

"*Empire* has a few socially conscious moments. However, they are outweighed by the negative and contrived efforts to force homosexuality on people."

"It overemphasizes the broken black family epidemic for the purposes of humor."

"These issues or depictions will go on whether the show existed or not. If the show disgusts a person that much, don't watch."

"White privilege has always filtered Black entertainment through its lenses of respectability. *Empire* does no more damage than reality TV shows and social media."

The common theme in many of these highlighted responses is that *Empire* is trash that is misrepresenting the black family, ruining the minds and self-image of black youth, perpetuating racist stereotypes, glorifying crime and dysfunctional behavior, and forcing homosexual lifestyles down our throats. According to some respondents, the series is the opposite of being "woke," which is ironic considering the fact the third season goes out of its way to attach itself to the social consciousness movement. Examples of this include the introduction of a new character, Angelo Dubois, who oversees a youth program called WOKE (We Organize for Knowledge and Empowerment) and a song titled "Woke" by the show's newest character Nessa. Jamal and Nessa's anti-gun violence anthem, "Need Freedom," references the Orlando mass shooting and the deaths of Alton Sterling, Philando Castille, Sandra Bland, Trayvon Martin, and Michael Brown.

The use of the word "monkeys" to describe the black actors in the series is very problematic. You should not call something racist by beginning your argument with historically racist terminology. The remark that the series forces homosexuality on people speaks to a greater hypocrisy in the black community. For years we complained about the lack of black images in Hollywood. We say that it is empowering to see people who look like us and stories that mirror our own. Yet, we have a problem when those images and stories come from the LGBTQ community. While I think some of the other respondents raise very valid arguments, I really appreciate the respondent who raised the issue of respectability. The percent of respondents who cited respectability politics as the cause for the show's dismissal by so many blacks was 56.42. Respectability politics have defined African American behavior and art since the 19th century. The National Association of Colored Women Clubs (NACWC), founded in 1896, adopted the motto "lifting as we climb." The organization preached that women could uplift the African American community and their men through education, community service, and respectable behavior that challenged stereotypes. According to Evelyn Brooks Higginbotham, respectability was not intended to be elitist. When poor black workers put on their Sunday best for protests during the 1950s and 1960s, they were demanding to be respected as human beings. Nonviolent civil rights activists refused to fight back to demonstrate that they were more respectable than their attackers. "Respectability," says Higginbotham, "is about character and one's moral compass."[26] Martin Luther King, Jr., dressed and spoke well to denote the respect that he had for himself. Malcolm X adhered to respectability politics to uplift other black men. "Malcolm X, dressed in a business suit, his tie dangling, one hand parting a window shade, the other holding a rifle. The portrait communicated everything I wanted to be—controlled, intelligent, and beyond fear," says Ta-Nehisi Coates.[27]

In an interview with *For Harriet*, Higginbotham acknowledges that there is a conservative side of respectability politics that demands that individuals live by a set standard of what is considered "appropriate" behavior.[28] Some in the black intelligentsia condemned Paul Robeson for singing Negro spirituals because that music was thought to lack sophistication and class.[29] Alain Locke, former chair of the Department of Philosophy at Howard University and the father of the Harlem Renaissance (1920s-1930s), believed that blacks should use the arts and entertainment for the sole purpose of inspiring social consciousness and uplifting the race.[30] The 1929 film *Hell-Bound*, directed by black directors Eloyce King Patrick and James Gist, warned black audiences that premarital sex, promiscuity, gambling, socializing in pool halls, and drinking alcohol would send them to hell. You had some black elites and intelligentsia who associated respectability with Social Darwinism.[31]

According to historian Kevin Gaines, 19th century black elites developed a racial uplift ideology centered on the collective advancement of the race. However, by the dawn of the 20th century, elites began focusing more on advancing themselves and drawing distinct divisions based on class.[32] This racial uplift ideology inspired the boycotts led by black newspapers and civil rights organizations such as *The Pittsburgh Courier* and the NAACP, respectively, to ban *The Beulah Show* and *The Amos 'n' Andy Show* from radio and television for their exaggeration of uneducated, lower class blacks.[33] Bill Cosby once admitted in an interview that while shows like *Amos 'n' Andy* were fine for blacks to enjoy and laugh at amongst themselves, they were inappropriate to watch in the company of white people.[34] Cosby's statement hints at W.E.B. Du Bois' argument of the double-consciousness of black folk: the notion that black people are always viewing themselves through the gaze of those outside their community.[35]

Respectability politics was one driving force behind criticism of Blaxploitation cinema in the 1970s and the cinematic adaptation of *The Color Purple* in the 1980s. When honorable figures like the Rev. Calvin Butts, pastor of the historic Abyssinian Baptist Church in Harlem, and civil rights leader C. Delores Tucker spoke out against hip-hop. The Reverend Butts went as far as to hold a public demonstration in which he threatened to drive a steamroller over boxes of rap CDs placed on the ground.[36] Mrs. Tucker filed a $10 million lawsuit against the estate of Tupac Shakur claiming that his vile lyrics caused her to suffer emotional distress.[37] When I was a graduate student at Howard University, I heard a black U.S. congressman advising students not to watch *The Wire* because it was nothing but white liberals marginalizing blacks as drug dealers and addicts, welfare recipients, single mothers, and strippers. Back in the introduction, I highlighted the controversy surrounding Lee Daniels' earliest films, *Monster's Ball* (2001) and *Precious* (2009). "Not since 'The Birth of a Nation' has a mainstream movie demeaned the idea of black American life as much as 'Precious,'" wrote Armond White in his critique of the film. "Full of brazenly racist clichés (Precious steals and eats an entire bucket of fried chicken), it is a sociological horror show."[38] Critics have expressed equally scathing assessments of Tyler Perry for his Madea films, television programs, and depiction of black women.[39] Spike Lee has called Perry's work coonery and buffoonery.[40]

According to Michael Eric Dyson, there is a "dirty-laundry theory of racial politics" that exists in the African American community. Anything that makes the race look bad must remain hidden in the secrecy of individual black homes and institutions.[41] James Peterson counters this argument by suggesting that blacks, in past decades, wanted to keep their dirty laundry out of the public's view because they knew that it was added fuel for white supremacists trying to keep the race down.[42] As far back as the Harlem Renaissance distinguished blacks were willing to risk ridicule from white supremacists and black leaders to tell their stories. African American sexuality was often muted in literature and art in this "New Negro" era to combat the stereotype of hyper-sexuality. Langston Hughes, Zora Neal Hurston, Wallace Thurman, and other progressive black writers rejected this ideology, refusing to self-censor their work. Their 1926 magazine, *Fire*, dealt with touchy issues such as the earliest examples of the black underclass, prostitution, and homosexuality. Hughes further addressed this issue of appropriate art work in his essay, "The Negro Artist and the Racial Mountain," published in the June 23, 1926, issue of *The Nation*. Hughes wrote the following statement concerning criticism of Jean Toomer's novel *Cane* about black southern folk culture, black urban life in Washington, D.C., and discord between black northerners and southerners:

> The Negro artist works against an undertow of sharp criticism and misunderstanding from his own group and unintentional bribes from the whites. "Oh, be respectable, write about nice people, show how good we are," say the Negroes. "Be stereotyped, don't go too far, don't shatter our illusions about you, don't amuse us too seriously. We will pay you," say the whites. Both would have told Jean Toomer not to write Cane. The colored people did not praise it. The white people did not buy it. Most of the colored people who did read Cane hated it. They are afraid of it.[43]

Other ethnic groups have experienced similar debates over their representation in popular culture. The HBO series *The Sopranos* has been the named the greatest scripted series in television history by most Hollywood critics. Scholars have written books and taught college courses about the series.[44] The majority of Americans are probably unaware of the firestorm initially surrounding the series. David Chase, the Italian American creator of *The Sopranos*, found himself in the same predicament as Lee Daniels, having to defend his series against charges of racism. Frank Guarini, chairman of the National Italian American Foundation, led a boycott to ban the series from the airwaves because it perpetuated the myth of Italian Americans' association with the Mafia. The Rev. Al Sharpton and the National Ethnic Coalition of Organizations were among the boycott's supporters.[45] During a 2001 C-Span panel on Italian American stereotypes Camila Paglia, a media studies scholar, denounced the series as a "piece of crap" that misrepresented Italians and exaggerated the "psychopathology of urban life."[46] Republican Representative Marge Roukema from New Jersey declared that Americans would be marching in the streets if the show was about African Americans or Latinos.[47]

I do not deny the diversity issues and inherent racism that exist within Hollywood. "Moonlight" (2017), Jay-Z's music video/parody of NBC's *Friends* sitcom, addresses this problem.[48] Todd Boyd, the endowed chair for the Study of Race and Popular Culture at the University of Southern California, points out that *Birth of a Nation* planted the seeds of cultural bias in Hollywood. As a result, racist stereotypes are the norm in the depiction of all minorities: African Americans, Latinos, Asians, Native Americans, and

Muslims. The premium channel Showtime has a poster for its award-winning series *Homeland* (2011–), which portrays the show's protagonist Claire Danes, a beautiful blond white woman, dressed like Little Red Riding Hood standing helplessly in the presence of *scary* Muslim women wearing black burkas.

One major problem is that white executives in Hollywood often do not realize when they are engaging in racist depictions of minorities. On the TNT docuseries, *American Race* (2017), retired NBA superstar Charles Barkley interviewed a white casting director in Los Angeles named Sande Alessi. Alessi does not believe that racism exists in Hollywood. She said that stereotypes are used to cast minorities for roles, but in her eyes, those stereotypes are required to make stories more realistic. Keep in mind that in the film industry the CEOs are 94 percent white and 100 percent male. They decide if black projects get made. The NWA biopic *Straight Outta Compton* (2015) earned $201.6 million at the box office—it only cost $50 million to make— and received an Academy Award nomination for Best Original Screenplay. Nevertheless, Hollywood executives were originally skeptical about making it.[49] Black audiences have repeatedly proved that they will support their products if they are good quality. On television, the CEOs are 96 percent white and 71 percent male. *Variety* reported that for all the new scripted television series for the 2016–17 season 90 percent of the showrunners were white and 80 percent were male. Showrunners are the people who manage the direction of a series. Only two black women were showrunners for the season.[50] Minorities account for just 8 percent of the lead roles in television.[51] Therefore, programs like *Empire*, carry a huge burden to speak for and correctly represent diverse voices within that minority group. Sadly, minority groups such as blacks are still prejudged by media images.

Eric Deggans, a black television critic for National Public Radio (NPR), published one of the earliest articles to question *Empire*'s value to the African American community. "For some, Cookie is the embodiment of all the stereotypes black women face on TV. Dressed flamboyantly in floor-length furs, color-coded nails … she's quick to anger and ready to throw down at a moment's notice," wrote Deggans.[52] Darnell Hunt, the co-author of UCLA's Ralph J. Bunche Center for African American Studies' annual report on TV and film diversity, says that many critics fail to realize that *Empire*'s characters are not one-dimensional. If viewers can look beyond Cookie's attire and attitude they will see a woman who rebuilt her life after 17 years of incarceration. Hunt also points out the fact that *The Cosby Show* was a watershed moment in the portrayal of black families. The Huxtables were placed in an upper middle-class environment as opposed to the disenfranchised ghettos of 1970s black sitcoms. At the same, Hunt says, *The Cosby Show* gave white conservatives an excuse to pretend that racism no longer existed and that the black poor were victims of their own unseized opportunities. Viola Davis once said in a 2013 interview with Oprah (*Oprah's Next Chapter* episode 235) that this emphasis on perfection stifles black artists. "Art is about truth. Art is about what is ugly and human."

Why does *Empire*, a series that is rife with stereotypes, do so much better than a series like *Frank's Place* in terms of Nielsen ratings? *Frank's Place* was a comedy-drama that aired on CBS during the 1987/1988 season. Comedian Tim Reid played an elite black professor at Brown University who became the owner of a black restaurant in New Orleans, Louisiana. The series was noteworthy for its emphasis on black folklore, New Orleans' culture, and its willingness to tackle sensitive topics like the color caste system in the city's black community. *Frank's Place*, which avoided all stereotypes, received an Emmy Award, Golden Globe Award, NAACP Image Award, and a Humanitas Prize for programs that "affirm human dignity and probe the meaning of life."[53] Yet, it was cancelled after only 22 episodes due to low viewership. I could point to CBS's failure to market this show properly, the absence of a laugh track, or the fact that the network changed the show's night and time slot three times. But I also must ask why more black viewers did not tune in or petition the network to keep *Frank's Place* on the air? NBC cancelled *The Carmichael Show*, a critically acclaimed black family sitcom dedicated to addressing social issues, after only three seasons. Certainly, this does not mean that blacks prefer shows with characters that some consider to be less intelligent or unrespectable. The success of *The Cosby* Show, *A Different World*, and *Black-ish* prove such a myth to be untrue. If anything, it could mean that some of those television programs considered "low quality" have more to offer than what appears on the surface and the "high quality" shows may need to do more to reach the masses (without sacrificing their content).

Lee Daniels and Danny Strong heard the criticism of their series. They addressed it on episode 46, "Absent Child," when Mrs. Dubois derides the Lyons as a setback for the (black) race.[54] Does *Empire* have a responsibility to do more than merely entertain audiences and make money? A frequent debate in sports today is that all prominent professional black athletes need to use their platform to address civil rights. In 2016, I published an article on Michael Jordan and social responsibility in *Spectrum: A Journal for Black Men*. There I argued that while I would applaud Jordan if he chose to follow the lead of outspoken athletes, Muhammad Ali and Arthur Ashe, I cannot condemn him if that is not in his heart. Some people are not cut out to be activists. Also, not every famous individual has something substantive to add to a dialogue on race or social issues. In terms of television, every black show does not need to be a platform for activism. At times, I only want to be entertained.

Empire is in an unmistakably unwinnable situation because it has proudly taken on the mantle to be a didactic drama that addresses issues of homophobia, mental illness, mass incarceration, policing, interracial relationships, religion, spirituality, family, gender roles, gun violence, Post-traumatic stress disorder (PTSD), and the illegal drug trade. One of my survey respondents said the show lacks focus because it tries to deal with every problem in the African American community. One of my challenges in writing this book was covering such a multitude of topics. I agree and believe that it would be better for *Empire* to narrow its scope to a few important issues. However, even if Lee Daniels limited the show's focus to a couple of issues some blacks would still complain because he chose to focus on LGBTQ issues and mental illness rather than Black Lives Matter. Others would complain if the focus was Black Lives Matter rather than black-on-black crime. Since *Empire* has chosen to deal with social issues on a weekly basis, its supporters cannot get by with the excuse that it is simply entertainment.

The fact that it is among the highest rated shows on one of the four major networks brings more scrutiny to it than if it was airing on a less watched cable or streaming network. To be sure, the series has some challenges because it appears on FOX. But the format of the series makes it difficult for it to be taken seriously; therefore, critics will always find room to attack it. *Empire* is a hip-hop musical soap opera. If you have watched *All My Children* (1970–2013), *General Hospital* (1963–), *Dallas* (1978–1991), or *Dynasty* (1981–1989), you should have noticed numerous commonalities. The storylines are outrageous, melodramatic, and often involve dysfunctional wealthy families, greed, violence, backstabbing, and sex. Ien Ang says of soap operas: "The most important characteristic is its economic marketability. Aiming at a very broad market means that content must be reduced to universally consumable motifs. This reduction to normal human aspects means that the content is recognizable to a wider audience, but it offers a stereotypical image of reality."[55] *Empire* has all of these elements plus a never-ending soundtrack and musical performances that make it feel more like musical series Glee (2009–2015), *Nashville* (2012–), and *The Get Down* (2016–2017) than a mind stimulating, thought-provoking drama. We should not be surprised if *Empire* repeatedly fails to receive a best drama nomination at the Golden Globes, Primetime Emmys, or Screen Actors Guild Awards.

I teach a university-level course called "Spike Lee's America" which uses Lee's filmography to study issues of race in America. Most of my students dismissed his films *School Daze* (1988) and *Chi-Raq* (2015), which use a musical format and satire to address serious issues that many believe are not laughing matters. They found the music and jokes distracting and unnecessary. *Empire* follows a similar format, which leads me to ask if it can ever be truly impactful. This same format is one reason that *Empire* tops the Nielsen Ratings on Wednesday nights and has earned multi-million-dollar sponsorship deals with Pepsi and the Lincoln Motor Company. For *Empire* to maintain ratings, it must keep this format. Perhaps the music, writing, and storytelling will improve in future seasons, but the format will most likely remain the same. If this continues, the show will never be able to live up to the expectations of the racial uplift ideology proponents. Lucious and Cookie cannot change their criminal backgrounds midway into the series. Andre will always have a bipolar disorder and a deceased white wife. Jamal will always be a proud gay black man. Hakeem may never grow up. The brand of music that the series promotes will always offend some people. Mississippi rapper and political activist David Banner says a lot of hip-hop is guilty of doing the work of white supremacists who tarnish the African American image.[56] Many *Empire* haters would accuse the series of doing just what David Banner despises about parts of the hip-hop industry.

What do I get out of watching *Empire*? I primarily tune into *Empire* to be entertained more than enlightened. Nevertheless, I must admit that the series has made me pay more attention to issues like mental illness, the incarceration of black women, and discrimination against gay black men than previously. As I stated earlier, if *Empire* was so toxic why would someone as highly respected as Phylicia Rashad attach herself to the series? My advice for Lee Daniels and his fellow writers is to go into more depth with their storylines when they are weaving in these social issues. Except for the LGBTQ issues, most of the time the show suffers because it only scratches the surface of the issues. Lucious went to prison for a couple of episodes in season two. The writers could have done more to address the scourge of mass incarceration and the treatment of imprisoned black bodies with those episodes than having a two-minute star-studded benefit concert to free Lucious. Andre gets arrested by two white police officers. He goes to court on the next episode, and then the series moves on. This is also true for Cookie's incarceration and the imprisonment of black women. Shonda Rhimes did more to address the horrors faced by imprisoned women in only a few episodes of *How to Get Away with Murder* than *Empire*'s first three seasons. *Empire*'s writers did a good job correcting this problem in its fourth season. Cookie's relationship with her inmates is a major subplot.

The series has always addressed the Black Lives Matter Movement, but it has never delved deeply into the multiple dimensions of the movement as other series have tried to do. Thus, Black Lives Matter, at times, is reduced to a slogan, a social media hashtag, or a verse in a song rather than something more substantive. The series would also benefit from a more nuanced portrayal of hip-hop rather than overemphasizing the materialistic, hyper-macho image of the culture. Why not have cameos from rappers like Lecrae, J. Cole, Kendrick Lamar and Chance the Rapper, who are actually promoting change with their music, in addition to French Montana and Birdman?

Conclusion

Does Lee Daniels hate black people? Of course not! He has publicly acknowledged his obligation to correctly represent and empower the African-American community. *Empire* does not need to be cancelled because it fails to show blacks in a pristine image. If the presence of a nearly perfect black family in the White House for eight years did not improve race relations or uplift all black people, neither will *Empire*'s cancellation. Yes, *Empire* would benefit from the addition of a few more positive characters. But even those characters would not be realistic for viewers if they were completely flawless. *Empire* is in a no-win situation. Just because I find it entertaining does not mean that I agree with all aspects of the show. I can applaud it for attempting to create change and still critique it for its shortcomings. Fortunately, we are no longer living in a time where we only have one image of blacks on television and other venues of popular culture.

6

The *Empire* Effect
The Revolution Will Be Televised!

For this final section, I discuss what I call "the *Empire* Effect." *Empire*'s success is manifested in the new scripted black programming between June 2015 and June 2018. This television revolution reflects the growing influence of blacks in Hollywood and historic feats in cinema. How do these new series compare and contrast with *Empire*? How do they reflect recent trends in the portrayal of the African American community? What is the overall value of *Empire* and similar programming to race relations in America?

Color by FOX

It did not surprise me to see FOX offer Lee Daniels a lucrative deal to develop more original programing based on *Empire*'s success. His first new series *Star*, debuting on December 14, 2016, follows the lives of two orphaned sisters (one white and the other biracial) and the pampered daughter of a black rock star who escape to Atlanta to follow their musical dreams. While the lead actress is white, most of the cast is African American and Latino. Just as he did with *Empire*, Daniels uses *Star* to tear down walls of injustice and promote tolerance. Transgender model Amiyah Scott, born Arthur Scott, was given a role in the series as Cotton, the daughter of Carlotta Brown (Queen Latifah). Scott preceded Laverne Cox on CBS's *Doubt*, as the first black transgender actress on a broadcast network scripted series.[1] Cross-dressing reality television personality and hairstylist Miss Lawrence was also cast in the series. Scott's character, Cotton, works in Carlotta's hair salon, but also strips and prostitutes on the side for extra money for her transitional surgeries. One of the more poignant episodes of season one features a heart-wrenching scene in which her mother's pastor, Bobby Harris (Tyrese Gibson), performs an exorcism on Cotton to pray the "demon" out of her soul. "I am a man ... say it," he shouts at her.² The incident leads Cotton to put a gun to her head as she contemplates suicide. The American Foundation for Suicide Prevention and Williams Institute reports that 41 percent of transgender individuals attempt suicide at some point in life.³

Star, like *Empire*, is a musical that touches numerous social issues such as rape, drug addiction, religion, domestic violence, policing, and human trafficking. *Star* delves deeper into the Black Lives Matter Movement than *Empire*. After a young mother is murdered by a white police officer, who goes unpunished, the girls sing at a protest rally. A group of outside agitators infiltrates the rally and begins attacking police officers. The rally's organizer, Derek (Quincy Brown), is wrongly arrested when he tries to aid the battered officer. He goes to jail and is forced to contemplate taking a plea deal to avoid a lengthy prison sentence. Derek's dilemma dramatizes famous legal cases involving black males, such as Kalief Browder, who were persuaded to admit to crimes that they did not commit. Thus far *Star* has failed to live up to the lofty expectations of its predecessor. The media unanimously bashed the pilot episode.⁴ Perhaps in an attempt to boost ratings FOX moved *Empire* up one hour and placed *Star* behind it in the 9:00p.m. time slot.

The African American presence has noticeably increased in other new FOX programming geared towards more diverse audiences. *Lethal Weapon*, which debuted on September 21, 2016, before *Empire*'s season three premiere, stars comedian Damon Wayans and has five other black cast members in prominent roles. FOX debuted *24: Legacy*, a new installment of the popular *24* series, following Super Bowl LI between on February 5, 2017. Corey Hawkins, the star of *Straight Outta Compton*, replaced Kiefer Sutherland in the lead role. Hawkins plays Eric Carter, an ex-Army Ranger. Senegalese actress Anna Diop plays his wife Nicole Carter. Other black men and women have minor roles. *Shots Fired*, a racially charged miniseries, staring film star Sanaa Lathan, about the investigation of fictional police shootings in a rural North Carolina community, debuted on March 22, 2017, an hour before *Empire*'s season three spring premiere.

Decoding "The Empire *Effect"*

"The *Empire* Effect" extends beyond FOX. Since June 2015 there has been an explosion of new cutting edge black programming on network television, basic cable, HBO, and the digital streaming service Netflix. I am not suggesting that *Empire* deserves credit for all of these programs. To the contrary, the hit HBO comedy *Insecure* is partly the byproduct of that network's campaign to diversify programming.⁵ FX began developing *Atlanta* in early 2013, although the series was not picked up until October 2015. It debuted a year later. The process to get a new series on air is quite lengthy. In June a proposal for a television pilot, or standalone episode, is pitched to a producer and a studio. Next the studio takes the pilot to a network. Writers are hired to create a script. A casting call takes place to find actors. The average cost for a 30-minute comedy pilot is $2 million. An hour-long drama ranges from $5.5 to $20 million. If the network likes a pilot it will order a full series. Sometimes, a network will order 8–13 episodes without seeing a pilot. *The Last O.G.*, starring Tracey Morgan as an ex-convict returning home after a 15-year sentence for selling crack, was originally ordered by FX in 2016, but ended up airing on TBS in 2018.

I think it is fair to say that *Empire*'s popularity has made networks more eager to have the "hot" new black show or at least cast blacks in leading roles. "When *Empire* hit, executives in Hollywood were openly looking for the next shit," says Irv Gotti, creator of the new BET series *Tales* (2017–). I also think that *Empire*'s success has made it easier for this cutting edge programming to tackle uncomfortable topics on a weekly basis that would either have been avoided or given less emphasis in years past. Keep in mind that minorities account for just 8 percent of the lead roles in television.⁶ Therefore, this "*Empire* Effect" should not be taken lightly. The "*Empire* Effect" may be a 21st century phenomenon, but we have seen such trends in Hollywood before. After the success of *Sanford and Son* in 1972 there was a plethora of television programming targeting black viewers throughout the 1970s. The same was true following the success of *The Cosby Show* in the 1980s. In the 1990s and early 2000s upstart networks UPN and The WB began clamoring to attract younger "urban" black audiences in an attempt to model themselves after FOX which hit it big with *Martin* and *Living Single*.

Many of these new series, debuting between 2015 and 2018, used social media and marketing strategies in a fashion similar to *Empire* to attract viewers. The OWN drama *Greenleaf* used a promotional poster that featured the cast and the caption: "The Kingdom. The Family. The Fall." The poster was almost identical to one of *Empire*'s season one posters featuring the cast and the caption "Music. Family. Power." The FX dramedy *Atlanta* spent months running short teasers featuring Rihanna's song "Same Ol' Mistakes." For *Empire*'s initial advertising campaign FOX ran several teasers during commercial breaks with music from another hip-hop superstar, Kanye West. As previously discussed in the introduction social media has been a contributing factor in *Empire*'s success. Cast members encourage fans to live tweet during episodes and follow them on various social media sites. *Atlanta* built a potent following on social media in its inaugural season. FX posted the pilot episode on Facebook and YouTube. The episode received 1.4 million views on Facebook and another 1 million views on YouTube.

These new series share common themes such as family, gender (especially black women), homophobia, romance, music, class, crime, anti-heroes, and social activism. While some series copy *Empire*'s flaws others excel where it fails, thus providing a broader view of blackness. Although the majority of the programming that I will focus on is scripted dramas and comedies, I want to mention three reality series. BET debuted a new docuseries entitled *Music Moguls* in June 2016 about real life hip-hop moguls Brian "Birdman" Williams, Damon Dash, Jermaine Dupri, and Snoop Dogg. The cable network Bravo premiered *The First Family of Hip Hop* on January 15, 2017. The docuseries focuses on the family of rap music pioneers Sylvia and Joe Robinson, the founders of Sugarhill Records in the late 1970s. Sugarhill released the first rap song to achieve mainstream success, "Rapper's Delight" and gave us rap's first socially conscious anthem, "The Message." Sylvia Robinson, affectionately called the mother of hip-hop, passed away in 2011. Bravo viewers witness the efforts of the Robinsons' son, Leland Robinson, Sr., and his relatives to continue running the business in her absence. As is the case in *Empire* there is a feisty woman who believes that she deserves to wear the crown and run the family enterprise. LeAnetta "LeA" Robinson, is Slvia's granddaughter. The pilot episode was titled "The Empire Strikes Back." Another cable network, WE television, is home to *Growing Up Hip Hop* documenting the lives of the children of hip-hop moguls like Russell Simmons, Rev. Run, and Master P. In the summer of 2017 Facebook began airing *Ball in the Family*. Arguably the closest thing to *Empire*, the series follows an overbearing father's (LaVar Ball) efforts to build his Big Baller Brand (BBB) empire through the basketball exploits of his three sons: Lonzo, LiAngelo, and LaMelo.

The first two scripted series to appear on television following *Empire*'s first season were HBO's *Ballers* and NBC's *The Carmichael Show* in the summer of 2015. Unlike the majority of these new series that I will discuss *Ballers* is written, directed, and produced solely by whites. Mark Wahlberg, the executive producer of previous HBO hits *Entourage* (2004–2011) and *Boardwalk Empire* (2010–2014), produces *Ballers*. The show's creator Stephen Levinson does his best to attract black audiences and younger white males who enjoy sports and hip-hop. The term "ballers" is a slang expression for the nouveau riche made popular in 1990s rap songs. The opening theme song is "Right Above It" performed by Lil Wayne and Drake. *Ballers* stars Dwayne "The Rock" Johnson, as Spencer Strasmore, a retired NFL player for the Miami

Dolphins turned financial consultant to star athletes. The Rock is biracial and most of the cast members are African American. John David Washington, son of Denzel Washington, plays the cocky wide receiver Ricky Jerret, who exhibits all of the stereotypical traits of young black athletes. He spends his money on Lamborghinis, name brand luxury sneakers, jewelry, and extravagant vacations. Ricky enjoys "making it rain" at the strip club and has a "fun room" in his mansion for his lewd sexual escapades.[7] There is Reggie (London Brown), the best friend and assistant of Dallas Cowboys' Vernon Littlefield (Donovan W. Carter), who drives a $400,000 Rolls Royce despite not having a personal checking account or health insurance. Vernon blows his money on foreign sports cars and lavish lobster dinners with his large entourage of friends and family. Although *Ballers* occasionally grapples with serious topics like the absence of Ricky's father for much of his life, most episodes lack meaningful substance. I blame the absence of black screenwriters and producers for these marginal portrayals of black men, which end up being little more than simplistic caricatures of black masculinity.

The Carmichael Show (2015–2017) fares much better than *Ballers*. Unlike the Huxtable-like Johnson family on ABC's *Black-ish* and the absurdly dysfunctional Lyons on *Empire,* the Carmichaels are your average middle-class black family. The mother, Cynthia (Loretta Devine), is deeply religious. The father, Joe (David Alan Grier), is politically incorrect, old fashioned, and set in his ways. He is a modern day Archie Bunker who proudly voted for Donald Trump. He does have an adult child out of wedlock, but that is not revealed until season three. The family's youngest son Jerrod (Jerrod Carmichael) is a progressive thinker who sees the world through a very cynical lens. He lives with his biracial girlfriend Maxine (Amber Stevens West). Maxine is a graduate student who is always trying to impose her liberal and feminist views on Jerrod's family. Jerrod's older brother Bobby (Milton "Lil Rel" Howery) is a simple-minded underachiever still living with his estranged wife Nakeisha (Tiffany Haddish). Although *The Carmichael Show* follows a traditional format for family sitcoms dating back to 1960s, it succeeds in handling race and other social issues in a nuanced manner missing from network television sitcoms with the exception of *Black-ish*. Viewers are privy to uncomfortable conversations found in black households on topics ranging from questioning the value of Black Lives Matter protests to the appropriateness of watching *The Cosby Show* reruns despite Bill Cosby's rape scandal. Other topics ranging from gun control, depression, euthanasia and atheism to Islamophobia, patriotism, rape, the N-Word, stripping, and transgender lifestyles are also debated.

We Are Family

The Carmichael Show is a breath of fresh air that does not try to emulate Empire in any way. Well, there are two exceptions. On its third episode, titled "Kale," Joe tells the family that he will choose a son to lead the family in the advent of his death. "I watch TV. Dad's trying to Empire us," says Bobby.[8] On another episode Bobby suggests that his dying grandmother watch Empire before she passes away from suicidal overdosing. Perhaps the lack of similarities contributed to its lower viewership and cancellation. The series was averaging just 2.25 million viewers at the end of its sophomore season compared to Empire's 9 to 10 million. One new series that has successfully modeled itself after Empire is Greenleaf, the first of two poignant dramas to premiere on the Oprah Winfrey Network (OWN) between June and September 2016. Labeled by the Los Angeles Times as "Empire in choir robes," Greenleaf focuses on the first family of the fictional Greenleaf World Ministries in Memphis. Greenleaf is written, directed, and produced by Craig Wright, who is white, but co-produced by Oprah and Clement Virgo. Virgo is a Jamaican born Canadian black filmmaker and screenwriter, best known for his work on the Peabody Award nominated BET miniseries The Book of Negroes (2015). In the public's eye the Greenleaf family appears to be fighting sin's hold on mankind, but they are really engaged in an inner struggle to tear down Satan's kingdom in their own home. They are religious in public but "ratchet" in private. Bishop James Greenleaf (David Craig) is being audited by the FBI on suspicion of misappropriating the church's funds. The Bishop's Roundtable is for all church members who donate $10,000 or more above their tithes. One has to wonder if these donations are being used for the church's "building fund" or the family's private jet. During the season two premiere viewers learn that Bishop, when he was a young man, ordered his right hand man to burn down his old church in an attempt to collect insurance to pay off debts and purchase a larger building. Unbeknownst to the Bishop at the time the church's caretaker, Darryl James, died in the fire. The man's son grew up to become the Bishop's arch nemesis, the shady Pastor Basie Skanks (Jason Dirden).

The 60-year-old Bishop is hiding early stages of Parkinson's disease from the church. Empire's patriarch, Lucious, is also fighting health problems. As the Bishop's health deteriorates his wife, Lady Mae (Lynn Whitfield), takes on a larger role at church and home. Lady Mae proudly mirrors the traditional role of the elitist wife as her husband's charming accessory. Yet, this is only an act to mask her true personality. In the words of Lynn Whitfield, Lady Mae is "the queen of her kingdom.... Each episode you get a little bit more of who she is and the tenacity with which she is determined to hold onto the family and its legacy."⁹ Family legacy is just as vital for *Empire*'s Cookie. Lady Mae fires the choir director because his same-sex marriage is provoking the church trustees to stop paying their tithes. Her insistence upon keeping up appearances contributed to the molestation and suicide of her daughter Faith. Lady Mae's complicit silence and feigned ignorance surrounding Faith's tragic demise even as she preaches the crucial necessity of the virtuous woman mark her as a sanctimonious fraud. Her estranged, alcoholic sister Mavis McCready (Oprah) despises her for allowing their brother, Robert "Uncle Mac" McCready (Gregory Alan Williams), an incestuous pedophile, to rape Faith during her teenage years. Mac, the bishop's right hand man and Memphis's man of the year, has raped and molested multiple teenage girls from the church. One of his victims had an abortion and was given church scholarship money to keep her quiet. Upon learning the news of Mac's wrongdoings the Bishop shoots him in his church office. Mac is jailed temporarily then returns to his old habits until the bishop's eldest daughter Grace (Merle Dandridge) fatally stabs him in self-defense.

Grace Greenleaf returned home after 20 years with her teenage daughter Sophia (Desiree Ross), whom she conceived out of wedlock by a white man, to investigate the death of her sister. Faith apparently was a drug addict and prostitute before her death. Grace, a gifted preacher, has sex with her engaged ex-boyfriend Noah (Benjamin Patterson) days before his wedding. The bishop's youngest daughter Charity (Deborah Joy Winans) is preparing to have twins with her husband Kevin (Tye White) who is a closeted homosexual addicted to online gay pornography. The danger of gay anonymity is grimly present in the moment of Kevin's agonizing revelation to Charity of his desire for men. Overwhelmed by Kevin's confession of his noxious charade, Charity hits and shoves him grief-stricken and baffled; but in her raging attempt to drive him away she falls. The fall results in the death of one of her twins. Charity puts Kevin out of the house, forcing him to stay at a hotel for months. He joins a Christian counseling group that encourages him to take a dose of what appears to be an herbal mixture whenever he feels the urge to look at other men. Yet his efforts to win Charity back prove unfruitful and they end up in divorce court. Unable to cure himself Kevin decides to disappear rather than risk shame from family and church members.

The bishop's only son, Jacob (Lamman Rucker), undergoes marital counseling with his wife, Kerissa (Kim Hawthorne), for his infidelity. On the pilot episode Jacob has sex with the bishop's white executive assistant in a church office as 4,000 worshipers are assembled in the sanctuary for Sunday service. Jacob, also a pastor, views the church as an expansionist entrepreneurial enterprise rather than a source of salvation. Jacob believes that he is entitled to be his father's heir apparent in the ministry; however, the bishop favors Jacob's sister Grace. The bishop's refusal to advance Jacob's career causes him to take a position at Pastor Basie Skanks' mega church, Triumph. Meanwhile, Jacob's teenage daughter Zora (Lovie Simone) is secretly experimenting with drugs and having sex with a famous teenage gospel music singer.

Greenleaf is *Empire* minus the drug dealers, gangsters, and melodramatic storylines. The coarse language, violence, gay love scenes, and raunchy behavior that is overflowing on *Empire* each week is toned down. Gospel musical performances replace the rap and pop music. The Greenleafs' classy demeanor contrasts boldly with the gravity of their breakdown and deceit which likely makes the series easier for some blacks to stomach. Bishop Greenleaf has deployed unscrupulous means to build his empire, but he is not a gangster in the same vein as Lucious. Lady Mae is more devious than Cookie, lacks her loving maternal skills, and treats both of her daughters with contempt. But the fact that she is not a formerly convicted drug dealer with ostentatious attire and a foul mouth makes her more acceptable for some in the African American community. Nevertheless, as gospel musician Erica Campbell from the duo Mary Mary told *The Tom Joyner Morning Show* in a 2016 interview, many black Christians will find the negative depictions of the church off-putting.[10] A minister, also sensing an undercurrent of cynical intent, told me she refuses to watch *Greenleaf* because it "glorifies myths" about black preachers, their churches, and their families.

Greenleaf shines a spotlight on issues never before explored in such depth on scripted television (or in cinema). These issues include the financial aspect of church politics, sexism and homophobia in the African American church, pedophilia, incest, and other interpersonal problems that Christians wrestle with in their private lives. Prior to *Greenleaf* the only popular television programming about black Christians was the family friendly sitcom *Amen* (1986–1991), the controversial *Preachers of L.A.* (2013–2014) reality show, and Bounce TV's salacious drama *Saints & Sinners* (2016–). Much of *Greenleaf*'s narrative reads like pages from Jonathan Walton's *Watch This! The Ethics and Aesthetics of Black Televangelism*. Walton's 2009 study on black megachurch televangelists T.D. Jakes, Creflo Dollar, and others manifests many of the same examples of worship style and the extravagant lifestyles found in the OWN drama.[11] Walton devotes a chapter to the late Bishop Eddie Long who was involved in a steamy sex scandal. Bishop Long's past homophobic remarks rival those of Lucious and explain why men like Bishop Greenleaf's son-in-law Kevin live in perpetual mental anguish that can bring horrendous detriment to themselves as well as others.

For its sophomore season, in the spring of 2017, *Greenleaf* began airing an hour after *Empire* on Wednesdays, making Wednesdays the new unofficial night for black programming. *Black-ish* aired over on ABC in between these two programs. *Shots Fired* aired on FOX right before *Empire*. When all of these programs went on summer break NBC ran new episodes of *The Carmichael Show* from 9 until 10 p.m. This show was proceeded by *Little Big Shots: Forever Young* (2017–) hosted by Steve Harvey.

As OWN fans watched the first season of *Greenleaf* over the summer of 2016 they could not avoid the frequent ads for OWN's next hit scripted prime-time drama *Queen Sugar*, debuting in the fall. Based on the novel *Queen Sugar* by Natalie Baszile, the adaptation follows the efforts of three young adult siblings (Charley, Nova, and Ralph Angel Bordelon) to save their father Earnest's (Glynn Turman) 800-acre sugarcane farm in rural Louisiana following his unexpected death. The sisters Charley and Nova have a volatile relationship which stems partly from their having different mothers. Charlotte "Charley" Bordelon (Dawn-Lyen Gardner) is viewed by Nova (Rutina Wesley) as the stuck-up sibling who turned her back on the family. Charley lives in a lavish Los Angeles mansion with her NBA superstar husband Davis West (Timon Kyle Durrett) and their 15-year-old son Micah (Nicholas L. Ashe). Charley, who manages Davis's career for a living, has her world rocked to the core after he is accused of participating in a gang rape of a younger Latina escort at a hotel. Upon learning the shocking news on her cell phone in the midst of a televised game Charley leaves her front row seats to accost him on the middle of the court. I had a debate with a group of highly educated black women about the realism of Charley's action. They all agreed that her action was not only realistic, but symbolic of the anger experienced by countless black women confronted by the revelation of their spouses' infidelity. In their opinion Charley was standing up for all black women suffering in silence and out of the camera's lens. Besides her marital woes Charley's son Micah is expelled from his prestigious private school after a picture of a penis appears on his white girlfriend's cell phone.

Charley's return to the farm after her father's death brings up several issues within the family. First there is a class divide between Charley and her less fortunate relatives. She disagrees with her Aunt Violet (Tina Lifford), the designated family matriarch following her father's death, over sending Micah to a predominantly white high school in Louisiana with a $36,000 annual tuition. Aunt Vi believes that Micah can receive a fine education at a less expensive school and earn a scholarship to nearby Tulane University. But Charley is obsessed with sending Micah to Harvard or Stanford so that he can have a better lifestyle than his relatives in Louisiana. She views her family with disdain for not doing better with their lives. Her family and friends in Louisiana question her views on the American Dream and living by mainstream (white) standards. This class issue within the black family has consistently been an important theme of *Empire*. Andre's Ivy League pedigree and his white wife Rhonda make him a black sheep in the Lyon family. Andre becomes aware of his blackness after becoming a victim of racial profiling after Rhonda's death. He even begins dating a dark skinned black woman with a natural hairstyle. *Queen Sugar* follows the same trajectory. In the midst of his father's scandal and his time in Louisiana, Micah gains an appreciation for southern black culture and the Black Lives Matter Movement, learns about racial bias, and begins dating a dark skinned black girl named Stella (True O'Brien) from the local public high school. On the season two premiere Micah, like Andre, is wrongfully arrested and harassed by a racist white police officer. The officer pulled him over for speeding in an expensive car that his father bought for his birthday. Unlike Andre, who chooses to begin acting like a stereotypical thug in the face of racial injustice, Micah becomes further aware of his complex reality as a young black man in America. His newfound sense of activism causes him to get suspended from his new school for speaking out against Confederate symbols displayed proudly on the campus.

Colorism is never directly discussed in the first season of *Queen Sugar*, but it is clearly evident. Charley, whose mother is a white woman from California, Micah, and her husband Davis are light skinned. They live in the big city and have a glamorous life at the start of the series. Charley becomes the first black woman to own a sugar mill in Louisiana. The rest of the family members, with the exception of Ralph Angel's son and his son's mother, are darker skinned. This harkens back to slavery and the early Jim Crow era when the blacks with fair complexion routinely had better opportunities for education, employment, and mainstream acceptance because their appearance was closer to whites. Critics of *Empire* have pointed out the fact that all of the Lyon family members have a fair complexion. Until the introduction of Taye Diggs' character, Angelo Dubois, in season three all of the regular dark skinned actors (Ta'Rhonda Jones, Derek Luke, Gabourey Sidibe, and Malik Yoba) played roles of often-disrespected assistants to the Lyons and were given little opportunity to develop their own voice. Cookie's darker sister Carol (Tasha Smith) is a working class single mother and recovering crack addict. Lucious' former dark skinned assistant Becky must constantly acquiesce to others and overcome rejection on her way up the corporate ladder.

Back on *Queen Sugar*, Charley's siblings have their own set of issues shaping their personal lives. Nova is an herbal healer and socially conscious journalist who writes about the racially biased corruption in the New Orleans' police department and the local justice system. She speaks on panels with scholars. Her public image as a socially conscious activist belies her private lifestyle as a distributor of illegal marijuana from her home. Nova is also engaging in an affair with a married white police officer named Calvin (Greg Vaughan) on the same force that she is investigating. After the affair ends she jumps into a romantic relationship with Chantal (Reagan Gomez-Preston), a lesbian activist in the Black Lives Matter Movement. *Queen Sugar* does not place the same scrutiny on Nova's sexual preference as *Empire* and *Greenleaf* do with Jamal and Kevin. Charley has a bigger problem with Nova's selling drugs and sleeping with a married man, given her own marital issues, than she does seeing her with a female partner. In season two Nova meets a potential love interest named Robert DuBois (Alimi Ballard) which mirrors Cookie's season three love interest Angelo Dubois in some ways.

Charley and Nova's younger brother Ralph Angel (Kofi Siriboe), like *Empire*'s Cookie in season one, is adjusting to life after prison. But he does not have a multi-million dollar company waiting for him upon his release. He robs a store at gunpoint in the opening minutes of the first episode to acquire some money. Charley did him no favors while he was incarcerated for four years. Ralph Angel finds it hypocritical that Nova makes it her personal mission to fight for the rights of a local teen who has been wrongly imprisoned, since she did nothing to help him. Throughout season one Ralph Angel struggles to find steady work, prove his manhood, stay out of trouble, raise his sexually uncertain son Blue (Ethan Hutchinson) who is bullied by classmates for playing with dolls, and reconcile with Blue's mother Darla (Bianca Lawson), a recovering drug addict.

Ralph Angel is in a constant fight to prove to the domineering women in his family that he deserves their respect and trust in his ability to manage the farm. He breaks down in tears on the season one finale because he is tired of being sick and tired. The world is constantly beating him down. He tries to get a legitimate job only to learn that his manager wants him to commit crimes. Ralph Angel cannot fulfill the slightest of fatherly duties such as signing a permission slip for Blue to go on a school field trip to the zoo. He must fight with his Aunt Vi to convince her to sign over Blue's legal guardianship rights. Ralph Angel is in a similar predicament as the Lyon sons: he wants to be treated like a man. Although this series is female-centered, Ralph Angel offers one of television's best three-dimensional characterizations of black manhood to date. He proves that a heterosexual black man can be strong yet emotional. The father-son relationships between him and his late father, and Ralph Angel and Blue are based on love and friendship, not the contempt or rivalry found in *Empire*. This is never more evident than on the season one finale when we learn that Ralph Angel's father left the farm to him in his will. And again in season two when he defends Blue's right to play with dolls rather than toys deemed to be more gender appropriate. His love for Blue remains steadfast even after learning the shocking news that he is not the biological father.

Queen Sugar was created, produced, and directed by the brilliant African American filmmaker Ava DuVernay. DuVernay has shifted the paradigm in filmmaking with her beautifully crafted films *Selma* (2014) and *13th* (2016), and by hiring only women of color to direct the episodes of *Queen Sugar*'s first season. This primetime drama explores issues of family, gender, race, mental illness, therapy, rape, and mass incarceration. The ordeal of Too Sweet, the teen that Nova is helping, might be another nod to Kalief Browder, a 16-year-old black New York City high school student wrongly accused of robbery and left to rot away in Rikers Island for three years awaiting trial. DuVernay covers Browder's story in her documentary *13th* about mass incarceration.

The mistreatment of migrant field workers is another topic in *Queen Sugar*. There is great irony in the fact that the Bordelon family hires undocumented Spanish workers to toil day and night on their land. On episode nine, "Next to Nothing," two workers die in a tropical storm because Charley refuses to let them go home for safety. Charley finds their dead bodies on her property after the storm passes. Her treatment of her workers is reminiscent of the white plantation owners and overseers who overworked their poor black laborers working in the fields two centuries ago. Nova once compared the family's business to slavery. She says the black bodies in the sugarcane fields have now been replaced by brown bodies. Another brilliant addition to the narrative, besides the mistreatment of migrant workers, was the emphasis on the historical exploitation of African American farmers. On the tenth episode, "So Far," viewers learn that the two wealthy white families, the Bourdreaux and the Landrys, are trying to buy the Bordelon's land for $4 million. As it turns out these families previously owned the land and the Bordelon family during slavery. After the Bourdreaux/Landry clan met financial hardship they sold a significant portion of acres to the newly freed Bordelons. Years later the Bourdreaux/Landry clan tried to reclaim their land by lynching members of the Bordelon family. The discrimination experienced by these generations of black farmers is a new subject on primetime television. *Queen Sugar* follows *Empire*'s pattern of presenting its audience with numerous topics from multifaceted perspectives. One of the characters is also struggling with bipolar disorder. But the OWN series lacks the frenetic paced storytelling that caused *Empire* to lose viewers in its second season. Since this is not a soap opera it also does not try to be funny, salacious, or overly melodramatic to attract a wider audience. *Queen Sugar* is a traditional drama that unfolds slowly like a well-written piece of literature.

The Curious Case of the Black Millennial

Queen Sugar gives a voice to black life in the rural South. This can also be said of the FX comedy *Atlanta*, the highest acclaimed of all these post *Empire* programs. Since its debut on September 6, 2016, *Atlanta* has become an instant cult classic for black Millennials winning a 2017 Golden Globe Award and Primetime Emmy for best television comedy series. *Atlanta*'s Donald Glover won a 2017 Golden Globe Award for best actor in a comedy series. Every Thursday night viewers are given a mini tour of the African American experience in "The A." Arguably the most insightful comedy on television, since Aaron McGruder's *The Boondocks* (2005–2014), *Atlanta* blends intellectually stimulating satire with Atlanta trap music to provide a nuanced coming of age tale of southern black manhood.[12] Only Showtime's acclaimed drama *The Chi* (2018–), about life in the South Side of Chicago, rivals *Atlanta*'s coming of age narrative.

Atlanta follows the life of Earnest "Earn" Marks (Glover), a homeless Princeton University dropout who is so broke that he has to order from the kid's menu at the fast food restaurant. In a desperate attempt to provide for his ex-girlfriend Vanessa "Van" (Zazie Beetz) and their baby daughter, he becomes the manager for his cousin, rapper Alfred "Paper Boi" Miles (Brian Tyree Henry). Donald Glover's canny use of dark comedy allows his series to address many of the same controversial subject matter explored in *Empire*. On the second episode, "Go for Broke," Earn is arrested for the first time, an unfortunate rite of passage for many young black males, after Paper Boi shoots another black man outside a nightclub for side swiping his car window. Earn encounters an array of eccentric characters during his Alice in Wonderland-like adventure to the county jail. He meets a gentleman badmouthing his friend Grady for getting him arrested. The laughs come from the fact that Grady is sitting right in front of him the entire time. Next, Earn witnesses a man dressed in a hospital robe dancing around the room. He overhears one of the prisoners say that the dancer is a regular at the jail. Earn remarks that the man needs to be receiving therapy in a mental hospital not sitting in jail. The other men, waiting to be processed before they are sent to a cell, find humor in watching his odd behavior, which includes drinking from a paper cup filled with toilet water. They could not care less about the poor man's mental state. Their amusement abruptly turns to shock after a white correctional officer beats the man with his nightstick for spitting in his face. As the officers carry the man away his screams grow louder and louder. The scene not so subtly alludes to the absence of discussions about mental health amongst black men.

Later in his visit Earn finds himself sitting between two distant lovers catching up on old times. What makes this scene interesting is the fact that the man doing most of the flirting does not realize that his ex-girlfriend is a transvestite. Earn just awkwardly sits there trying to avoid making eye contact with either of the men. The conversation disgusts the other men in the holding area. "This nigga gay as hell," shouts out one of the onlookers.[13] The young man is clearly embarrassed and tries to defend his manhood by pretending that he did not realize he was being duped. "I ain't on that faggot shit," he says in an exaggerated bass voice. He goes on to rebuke the other men for supposedly engaging in homosexual activity during their time in jail. One of the men counters his criticism by differentiating between gay sex in jail and openly embracing it by choice outside of jail. Earn tries to help him feel less shamed by telling him "sexuality is a spectrum."[14] Such conversation between black men about the parameters of sexuality is seldom heard on television, except for shows like *Empire*.

On the season one finale, "The Jacket," Earn loses his jacket one night partying with Paper Boi and their friend Darius (LaKeith Stanfield). Earn spends the next day, on a *Hangover*-like attempt to retrace the steps he and his wolf pack made the night before, searching for his jacket. Along the way he meets a stripper in her early twenties looking to better herself by becoming a rap music video vixen. He witnesses a group of police officers gun down a young man, in front of his girlfriend and child, during a drug bust. Instead of being concerned about the man that was shot, Earn asks the cops if he can check the pockets of the jacket that their victim is wearing to see if it contains a key to a temporary place at which he plans to sleep later that night. The scene highlights the importance that Earn places on that room key and how desensitized many black Millennials have become to gratuitous violence and police shootings. Professor Salamishah Tillet says shows like *Atlanta* highlight the vulnerability and downward mobility of today's black middle class. The Ivy League educated Earn, who is jobless and homeless, is too concerned with finding a place to lay his head to be traumatized by this potentially unjust act of violence.[15]

In the ninth episode, "Juneteenth," Van makes Earn accompany her to a private party celebrating the annual commemoration of Juneteenth, the day that African Americans learned of their emancipation in 1865. The party is held at a mansion owned by Monique Allen, a pretentious black woman unhappily married to a wealthy white optometrist named Craig. Monique looks down on her black kitchen attendants and valet parkers. In his attempt to tackle his white guilt, Craig unknowingly transforms himself into a walking version of the white Negro. He tries very hard to act knowledgeable of and empathetic towards the African American experience but it amounts to little more than appropriation. He quotes Malcolm X, performs asinine spoken word pieces about "Negro" suffering, paints a portrait of a black man slaying a hawk, and hangs pictures on the wall of his pilgrimages to Africa. The awkward exchange between Craig and Earn is close to the scene from the popular film *Get Out* (2017), in which a young black man meets his white girlfriend's *liberal* father for the first time.

The Juneteenth partygoers consist of Jack and Jill club members, an eccentric playwright, a megachurch pastor, and fancy women resembling extras from *The Real Housewives of Potomac* (2016–). Earn and Van pretend to be a happily married buppie couple to fit in at the high saditty affair.[16] After Monique learns that Earn is Paper Boi's manager, she scoffs at the thought of rap being a serious career path. When Craig, the *expert* on underground hip-hop mix tapes, mentions that Paper Boi's arrest was all over the news, Monique sarcastically asks Earn if he plans to shoot up her party. This hilarious episode provides a thought provoking assessment of class differences within the African American community. Earn and Van exhibit the same feeling of discomfort as Cookie when she initially encounters the elite Dubois family and their friends.

Atlanta is an excellent case study in why blacks need to tell their own stories. Throughout the early portion of the first season Earn is the stereotypical absentee black father that Chris Rock makes fun of for wanting credit because he occasionally takes care of his kids.[17] Earn turns Paper Boi's couch and his parents' spare bedroom into his temporary shelter when Van is unwilling to let him crash at her place. Paper Boi sells drugs, smokes marijuana daily, lives with his eccentric unemployed best friend Darius, polishes his guns, calls women out of their name, and settles his problems with violence. Paper Boi is the embodiment of the "thugged-out" masculine performance that *Empire*'s Hakeem unsuccessfully tried to mimic early on. FX, a sister network of FOX, is not a premium channel, but it has few restrictions on what it allows. As a result, weed smoking, the use of the N-word, and strong profanity are common in *Atlanta*.

In the hands of white scriptwriters *Atlanta* could potentially suffer the fate of *Ballers*. But this does not happen thanks to Donald Glover. The 33-year-old Glover is a budding movie star, standup comedian, the former writer for the NBC sitcom *30 Rock*, and a Grammy nominated alternative hip-hop artist who goes by the moniker Childish Gambino. All but two of *Atlanta*'s ten episodes in its first season were written by him or his younger brother Stephen. The Glover brothers add an authentic touch to their storylines that highlights Atlanta's rich culture while allowing their characters to develop as multifaceted men and women. *Atlanta,* much like *Empire,* succeeds in humanizing stereotypes. *Atlanta,* however, does not present the glamourous side of the hip-hop industry found in *Empire.* Glover chose to emphasize the unsexy lifestyle of an underground rap artist, with one foot still in the streets, as he begrudgingly attempts to gain mainstream acceptance. Earn's pragmatic management style and understated demeanor is the perfect antithesis to the over the top maneuvers of Lucious and Cookie.

If *Atlanta* is the black Millennial male's answer to the unrealistic thugs, ballers, and hustlers in popular culture, then HBO's *Insecure* is the black Millennial woman's counter to Cookie and the other black superwomen in primetime. *Insecure,* created by Jo-Issa "Issa" Rae Diop and Larry Wilmore, debuted on HBO on October 9, 2016.[18] This is the first scripted HBO series to have an all-black cast and black screenwriters. It is based on Issa Rae's YouTube series *The Mis-Adventures of Awkward Black Girl* (2011–2013). In the summer of 2017 it joined HBO's Sunday night lineup, airing after *Game of Thrones* and *Ballers.* The series centers around two successful black women in their early thirties living in Los Angeles. Issa Dee and her best friend Molly Carter navigate their professional and personal lives. Considering the fact that HBO is a premium network consisting of mostly upper middle-class white subscribers, *Insecure* provides an eye-opening look at what it means to be an unmarried, college educated black woman, with a good job, in the 21st century. Viewers see how these two beautiful dark skinned women routinely engage in code switching when they are around their white colleagues versus their black friends. As the only black employees at their jobs they must go out of their way to avoid all stereotypically black behavior. Yet they listen to hip-hop and engage in the dozens when they are with their black friends. Issa Dee is not loud and sassy like Cookie. She does not carry a gun in her designer purse, never went to prison, or sold crack. She does not run her own record label. She does not fix everybody's problems while wearing Gucci like *Scandal*'s Olivia Pope. Nor is she a devious Ivy League educated attorney or celebrity reporter like Annalise Keating or Mary Jane Paul. Issa is representative of the women who do not fit superheroine criteria and walk through town like Beyoncé proudly chanting, "I woke up like this."[19]

Insecure is "Must See TV" for the majority of black women that I know under the age of 40. They see a bit of themselves in its characters and storylines. This is one of the few television series that depicts black women as close friends instead of rivals. Kellee Terrell writes in *Vogue:*

> Reality series like *The Real Housewives of Atlanta* and *Love & Hip Hop* show black women throwing shade (and Champagne bottles) at one another. *Scandal, How to Get Away with Murder,* and *Empire* all have amazing and complicated black female leads with meaty roles and interesting plot twists—but seemingly no black girlfriends. (I often wonder how Olivia survives all that White House drama without having anyone to decompress with over a glass of Cabernet and to be like, "Girl, let me tell you what these crazy white people did at work today." I know I couldn't.)[20]

Terrell's point is in line with Katrina McDonald's assessment of black women in her book *Embracing Sisterhood*. McDonald says that the concept of sisterhood for black women grew out of a reaction to racism and sexism. Once some women were able to advance to a higher social class that fragile bond of sisterhood broke. Thus, you get the petty divisions between women like Cookie, Anika, and Mrs. Dubois on *Empire*. Furthermore, the bitter rivalries among black women on *Empire* mirror real-life issues. Gabrielle Union made headlines by admitting in a 2013 *Essence* magazine speech that she rooted against other successful black women in Hollywood, took joy at their setbacks, and tap danced on their misery.

But not everyone loves *Insecure*. In her review journalist Maiysha Kai accused *Insecure* of preying on black women's insecurities for laughs and perpetuating the trope of the successful black women as incapable of finding a husband.[21] The show's protagonist Issa Dee is unhappy with her boyfriend Lawrence's (Jay Ellis) lack of steady employment and perceived lack of ambition throughout much of the debut season. Lawrence, a bright Georgetown University graduate, has an entry-level job at Best Buy. His situation, while not as dire as *Atlanta*'s Earn, still speaks to financial struggles facing black Millennials. The second season revolves around Issa's life as a newly single woman following her breakup with Lawrence. Issa's best friend Molly (Yvonne Orji) has to search dating websites to find a mate. After being dumped she finds herself having to contemplate being lonely or settling for another guy who did not attend college and might be bi-sexual. In her review of *Insecure* Tillet credits the series for addressing this perceived trope. Tillet references the book *Inequalities of Love: College-Educated Black Women and the Barriers to Romance and Family* by Averil Y. Clarke, which argues that "black women's class aspirations are more likely to be unfulfilled than white women, their femininity and sense of value more likely to feel under assault."[22]

Insecure, in contrast to *Empire,* provides young college educated black women a character with whom they may have more in common. It shows white viewers, lacking significant interaction with black people, that all black women are not as naturally fabulous as Cookie. All are not unbreakable forces unto themselves. *Insecure* shines light on the various challenges faced by young professional black women. When Molly tells her girlfriends that she must stop dating this guy named Jared (Langston Kerman) because he admitted to having one homosexual encounter, which automatically makes him gay in her mind, they ask if she ever kissed a woman. Molly says yes, but she is not bi-sexual because it is okay for women to have such casual encounters. Issa challenges Molly's double standard and asserts that Jared is simply refusing to "subscribe to the heteronormative rejection of sexual fluidity." Her Friend Kelli (Natasha Rothwell) jokes, "So it's like straight, straight, straight, straight, Lee Daniels."[23] The scene is captivating because it points back to the argument that I made in Chapter 4. Issa and her girlfriends, like Cookie, do not project the perfect image of feminists or womanists. Some might call them postfeminists who are more concerned with their individual struggle for happiness.[24] The third episode of *Insecure*'s sophomore season, "Hella Open," is all about Molly teaching Issa to be "a hoe" (promiscuous). Molly has sex with her married male friend. In fact, it is unclear if they want these labels. They are too busy making their way in the world to carry a feminist flag. The same is true of the millennial women on Netflix's *Dear White Pople* and *She's Gotta Have It*.

Super Heroes and Wonder Women

Luke Cage debuted on September 16, 2016, on the online video streaming service Netflix. The new series began airing a few months after the first season of the channel's hip-hop musical series *The Get Down*. *Luke Cage* is an adaptation of the 1972 Marvel comic book series of the same name. The comic book was published at the height of the Blaxploitation Cinema era and Donald Goines' street literature craze. The character Luke Cage was a perfect bookend to John Shaft, Kenyatta, Slaughter, Black Belt Jones, and the other black superheroes of the decade. Luke Cage, also known as Power Man, was the fourth comic hero of African American descent behind Marvel's Black Panther (1966) and Falcon (1969), and DC Comics Green Lantern John Stewart (1971). Adilifi Nama, in his 2011 book *Super Black: American Pop Culture and Black Superheroes*, discusses the influence of the black prison reform movement, highlighted by the Free Angela Davis Movement and the writings of Eldridge Cleaver (*Soul on Ice*) and George L. Jackson (*Soledad Brother: The Prison Letters of George Jackson*) on the comic's narrative.[25]

The Netflix series was created by Cheo Hodari Coker, a black music journalist and screenwriter best known for creating *Notorious*, the 2009 biopic of The Notorious B.I.G. Coker infuses a heavy dosage of 1990s hip-hop into the soundtrack. Michael Colter plays Carl Lucas, a Chicago police officer wrongfully incarcerated for months at Seagate, a private prison in Georgia. Seagate is controlled by racist guards who force the inmates to engage in arena style fighting. After Luke is nearly beaten to death by two fellow inmates the prison doctor conducts an illegal scientific experiment to save his life. The experiment not only prevents his death, but it gives him supernatural strength and bulletproof skin. He changes his name from Carl Lucas to Luke Cage. Back in Harlem he takes up work sweeping the floors of Pop's barbershop. Henry Hunter, better known as Pop (Frankie Faison), is a reformed gangster and ex-convict, who, after serving ten years in prison, is now dedicated to uplifting his community and keeping other young men positively engaged. Pop is always encouraging Luke to do something positive with his superpowers, but Luke refuses to heed his advice. "Forward never backwards" is Pop's famous mantra. After Pop is murdered by Cottonmouth's goons Luke is forced into action.

Cornel "Cottonmouth" Stokes (*Moonlight*'s Academy Award winning actor, Mahershala Ali) is Marvel's version of Lucious Lyon.[26] Cottonmouth is a talented musician turned ruthless gangster. He appears before the public attired in dapper three-piece suits. He prefers to be called Mr. Stokes rather than by his street moniker. His nightclub, Harlem's Paradise, is the hottest black owned late-night establishment in the city. Glitzy partygoers fill the club to drink, dance, and enjoy live performances by R&B, Neo Soul, funk, and Hip-Hop artists such as Raphael Saaidiq, Faith Evans, Charles Bradley, and Jidenna. But all this glitz masks Mr. Stokes' real profession as an outlaw. He stashes his illegal gun shipments at a private location named after Crispus Attucks, a free black man and the first person to die in the American Revolution. Cottonmouth has been involved in the underworld since Mama Mabel, the former head of Harlem's black underworld, introduced him to the game. On the pilot episode Cottonmouth beats a young man to death with his fists, getting blood all over his crisp white dress shirt. A large portrait of the Notorious B.I.G. wearing a crooked gold crown upon his head hangs above the wall in his office where the fatal beating takes place. (Lucious has a similar portrait of himself hanging in his office.) Cottonmouth believes that his deviant lifestyle is symbolic of what his ancestors fought for: respect, self-determination, and power. His pursuit of the American Dream by any means necessary is identical to that of Lucious.'

Alfre Woodard (who portrays Cookie's mother on *Empire*) plays Cottonmouth's cousin Mariah, a councilwoman preaching black power, and halting gentrification. Mariah raised Cottonmouth and has been a surrogate big sister to him from the time he was a very young kid. Cottonmouth wished to pursue a musical career, but was forced into selling drugs as a teenager by Mama Mabel. His illegal earnings from gun smuggling help to fund many of Mariah's affordable housing initiatives for the poor residents in the projects. After Cottonmouth accuses Mariah of welcoming her Uncle Pete's molestation when she was a teenager, an uncontrollable rage consumes her causing Mariah to push him through a window and beat him to death with a stanchion. Mariah is corrupted and begins working for Harlem's most feared gangster Willis Stryker, better known as Diamondback. Diamondback (Erik LaRay Harvey) is Luke's jealous half-brother, the product of their preacher father's affair with a woman at his church. Luke and Diamondback's modern-day Cain and Abel narrative is similar to that of Lucious and his half-brother Tariq. Mariah helps Diamondback frame Luke for the murders of Cottonmouth and a white police officer. Although the NYPD and City Hall cast him as an outlaw, Luke becomes an anti-hero for Harlem's black residents.

Ellen McGirt, a writer for *Fortune* magazine, hailed the series as "part of a new, quiet revolution in entertainment."[27] Lawrence Ware, a writer for *The Root*, named Cage "a bulletproof black man in the Black Lives Matter era."[28] Just like *Empire* and the other previously mentioned programs, *Luke Cage* proudly embraces its blackness. It does not present a fairytale postracial world. Luke often wears a hoodie, which some believe honors the memory of the slain teenager Trayvon Martin. On episode twelve, "Soliloquy of Chaos," Wu Tang Clan Member Method Man tells hip-hop radio personality Sway Calloway that there is "something powerful about seeing a black man that is bulletproof and unafraid."[29] During an episode of ESPN's *The Undefeated* "All Day" podcast Jill Hudson remarked to her co-host Clinton Yates that her pre-teenage son asked her if a black man has to be bulletproof and immortal just to walk down the street these days wearing a hoodie.

Luke Cage may have some of the stereotypical features of *Empire*, but it also makes it a habit to provide brief lessons in African American history. Crispus Attucks, Adam Clayton Powell, Jr., Shirley Chisholm, Madam C.J. Walker, Bill Russell, the Harlem Renaissance, and literary icons Zora Neal Hurston, Langston Hughes, and Chester Himes are just some historical topics. On the second episode Luke gives a teenage black male attempting to rob him at gun point a passionate lecture on the self-destructive use of the N-word before snatching the gun from his hand. Other episodes address colorism, rape, education, black manhood, the illegal drug trade, police brutality, racial profiling, and the prison industrial complex. The series not only pays homage to ole school rap legends, it shows love to a variety of black musical genres: soul, rhythm and blues, and neo-soul. The live musical performances found in *Empire* resurface on *Luke Cage* at Harlem's Paradise.

Luke Cage has its own version of strong wonder women of color. Mariah is a powerful business-minded woman who benefits and suffers from her ties to bad men. Detective Misty Knight (Simone Missick) has superpowers that allow her to look back into the past and see what happened at crime scenes. On *Empire*, we see Cookie out trash talking and out drinking with a group of wannabe thugs to sign an artist. On *Luke Cage* Misty out plays a young man on the basketball court, in front of all his friends, in order to get him to cooperate with the police. She is adept at handling a gun and using her fists in a fight. Misty, working undercover at Cottonmouth's nightclub, has a one-night stand with Luke before learning of his true identity. She finds herself in a similar predicament as Cookie, having feelings for a man that she cannot be with. Misty comes in second place to a Puerto Rican woman named Claire Temple (Rosario Dawson) for Luke's affection. Claire is a night nurse who treats Luke's wounds and assists him in fighting Diamondback.

Many of these new series build upon the narrative of powerful black women and divas like Cookie Lyon. VH1's *The Breaks*, BET's *The Quad*, CW's *Black Lightning*, TV One's *Media*, and TNT's *Claws* focus on powerful women. VH1 debuted an original film in 2016 about the rap industry during the Golden Age of hip-hop in New York City called *The Breaks*, which became a primetime series in February 2017. *The Breaks*, produced by iconic hip-hop producer DJ Premier, is based on the book *The Big Payback: The History of the Business of Hip-Hop* written by Dan Charnas, a former writer for hip-hop's first magazine, *The Source*. Afton Williamson plays Nikki Jones, the new executive assistant to Barry Fouray (Wood Harris). Nikki is a younger, college educated, unmarried version of Cookie making her way in the music business. She is not glamorous like the *Empire* diva, but she exhibits the same hustle and determination. Nikki will do whatever it takes to achieve her goals, from throwing a drink in her future boss's face to force him to interview her; tracking down an intoxicated rapper to make him get back in the studio; or helping an outed gay artist come to grips with his sexuality and keep from committing suicide. Over the course of the first season Nikki gets fired from Fouray's new music label, begins working for a rival label, gets an offer to come back to Fouray as the head of the Artists and Repertoire (A&R) department, and eventually decides to partner with an older Jewish record producer to establish her own label.

The BET series *The Quad* (2017–) began as a made-for-television film. Tony Award-winning actress Anika Noni Rose plays Dr. Eva Fletcher, the new president of the fictional HBCU Georgia A&M University. The 43-year-old Ivy League educated, married mother of a college age daughter looks more like a model than the typical university president. Her jaw dropping looks and rogue attitude get her in trouble. She is trying to end an affair with an obsessed male graduate student who is nearly 20 years younger than her. She is guilty of paying the student a larger than usual stipend as hush money. Eva, like Cookie, is an anti-hero willing to take unconventional measures to achieve her goals. For example, she forms a business partnership with a wealthy alumnus/strip club owner to secure the millions needed to keep the school afloat and provide her job security.[30] Eva's confident attitude puts her at odds with the school's male administrators who are uncomfortable with taking orders from a woman. Unlike Cookie, she is outspoken on issues affecting women. After a video goes viral of her daughter Sydney (Jazz Raycole) being raped by the football team's star quarterback, Eva makes it her mission to fight rape culture on the campus. The CW's *Black Lightning*, created by Mara Brock Akil, is an adaptation of the 1970s DC Comic book series. *Black Lightning* presents some of television's most ground breaking black female character. Nafessa Williams plays Anissa Pierce, a medical school student, Black Lives Matter activist, and part-time high school teacher. She is the daughter of the vigilante superhero Black Lightning. When she learns of her superpowers she becomes Thunder. Thunder is television's first black queer superheroine. Her younger sister is also a crime fighter and her mother is a brilliant neuroscientist.

Media, loosely based on Radio One and TV One founder Cathy Hughes, debuted as a made-for-television film on TV One on February 25, 2017. At the completion of this book reports stated that the network was planning to expand the film into a weekly primetime soap opera. *Media*, or *Empire* by another name, is a glossy soap opera dealing with a wealthy family in the entertainment industry. Ironically, TV One was the first network to air *Empire* in syndication, beginning in the summer of 2016. *Media* has a stylish, good-looking cast and cameos by music celebrities. Themes of family, greed, violence, sex, and power run throughout the narrative. Following in the tradition of *Dallas* and *Empire* you have two warring wealthy families, the Jones and the Randolphs. Jackie Jones (Penny Johnson Jerald) is the CEO and founder of Jones Universal Media Properties (JUMP), the world's largest urban media conglomerate. Jackie, like Cookie, will do anything to protect her throne and her family's legacy. She has three adult sons and one adult daughter. All her children play a role in the family business except for her eldest son Michael (Brian White), a prosecutor. Michael, riding the momentum of convicting the city's biggest mobster, is running for mayor. Jackie also resembles Lucious in her cutthroat tactics to maintain power. She secretly plots the murder of her irascible son Clay (Marion "Pooch" Hall, Jr.) after he becomes a liability to her business. Michael is forced to assume control of JUMP while dealing with Clay's death and a growing violent rivalry with the wealthy Randolph family.

Media not only continues the trend of putting strong black mothers at the forefront, it presents multifaceted portrayals of upper class black men. Brotherly love among both sets of families is a major underlying theme as it is in *Empire*. Michael's youngest brother Anthony (Blue Kimble), reminiscent of the Lyon sons, is in a constant struggle to prove his worth to the family business. His hard-partying ways and use of drugs as a coping mechanism land him in rehab. Michael, like Andre, is the most responsible and best-educated sibling. He has a wife, but his marriage also dissolves. In the Randolph family Jabbar (Gary Dourdan) and his younger brother Will (Stephen Bishop) have a falling out over Jabbar's gangster-like business practices and Will's secret marriage to Michael's younger sister Crystal Jones (Chrystee Pharris). *Media* shares many of the same flaws about which *Empire* is criticized. Once again you have a familiar narrative of wealthy dysfunctional black families. Colorism is worse in *Media* than in *Empire*. All members of the Jones and Randolph families are fair-skinned. The two dark-skinned female characters are portrayed as whores, untrustworthy, emotionally unstable, or violent. The two dark-skinned male characters in the film are ignorant, inarticulate, sexually deviant, or thuggish.

The TNT dramedy *Claws* debuted on June 11, 2017. Niecy Nash was cast in the lead role as Desna Simms, a feisty nail salon owner in Palmetto, Florida, where she serves as the queen mother to her ladies—Jen (Jenn Lyon), Polly (Carrie Preston), Quiet Ann (Judy Reyes) and Virginia (Karrueche Tran). Her crew consists of two ex-convicts, a stripper/escort, a lesbian, and the wife of an aspiring gangster. She has overcome a crack addicted mother, absentee father, and abusive white foster parents. She began her craft designing the nails of dancers in a strip club. The show's producer, Rashida Jones, describes Desna as fiercely loyal and protective. "She is a badass. She is a mobster. She is a lover," says Jones.[31] Desna, like Cookie, is a woman who has had her dreams broken repeatedly. Both women often find themselves underappreciated by the men in their lives who refuse to acknowledge the vital role that they play in their fortunes. Desna has spent the past years helping to run a money laundering scheme and drugs out of a health clinic for her white boyfriend Roller (Jack Kesy), who tries way too hard to act *stereotypically* black, and his boss Clay, better known as Uncle Daddy (Dean Norris). Uncle Daddy is a strip club owner and the head of a local crime syndicate called the Dixie Mafia. Roller is his top earner and henchman. Desna's plan is to take the $20,000 that Roller and Uncle Daddy owe her for taking all the risks to escape the criminal underworld, open a state of the art nail salon, and buy a new home for her autistic brother Dean (Harold Perrineau).

Desna is a politically incorrect, gun packing diva with an eye for high-end fashion. The majority of her wardrobe accentuates her large breasts and butt. Like Cookie, she finds herself in predicaments where she must break the rules to survive. When Roller refuses to get her the money he promised she attempts to drown him in the swimming pool of his mansion. He overpowers her and begins punching her profusely in the face. Fortunately, Desna's new employee Virginia, a 29-year-old former stripper who is sleeping with Roller behind her back, comes to her rescue and shoots him. The two women put his body on a boat and set it on fire. Desna now must outsmart gangsters searching for Roller's killer, befriend and mother his trifling mistress, hustle to get her girls out of Uncle Daddy's money laundering racket, care for her mentally ill brother Dean, and grow her nail empire from the ground up. Along the way she orders the murder of her foster parents for molesting Dean when they were children. She begins dating a sophisticated doctor from Haiti who initially appears to be out of her league. Aspects of their relationship resemble that of Cookie and Angelo. Desna, like Cookie, is a complex figure that you want to root for even though you may detest several aspects of her character. In an article for *Madamenoir* Niecy Nash talks about the importance of roles like hers that focus on black ownership and powerful black women. While Desna is not an ideal role model, she is indicative of evolving images of black womanhood on television.

The Big Payback

What I find revolutionary about much of this new programming is the impact it is having on Hollywood and popular culture. Audiences are given the opportunity to see a kaleidoscope of black images from all walks of life and witness the changing realities of their communities. While these characters have experiences that are unique to black folk, they are no less relatable to the general public. You do not have to be black to deal with mental illness, rape, homophobia, spirituality, career development, or family drama. Moreover, this renaissance in black programming is providing new opportunities for black directors, producers, screenwriters, show runners, costume designers, musicians, grips, and publicists. Blacks have a level of power, not seen in previous decades, because they have control over every aspect of their series. All these advancements on television come at a time in which blacks are also making history in cinema with critically acclaimed films: Marvel's

Black Panther, Detroit, *Fences*, *Get Out*, *Girl's* Trip, Hidden *Figures*, *I Am Not Your Negro*, and *Moonlight*. *Hidden Figures* and *Get Out* each grossed over $150 million at the box office. *Get Out* (2017), one of the few successful mainstream horror films to be directed by a black man, earned a 99 percent fresh rating on Rotten Tomatoes and received an Academy Award nomination for Best Picture in 2017. *Hidden Figures*, starring Taraji P. Henson as the lead actress, won the Screen Actors Guild Award for outstanding performance by a cast in a motion picture. The 2017 Academy Awards ceremony featured three black films nominated for best picture, six black actors nominated for awards, one nomination for best director and nominations for cinematography and editing.[32] *Moonlight* won the Oscar for Best Picture and Best Adapted Screenplay. *Moonlight*'s actors also won or were nominated for multiple awards. Ezra Edelman's documentary film *O.J.: Made in America* beat out two other films also directed by blacks in the category for Best Documentary Film. *Girls Trip* (2017), an R-rated comedy about black women, earned over $100 million in its first three weeks. *Girls Trip* was directed, written and produced by black men. Marvel's *Black Panther* shattered records grossing over $1 billion globally in four weeks. With its unapologetic embrace of African culture and black excellence *Black Panther* is a paradigm shift. Call it the Wakanda Effect. Perhaps polarizing images of blacks in film and television will soon become outdated.

In closing, *Empire* has a complicated legacy. It has been a godsend for FOX by boosting the network's overall ratings for the 18-to-40-year-old demographic. The series has elevated the careers of Lee Daniels, Taraji P. Henson, and Terrence Howard. It has made lesser-known actors household names. It has placed veteran black celebrities back in the forefront and introduced them to a new generation. While building on other past and present pop cultural examples it has offered nuanced multifaceted representations of blackness. *Empire* has initiated much needed dialogue on various issues within the African American community, yet it has been a source of an intense, dismissive scrutiny in black homes, classrooms, churches, and on social media. Some of the ridicule is justified; however, much of it is cloaked in respectability politics.

Empire's greatest contribution to popular culture and African American history is the revolution that its success has sparked in scripted television. In a matter of two years television has seen an astonishing increase in the variety of black programming available to audiences. While none of these shows is perfect each presents different aspects of the overall African American experience and proves that blackness is not a monolith. I can watch *Empire* and say, "yeah, I recognize that as part of black life." But I can watch

Queen Sugar and say, "I recognize that, too." I suppose that their success will lead to further programming and job opportunities for blacks over the next few years. Hopefully this new programming will not only entertain the masses, but will also contribute to the healing of race relations in America. The country is so divided right now. This is magnified by incidents like the tragic 2017 white nationalist rally in Charlottesville, Virginia, and protests over the playing of the national anthem in sports.[33] Most Americans who are not living in black households do not fully grasp the role that race plays in partisan politics, the judicial system, the economy, and the media. In this anxious political age, television and other mediums of popular culture, such as cinema and music, will be more vital than ever in shaping attitudes and the ability of Americans to coexist despite their differences.

Chapter Notes

Preface

1. Rorke, "How 'Empire' Changed Primetime Diversity for the Better." *New York Post*. October 29, 2015. http://nypost.com/2015/10/29/how-empire-changed-prime-time-diversity-for-the-better/. Accessed on November 29, 2016.

2. *Generations* (1989–1991) was the first American daytime soap opera to have an entirely multi-racial cast and African Americans in prominent roles.

3. Browne is a former Professor Emeritus at Bowling Green State University (BGSU) and the founder of the academic study of popular culture in the United States. He also founded the Popular Culture Association, the American Culture Association, the *Journal of Popular Culture*, and the *Journal of American Culture*.

Introduction

1. Episode no. 16, first broadcast October 14, 2015 by FOX. Directed and written by Daniel Strong. "G" is short for "gangster," while "OG" means "original."

2. Gray, *Watching Race: Television and the Struggle for Blackness* (Minneapolis: University of Minnesota Press, 1995), 9.

3. *Ibid.*, 8.

4. Green, "'Birth of A Race': The Obscure Demise Of A Would-Be Rebuttal To Racism." *NPR*. October 25, 2015. http://www.npr.org/2015/10/25/451717690/birth-of-a-race-the-obscure-demise-of-a-would-be-rebuttal-to-racism. Accessed on November 24, 2016.

5. Bogle, *Toms, Coons, Mulattoes, Mammies, and Bucks: An Interpretive History of Blacks in American Films*. 4th Edition (New York: Bloomsbury Academic, 2001), 102–103.

6. Butters, *Black Manhood on the Silent Screen* (Lawrence: University of Kansas Press, 2002).

7. Gray White, Mia Bay, and Waldo E. Martin Jr. *Freedom on My Mind: A History of African Americans with Documents,* Vol. 2: Since 1865 (New York: Bedford/St. Martin's, 2012), 510.

8. *Ibid.*, 512.

9. Perry's stage name Stepin Fetchit was derived from a race horse named Step and Fetch It.

10. July 7, 1951, Gloster B. Current, director of the NAACP Branch and Field Services, sent a memorandum to all members of the executive committee and advisory board notifying them that the annual convention had voted to condemn *Amos 'n' Andy* along with *The Beulah Show* for negatively depicting black men and women.

11. Ralph Ellison, "Change the Joke and Slip the Yoke," in *Shadow and Act* (New York: Random House, 1972), 48.

12. *Amos 'n' Andy: Anatomy of a Controversy*, DVD, directed by Stanley Sheff, 2008; New York, NY: Scott Entertainment, 1983.

13. Kiuchi, *Struggles for Equal Voice: The History of African American Media Democracy* (Albany: State University of New York Press, 2013), 28–29.

14. script from an episode of *Good Times* archived at The Browne Popular Culture Library at Bowling Green State University in Bowling Green, Ohio, has the transcript of an episode about the growing concern over heroin use in poor black communities.

15. Acham, *Revolution Televised: Prime Time and the Struggle for Black Power* (Minneapolis: University of Minnesota Press, 2005), 93.

16. Paterniti, "Norman Lear: The Comedy Godfather of Television." *GQ*. May 24, 2017. http://www.gq.com/story/norman-lear-the-comedy-godfather-of-television (Accessed on May 30, 2017).

17. *Ibid.*, 89.

18. *Ibid.*, 67.

19. May 28, 1999, the *Los Angeles Times* reported that none of the 26 new sitcoms in the

upcoming fall television lineup on the 4 major networks had African American actors in leading roles.

20. Taylor and Austen, 188.

21. Accessed on October 28, 2015. http://www.biography.com/people/lee-daniels-516876#career-in-healthcare.

22. Birnbaum, "Remote Controlled: Lee Daniels on 'Star,' 'Empire' and the Mistakes He Regrets." *Variety*. December 15, 2016. Accessed on December 20, 2016. http://variety.com/2016/tv/news/remote-controlled-lee-daniels-empire-star-roseanne-1201943597/.

23. Wickham, "Bassett Criticism Has Its Merits." *USA Today*. July 8, 2002. Assessed on December 1, 2015. http://usatoday30.usatoday.com/news/comment/columnists/wickham/2002-07-09-wickham.htm.

24. Mary Pols, "Precious Review: Too Powerful for Tears." *Time*. November 16, 2009. Accessed on December 20, 2016. http://content.time.com/time/magazine/article/0,9171,1935116,00.html.

25. F. Smith, "Does Hollywood Still Have a Brown Paper Bag Test?" *The Root*. November 12, 2009. Accessed on January 19, 2016. http://www.theroot.com/articles/culture/2009/11/all_the_darkskinned_stars_in_precious_are_bad_all_the_lightskinned_stars_in_precious_are_good/.

26. Louis Gates, Jr., and Cornel West, *The Future of the Race* (New York: Vintage, 1997).

27. Cummings-Yeates, "Runaway Hit Show 'Empire' Upholds Light-Skin Vs. Dark-Skin Power Divide." *AlterNet*. March 21, 2015. Accessed on June 13, 2016. http://www.alternet.org/media/runaway-hit-show-empire-upholds-light-skin-vs-dark-skin-power-divide.

28. Lauren Duca, "How Doyle From 'Gilmore Girls' Came Up With The Idea For 'Empire.'" *The Huffington Post*. January 10, 2015. Accessed on December 20, 2016.http://www.huffingtonpost.com/2015/06/10/danny-strong-doyle-empire_n_7542820.html.

29. Espinoza, "Diddy and Jay Z Lead Forbes List' Wealthiest Hip-Hop Artists of 2017 List." *Complex*. May 10, 2017. Accessed on May 14, 2017. http://www.complex.com/music/2017/05/forbes-releases-list-of-wealthiest-hip-hop-artists-2017.

30. Bradley, *Shakespearean Tragedy: Lectures on Hamlet, Othello, King Lear, and Macbeth* (London: Penguin, 1991), 235.

31. Feuer, "Melodrama, Serial Form and Television Today." *Screen*. Volume 25, Issue 1. January-February 1984. 4–17.

32. Geraghty, *Women and Soap Opera* (Cambridge, MA: Polity Press, 1991), 43–52; Tania Modleski, *Loving with a Vengeance: Mass Produced Fantasies for Women* (New York: Routledge, 2007), 102.

33. Ang, *Watching "Dallas": Soap Opera and the Melodramatic Imagination* (New York: Routledge, 1986), 41–42.

34. *Ibid.*, 34 and 41.

35. *Ibid.*, 93.

36. Brian Grazer: "'Empire' Is 'Better Than Any Other Success I've Had.'" *The Huffington Post*. April 16, 2015. Accessed on December 20, 2016. http://www.huffingtonpost.com/2015/04/16/empire-producer-brian-grazer-success_n_7073336.html.

37. L. Datcher, "Chicago's Talent Behind 'Empire.'" *Chicago Defender*. October 3, 2015. Accessed on June 16, 2016. http://newpittsburghcourieronline.com/2015/10/03/chicagos-talent-behind-empire/.

38. Robinson, "Catch Up with Timbaland, the Man Behind *Empire*'s Infectious Beats." *Vanity Fair*. April 2015. Accessed on June 20, 2016. http://www.vanityfair.com/magazine/2015/03/timbaland-empire-music.

39. Ben Dandridge-Lemco, "Timbaland Leaves *Empire* TV Series Rodney "Darkchild" Jerkins and Ester Dean have joined Fox's Hit Show." *The Fader*. September 14, 2016. Accessed on October 19, 2016. http://www.thefader.com/2016/09/14/timbaland-exits-empire-season-3-darkchild.

40. Eddie Roche, "Meet Empire's Costume Designer Paolo Dieddu." November 19, 2015. Accessed on December 21, 2016. https://fashionweekdaily.com/meet-empires-costume-designer-paolo-nieddu/.

41. Fawnia Soo Hoo, "How the 'Empire' Costume Designer is Dressing the Lyon Family in Season 2." *Fashionista*. September 16, 2015. Accessed on December 21, 2016. http://fashionista.com/2015/09/empire-costumes-paolo-nieddu.

42. Kristina Rodulfo, "Soon Your Face Can Be Obsessed With 'Empire' Too. Thank you, Covergirl!" *Elle*. March 22, 2016. Accessed on May 1, 2016. http://www.elle.com/beauty/makeup-skin-care/news/a35033/covergirl-empire-collaboration/.

43. Steve Baron, "Wednesday Final Ratings: 'Arrow' & 'Survivor' Adjusted Up; 'Supernatural' Adjusted Down & Final 'Empire' Numbers." March 19, 2015. Accessed on June 19, 2016. http://tvbythenumbers.zap2it.com/2015/03/19/wednesday-final-ratings-arrow-supernatural-adjusted-down-final-empire-numbers/377077/.

44. "Why Can't We Stop Watching 'Empire'?" *The New York Times Magazine*. March 18, 2015.

Accessed on April 1, 2015. http://www.nytimes.com/2015/03/18/magazine/why-cant-we-stop-watching-empire.html?_r=0.

45. Jason Lynch. "How Fox's Marketing Fanned the Flames of Empire, One of the Biggest New Shows in Years. The Strategy Behind a Breakout Hit." *Adweek*. January 29, 2015. Accessed on June 19, 2016. http://www.adweek.com/news/television/how-foxs-marketing-fanned-flames-empire-one-biggest-new-shows-years-162612.

46. *Ibid*.

47. Cynthia Littlejohn, "TV One Grabs 'Empire' Reruns from Fox." *Variety*. April 13, 2016. Accessed on June 18, 2016. http://variety.com/2016/tv/news/empire-tv-one-fox-rerun-rights-1201753238/.

48. Lorenza Munoz, "The Hollywood Gospel According to Tyler Perry." *Los Angeles Times*. February 19, 2006. http://articles.latimes.com/2006/feb/19/business/fi-tylerperry19. Accessed on June 20, 2016.

49. Cory Barker, "Is 'Empire' in Trouble?" *Complex*. November 13, 2015. http://www.complex.com/pop-culture/2015/11/empire-ratings-decline. Accessed on June 20, 2016.

50. *Ibid*.

51. Alice Fuller, "What Fox's 'Empire' Teaches Us About Social Media Marketing." April 1, 2015. http://sheersocial.com/what-foxs-empire-teaches-us-about-social-media-marketing/#.V03kPvkrKM8. Accessed on June 17, 2016. A hashtag is a type of label or metadata tag used on social network and microblogging services that makes it easier for users to find messages with a specific theme or content.

52. #SayHerName is a gender-inclusive racial justice movement that campaigns against police brutality and anti-black violence against black women in the United States.

53. "Young, Connected and Black" *Nielsen*. October 17, 2016. Accessed by December 22, 2016. http://www.nielsen.com/us/en/insights/reports/2016/young-connected-and-black.html.

54. Lisa Fraser, "Beyond Black Twitter: Black Millennials Rule the Internet." *Black Enterprise*. October 22, 2016. Accessed on December 22, 2016. http://www.blackenterprise.com/news/black-Millennials-powerful-rule-internet/.

55. Donovan X. Ramsey, "The Truth About Black Twitter." *The Atlantic*. April 10, 2015. Accessed on December 22, 2016. http://www.theatlantic.com/technology/archive/2015/04/the-truth-about-black-twitter/390120/

56. Marc Silver, "How 'Empire' Became Social Media's Most Talked-About TV Show." *The Washington Post*. October 26, 2016. Accessed on December 22, 2016. https://www.washingtonpost.com/express/wp/2016/10/26/how-empire-became-social-medias-most-talked-about-tv-show/?utm_term=.d860f458fc91.

57. Tanya Gazdik, "African American Buying Power Tops $1 Trillion." *MarketingDaily*. October 3, 2016. Accessed on December 30, 2016. http://www.mediapost.com/publications/article/285767/african-american-buying-power-tops-1-trillion.html.

58. Eriq Gardner, "Fox Gets to Keep 'Empire' Series Title After Beating Hip-Hop Record Label in Court." *Hollywood Reporter*. February 3, 2016. Accessed on June 20, 2016. http://www.hollywoodreporter.com/thr-esq/fox-gets-keep-empire-series-861607.

59. Kevin Fallon, "The 'Real' Cookie Lyon Sues 'Empire' For $300 Million, Claiming Fox Series Is Based on Her Life." *The Daily Beast*. August 4, 2015. Accessed on June 20, 2016. http://www.thedailybeast.com/articles/2015/08/04/the-real-cookie-lyons-sues-empire-for-300-million-claiming-fox-series-is-based-on-her-life.html.

60. Janet Stilson, "How Lee Daniels Drew on His Own Life to Shape Empire, TV's Surprise Hit." *ADWEEK*. May 18, 2015. Accessed on June 30, 2015. http://www.adweek.com/news/television/how-lee-daniels-drew-his-own-life-shape-empire-tvs-surprise-hit-164824.

61. *Ibid*.

62. A TV One documentary series about actors, films, and television shows that were hot but never reached their full potential.

Chapter 1

1. *Empire*, "Rise by Sin." Episode no. 29. Directed by Paul McCrane and written by Ayanna Floyd Davis and Jamie Rosengard. FOX, May 11, 2016.

2. African Americans who lost their biological kinfolk during slavery to sale or migration often created new family connections by embracing nonrelatives as fictive kin.

3. "The Lakewood Story: History, Traditions, and Values." Accessed on June 21, 2016. http://www.lakewoodcity.org/about/history/history/default.asp.

4. David Goldfield, Carl Abbott, Virginia DeJohn Anderson, Jo Anne Argersinger, Peter Argersinger, and William Barney. *The American Journey: A History of the United States* (Boston: Pearson, 2017), 786.

5. Eric Foner and John A. Garraty, *The Reader's Companion to American History* (New

York: Houghton Mifflin Harcourt Publishing Company, 1991).

6. Jennifer M. Fogel, "In Contemporary Television Series." (Ph.D. diss., The University of Michigan, 2012).

7. The white residents of Levittown were interviewed in 1957 by Professor Dan W. Dodson, director of the Center for Human Relations and Community Studies at New York University. Interviewees expressed mixed opinions on the prospect of black families moving into their neighborhoods.

8. Chris Gladora, "History: Housing Policy and Segregation in Baltimore." Summer 2006 Issue I. Accessed on November 18, 2015. https://indyreader.org/content/history-housing-policy-and-segregation-baltimore.

9. Tammy L. Brown, "An Interview with James Amos," in African *Americans on Television: Race-ing for Ratings*, ed. David J. Leonard and Lisa A. Guerrero (Santa Barbara, CA: Praeger, 2013), 39.

10. Donald Bogle, *Toms, Coons, Mulattoes, Mammies, and Bucks: An Interpretive History of Blacks in American Films*. 4th Edition (New York: Bloomsbury Academic, 2001), 200.

11. Howard University Commencement Address delivered by Lyndon B. Johnson on June 4, 1965. Accessed on June 21, 2016. http://www.c-span.org/video/?326895–1/president-lyndon-b-johnson-commencement-address-howard-university.

12. E. Franklin Frazier, *The Negro Family in the United States* (New York: The Dryden Press, 1951), 103.

13. Herbert Gutman, *The Black Family in Slavery and Freedom, 1750–1925* (New York: Vintage, 1977).

14. Daniel P. Moynihan, *The Negro Family: The Case for National Action*. Washington, D.C., Office of Policy Planning and Research, U.S. Department of Labor, 1965.

15. Ulf Hannerz, "What Ghetto Males Are Like: Another Look," in *Afro American Anthropology: Contemporary Perspectives*, ed. Norman E. Whitten, Jr. (New York: The Free Press, 1970), 313.

16. William Ryan, *Blaming the Victim* (New York: Pantheon, 1971).

17. Andrew Billingsley, *Black Families in White America* (New York: Touchstone Books, 1998).

18. All of J.J.Walker's paintings featured in *Good Times* were created by the African American artist Earnie Barnes.

19. Thurgood Marshall was an Associate Justice of the United States Supreme Court. He was the first African American to sit on the Supreme Court. Marshall served on the court from 1967 until 1991.

20. *Ibid.*, 202.

21. Yesha Callahan, "John Amos Says He Was Kicked Off Good Times Because He Didn't Agree With the Shucking and Jiving." *The Root*. June 4, 2015. Accessed on June 22, 2016. http://www.theroot.com/blog/the-grapevine/john_amos_says_he_was_kicked_off_good_times_because_he_didn_t_agree_with/.

22. Bonnie Allen, "Movin' On Up: The Jeffersons," *Essence*. October 1981.

23. Gray, xxi.

24. *Why We Laugh*, DVD, directed by Robert Townsend, 2010; Universal City, CA: Codeblack Entertainment, 2009.

25. Denise's struggles at Hillman College were depicted in the first season of *A Different World*, a spin-off of *The Cosby Show*.

26. *The Cosby Show* was discussed in the 2016 CNN miniseries, *The Eighties*.

27. Robert Ehrlich, "A Permanent Family Crisis: The Problem of Fatherless Children Persists Half a Century After the Moynihan Report." *National Review*. October 11, 2014. Accessed on June 22, 2016. http://www.nationalreview.com/article/390111/permanent-family-crisis-robert-ehrlich.

28. Josh Levin, "The Welfare Queen." *Slate*. December 19, 2013. http://www.slate.com/articles/news_and_politics/history/2013/12/linda_taylor_welfare_queen_ronald_reagan_made_her_a_notorious_american_villain.html. Access on October 3, 2016.

29. Bill Cosby has a history of promoting African American history, culture, and education. Over the years has been major philanthropist for HBCUs. He helped to finance Melvin Van Peebles' *Sweet Sweetback's Baadasssss Song* (1971) and Spike Lee's *Malcolm X* (1992). Mr. Cosby and his wife Camille donated an art exhibit to the National Museum of African Art.

30. John Hughes directed and produced several notable comedic films about suburban white teenagers and families in the 1980s and early 1990s.

31. *The Cosby Show*, "Physician of the Year." Episode no. 15. Directed by Jay Sandrich and written by John Markus. NBC, January 17, 1985.

32. Dale Maryclaire, "Bill Cosby Charged with Sexually Assaulting a Woman." *Associated Press*. December 30, 2015. Accessed on June 22, 2016. http://bigstory.ap.org/article/df3cf7cb94494542bcbd58e3dc2b9748/results-bill-cosby-criminal-inquiry-be-announced.

33. Manuel Roig-Franzia, "Mistrial Declared

in Bill Cosby's Sex-Assault Trial." *The Washington Post.* June 17, 2017. Accessed on June 17, 2017. https://www.washingtonpost.com/lifestyle/style/mistrial-is-declared-in-sexual-assault-trial-of-entertainer-bill-cosby/2017/06/17/6d6d70f2-5114-11e7-be25-3a519335381c_story.html?utm_term=.61be6e0639db&wpisrc=nl_most-draw16&wpmm=1.

34. Whitney Friedlander, "Bounce TV Pulls 'Cosby' Reruns, BET's Centric Yanks 'The Cosby Show.'" *Variety.* July 7, 2015. Accessed by June 22, 2016. http://variety.com/2015/tv/news/cosby-reruns-bounce-tv-1201535254/.

35. Audio recording of Goldie Taylor's NPR interview with Kelly McEvers on October 16, 2015. Accessed on June 22, 2016. http://www.npr.org/2015/10/16/449238092/ebony-magazine-explores-the-cosby-shows-tainted-legacy.

36. Notable hip-hop labels (Death Row, Black Mafia Family Entertainment, Murder Inc., and Roc-A-Fella) founded in the 1990s had ties to prominent drug dealers.

37. *The Jerry Springer Show* is a syndicated talk show characterized by absurd guests and lewd behavior which gained notoriety in the 1990s because of the physical altercations between guests.

38. Stephanie Coontz, *The Way We Never Were: American Families and the Nostalgia Trap* (New York: Basic Books, 2000), 222–223.

39. Judith Halberstam, *Female Masculinity* (Durham, NC: Duke University Press, 1998), 1.

40. Robert A. Humphrey, "Representing Race, Gender, and Sexuality in Empire: (Counter) Hegemonic Masculinity, Black Fatherhood, and Homosexuality in Primetime Television." (Master's thesis, Bowling Green State University, 2016), 46–47.

41. Patricia Hill Collins, "Booty Call: Sex, Violence, and Images of Black Masculinity," in *Media and Cultural Studies: Keyworks,* edited by Meenakshi Gigi Durham and Douglas M. Kellner (Oxford, United Kingdom: Wiley Blackwell, 2012), 318–337.

42. *Empire,* Episode no. 25, first broadcast April 13, 2016 by FOX. Directed by Paris Barclay and written by Attica Locke and Joshua Allen.

43. *Empire,* Episode no. 17, first broadcast October 21, 2015 by FOX. Directed by Kevin Bray and written by Wendy Calhoun and Janeika James.

44. Henry Louis Gates, Jr., "TV's Black World Turns—But Stays Unreal." *The New York Times.* November 12, 1989. Accessed on June 23, 2016. http://www.nytimes.com/1989/11/12/arts/tv-s-black-world-turns-but-stays-unreal.html.

45. Bogle, 189.

46. Sut Jhally and Justin Lewis, *Enlightened Racism: The Cosby Show, Audiences and the Myth of the American Dream* (Boulder, Colorado: Westview Press, 1992).

47. The Central Park jogger case, 1989, involved five juvenile males—four black and one Hispanic—who were falsely accused of the rape and sodomy of a white 28-year-old female investment banker in New York City's Central Park.

48. *Planet Rock: The Story of Hip Hop and the Crack Generation.* Directed by Richard Lowe and Martin Torgoff, 2011, VH1.

49. Emily Dufton, "The War on Drugs: How President Nixon Tied Addiction to Crime." *The Atlantic.* March 26, 2012. Accessed on September 16, 2016. http://www.theatlantic.com/health/archive/2012/03/the-war-on-drugs-how-president-nixon-tied-addiction-to-crime/254319/.

50. Michelle Alexander, *The New Jim Crow: Mass Incarceration in the Age of Colorblindness* (New York: New Press, 2012), 52–53.

51. From the Reconstruction through the Second World War, southern states enacted laws to imprison black men for unjustifiably long sentences for trivial offenses such as stealing chickens, owing a debt, playing dice, or behaving uppity. Under this system of forced labor black male prisoners were leased by southern state, county, and local governments to the coal mining, steel, railroad, and lumber industries for profit. States such as Alabama would lease black convicts to private industries for as little as nine dollars a month. In 1874 the state of Alabama earned $164,000 in revenue from convict leasing.

52. Ta-Nehisi Coates, "The Black Family in the Age of Mass Incarceration." *The Atlantic.* October 2015. http://www.theatlantic.com/magazine/archive/2015/10/the-black-family-in-the-age-of-mass-incarceration/403246/. Accessed on December 14, 2016.

53. Shoshannay Sayers, "Mass Incarceration & People of Color." *Social Coalition for Social Justice.* April 9, 2014. Accessed on December 14, 2016. http://www.southerncoalition.org/mass-incarceration-people-color/.

54. Herron Keyon Gaston, "Mass Incarceration's Impact on Black and Latino Women and Children." *The Huffington Post.* April 22, 2015. Accessed on December 14, 2016. http://www.huffingtonpost.com/herron-keyon-gaston/mass-incarcerations-impact-black-latino_b_6702900.html.

55. Chauncey DeVega, "In Cosby, Americans Mourn the Loss of an Innocent Part of Their

Youths. But There's a Problem with That Nostalgia." *Slate*. July 12, 2015. Accessed on April 16, 2017. http://www.salon.com/2015/07/12/how_the_cosby_show_duped_america_the_sitcom_that_enabled_our_ugliest_reagan_era_fantasies/.

56. Michael Eric Dyson, "Punishment or Child Abuse?" *The New York Times*. September 17, 2014. Accessed on January 17, 2018. https://www.nytimes.com/2014/09/18/opinion/punishment-or-child-abuse.html.

57. David A. Love, "Beating Our Black Children Furthers the Legacy of Slavery." *The Grio*. September 15, 2014. Accessed on June 23, 2016. http://thegrio.com/2014/09/15/adrian-peterson-child-abuse-slavery/.

58. Ayah Nuriddin, Johns Hopkins University. "'Something Needed to be Done for the Black Patients': Integrating the Crownsville State Hospital, 1945–1970." Ms. Nuriddin was a panelist in a session on African Americans and Mental Health Issues.

59. King Davis was a panelist in a session on African Americans and Mental Health Issues at the annual meeting of ASALH in Richmond, VA on October 6, 2016.

60. Kevin White, *An Introduction to the Sociology of Health and Mental Illness* (Thousand Oaks, CA: SAGE, 2002), 41–42.

61. Jim Downs, *Sick from Freedom: African American Illness and Suffering During the Civil War and Reconstruction* (New York: Oxford University Press, 2012).

62. Nia Hamm, "Black Folks and Mental Health: Why Do We Suffer in Silence?" *Ebony*. October 1, 2012. Accessed on June 23, 2016. http://www.ebony.com/wellness-empowerment/black-folks-and-mental-health-610#axzz4CS8uOQT0.

63. Keli Goff, "Do Whites Have a Mental-Health Edge?" *The Root*. May 8, 2013. Accessed on June 23, 2016. http://www.theroot.com/articles/culture/2013/05/mental_health_illness_in_blacks_failure_to_seek_treatment_may_be_holding_us_back.3.html.

64. Carina Storrs, "Suicide Rates Among Young Black Boys on the Rise." *CNN*. May 19, 2005. Accessed on January 14, 2017. http://www.cnn.com/2015/05/19/health/suicide-youth/.

65. Kasey Woods, "The Beautiful Face of Mental Illness." *Ebony*. February 18, 2014. Accessed on December 28, 2016. http://www.ebony.com/wellness-empowerment/the-beautiful-face-of-mental-illness-042#axzz4U9IxQ9lf.

66. Elaine G. Flores, "What *Empire* Gets Wrong (and Right) About Bipolar Disorder." *The Root*. March 6, 2015. Accessed on June 23, 2016. http://www.theroot.com/articles/culture/2015/03/what_empire_gets_wrong_and_right_about_bipolar_disorder.html.

67. Kimberly Farris documents the gaps in collaborative efforts between formal mental health care providers and black clergy members in her 2012 paper, "Innovative Ways to Address Mental Health Needs of African Americans: Examining the Importance of How Pastors Conceptualize Mental Illness."

68. King Davis and Albert Thompkins, "Mental Health Education in African American Divinity/Theology Schools." September 2012 policy report for The Institute for Urban Policy Research and Analysis.

69. The New King James Version of the Bible.

70. The Rev. Danielle Graham was interviewed on January 7, 2017.

71. Kevin Gaines, *Uplifting the Race: Black Leadership, Politics and Culture in the Twentieth Century* (Chapel Hill: University of North Carolina Press, 1996).

72. Margo Jefferson, *Negroland: A Memoir* (New York: Pantheon Books, 2015).

73. Lawrence Otis Graham, *Our Kind of People: Inside America's Black Upper Class* (New York: HarperCollins, 1999), 22, 63, and 89.

74. Ibid., 102, 128–130, and 152.

75. Audrey Elisa Kerri, *The Paper Bag Principles: Class, Colorism, and Rumor and the Case of Black Washington, Part 3* (Knoxville: University of Tennessee Press, 2006), 93.

76. Graham, 3.

77. *Empire*, "My Bad Parts." Episode no. 20. Directed by Sanaa Hamri and written by Malcolm Spellman. FOX, November 18, 2015.

78. Throwing shade is an urban slang term, popular in hip-hop culture, meaning an action of disrespecting another individual.

79. *Empire*, Episode no. 45, first broadcast May 3, 2017 by FOX. Directed by Howard Deutch and written by Illene Chaiken and Carlito Rodriguez.

80. The Hatfield-McCoy rivalry involved two feuding rural white families in the West Virginia-Kentucky area during the Civil War era.

81. Michael Eric Dyson, "What's Behind Steph Curry's MVP Life: Faith, Fatherhood, Ayesha's Feminism and Family." *The Undefeated*. June 2, 2016. Accessed on June 24, 2016. https://theundefeated.com/features/whats-behind-steph-currys-mvp-life/.

82. Emily Nussbaum, "In Living Color: With "Black-ish," Kenya Barris rethinks the family sitcom." *The New Yorker*. April 25, 2016.

83. Ang, 69.

Chapter 2

1. *Empire*, "Pilot." Episode no. 1. Directed by Lee Daniels. Written by Lee Daniels and Daniel Strong. FOX, January 7, 2015.
2. Ibid.
3. James Truslow Adams, *The Epic of America* (Boston: Little Brown & Company, 1931), 214–215.
4. W.E.B. Du Bois, "The Talented Tenth," in *The Negro Problem: A Series of Articles by Representative Negroes of Today* (1903), ed. Booker T. Washington (Bloomington: Indiana University, 1903).
5. Ta-Nehisi Coates, "The Case for Reparations." *The Atlantic*. June 2014. Accessed on February 7, 2017. http://www.theatlantic.com/magazine/archive/2014/06/the-case-for-reparations/361631/.
6. Eric Foner, *Reconstruction: America's Unfinished Revolution* (New York: HarperCollins, 1988).
7. Ta-Nehisi Coates, *Between the World and Me* (New York: Spiegel & Grau, 2015).
8. James H. Cone, *Martin & Malcolm & America: A Dream or a Nightmare* (Maryknoll, NY: Orbis Books, 2012), 111–119.
9. Malcolm X delivered the speech "The Ballot or the Bullet" on April 3, 1964, at Cory Methodist Church in Cleveland, Ohio.
10. Excerpts of lyrics from the 1939 Billie Holiday song "Strange Fruit" about southern lynchings.
11. Malcolm X with Alex Haley, *The Autobiography of Malcolm X* (New York: Ballantine Books, 1992), 119–120.
12. The term bolita is used in Spanish to describe a little ball used in a type of lottery that was popular among the working class in Cuba and parts of America during the 19th and early 20th century.
13. The Moguldom Studios 2015 documentary *A Genius Leaves The Hood: The Unauthorized Story of Jay-Z* is available on Netflix.
14. Mark Jacobson. "The Return of Superfly," *New York Magazine*. August 14, 2000. Accessed on June 28, 2016. http://nymag.com/features/3649/
15. Chris Rovzar, "Frank Lucas Shouldn't Have Worn That Floor-Length Chinchilla Coat." *New York Magazine*. June 7, 2010. Accessed on May 1, 2017. http://nymag.com/daily/intelligencer/2010/06/frank_lucas_shouldnt_have_worn.html.
16. A maximum security correctional facility in Ossinng, New York.
17. I conducted a phone interview with Dr. Cecil Brown on June 26, 2011.
18. Michelle Alexander, *The New Jim Crow: Mass Incarceration in the Age of Colorblindness*. (New York, New York: The New Press, 2012), 44–47.
19. Dan Baum, "Legalize It All: How to Win the War on Drugs." *Harper's*. April 2016. http://harpers.org/archive/2016/04/legalize-it-all/. Accessed on April 12, 2017.
20. African American track and field sprinters Tommie Smith and John Carlos made a black power salute on the podium after winning the gold and bronze medals in the 200 meter dash at the 1968 Summer Olympics in Mexico City, Mexico. The gestured was repeated by several black NFL players in the wake of the Colin Kaepernick Black Lives Matter protests in 2016.
21. Mark Jacobson, "Lords of Dopetown," *New York*. October 29, 2007. Accessed on June 28, 2016. http://nymag.com/guides/money/2007/39948/.
22. "Mister Untouchable." *The New York Times Magazine*. June 5, 1977.
23. Chapter Two: "Ananse: Spinner of Ashanti Doubleness" in Robert Pelton, *The Trickster in West Africa: A Study of Mythic Irony and Sacred Delight* (Berkeley: University of California Press, 1980), 26–27.
24. Lawrence Levine, *Black Culture and Black Consciousness: African American Folk Thought from Slavery to Freedom* (Oxford, United Kingdom: Oxford University Press, 1977), 82.
25. Roger D. Abrahams, *Deep Down in the Jungle: Negro Narrative Folklore from the Streets of Philadelphia* (Chicago: Aldine, 1970), 64.
26. John W. Roberts, *From Trickster to Badman: The Black Folk Hero in Slavery and Freedom* (Philadelphia: University of Pennsylvania Press, 1989), 24.
27. John Hope Franklin and Loren Schweninger, *Runaway Slaves: Rebels on the Plantation* (Oxford, United Kingdom: Oxford University Press, 1999).
28. Scott Leonard and Michael McClure, *Myth and Knowing: An Introduction to World Mythology* (New York: McGraw-Hill Education, 2003), 250–251.
29. *The Mack*, DVD, directed by Michael Campus, 1973; New York; New Line Home Video, 2002.
30. Hine, 548.
31. M. Wesley Swearigan, *FBI Secrets: An Agent's Expose* (Boston: South End Press, 1995).
32. Interview with Robin D.G. Kelley conducted in July 2009.
33. Jacques Kelly, "'Little' Melvin Williams, Baltimore Drug Kingpin Who Appeared on 'The Wire,' Dies." *The Baltimore Sun*. July 12,

2016. Accessed on June 28, 2016. http://www.baltimoresun.com/news/obituaries/bs-md-ob-melvin-williams-20151203-story.html.

34. Dan Morain, "Garish Oakland Funeral: 1,000 Witness Last Ride of Slain Drug Kingpin." *Los Angeles Times*. August 30, 1986. http://articles.latimes.com/1986-08-30/news/mn-14145_1_oakland-funeral. Accessed on July 17, 2016.

35. Todd Boyd, *The Notorious Ph.D.'s Guide to the Super Fly '70s* (New York: Broadway Books, 2007), 31.

36. The Acts of the Apostles tells the story of Paul, a man who experiences a life changing conversion on the road to Damascus causing him to cease his persecution of Christians and give his life to Jesus Christ.

37. An excerpt from the Langston Hughes 1951poem "Harlem (A Dream Deferred)."

38. Ibid.

39. Mark Anthony Neal, *Looking for Leroy: Illegible Black Masculinities* (New York: New York University Press, 2013), 99.

40. Ernest L. Gibson III, "For Whom the BELL Tolls: *The Wire's* Stringer Bell as Tragic Intellectual." *Americana: The Journal of American Popular Culture (1900–Present)*, Spring 2011, Volume 10, Issue 1. http://www.americanpopularculture.com/journal/articles/spring_2011/gibson.htm.

41. Mark Anthony Neal, *Looking for Leroy: Illegible Black Masculinities* (New York: New University Press, 2013), 98–100.

42. Omari Hardwick was interviewed on ESPN's radio's *Russillo & Kanell* on July 15, 2016.

43. Michael Eric Dyson, *Tears We Cannot Stop: A Sermon to White America* (New York: St. Martin's Press, 2017).

44. Marion "Suge" Knight is the co-founder of Death Row Records and hip-hop mogul from the 1990s. He is best known for his violent treatment of his artists and running his record label like a crime mob boss.

45. *Inside the Label*. Episode no. 3, first broadcast May 25, 2016 by BET.

46. Ibid.

47. *Jack City*, DVD, directed by Mario Van Peebles, 1991; Burbank, CA: Warner Home Video, 1998.

48. By the early 1980s, Cornell "the Ghost" Jones, was the top distributor for powder cocaine to the Washington elite on Capitol Hill and in the exclusive Georgetown neighborhood. He turned the Hanover Place neighborhood in Washington, DC, into the city's 24-hour emporium for illegal narcotics such as imported heroin from Amsterdam and Thailand. Cornell began to transition out of the underworld completely by opening a real estate management company. He was eventually found guilty and sentenced to nine years at Leavenworth Federal Penitentiary in Kansas.

49. Henri E. Cauvin, "A Drug Kingpin's Hot-Selling Story." *The Washington Post*. July 22, 2005. Accessed on September 16, 2016. http://www.washingtonpost.com/wp-dyn/content/article/2005/07/21/AR2005072102517.html.

50. James Peterson, "'It's Yours': Hip-Hop Worldviews in the Lyrics of Nas," in *Born To Use Mics*, ed. Michael Eric Dyson and Sohail Daulatzai (New York: Basic Civitas Books, 2010), 75–78.

51. Spike Lee's Lil' Joints: *$15 kicks*. Posted on www.theundefeated.com on June 28, 2016.

52. Excerpts from Jay-Z's interview were taken from the short film, *Footnotes to "The Story of O.J."* available on Tidal.

53. Jason Read, "Stringer Bell's Lament: Violence and Legitimacy in Contemporary Capitalism," in *The Wire: Urban Decay and American Television*, ed. Tiffany Potter and C.W. Marshall (New York: Continuum, 2011), 122.

54. Toure, "The Book of Jay," *Rolling Stone*, December 11, 2005.

55. "A Bootlegger's Story I. How I Got Started." *The New Yorker*. September 25, 2016. Accessed on January 1, 2017. http://www.newyorker.com/magazine/1926/09/25/a-bootleggers-story-i-how-i-started.

56. William Julius Wilson, *When Work Disappears: The World of the New Urban Poor* (New York: Vintage, 1997).

57. Joe D'Angelo, "Jay-Z Pleads Guilty to Stabbing, Faces Three Years' Probation." *MTV*. October 17, 2001. Accessed on June 30, 2016. http://www.mtv.com/news/1450090/jay-z-pleads-guilty-to-stabbing-faces-three-years-probation/.

58. Joe Coscarelli, "Jay Z to Be the First Rapper in the Songwriters Hall of Fame." *The New York Times*. February 22, 2017. Accessed on June 16, 2017. https://www.nytimes.com/2017/02/22/arts/music/jay-z-songwriters-hall-of-fame.html?_r=0.

59. Lucy Handley, "Jay Z's latest Ace of Spades Champagne Will Cost $850, Only 2,333 Bottles Available." *CNBC*. April 6, 2017. Accessed on May 11, 2017. http://www.cnbc.com/2017/04/06/jay-zs-latest-ace-of-spades-champagne-will-cost-850.html.

60. Stuart Dredge, "Jay Z Aims to Topple Spotify with Music Streaming Service Tidal." *The Guardian*. March 31, 2015. Accessed on June 30, 2016. https://www.theguardian.com/music/

2015/mar/31/jay-z-spotify-music-streaming-relaunch-tidal-support-artist.

61. Zack O'Malley Greenburg, "Spring Buys 33% of Jay Z's Tidal for a Reported $200 Million." *Forbes.* January 23, 2017. Accessed on January 24, 2017. http://www.forbes.com/sites/zackomalleygreenburg/2017/01/23/sprint-buys-33-of-jay-zs-tidal-for-a-reported-200-million/#33c2eaa51471.

62. Mike Fleming, Jr., "Jay Z Makes 2-Year Overall Movie & TV Deal With Weinstein Company." *Deadline.* September 29, 2016. Accessed on September 29, 2016. http://deadline.com/2016/09/jay-z-movie-tv-deal-weinstein-company-1201828241/.

63. Zack O'Malley Greenburg, "The Forbes Five: Hip-Hop's Wealthiest Artists 2017." *Forbes.* May 10, 2017. https://www.forbes.com/sites/zackomalleygreenburg/2017/05/10/the-forbes-five-hip-hops-wealthiest-artists-2017/#1d7759002273. Accessed on May 10, 2017.

64. Zack O'Malley Greenburg, "Sprint's Investment in Jay Z's Tidal: Prelude to a Bigger Deal?" *Forbes.* January 24, 2017. Accessed on February 5, 2017. http://www.forbes.com/sites/zackomalleygreenburg/2017/01/24/sprints-investment-in-jay-zs-tidal-prelude-to-a-bigger-deal/#6222852470b2.

65. Mark Anthony Neal, *Looking for Leroy: Illegible Black Masculinities* (New York: New York University Press, 2013), 48–53, 56.

66. Miles Raymer, "Jay-Z and the New Age of Rap." *Esquire.* July 8, 2013. Accessed on June 30, 2016. http://www.esquire.com/entertainment/music/a23398/jay-z-magna-carta-holy-grail/.

67. Serving as the head of a publicly traded company is a major accomplishment. When I was a graduate student at Howard University hip-hop mogul Kevin Liles addressed the students on campus. During his talk he spent a considerable amount of time talking about his role as the executive vice president of the Warner Music Group, a publicly traded company. This was my first time learning about publicly traded companies and initial public offerings.

68. Gustav Klimt was a famous 19th century Austrian symbolist painter.

69. Anne T. Donahue, "'Empire' Costume Designer Rita McGhee Explains Cookie's Fur and Lucious's Scarves." *Cosmopolitan.* February 4, 2015. Accessed on June 30, 2015. http://www.cosmopolitan.com/entertainment/tv/a36077/empire-costumer-rita-mcghee-interview/.

70. Ibid.

71. Monica L. Miller, *Slaves to Fashion: Black Dandyism and the Styling of Black Diasporic Identity* (Durham, NC: Duke University Press, 2009).

72. Conk was a relaxer that was made at home, by mixing lye, eggs, and potatoes. The applier used gloves to rub it into the receiver's head. The receiver's head had to be rinsed thoroughly after application to avoid chemical burns.

73. *Empire,* "The Lyon's Roar." Episode no. 8. Directed and written by Danny Strong. FOX, February 25, 2015.

74. Nash Jenkins, "Jay-Z Responds to Pundit Who Called Him a 'Drug Dealer' in New Track." *Time.* May 31, 2016. Accessed on February 6, 2017. http://time.com/4353218/jay-z-drug-dealers-anonymous-pusha-t/.

75. Excerpts from a conversation between Jay-Z and Dean Baquet for the *New York Times Style Magazine* on September 29, 2017.

76. Carvell Wallace, Mahershala Ali Thinks We Can Still Make This Country Great." *GQ.* June 19, 2017. Accessed on July 10, 2017. http://www.gq.com/story/mahershala-ali-moonlight-and-america.

Chapter 3

1. *Empire,* "The Outspoken King." Episode no. 2. Directed by Lee Daniels and written by Danny Strong and Ilene Chalken. FOX, January 14, 2015.

2. Taraji P. Henson acceptance speech at the 2016 Golden Globe Awards broadcasted on NBC on January 10, 2016.

3. Tajari P. Henson hosted NBC's *Saturday Night Live* on April 11, 2015.

4. *Black-ish,* Episode no. 32, first broadcast November 18, 2015, by ABC. Directed by John Putch and written by Hale Rothstein.

5. Ana Cottle, "'The Handmaid's Tale': A White Feminist's Dystopia." *Alternet.* May 28, 2017. Accessed on June 2, 2017. http://www.alternet.org/culture/handmaids-tale-white-feminists-dystopia.

6. Lorena Blas, "More Women Are Behaving Badly on TV, and They're Not All 'Real Housewives.'" *USA Today.* July 6, 2016. https://www.usatoday.com/story/life/tv/2016/07/06/more-women-behaving-badly-tv-and-not-just-housewives/86572768/. Accessed on June 1, 2017.

7. Zeba Blay, "How Feminist TV Became The Normal." *The Huffington Post.* June 18, 2015. Accessed on July 7, 2016. http://www.huffingtonpost.com/2015/06/18/how-feminist-tv-became-the-new-normal_n_7567898.html.

8. Rachet is a slang term in hip-hop used to describe a person who acts stereotypically "ghetto." This person is considered to lack class, prone to anger and fighting, and unable to use proper grammar when speaking.

9. Bogle, 15.
10. Powell represented Harlem in the United States House of Representatives from 1945–1971.
11. Bogle, 33.
12. The oppositional gaze, is a term coined by bell hooks, to describe political resistance against the repression of black people's right to gaze or view themselves. In feminist film theory it criticizes the male gaze through Michael Foucault's relations of power. Laura Mulvey coined the phrase male gaze in 1975 to describe the depiction of (white) women in literature and visual arts from the masculine view point.
13. Mae Jamison was a member of the National Aeronautics and Space Administration (NASA) crew to travel outer space on the Space Shuttle *Endeavor* on September 12, 1992. She made a guest appearance on *Star Trek: The Next Generation* in 1993.
14. In *Loving v. Virginia* (1967) the U.S. Supreme Court ruled that anti-miscegenation laws were unconstitutional and violated interracial couples' civil rights.
15. The Oxford English Dictionary defines Ebonics as "American black English regarded as a language in its own right rather than as a dialect of standard English."
16. Brian Stelter, "Shonda Rhimes is Leaving ABC for Netflix." *CNN*. August 14, 2017. Accessed on August 15, 2017. http://money.cnn.com/2017/08/14/media/shonda-rhimes-netflix/index.html.
17. Brandon Maxwell, "Olivia Pope and the Scandal of Representation." *The Feminist Wire*. February 7, 2013. Accessed on July 7, 2016. http://www.thefeministwire.com/2013/02/olivia-pope-and-the-scandal-of-representation/.
18. Lesley Kennedy, "No Office Scandal Here: How to Get Olivia Pope's Work Look for Less." *USA Today*. September 26, 2014. Accessed on July 7, 2016. http://www.today.com/style/get-olivia-popes-scandal-style-less-2D80176913.
19. Robin Givhan, "On 'Scandal,' Olivia's New Red Leather Trenchcoat Means Everything You Think It Does." *The Washington Post*. February 10, 2016. Accessed on July 7, 2016. https://www.washingtonpost.com/news/arts-and-entertainment/wp/2016/02/10/on-scandal-olivias-new-red-leather-trenchcoat-means-everything-you-think-it-does/.
20. Tiya Miles, "Black Women, Interracial Dating, and Marriage: What's Love Got to Do With It?" *The Huffington Post*. November 5, 2013. Accessed on December 1, 2013. http://www.huffingtonpost.com/tiya-miles/interracial-dating-and-marriage_b_4213066.html.
21. Aisha Harris, "Why *Scandal's* Ferguson-Themed Episode Was So Frustrating." *Slate*. March 6, 2015. Accessed on July 7, 2016. http://www.slate.com/blogs/browbeat/2015/03/06/scandal_police_brutality_episode_the_lawn_chair_tackles_michael_brown_video.html.
22. Metaphorically speaking an individual puts on a cape when he or she comes to the rescue or fights unceasingly for someone or something in the manner of a comic book super hero.
23. Mara Brock Akil shared these feelings about her characters in the television series *Girlfriends* and *Being Mary Jane* during a October 2015 interview with *The New York Times*.
24. At the 2016 Republican National Convention First Lady Melania Trump was discovered to have plagiarized passages from a 2008 speech given by Michelle Obama.
25. Alexander Cooper Hawley, "An Image Rarely Seen: The Real Housewives of Atlanta and the Televisual Image of the African American Woman." (Ph.D. diss., University of Iowa, 2014).
26. Robin Boylorn, "Brains, Booty and Bizness": Identity Politics, Ratchet Respectability, and The Real Housewives of Atlanta. In *The Fantasy of Reality: Critical Essays on the Real Housewives*, ed. (Rachel E. Silverman. Frankfurt, Germany: Peter Lang Inc., 2015), 35.
27. Ibid., 36.
28. Robin Givhan, "How 'Empire' Charts the Rise of Hip-Hop Through Fabulous Fashion." *The Washington Post*. February 3, 2015. Accessed on June 30, 2016. https://www.washingtonpost.com/news/arts-and-entertainment/wp/2015/02/03/how-empire-charts-the-rise-of-hip-hop-through-fabulous-fashion/.
29. Anne T. Donahue, "'Empire' Costume Designer Rita McGhee Explains Cookie's Fur and Lucious's Scarves." *Cosmopolitan*. February 4, 2015. Accessed on July 8, 2015. http://www.cosmopolitan.com/entertainment/tv/a36077/empire-costumer-rita-mcghee-interview/.
30. *Empire*, Episode no. 6, first broadcast February 11, 2015, by FOX. Directed by Michael Engler and written by Malcolm Spellman.
31. *Empire*, "Dangerous Bonds." Episode no. 5. Directed by John Singleton and written by Eric Haywood. FOX, February 4, 2015.
32. Julee Wilson, "The Meaning of #BlackGirlMagic, and How You Can Get Some of It." *The Huffington Post*. January 13, 2016. Accessed on July 8, 2016. http://www.huffingtonpost.com/entry/what-is-black-girl-magic-video_us_5694dad4e4b086bc1cd517f4.
33. Geraghty, 65.
34. Kristal Brent Zook, "Cookie Don't Crumble." *The Nation*. March 18, 2015. Accessed on

July 8, 2016. https://www.thenation.com/article/cookie-dont-crumble/.

35. "On Moya Bailey, Misogynoir, and Why Both Are Important." May 27, 2014. Accessed on December 27, 2016. http://www.thevisibilityproject.com/2014/05/27/on-moya-bailey-misogynoir-and-why-both-are-important/.

36. Viola Davis, in the role of Annalise Keating, brilliantly plays a woman on the verge of mental and emotional collapse as she fights to maintain her innocence and dignity at a Philadelphia prison for women. She is verbally abused and sexually harassed by the other far less privileged black women in the cells and showers.

37. Shoshannah Sayers, "Mass Incarceration & People of Color." April 9, 2014. Accessed on July 9, 2014. http://www.southerncoalition.org/mass-incarceration-people-color/.

38. Desiree Adaway, "You Want the Power But Not the Pain: Some Notes for White Women Who Love Cookie." *The Feminist Wire*. October 22, 2015. Accessed on July 6, 2016. http://www.thefeministwire.com/2015/10/you-want-the-power-but-not-the-pain-some-notes-for-white-women-who-love-cookie/.

39. Herron Keyon Gaston, "Mass Incarceration's Impact on Black Women and Children." *The Huffington Post*. April 22, 2015. Accessed on July 9, 2016. http://www.huffingtonpost.com/herron-keyon-gaston/mass-incarcerations-impact-black-latino_b_6702900.html.

40. David A. Graham, "Sandra Bland and the Long History of Racism in Waller County, Texas." *The Atlantic*. July 21, 2015. Accessed on July 10, 2016. http://www.theatlantic.com/politics/archive/2015/07/sandra-bland-waller-county-racism/398975/.

41. "Say Her Name: Families Seek Justice in Overlooked Police Killings of African American Women. *Democracy Now*. May 20, 2015. Accessed on July 10, 2016. http://www.democracynow.org/2015/5/20/say_her_name_families_seek_justice.

42. Henry Louis Gates, Jr., addressed this topic during a television series *Upon Reflection* in 1994. He was reacting to a claim by another black scholar. He stated that he did not support this argument.

43. *Foxy Brown*, DVD, directed by Jack Hill, 1974; Los Angeles, CA: MGM, 2001.

44. John Petkovic, "Pam Grier, Queen of 1970s Blaxploitation Films, Speaks in Cleveland on Her Book Tour." *The Plain Dealer*. September 10, 2010. Accessed on October 12, 2016.http://www.cleveland.com/goingout/index.ssf/2010/09/pam_grier_queen_of_1970s_blaxp.html.

45. Lucille Ball played the unhappy housewife Lucille Ball on the popular television series *I Love Lucy* (1951–1957).

46. Brook Obie, "Woman in Viral Photo from Women's March to White Female Allies: 'Listen to Black Woman.'" *The Root*. January 23, 2017. Accessed on January 24, 2017. http://www.theroot.com/woman-in-viral-photo-from-women-s-march-to-white-female-179152461.

47. Alia E. Dastagir, "What Is Intersectional Feminism? A Look at the Term You May Be Hearing a Lot." *USA Today*. January 19, 2017. Accessed on January 26, 2017. http://www.usatoday.com/story/news/2017/01/19/feminism-intersectionality-racism-sexism-class/96633750/.

48. Patricia Hill Collins, *Black Feminist Thought: Knowledge, Consciousness and the Politics of Empowerment*. New York, NY: Routledge, 1999), 19–38.

49. Melissa Brown, "Ready to Ditch White Feminism? Here Are 6 Black Feminist Concepts You Need to Know." December 2, 2016. https://dailyprogressive.org/2016/12/ready-ditch-white-feminism-6-black-feminist-concepts-need-know/?utm_source=EverydayFeminism&utm_campaign=ef-fb-page. Accessed on December 28, 2016.

50. Clenora Hudson-Weems, *Africana Womanism: Reclaiming Ourselves* (Gordonsville, VA: Bedford/St. Martin's, 2004).

51. Ashley Daniels, "For Colored Girls Considering Womanism When Feminism Isn't Enough." *For Harriet*. February 2015. Accessed on April 2, 2017. http://www.forharriet.com/2015/02/a-colored-girl-considering-womanism.html#ixzz4d7ucQd4W.

52. Allison P. Davis, "Regular, Degular, Shmegular Girl From the Bronx." *New York Magazine*. November 12, 2017.

53. Nicole Martin "Women Key in Shaping Black Panther Party." January 6, 2014. Accessed on July 11, 2016. http://gender.stanford.edu/news/2014/women-key-shaping-black-panther-party.

54. Both of these women, outspoken activists, became fugitives from the law following the deaths of law officials. Davis was eventually found innocent after trial. Shakur has been living in Cuba under political asylum since 1984.

55. Yvonne D. Sims, *Women of Blaxploitation: How the Black Action Film Heroine Changed American Popular Culture* (Jefferson, NC: McFarland & Company, 2006), 1–6 and 13.

56. *Ibid.*, 81.

57. Celia L. Smith, "Fashion Flashback: Pam Grier." *Essence*. February 23, 2012. Accessed on

July 11, 2016. http://www.essence.com/2012/02/23/fashion-flashback-pam-grier.

58. *Empire*, "The Outspoken King." Episode no. 2. Directed by Lee Daniels and written by Danny Strong and Ilene Chaiken. FOX, January 14, 2015. In 2014 Ray Rice was released from the Baltimore Ravens professional football team and indicted for third-degree aggravated assault after TMZ released a video of him punching his then fiancé in an elevator.

59. Retired NBA coach and New York Knicks president Phil Jackson found himself in hot water after he referred to LeBron James's entourage as a posse. James and his business associate Maverick Carter accused Jackson of using the term in a derogatory fashion to categorize LeBron's closest black friends as hoodlums mooching off his success.

60. *Empire*, "A High Hope for a Low Heaven." Episode no. 18. Directed by Mario Van Peebles and written by Robert Munic. FOX, November 4, 2015.

61. Chimamanda Ngozi Adichie, *We Should All Be Feminists* (New York, NY: Anchor Books, 2012), 47.

62. Zeba Blay, "The Imperfect But Important Feminism of Cookie Lyon." *The Huffington Post*. September 24, 2015. Accessed on July 13, 2016. http://www.huffingtonpost.com/entry/the-imperfect-but-important-feminism-of-cookie-lyon_us_56005a09e4b08820d919a8e5.

63. Excerpts from a radio interview with President Barack Obama on the *Rickey Smiley Morning Show* on February 2, 2015.

64. Barbara Smith's March 27, 2015, interview with Janet Mock is available at http://www.msnbc.com/so-popular-/watch/feminist-icon-barbara-smith-on--empire----more-4192108 19704. Accessed on July 13, 2016.

65. Zia Jaffrey, "The Salon Interview—Toni Morison." *Salon*. February 2, 1998. Accessed on February 11, 2017. http://www.salon.com/1998/02/02/cov_si_02int/.

66. Beyoncé repeats the phrase "I slay" in her hit 2016 song "Formation" from her *Lemonade* album.

67. Zack O'Malley Greenburg, "Beyoncé's Net Worth: $265 Million in 2016." *Forbes*. June 1, 2016. Accessed on July 13, 2016. http://www.forbes.com/sites/zackomalleygreenburg/2016/06/01/Beyoncés-net-worth-265-million-in-2016/#62e584f6689d.

68. Janell Hobson, "Beyoncé's Fierce Feminism." *Ms*. March 7, 2015. Accessed on July 13, 2016. http://msmagazine.com/blog/2015/03/07/Beyoncés-fierce-feminism/.

69. Syreeta McFadden, "Beyoncé's Lemonade Is #blackgirlmagic at Its Most Potent." *The Guardian*. April 24, 2016. Accessed on July 13, 2016. http://www.theguardian.com/music/2016/apr/24/Beyoncé-lemonade-album-video-black-girl-magic-womanhood-america.

70. Excerpts in these sentences were inspired by the singles "Hold Up" and "Sorry" from Beyoncé's 2016 album *Lemonade*. "Becky with the good hair" is a nickname that Beyoncé gives to her lover's mistresses.

71. Yohana Detesta, "How Beyoncé's *Lemonade* Helped Bring a Groundbreaking Film Back to Theaters." *Vanity Fair*. August 22, 2016. Accessed on March 30, 2017. http://www.vanityfair.com/hollywood/2016/08/daughters-of-the-dust-exclusive.

72. Malcolm X delivered this speech in Los Angeles, CA on May 5, 1962. Video footage of the speech is available on www.youtube.com.

73. *Empire*, Episode no. 40, first broadcast March 22, 2017, by FOX. Directed by Craig Brewer and written by Eric Haywood and Carlito Rodriguez.

74. Kamaria Roberts and Kenya Downs, "What Beyoncé Teaches Us About the African Diaspora in 'Lemonade.'" *PBS News Hour*. April 29, 2016. Accessed on April 1, 2017. http://www.pbs.org/newshour/art/what-Beyoncé-teaches-us-about-the-african-diaspora-in-lemonade/.

75. Roxane Gay, *Bad Feminist: Essays* (New York: Harper Perennial, 2014).

76. Kellee Terrell, "Why It's Important to Show Black Female Friendship on Television." *Vogue*. July 21, 2017. Accessed on August 16, 2017. http://www.vogue.com/article/insecure-issa-rae-yvonne-orji-black-female-friendship-onscreen.

77. Josie Pickens, "The Respectability Politricks of Ayesha Curry." *Ebony*. December 10, 2015. Accessed on July 13, 2016. http://www.ebony.com/entertainment-culture/the-respectability-politricks-of-ayesha-curry-323#ixzz4CS8Nuodg.

78. Brittney Cooper, *Beyond Respectability: The Intellectual Thought of Race Women*. (Urbana, IL: University of Illinois, 2017), 37.

79. Leah Mullings, *On Our Own Terms: Race, Class, and Gender in the Lives of African American Women*. (New York: Routledge, 1997), 112–113.

80. Patricia Hill Collins, *Black Sexual Politics: African Americans, Gender and the New Racism*. (New York: Routledge, 2004), 98.

81. NAACP collection at the Library of Congress in Washington, DC. Box II A 499 Folder 2. Publicity Protests—Conference with Sig Mickelson (Amos 'n' Andy), 1951.

82. Jack Haverstraw, "The Making of a Movie Star." *Sepia*. May 1975.

83. Stephanee Dunn, *"Baad Bitches" & Sassy Supermamas: Black Power Action Films* (Urbana and Chicago: University of Illinois, 2008), 111.

84. Kat George, "Why Missy Elliot's Feminist Legacy is Criminally Underrated." *Dazed.* January 22, 2016. Accessed on April 2, 2017. http://www.dazeddigital.com/music/article/29353/1/why-missy-elliott-s-feminist-legacy-is-criminally-underrated.

85. Tracy Clark-Flory, "Feminists Can Twerk Too: What Annie Lennox Misunderstands About Beyoncé." *Salon.* October 22, 2014. Accessed on April 23, 2017. http://www.salon.com/2014/10/22/feminists_can_twerk_too_what_annie_lennox_misunderstands_about_Beyoncé/.

86. The New School presents a conversation with bell hooks, scholar-in-residence at Eugene Lang College the New School for Liberal Arts: "Are You Still a Slave? Liberating the Black Female Body." May 7, 2014.

87. Elaine Richardson, "Lil' Kim, Hip-Hop Womanhood and the Naked Truuf," in *Home Girls Make Some Noise! Hip-Hop Feminism Anthology,* edited by Gwendolyn Pough, Elaine Richardson, Aisha Durham, and Rachel Raimist (Mira Loma, CA: Parker Publishing, 2007), 187–191.

88. Brianne A. Painia, "'My Crown Too Heavy Like the Queen Neferti': A Black Feminist Analysis of Erykah Badu, Beyoncé Knowles, Nicki Minaj, and Janelle Monae." Thesis. George Washington University. May 18, 2014.

89. Evette Dionne, "The Twerking Feminist." *Mic.* October 25, 2013. Accessed on December 28, 2016. https://mic.com/articles/69657/the-twerking-feminist#.uYwRdWyFE.

90. Viola, "Who Needs Hip-Hop Feminism?" *Medium.* April 28, 2015. Accessed on December 28, 2016. https://medium.com/black-feminism/who-needs-hip-hop-feminism-394c40af8f35#.ld08ej60v.

91. "Love, Hip Hop, and Ratchet Respectability (Something Like A Review)." *Crunk Feminist Collective.* September 10, 2015. Accessed on July 14, 2016. http://www.crunkfeministcollective.com/2015/09/10/love-hip-hop-and-ratchet-respectability-something-like-a-review/.

Chapter 4

1. *Empire,* Episode no. 18, first broadcast November 4, 2015, by FOX. Directed by Mario Van Peebles and written by Robert Munic.

2. "Actor Trai Byers: Committed to Shedding Light on Mental Health." July 19, 2016. Accessed on July 20, 2016. http://blackdoctor.org/495084/actor-trai-byers-committed-to-shedding-light-on-mental-health/.

3. *Empire,* "The Lyon's Roar." Episode no. 8. Directed and written by Danny Strong. FOX, February 25, 2015.

4. Dave Schilling, "Black Gatsbys: Interracial Marriage, Black Social Climbing, and the Rise of Andre on 'Empire.'" *Grantland.* February 26, 2015. Accessed on July 19, 2016. http://grantland.com/hollywood-prospectus/black-gatsbys-interracial-marriage-black-social-climbing-and-the-rise-of-andre-on-empire/.

5. Alex P. Keaton was a fictional character on the NBC sitcom *Family Ties* (1982–1989). who symbolized the conservatism of the Ronald Reagan presidential administration during the 1980s.

6. Rana Campbell, "Black Men at Princeton Share Their Experiences." *The Huffington Post.* June 19, 2014. Accessed on July 20, 2016. http://www.huffingtonpost.com/rana-campbell/black-men-at-princeton-sh_b_5352980.html.

7. *Empire,* "Pilot." Episode no. 1. Directed by Lee Daniels and written by Lee Daniels and Danny Strong. FOX, January 7, 2015.

8. Barack Obama, *Dreams from My Father: A Story of Race and Inheritance* (New York: Tree Rivers Press, 2004), 79.

9. *Black-ish,* "Pilot." Episode no. 1. Directed by James Griffiths and written by Kenya Barris. ABC, September 24, 2014.

10. Jay-Z criticizes O.J. Simpson's failed attempts to transcend race and juxtaposes him an animated character, Jaybo, based on the racist children's book *Little Black Sambo* (1899) in the 2017 music video for "The Story of O.J."

11. ESPN 30 for 30 *O.J.: Made in America* part I. 2016.

12. This short film contains interviews with famous black men about success and race in America. The film is available exclusively on Tidal.

13. Jessica Ann Mitchell, "Kanye's Frantz Fanon Complex." December 2, 2013. Accessed on December 18, 2016. https://ourlegaci.com/2013/12/02/kanyes-frantz-fanon-complex/.

14. Toure, *Who's Afraid of Post-Blackness: What It Means to Be Black Now* (New York: Free Press, 2011), 9–10.

15. Ibid., 19–20.

16. Colleen Long, "Former Tennis Player James Blake Agrees Not to Sue New York City." *Chicago Tribune.* June 21, 2017. Accessed on June 23, 2017. http://www.chicagotribune.com/sports/international/ct-tennis-james-blake-nypd-settlement-20170621-story.html.

17. *Empire,* "Sins That Amends." Episode no.

18. Christopher Mathias, "Kalief Browder, NYC Teen Jailed For Years With No Conviction, says Rikers Guard 'Starved' Him." *The Huffington Post*. September 15, 2016. Accessed on October 21, 2016. http://www.huffingtonpost.com/2013/12/02/kalief-browder_n_4373544.html.

19. Matt Pearce. "Kalief Browder, Jailed for Three Years Without a Trial at Rikers Island in New York, Commits Suicide." *Los Angeles Times*. June 7, 2015. Accessed on October 22, 2016. http://www.latimes.com/nation/.

20. Glenn Kessler, "The Stale Statistic That One in Three Black Males 'Born Today' Will End Up in Jail." *The Washington Post*. June 16, 2015. Accessed on October 22, 2016. https://www.washingtonpost.com/news/fact-checker/wp/2015/06/16/the-stale-statistic-that-one-in-three-black-males-has-a-chance-of-ending-up-in-jail/.

21. Ta-Nehisi Coates, "The Black Family in the Age of Mass Incarceration." *The Atlantic*. October 2015. Accessed on December 12, 2016. http://www.theatlantic.com/magazine/archive/2015/10/the-black-family-in-the-age-of-mass-incarceration/403246/.

22. Emily Shapiro, "OJ Simpson Granted Parole for Las Vegas Robbery." *ABC News*. July 20, 2017. Accessed on July 22, 2017. http://abcnews.go.com/US/oj-simpson-granted-parole-las-vegas-robbery/story?id=48689499.

23. In the classic 1972 film mafia leader Vito Corleone sends his consigliere Tom Hagen to negotiate a deal with Jewish film producer Jack Woltz to release his singer Johnny Fontane from his oppressive contract. Woltz is disrespectful in his refusal of Hagen's offer. The following morning he wakes up screaming in horror to find his bed sheets covered in the blood from the severed head of his prize racehorse.

24. The American Sound Awards is a fictional musical award show on *Empire*.

25. *Empire*, "Pilot." Episode no. 1. Directed by Lee Daniels and written by Lee Daniels and Danny Strong. FOX, January 7, 2015.

26. Joe Satran, "50 Cent Blames 'Empire' Ratings Dip On 'Gay Stuff.'" *The Huffington Post*. October 6, 2015. Accessed on July 21, 2016. http://www.huffingtonpost.com/entry/50-cent-empire-ratings_us_5612c235e4b0af3706e19b3f.

27. A meme is "a concept or catchphrase which spreads, often as mimicry, from person to person" across the internet.

28. Louis Farrakhan was interviewed on the Power 105.1 morning radio series *The Breakfast Club* on May 24, 2016.

29. Shenna C. Howard, "Dr. Boyce Watkins Charges Lee Daniels With Having A 'Gay Agenda.'" *The Huffington Post*. May 5, 2015. Accessed on July 21, 2016. http://www.huffingtonpost.com/sheena-c-howard/boyce-watkins-empire-gay_b_6781362.html.

30. Bill Chappell, "Supreme Court Declares Same-Sex Marriage Legal In All 50 States." *NPR*. June 26, 2015. Accessed on July 28, 2016. http://www.npr.org/sections/thetwo-way/2015/06/26/417717613/supreme-court-rules-all-states-must-allow-same-sex-marriages. Ralph Ellis, Ashley Fantz, Faith Karimi, and Elliott C. McLaughlin, "Orlando Shooting: 49 Killed, Shooter Pledged ISIS Allegiance." *CNN*. June 13, 2016. Accessed on July 28, 2016. http://www.cnn.com/2016/06/12/us/orlando-nightclub-shooting/.

31. Lindsay Kimble, "Empire's Homophobic Story Line Was Ripped From Co-Creator Lee Daniels' Own Childhood." *Us*. February 26, 2015. Accessed on July 21, 2016. http://www.usmagazine.com/entertainment/news/empires-homophobic-story-line-inspired-by-co-creator-lee-daniels-2015262.

32. Justin D. Edwards and Rune Graulund. *Grotesque* (New York, NY: Routledge, 2013), 109.

33. *Brother Outsider: The Life of Bayard Rustin*, DVD, directed by Nancy Kates and Bennett Singer, 2010; Warren, NJ: Passion River, 2003.

34. E. Patrick Johnson, *Sweet Tea: Black Gay Men of the South* (Chapel Hill: University of North Carolina Press, 2011), 182–200.

35. Alex Medeiros and Chandrika Narayan, "Controversial Megachurch Pastor Eddie Long Dies." *CNN*. January 15, 2017. Accessed on January 16, 2017. http://www.cnn.com/2017/01/15/us/bishop-eddie-long-dead/index.html.

36. Jonathan L. Walton, *Watch This! The Ethics and Aesthetics of Black Televangelism* (New York: New York University Press, 2009), 126.

37. In 2011 Bishop Long settled lawsuits out-of-court with four young men at New Birth who claimed to have been taken advantage of sexually by him as teenagers.

38. Curtis M. Wong, "Andrew Caldwell, Who Claimed To Have Been 'Delivered' From Homosexuality, Insists Viral Video Is Legitimate." *Huffington Post*. November 14, 2014. Accessed on July 22, 2016. http://www.huffingtonpost.com/2014/11/14/andrew-caldwell-homosexuality-video-_n_6159278.html.

39. Veronica Wells, "Why The 'Empire' Donnie McClurkin Jab Took Things A Little Too Far." *MadameNoire*. September 24, 2015. Accessed on July 22, 2016. http://madamenoire.com/589108/why-the-empire-donnie-mcclurkin-jab-took-things-a-little-too-far/.

32. Directed by Craig Brewer and written by Eric Haywood and Carlito Rodriguez. FOX, March 22, 2017.

40. "Throwing shade" is a popular hip-hop slang term used to say that someone or something is being denounced or disrespected.

41. *Hip Hop: Beyond Beats and Rhymes*, DVD, directed by Byron Hurt, Alexandria, VA: PBS Independent Lens, 2006.

42. R. Kurt Osenlund, "Lee Daniels on How Empire's Gay Content is Changing Minds," *Out*. January 23, 2015. Accessed on June 4, 2017. http://www.out.com/entertainment/television/2015/01/23/lee-daniels-howempires-gay-content-changing-minds.

43. Marc Lamont Hill, "Scared Straight: Hip-Hop, Outing, and the Pedagogy of Queerness," in *That's the Joint!: The Hip-Hop Studies Reader* (New York: Routledge, 2004), 388.

44. Guy Trebay, "Homo Thugz Blow Up the Spot," *The Village Voice*. February 8, 2000.

45. On July 4, 2012, Frank Ocean revealed that his first love was a man in an open letter posted as a blog on the social media site Tumblr.

46. Clover Hope, "Empire: Jamal Lyon Comes Out, Gives the World a Show." *The Muse*. February 26, 2015. Accessed on June 5, 2017. http://themuse.jezebel.com/empire-jamal-lyon-comes-out-gives-the-world-ashow-1688209305.

47. Sam Delaney, "Omar Little Is the Gay Stick-up Man Who Robs Drug Dealers for a Living in the Wire." *The Guardian*. July 19, 2008. Accessed on July 22, 2016. https://www.theguardian.com/culture/2008/jul/19/television.wire.

48. Humphrey, 52.

49. Alton Sterling and Philando Castile were two black men fatally shot by police officers on July 5 and 6, 2016 in Baton Rouge, LA and Falcon Heights, MN. The shootings led to nationwide protests in conjunction with the Black Lives Matter Movement.

50. The Oedipus Complex refers to a child's repressed desire to have sexual relations with the parent of the opposite sex.

51. Accessed on December 8, 2016. https://en.oxforddictionaries.com/.

52. Rivals Tupac Shakur and Christopher Wallace (The Notorious B.I.G.) were gunned down between September 1996 and March 1997, respectively.

53. *Hip Hop: Beyond Beats and Rhymes*.

54. Richard Majors and Janet Mancini Billson, *Cool Pose: The Dilemmas of Black Manhood in America* (Lanham, MD: Lexington Books, 1992).

55. bell hooks, *We Real Cool: Black Men and Masculinity* (New York: Routledge, 2003).

56. Patrick Ryan, "Is Kanye West the Greatest Artist of the 21st Century?" *USA Today*. February 9, 2016. Accessed on July 26, 2016. http://www.usatoday.com/story/life/music/2016/02/09/kanye-west-new-album/79814890/#.

57. The term "everyman" comes from an English play, *Everyman*, which is written in a fashion that allows readers to see themselves in the protagonist.

58. "How Drake's 'Hotline Bling' makes it OK to be dorky." *Melissa Harris-Perry*. Originally aired on MSNBC on October 25, 2015.

59. "How Drake's 'Hotline Bling' makes it OK to be dorky." *Melissa Harris-Perry*. Originally aired on MSNBC on October 25, 2015.

60. Trap music is a genre of hip-hop that speaks to this reality in the South. The Trap is a slang term used in the South for the dope house.

61. Michael P. Jeffries, "Drake, Childish Gambino, and the Specter of Black Authenticity." *The Atlantic*. November 22, 2011. Accessed on July 26, 2016. http://www.theatlantic.com/entertainment/archive/2011/11/drake-childish-gambino-and-the-specter-of-black-authenticity/248929/.

62. "Tony Parker Lawsuit. Club Sues Brown & Drake… They Should Pay!!!" *TMZ Sports*. March 17, 2013. Accessed on December 16, 2016. http://www.tmz.com/2013/03/17/chris-brown-drake-tony-parker-nightclub-lawsuit/.

63. *Empire*, no. 4, first broadcast January 28, 2015, by FOX. Directed by Rosemary Rodriguez and written by Wendy Calhoun.

64. *Empire*, "A High Hope for a Low Heaven." Episode no. 18. Directed by Mario Van Peebles and written by Robert Munic. FOX, November 4, 2015. Cash Money Records CEO Birdman popularized the phrase "put some respect on my name" during an argument with radio personality Charlamagne Tha God on the April 22, 2016 episode of Power 105.1 *The Breakfast Club*.

65. Spencer Kornhaber, "Hakeem Mans Up" *The Atlantic*. November 5, 2015. Accessed on July 28, 2016. http://www.theatlantic.com/entertainment/archive/2015/11/empire-season-2-episode-6-hakeem-masculinity/414247/.

66. *Empire*, "A High Hope for a Low Heaven." no. 18. Directed by Mario Van Peebles and written by Robert Munic. FOX, November 4, 2015.

67. Making it rain is a slang expression used in hip-hop to describe the act of throwing money in the air at a gentleman's club to watch it rain down on the women dancers.

Chapter 5

1. *Empire*, "The Outspoken King." Episode no. 2. Directed by Lee Daniels and written by Danny Strong and Ilene Chaiken. FOX, January 14, 2015.

2. Yesha Callahan, "Lee Daniels Responds to Tavis Smiley's Critique of *Empire*." *The Root*. April 9, 2015. Accessed on November 25, 2016. http://www.theroot.com/blogs/the_grapevine/2015/04/lee_daniels_responds_to_tavis_smiley_s_critique_of_empire.html.

3. The interview aired on April 26, 2017.

4. The symposium was held at Shiloh Baptist Church in Washington, DC, on September 19, 2015.

5. *Why We Laugh*, DVD, directed by Robert Townsend, 2010; Universal City, CA: Codeblack Entertainment, 2009.

6. Sara Magee, "High School is Hell: The TV Legacy of *Beverly Hills, 90210*, and *Buffy the Vampire Slayer*." *The Journal of Popular Culture* 47 (2014): 877–894.

7. Greg Braxton, "Farakhan Appearance on 'Arsenio' Sparks Furor," *Los Angeles Times*. February 25, 1994. Accessed on August 6, 2016. http://articles.latimes.com/1994-02-25/entertainment/ca-27285_1_louis-farrakhan.

8. Herman Gray, *Watching Race: Television and the Struggle for Blackness* (Minneapolis: University of Minnesota Press, 2004), 131.

9. *Ibid.*, 137.

10. Pullman Porters were men who worked on railroad sleeping cars. The Pullman Porters played a significant role in the black middle class between the 1860s and the 1960s.

11. A hood rat is a slang term for a low class (black) woman in the ghetto who exhibits trifling behavior and appearance. This woman was often derided for being promiscuous.

12. Ronda Racha Penrice, "Unsung Hollywood: Before Empire, Fox Had New York Undercover, the Original Hip Hop Drama." *The Root*. March 23, 2016. Accessed on August 14, 2017. http://www.theroot.com/unsung-hollywood-before-empire-fox-had-new-york-under-1790854715.

13. Kristal Brent Zook, *Color by Fox: The Fox Network and the Revolution in Black Television* (Oxford, United Kingdom: Oxford University Press, 1994).

14. Christine Acham, *Revolution Televised: Prime Time and the Struggle for Black Power*. Minneapolis: University of Minnesota Press, 2004), 68.

15. Yuval Taylor and Jane Austen, *Darkest America: Black Minstrelsy From Slavery to Hip-Hop* (New York: W.W. Norton & Company, 2012), 188.

16. Quiana M. Cutts, "The Black Family in the New Millennium: *The Bernie Mac Show, My Wife and Kids*, and *Everybody Hates Chris*, in *African Americans on Television: Race-in for Ratings* (Santa Barbara, CA: Praeger, 2013), 193.

17. Tyler Hansen, "Fox Blames Obamacare for Fictional Layoffs at Cleveland Clinic," Blog November 25, 2013. Accessed on January 4, 2014. http://mediamatters.org/blog/2013/11/25/fox-blames-obamacare-for-fictional-layoffs-at-c/197048.

18. Glenn Beck appeared on *Fox & Friends* on July 29, 2009. Beck apologized for his comments about the president during a 2016 interview with *The New Yorker*.

19. Jamelle Bouie, "Don't Forget That Megyn Kelly Is a Racial Demagogue." *Slate*. January 4, 2017. http://www.slate.com/articles/news_and_politics/politics/2017/01/megyn_kelly_is_a_racial_demagogue.html. Accessed on February 2, 2017.

20. PBS *Frontline: Divided States of America*. January 17–18, 2017.

21. Alternative facts is a phrase coined by Kellyanne Conway, counselor to President Donald Trump, to defend statements by White House press secretary Sean Spicer that were universally considered to be false.

22. Roger Ailes resigned from his post as the chairman and CEO of the Fox News Channel and the Fox Television Stations Group in July 2016 due to multiple charges of sexual harassment by female employees. Rupert Murdoch replaced Ailes as the chairman and acting CEO. Fox's biggest star Bill O'Reilly was terminated on April 19, 2017, for similar allegations. Since 2016 several popular female hosts including Megyn Kelly, Gretchen Carlson, and Andrea Tantaros left the network in 2016 due to sexual harassment. Roger Ailes passed away at the age of 77 on May 18, 2017.

23. Sydney Ember, "11 Sue Fox News, Citing 'Intolerable' Racial Bias." *The New York Times*. April 25, 2017. Accessed on May 1, 2017. https://www.nytimes.com/2017/04/25/business/media/fox-news-racial-discrimination-lawsuit.html?_r=0.

24. ABC, in 2016, made Channing Dungey the first African American to run one of the big four networks. ABC's lineup includes sitcoms and dramas about black women, Asian families, Jewish families, Indian women, Latinos, Muslims, undocumented immigrants, and the LGBTQ community.

25. *Ibid.*

26. Kimberly Foster, "Wrestling with Respectability in the Age of #BlackLivesMatter: A Dialogue." *For Harriet*. October 13, 2015. Accessed on January 2, 2016. http://www.forharriet.com/2015/10/wrestling-with-respectability-in-age-of.html#axzz4ojmTSMVY.

27. Ta-Nehisi Coates, *Between the World and Me* (New York: Spiegel & Grau, 2015), 35.

28. Evelyn Brooks Higginbotham, *Righteous*

Discontent: The Women's Movement in the Black Baptist Church, 1880–1920 (Cambridge, MA: Harvard University Press, 1994).

29. Cary D. Wintz, *Harlem Speaks: A Living History of the Harlem Renaissance* (Naperville, IL: Sourcebooks MediaFusion, 2006), 376.

30. *Ibid.*, 512.

31. Shantella Sherman, *In Search of Purity: Popular Eugenics & Racial Uplift Among New Negroes 1915–1935* (Createspace Independent Publishing Platform, 2016).

32. Kevin Gaines, *Uplifting the Race: Black Leadership, Politics and Culture in the Twentieth Century* (Chapel Hill: University of North Carolina Press, 1996).

33. Melvin Patrick Ely, *The Adventures of Amos 'n' Andy: A Social History of an American Phenomenon* (New York: The Free Press, 1991).

34. Taylor and Austen, 163.

35. W.E.B. Du Bois, *The Souls of Black Folk* (New York: Bantam Classic, 1903).

36. Clifford J. Levy, "Harlem Protest of Rap Lyrics Draws Debate and Steamroller." *The New York Times.* June 6, 1993. Accessed on August 10, 2016. http://www.nytimes.com/1993/06/06/nyregion/harlem-protest-of-rap-lyrics-draws-debate-and-steamroller.html.

37. "C. Delores Tucker Files $10 Million Lawsuit Against Tupac Shakur's Estate." *Jet.* September 1, 1997.

38. Felecia R. Leenov, "To Blacks, Precious Is 'Demeaned' Or 'Angelic.'" *The New York Times.* February 20, 2009. http://www.nytimes.com/2009/11/21/movies/21precious.html?_r=0. Accessed on August 8, 2016.

39. Bettina L. Love, "Tyler Perry Takes Over TV," in *African Americans on Television: Racing for Ratings* (Santa Barbara, CA: Praeger, 2013), 282–290.

40. Jimi Izrael, "Tyler Perry Vs. Spike Lee: A Debate Over Class and 'Coonery.'" *NPR.* April 22, 2011. Accessed on August 13, 2017. http://www.npr.org/sections/tellmemore/2011/04/22/135630682/tyler-perry-vs-spike-lee-a-debate-over-class-and-coonery.

41. Michael Eric Dyson, *Reflecting Black: African American Cultural Criticism* (Minneapolis: University of Minnesota Press, 1993).

42. James Peterson was interviewed by Henry Louis Gates in the 2016 PBS documentary *Black America Since MLK: And Still I Rise.*

43. *Cane* is a novel published by Jean Toomer in 1923 during the Harlem Renaissance. Toomer was a noted poet and artist during the time period.

44. Dana Polan, *The Sopranos* (Durham, NC: Duke University Press, 2009).

45. Donna Petrozzzello, "'Sopranos' Hits Wrong Note With Italian Americans." *New York Daily News.* September 8, 1999. http://articles.chicagotribune.com/1999-09-08/features/9909080134_1_italian Americans-jennifer-melfi-new-series-last-season. August 8, 2016.

46. Andrew Wallenstein, "No, 'Sopranos' Does Not Represent Italians." http://www.medialifemagazine.com:8080/news2001/june01/june04/5_fri/news4friday.html.

47. Raymond Hernandez, "Congresswoman Takes a Whack at 'The Sopranos' Stereotype." *The New York Times.* May 24, 2001. Accessed on August 8, 2016. http://www.nytimes.com/2001/05/24/nyregion/congresswoman-takes-a-whack-at-the-sopranos-stereotype.html. Accessed on August 8, 2016.

48. Siddhant Adlakha, "Jay-Z's MOONLIGHT Video: On Whiteness As American Export." August 11, 2017. Accessed on August 13, 2017. http://birthmoviesdeath.com/2017/08/11/jay-zs-moonlight-video-on-whiteness-as American-export.

49. LT Hutton and Benny Boom, the directors and producers of the 2017 Tupac Shakur biopic *All Eyez on Me*, discussed their struggles gaining acceptance in Hollywood during a June 14, 2017 interview on *The Breakfast Club* Power 105.1 FM.

50. Maureen Ryan, "Showrunners for New TV Season Remain Mostly White and Male." *Variety.* June 8, 2016. Accessed on October 20, 2017. http://variety.com/2016/tv/features/diversity-television-white-male-showrunners-stats-fox-nbc-abc-cbs-cw-study-1201789639/.

51. *American Race* episode no. 3, first broadcast May 13, 2017 by TNT.

52. Eric Deggans, "Does Fox's 'Empire' Break Bolster Black Stereotypes?" *NPR.* March 18, 2015. Accessed on August 10, 2016. http://www.npr.org/sections/monkeysee/2015/03/18/393785570/does-foxs-empire-break-or-bolster-black-stereotypes.

53. Bogle, 326.

54. *Empire*, "Absent Child." Episode no. 46. Directed by Millicent Shelton and written by Attica Locke and Malcolm Spellman. FOX, May 10, 2017.

55. Ien Ang, *Watching "Dallas": Soap Opera and the Melodramatic Imagination* (New York: Routledge, 1986), 93.

56. David Banner appeared on New York's Power 105.1 *The Breakfast Club* on April 21, 2017.

Chapter 6

1. Laverne Cox is the first transgender actress to earn a Primetime Emmy nomination for

her role on the Netflix series *Orange is the New Black*.

2. *Star*, "Pilot." Episode no. 8. Directed by Millicent Shelton and written by Gladys Rodriguez. FOX, February 15, 2017.

3. Laura Unger, "Transgender People Face Alarmingly High Risk of Suicide." *USA Today*. August 16, 2015. http://www.usatoday.com/story/news/nation/2015/08/16/transgender-individuals-face-high-rates—suicide-attempts/31626633/. Accessed on March 5, 2017.

4. Bethonie Butler, "'Star' Isn't Even the Good Kind of Bad. Lee Daniels's New Fox Drama Is Just Bad." *The Washington Post*. December 14, 2016. Accessed on December 16, 2016. https://www.washingtonpost.com/news/arts-and-entertainment/wp/2016/12/14/star-isnt-even-the-good-kind-of-bad-lee-danielss-new-fox-drama-is-just-bad/?utm_term=.474522d16eab.

5. Laura Berger, "HBO Launches Writing Fellowship to Find Diverse and Emerging Writers." *Indiewire*. February 27, 2015. Accessed on November 24, 2016. http://www.indiewire.com/2015/02/hbo-launches-writing-fellowship-to-find-diverse-and-emerging-writers-204434/.

6. *American Race*. Episode no. 3, TNT, May 13, 2017.

7. "Making it rain" is the act of throwing money in the air and watching it rain down on the exotic dancers at an African American gentlemen's club.

8. *The Carmichael Show*, "Kale." Episode no. 3. Directed by Michael Zinberg and written by Michael Royce. NBC, September 2, 2015.

9. Nadine Matthews, "Lynn Whitfield on Her New Role in OWN's 'Greenleaf.'" *The Afro American*. September 2, 2016. C1.

10. Chiqui Guyjoco, "Erica Campbell: Oprah's Greenleaf TV drama may be 'upsetting' for some churchgoers." *Christian Times*. July 10, 2016. Accessed on December 16, 2016. http://christiantimes.com/article/erica-campbell-says-oprahs-greenleaf-tv-drama-may-be-upsetting-for-some-church-people/58587.htm.

11. Jonathan L. Walton, *Watch This! The Ethics and Aesthetics of Black Televangelism* (New York: New York University Press, 2009), 1–2.

12. Trap music is a genre of hip-hop that speaks to this reality in the South. The Trap is a slang term used in the South for the dope house.

13. *Atlanta*, Episode no. 2, first broadcast September 6, 2016, by FX. Directed by Hiro Murai and written by Stephen Glover.

14. Ibid.

15. Salamishah Tillet, "What TV Says About Race and Money." *The New York Times*, January 6, 2017. Accessed on January 9, 2017. http://www.nytimes.com/2017/01/06/arts/television/what-tv-says-about-race-and-money.html?src=recg&_r=0.

16. A buppie is an abbreviation for a black urban professional. The term became en vogue in the 1980s. Saditty is a term in the African American vernacular used to describe a snobbish person belonging to the bourgeoisie.

17. Chris Rock mocks lazy African American fathers in his 1999 HBO standup comedy special *Bigger & Blacker*.

18. Issa Rae received a 2017 Golden Globe nomination for her performance in the series.

19. Beyoncé, "Flawless," *Beyoncé*. Parkwood-Entertainment/Columbia Records, 2013.

20. Kellee Terrell, "Why It's Important to Show Black Female Friendship on Television." *Vogue*. July 21, 2017. Accessed on August 16, 2017. http://www.vogue.com/article/insecure-issa-rae-yvonne-orji-black-female-friendship-onscreen.

21. Maiysha Kai, "Is *Insecure* Preying on Black Women's Insecurities? HBO Finally Has a Series with a Black Cast, but the Single-Black-Woman Trope Is Tiring." *The Root*. September 28, 2016. Accessed on November 18, 2016. http://www.theroot.com/articles/culture/2016/09/is-insecure-preying-on-black-womens-insecurities/.

22. Tillet.

23. *Insecure*, "Guilty as Fuck." Episode no. 6. Directed by Debbi Allen and written by Amy Aniobi. HBO, November 13, 2016.

24. Fien Adriaens and Sofie Van Bauwel, "*Sex and the City*: A Postfeminist Point of View? Or How Popular Culture Functions as a Channel for Feminist Discourse." *The Journal of Popular Culture*. 47 (2014): 179.

25. Adilifi Nama, *Super Black: American Pop Culture and Black Superheroes* (Austin: University of Texas Press, 2011), 55–56.

26. Mehershala Ali won the Academy Award for Best Supporting Actor for his role as Juan in the 2016 film *Moonlight*.

27. Ellen McGirt, "Netflix's 'Luke Cage' Part of a New, Quiet Revolution in Entertainment." *Fortune*. October 3, 2016. Accessed on November 18, 2016. http://fortune.com/2016/10/03/netflix-luke-cage-black-super-hero/.

28. Lawrence Ware, "Luke Cage: A Bulletproof Black Man in the Black Lives Matter Era." *The Root*. September 30, 2016. Accessed on November 18, 2016. http://www.theroot.com/articles/culture/2016/09/luke-cage-a-bulletproof-black-man-in-the-black-lives-matter-era/.

29. *Luke Cage*, Episode no. 12, first broadcast

September 30, 2016, by Netflix. Directed by Phil Abraham and written by Akela Cooper and Charles Murray.

30. William Harvey, president of Hampton University, publicly chided *The Quad* in an open letter for what he felt was a "bogus misrepresentation" of HBCUs as places where students, faculty, and administrators are "driven by sex, alcohol, marijuana, low self-esteem, parties, and a preoccupation with music."

31. Inside episode one of TNT's *Claws*.

32. Genatta M. Adams, "#OscarsSoBlack: Finally, Some Melanin-Proficient People Receive Nominations." *The Root*. January 24, 2017. Accessed on January 24, 2017. http://www.theroot.com/oscarssoblack-finally-some-melanin-proficient-people-1791557446.

33. Ben Jacobs and Warren Murray, "Donald Trump Under Fire After Failing to Denounce Virginia White Supremacists." *The Guardian*. August 13, 2017. Accessed on August 25, 2017. https://www.theguardian.com/us-news/2017/aug/12/charlottesville-protest-trump-condemns-violence-many-sides.

Bibliography

Abrahams, Roger D. *Deep Down in the Jungle: Negro Narrative Folklore from the Streets of Philadelphia*. Chicago, IL: Aldine, 1970.

Acham, Christine. *Revolution Televised: Prime Time and the Struggle for Black Power*. Minneapolis: University of Minnesota Press, 2005.

Adams, Genatta M. "#Oscarssoblack: Finally, Some Melanin-Proficient People Receive Nominations." *The Root*. January 24, 2017. Accessed on January 24, 2017. http://www.theroot.com/oscarssoblack-finally-some-melanin-proficient-people-1791557446.

Adams, James Truslow. *The Epic of America*. Boston, MA: Little Brown & Company, 1931.

Adaway, Desiree. "You Want the Power but Not the Pain: Some Notes for White Women Who Love Cookie." *The Feminist Wire*. October 22, 2015. Accessed on July 6, 2016. http://www.thefeministwire.com/2015/10/you-want-the-power-but-not-the-pain-some-notes-for-white-women-who-love-cookie/.

Adichie, Chimamanda Ngozi. *We Should All Be Feminists*. New York: Anchor Books, 2012.

Adlakha, Siddhant. "Jay-Z's Moonlight Video: On Whiteness as American Export." August 11, 2017. Accessed on August 13, 2017. http://birthmoviesdeath.com/2017/08/11/jay-zs-moonlight-video-on-whiteness-as-american-export.

Alexander, Michelle. *The New Jim Crow: Mass Incarceration in the Age of Colorblindness*. New York: New Press, 2012.

Allen, Bonnie. "Movin' on Up: The Jeffersons." *Essence*. October 1981.

Ang, Ien. *Watching "Dallas": Soap Opera and the Melodramatic Imagination*. New York: Routledge, 1986.

Barker, Cory. "Is 'Empire' in Trouble?" *Complex*. Accessed on June 20, 2016. November 13, 2015. http://www.complex.com/pop-culture/2015/11/empire-ratings-decline.

Baron, Steve. "Wednesday Final Ratings: 'Arrow' & 'Survivor' Adjusted Up; 'Supernatural' Adjusted Down & Final 'Empire' Numbers." March 19, 2015. Accessed on June 19, 2016. http://tvbythenumbers.zap2it.com/2015/03/19/wednesday-final-ratings-arrow-supernatural-adjusted-down-final-empire-numbers/377077/.

Baum, Dan. "Legalize It All: How to Win the War on Drugs." *Harper's*. April 2016. Accessed on April 12, 2017. http://harpers.org/archive/2016/04/legalize-it-all/.

Berger, Laura. "HBO Launches Writing Fellowship to Find Diverse and Emerging Writers." *Indiewire*. February 27, 2015. Accessed on November 24, 2016. http://www.indiewire.com/2015/02/hbo-launches-writing-fellowship-to-find-diverse-and-emerging-writers-204434/.

Billingsley, Andrew. *Black Families in White America*. New York: Touchstone Books, 1988.

Birnbaum, Debra. "Remote Controlled: Lee Daniels on 'Star,' 'Empire' and the Mistakes He Regrets." *Variety*. December 15, 2016. Accessed on December 20, 2016. http://variety.com/2016/tv/news/remote-controlled-lee-daniels-empire-star-roseanne-1201943597/.

Blas, Lorena. "More Women Are Behaving Badly on TV, and They're Not All 'Real Housewives.'" *USA Today*. July 6, 2016. Accessed on June 1, 2017. https://www.usatoday.com/story/life/tv/2016/07/06/more-women-behaving-badly-tv-and-not-just-housewives/86572768/.

Blay, Zeba. "How Feminist TV Became the Normal." *The Huffington Post*. June 18, 2015. Accessed on July 7, 2016. http://www.huffingtonpost.com/2015/06/18/how-feminist-tv-became-the-new-normal_n_7567898.html.

———. "The Imperfect but Important Feminism of Cookie Lyon." *The Huffington Post*. September 24, 2015. Accessed on July 13, 2016. http://www.huffingtonpost.com/entry/the-imperfect-but-important-feminism-of-cookie-lyon_us_56005a09e4b08820d919a8e5.

Bogle, Donald. *Toms, Coons, Mulattoes, Mam-

mies, and Bucks: An Interpretive History of Blacks in American Films. 4th Edition. New York: Bloomsbury Academic, 2001.

Bouie, Jamelle. "Don't Forget That Megyn Kelly Is a Racial Demagogue." *Slate.* January 4, 2017. Accessed on February 2, 2017. http://www.slate.com/articles/news_and_politics/politics/2017/01/megyn_kelly_is_a_racial_demagogue.html.

Boyd, Todd. *The Notorious Ph.D.'s Guide to the Super Fly '70s.* New York: Broadway Books, 2007.

Boylorn, Robin. "Love, Hip Hop, and Ratchet Respectability (Something Like a Review)." *Crunk Feminist Collective.* September 10, 2015. Accessed on July 23, 2017. http://www.crunkfeministcollective.com/2015/09/10/love-hip-hop-and-ratchet-respectability-something-like-a-review/.

Bradley, A.C. *Shakespearean Tragedy: Lectures on Hamlet, Othello, King Lear, and Macbeth.* London: Penguin, 1991.

Braxton, Greg. "Farrakhan Appearance on 'Arsenio' Sparks Furor." *Los Angeles Times.* February 25, 1994. Accessed on August 6, 2016. http://articles.latimes.com/1994-02-25/entertainment/ca-27285_1_louis-farrakhan.

Bristol, Keir. "On Moya Bailey, Misogynoir, and Why Both Are Important." May 27, 2014. Accessed on December 27, 2016. http://www.thevisibilityproject.com/2014/05/27/on-moya-bailey-misogynoir-and-why-both-are-important/.

Brown, Melissa. "Ready to Ditch White Feminism? Here Are 6 Black Feminist Concepts You Need to Know." Accessed on December 28, 2016. December 2, 2016. https://dailyprogressive.org/2016/12/ready-ditch-white-feminism-6-black-feminist-concepts-need-know/?utm_source=EverydayFeminism&utm_campaign=ef-fb-page.

Brown, Tammy L. "An Interview with James Amos," in African *Americans on Television: Race-ing for Ratings.* Edited by David J. Leonard and Lisa A. Guerrero, 34–44. Santa Barbara, CA: Praeger, 2013.

Butler, Bethonie. "'Star' Isn't Even the Good Kind of Bad. Lee Daniels's New Fox Drama Is Just Bad." *The Washington Post.* December 14, 2016. Accessed on December 16, 2016. https://www.washingtonpost.com/news/arts-and-entertainment/wp/2016/12/14/star-isnt-even-the-good-kind-of-bad-lee-danielss-new-fox-drama-is-just-bad/?utm_term=.474522d16eab.

Butters, Gerald. *Black Manhood on the Silent Screen.* Lawrence: University Press of Kansas, 2002.

Callahan, Yesha. "John Amos Says He Was Kicked Off Good Times Because He Didn't Agree with the Shucking and Jiving." *The Root.* June 4, 2015. Accessed on June 22, 2016. http://www.theroot.com/blog/the-grapevine/john_amos_says_he_was_kicked_off_good_times_because_he_didn_t_agree_with/.

_____. "Lee Daniels Responds to Tavis Smiley's Critique of *Empire.*" *The Root.* April 9, 2015. Accessed on November 25, 2016. http://www.theroot.com/blogs/the_grapevine/2015/04/lee_daniels_responds_to_tavis_smiley_s_critique_of_empire.html.

Campbell, Rana. "Black Men at Princeton Share Their Experiences." *The Huffington Post.* June 19, 2014. Accessed on July 20, 2016. http://www.huffingtonpost.com/rana-campbell/black-men-at-princeton-sh_b_5352980.html.

Cauvin, Henri E. "A Drug Kingpin's Hot-Selling Story." *The Washington Post.* July 22, 2005. Accessed on September 16, 2016. http://www.washingtonpost.com/wp-dyn/content/article/2005/07/21/AR2005072102517.html.

Chappell, Bill. "Supreme Court Declares Same-Sex Marriage Legal in All 50 States." *NPR.* June 26, 2015. Accessed on July 28, 2016. http://www.npr.org/sections/thetwo-way/2015/06/26/417717613/supreme-court-rules-all-states-must-allow-same-sex-marriages.

Clark-Flory, Tracy. "Feminists Can Twerk Too: What Annie Lennox Misunderstands About Beyoncé." *Salon.* October 22, 2014. Accessed on April 23, 2017. http://www.salon.com/2014/10/22/feminists_can_twerk_too_what_annie_lennox_misunderstands_about_beyonce/.

Coates, Ta-Nehisi. *Between the World and Me.* New York: Spiegel & Grau, 2015.

_____. "The Black Family in the Age of Mass Incarceration." *The Atlantic.* October 2015. Accessed on December 14, 2016. http://www.theatlantic.com/magazine/archive/2015/10/the-black-family-in-the-age-of-mass-incarceration/403246/.

_____. "The Case for Reparations." *The Atlantic.* June 2014. Accessed on February 7, 2017. http://www.theatlantic.com/magazine/archive/2014/06/the-case-for-reparations/361631/.

Collins, Patricia Hill. "Booty Call: Sex, Violence, and Images of Black Masculinity," in *Media and Cultural Studies: Keyworks.* Edited by Meenakshi Gigi Durham and Douglas M. Kellner. Oxford, United Kingdom: Wiley Blackwell, 2012.

Cone, James H. *Martin & Malcolm & America: A Dream or a Nightmare.* Maryknoll, NY: Orbis Books, 2012.

Coontz, Stephanie. *The Way We Never Were: American Families and the Nostalgia Trap.* New York: Basic Books, 2000.

Corinthios, Aurlie and Jessica Fecteau. "Taraji P. Henson Wins the 2016 Golden Globe for Best Actress in a Television Series, Drama." *People.* January 10, 2016. Accessed on March 9, 2016. http://www.people.com/people/package/article/0,,20972047_20978875,00.html.

Coscarelli, Joe. "Jay Z to Be the First Rapper in the Songwriters Hall of Fame." *The New York Times.* February 22, 2017. Accessed on June 16, 2017. https://www.nytimes.com/2017/02/22/arts/music/jay-z-songwriters-hall-of-fame.html?_r=0.

Cottle, Ana. "'The Handmaid's Tale': A White Feminist's Dystopia." *Alternet.* May 28, 2017. Accessed on June 2, 2017. http://www.alternet.org/culture/handmaids-tale-white-feminists-dystopia.

Cummings-Yeates, Rosalind. "Runaway Hit Show 'Empire' Upholds Light-Skin Vs. Dark-Skin Power Divide." *AlterNet.* March 21, 2015. Accessed on June 13, 2016. http://www.alternet.org/media/runaway-hit-show-empire-upholds-light-skin-vs-dark-skin-power-divide.

Cutts, Quiana M. "The Black Family in the New Millennium: The *Bernie Mac Show, My Wife and Kids,* and *Everybody Hates Chris,*" in *African Americans on Television: Race-In for Ratings.* Edited by David L. Leonard and Lisa A. Guerrero. Santa Barbara, Ca: Praeger, 2013.

D'angelo, Joe. "Jay-Z Pleads Guilty to Stabbing, Faces Three Years' Probation." *MTV.* October 17, 2001. Accessed on June 30, 2016. http://www.mtv.com/news/1450090/jay-z-pleads-guilty-to-stabbing-faces-three-years-probation/.

Dale, Maryclaire. "Bill Cosby Charged with Sexually Assaulting a Woman." *Associated Press.* December 30, 2015. http://bigstory.ap.org/article/df3cf7cb94494542bcbd58e3dc2b9748/results-bill-cosby-criminal-inquiry-be-announced.

Dandridge-Lemco, Ben. "Timbaland Leaves *Empire* TV Series Rodney 'Darkchild' Jerkins and Ester Dean Have Joined Fox's Hit Show." *The Fader.* September 14, 2016. Accessed on October 19, 2016. http://www.thefader.com/2016/09/14/timbaland-exits-empire-season-3-darkchild.

Daniels, Ashley. "For Colored Girls Considering Womanism When Feminism Isn't Enough." *For Harriet.* February 2015. Accessed on April 2, 2017. http://www.forharriet.com/2015/02/a-colored-girl-considering-womanism.html#ixzz4d7ucQd4W.

Dastagir, Alia E. "What Is Intersectional Feminism? A Look at the Term You May Be Hearing a Lot." *USA Today.* January 19, 2017. Accessed on January 26, 2017. http://www.usatoday.com/story/news/2017/01/19/feminism-intersectionality-racism-sexism-class/96633750/.

Datcher, Mary L. "Chicago's Talent Behind 'Empire.'" *Chicago Defender.* October 3, 2015. Accessed on June 16, 2016. http://newpittsburghcourieronline.com/2015/10/03/chicagos-talent-behind-empire/.

Deggans, Eric. "Does Fox's 'Empire' Break or Bolster Black Stereotypes?" *NPR.* March 18, 2015. Accessed on August 10, 2016. http://www.npr.org/sections/monkeysee/2015/03/18/393785570/does-foxs-empire-break-or-bolster-black-stereotypes.

Delaney, Sam. "Omar Little Is the Gay Stick-Up Man Who Robs Drug Dealers for a Living in the Wire." *The Guardian.* July 19, 2008. Accessed on July 22, 2016. https://www.theguardian.com/culture/2008/jul/19/television.wire.

Detesta, Yohana. "How Beyoncé's *Lemonade* Helped Bring a Groundbreaking Film Back to Theaters." *Vanity Fair.* August 22, 2016. Accessed on March 30, 2017. http://www.vanityfair.com/hollywood/2016/08/daughters-of-the-dust-exclusive.

DeVega, Chauncey. "How 'The Cosby Show' Duped America: The Sitcom That Enabled Our Ugliest Reagan-Era Fantasies" *Slate.* July 12, 2015. Accessed on April 16, 2017. http://www.salon.com/2015/07/12/how_the_cosby_show_duped_america_the_sitcom_that_enabled_our_ugliest_reagan_era_fantasies/.

Dionne, Evette. "The Twerking Feminist." *Mic.* October 25, 2013. Accessed on December 28, 2016. https://mic.com/articles/69657/the-twerking-feminist#.uYwRdWyFE.

Donahue, Anne T. "'Empire' Costume Designer Rita McGhee Explains Cookie's Fur and Lucious's Scarves." *Cosmopolitan.* February 4, 2015. Accessed on July 8, 2015. http://www.cosmopolitan.com/entertainment/tv/a36077/empire-costumer-rita-mcghee-interview/.

Downs, Jim. *Sick from Freedom: African-American Illness and Suffering During the Civil War and Reconstruction.* United Kingdom: Oxford University Press, 2012.

Dredge, Stuart. "Jay Z Aims to Topple Spotify with Music Streaming Service Tidal." *The Guardian.* March 31, 2015. Accessed on June 30, 2016. https://www.theguardian.com/music/2015/mar/31/jay-z-spotify-music-streaming-relaunch-tidal-support-artist.

Du Bois, W.E.B. *The Souls of Black Folk*. New York: Bantam Classic, 1903.

———. "The Talented Tenth," in *The Negro Problem: A Series of Articles by Representative Negroes of Today* (1903), edited by Booker T. Washington. Bloomington: Indiana University Press, 1903.

Duca, Lauren. "How Doyle from 'Gilmore Girls' Came Up with the Idea for 'Empire.'" *The Huffington Post*. January 10, 2015. Accessed on December 20, 2016. http://www.huffingtonpost.com/2015/06/10/danny-strong-doyle-empire_n_7542820.html.

Dufton, Emily. "The War on Drugs: How President Nixon Tied Addiction to Crime." *The Atlantic*. March 26, 2012. Accessed on September 16, 2016. http://www.theatlantic.com/health/archive/2012/03/the-war-on-drugs-how-president-nixon-tied-addiction-to-crime/254319/.

Dunn, Stephane. *"Baad Bitches" & Sassy Supermamas: Black Power Action Films*. Urbana and Chicago: University of Illinois, 2008.

Dyson, Michael Eric. *Reflecting Black: African-American Cultural Criticism*. Minneapolis: University of Minnesota Press, 1993.

———. *Tears We Cannot Stop: A Sermon to White America*. New York: St. Martin's Press, 2017.

———. "What's Behind Steph Curry's MVP Life: Faith, Fatherhood, Ayesha's Feminism and Family." *The Undefeated*. June 2, 2016. Accessed on June 24, 2016. https://theundefeated.com/features/whats-behind-steph-currys-mvp-life/.

Edwards, Justin D. and Rune Graulund. *Grotesque*. New York: Routledge, 2013.

Ehrlich, Robert. "A Permanent Family Crisis: The Problem of Fatherless Children Persists Half a Century After the Moynihan Report." *National Review*. October 11, 2014. Accessed on June 22, 2016. http://www.nationalreview.com/article/390111/permanent-family-crisis-robert-ehrlich.

Ellis, Ralph, Ashley Fantz, Faith Karimi, and Elliott C. McLaughlin. "Orlando Shooting: 49 Killed, Shooter Pledged Isis Allegiance." *CNN*. June 13, 2016. Accessed on July 28, 2016. http://www.cnn.com/2016/06/12/us/orlando-nightclub-shooting/.

Ellison, Ralph. "Change the Joke and Slip the Yoke," in *Shadow and Act*. New York: Random House, 1972.

Ely, Melvin Patrick. *The Adventures of Amos 'n' Andy: A Social History of an American Phenomenon*. New York: The Free Press, 1991.

Ember, Sydney. "11 Sue Fox News, Citing 'Intolerable' Racial Bias." *The New York Times*. April 25, 2017. Accessed on May 1, 2017. https://www.nytimes.com/2017/04/25/business/media/fox-news-racial-discrimination-lawsuit.html?_r=0.

Espinoza, Joshua. "Diddy and Jay Z Lead Forbes' List Wealthiest Hip-Hop Artists of 2017 List." *Complex*. May 10, 2017. Accessed on May 14, 2017. http://www.complex.com/music/2017/05/forbes-releases-list-of-wealthiest-hip-hop-artists-2017.

Fallon, Kevin. "The 'Real' Cookie Lyon Sues 'Empire' for $300 Million, Claiming Fox Series Is Based on Her Life." *The Daily Beast*. August 4, 2015. Accessed on June 20, 2016. http://www.thedailybeast.com/articles/2015/08/04/the-real-cookie-lyons-sues-empire-for-300-million-claiming-fox-series-is-based-on-her-life.html.

Feuer, Jane. "Melodrama, Serial Form and Television Today." *Screen*. Volume 25, Issue 1. January-February 1984.

Fleming, Mike, Jr. "Jay Z Makes 2-Year Overall Movie & TV Deal with Weinstein Company." *Deadline*. September 29, 2016. Accessed on September 29, 2016. http://deadline.com/2016/09/jay-z-movie-tv-deal-weinstein-company-1201828241/.

Flint, Joe. "Pepsi Gets Taste of 'Empire' Drama." *The Wall Street Journal*. November 19, 2015. Accessed on June 10, 2016. http://www.wsj.com/articles/pepsi-gets-taste-of-empire-drama-1447902181.

Flores, Elaine G. "What *Empire* Gets Wrong (and Right) About Bipolar Disorder." *The Root*. March 6, 2015. Accessed on June 23, 2016. . http://www.theroot.com/articles/culture/2015/03/what_empire_gets_wrong_and_right_about_bipolar_disorder.html.

Fogel, Jennifer M. "In Contemporary Television Series." Ph.D. diss., The University of Michigan, 2012.

Foner, Eric. *Reconstruction: America's Unfinished Revolution*. New York: HarperCollins, 1988.

Foner, Eric and John A. Garraty. *The Reader's Companion to American History*. New York: Houghton Mifflin Harcourt Publishing Company, 1991.

Foster, Kimberly. "Wrestling with Respectability in the Age of #Blacklivesmatter: A Dialogue." *For Harriet*. October 13, 2015. Accessed on January 2, 2016. http://www.forharriet.com/2015/10/wrestling-with-respectability-in-age-of.html#axzz4ojmTSMVY.

Franklin, John Hope and Loren Schweninger. *Runaway Slaves: Rebels on the Plantation*. United Kingdom: Oxford University Press, 1999.

Fraser, Lisa. "Beyond Black Twitter: Black Millennials Rule the Internet." *Black Enterprise.* October 22, 2016. Accessed on December 22, 2016. http://www.blackenterprise.com/news/black-millennials-powerful-rule-internet/.

Frazier, E. Franklin. *The Negro Family in the United States.* New York: The Dryden Press, 1951.

Friedlander, Whitney. "Bounce TV Pulls 'Cosby' Reruns, Bet's Centric Yanks 'The Cosby Show.'" *Variety.* July 7, 2015. Accessed by June 22, 2016. http://variety.com/2015/tv/news/cosby-reruns-bounce-tv-1201535254/.

Fuller, Alice. "What Fox's 'Empire' Teaches Us About Social Media Marketing." April 1, 2015. Accessed on June 17, 2016. http://sheersocial.com/what-foxs-empire-teaches-us-about-social-media-marketing/#.V03kPvkrKM8.

Fuller, James. "Taraji Henson's Son's Father Was Murdered & She Used to Be on Welfare." *Global Grind.* February 13, 2009. Accessed on July 12, 2015. http://globalgrind.com/2009/02/13/taraji-hensons-sons-father-was-murdered-she-used-to-be-on-welfare/.

Gaines, Kevin. *Uplifting the Race: Black Leadership, Politics and Culture in the Twentieth Century.* Chapel Hill: University of North Carolina Press, 1996.

Gardner, Eriq. "Fox Gets to Keep 'Empire' Series Title After Beating Hip-Hop Record Label in Court." *Hollywood Reporter.* February 3, 2016. Accessed on June 20, 2016. http://www.hollywoodreporter.com/thr-esq/fox-gets-keep-empire-series-861607.

Gaston, Herron Keyon. "Mass Incarceration's Impact on Black and Latino Women and Children." *The Huffington Post.* April 22, 2015. Accessed on December 14, 2016. http://www.huffingtonpost.com/herron-keyon-gaston/mass-incarcerations-impact-black-latino_b_6702900.html.

Gates, Henry Louis, Jr. "TV'S Black World Turns—But Stays Unreal." *The New York Times.* November 12, 1989. Accessed on June 23, 2016. http://www.nytimes.com/1989/11/12/arts/tv-s-black-world-turns-but-stays-unreal.html.

Gay, Roxane. *Bad Feminist: Essays.* New York: Harper Perennial, 2014.

Gazdik, Tanya. "African-American Buying Power Tops $1 Trillion." *MarketingDaily.* October 3, 2016. Accessed on December 30, 2016. http://www.mediapost.com/publications/article/285767/african-american-buying-power-tops-1-trillion.html.

Gealey, Grace. "The Empire Star Writes About the Lessons She Learned from a Near-Death Experience." *Essence.* March 20, 2015. Accessed on December 21, 2016. http://www.essence.com/2015/03/20/empire-star-grace-gealey-saying-goodbye.

George, Kat. "Why Missy Elliot's Feminist Legacy Is Criminally Underrated." *Dazed.* January 22, 2016. Accessed on April 2, 2017. http://www.dazeddigital.com/music/article/29353/1/why-missy-elliott-s-feminist-legacy-is-criminally-underrated.

Geraghty, Christine. *Women and Soap Opera.* Cambridge, MA: Polity Press, 1991.

Gibson, Ernest L., III. "For Whom the Bell Tolls: The *Wire's* Stringer Bell as Tragic Intellectual." *Americana: The Journal of American Popular Culture (1900–Present).* Spring 2011, Volume 10, Issue 1. Http://Www.Americanpopularculture.Com/Journal/Articles/Spring_2011/Gibson.Htm.

Givhan, Robin. "How 'Empire' Charts the Rise of Hip-Hop Through Fabulous Fashion." *The Washington Post.* February 3, 2015. Accessed on June 30, 2016. https://www.washingtonpost.com/news/arts-and-entertainment/wp/2015/02/03/how-empire-charts-the-rise-of-hip-hop-through-fabulous-fashion/.

_____. "On 'Scandal,' Olivia's New Red Leather Trenchcoat Means Everything You Think It Does." *The Washington Post.* February 10, 2016. Accessed on July 7, 2016. https://www.washingtonpost.com/news/arts-and-entertainment/wp/2016/02/10/on-scandal-olivias-new-red-leather-trenchcoat-means-everything-you-think-it-does/.

Gladora, Chris. "History: Housing Policy and Segregation in Baltimore." Summer 2006 Issue I. Accessed on November 18, 2015 https://indyreader.org/content/history-housing-policy-and-segregation-baltimore.

Goff, Keli. "Do Whites Have a Mental-Health Edge?" *The Root.* May 8, 2013. Accessed on June 23, 2016. http://www.theroot.com/articles/culture/2013/05/mental_health_illness_in_blacks_failure_to_seek_treatment_may_be_holding_us_back.3.html.

Goldfield, David, Carl Abbott, Virginia DeJohn Anderson, Jo Anne Argersinger, Peter Argersinger, and William Barney. *The American Journey: A History of the United States.* Boston, MA: Pearson, 2017.

Graham, David A. "Sandra Bland and the Long History of Racism in Waller County, Texas." *The Atlantic.* July 21, 2015. Accessed on July 10, 2016. http://www.theatlantic.com/politics/archive/2015/07/sandra-bland-waller-county-racism/398975/.

Graham, Lawrence Otis. *Our Kind of People: In-*

side America's Black Upper Class. New York: HarperCollins, 1999.

Gray, Herman. *Watching Race: Television and the Struggle for Blackness*. Minneapolis: University of Minnesota Press, 1995.

Green, R.H. "'Birth of a Race': The Obscure Demise of a Would-Be Rebuttal to Racism." *NPR*. October 25, 2015. Accessed on November 24, 2016. http://www.npr.org/2015/10/25/451717690/birth-of-a-race-the-obscure-demise-of-a-would-be-rebuttal-to-racism.

Greenburg, Zack O'Malley. "The Forbes Five: Hip-Hop's Wealthiest Artists 2017." *Forbes*. May 10, 2017. Accessed on May 10, 2017. https://www.forbes.com/sites/zackomalleygreenburg/2017/05/10/the-forbes-five-hip-hops-wealthiest-artists-2017/#1d7759002273.

———. "Sprint Buys 33% of Jay Z's Tidal for a Reported $200 Million." *Forbes*. January 23, 2017. Accessed on January 24, 2017. http://www.forbes.com/sites/zackomalleygreenburg/2017/01/23/sprint-buys-33-of-jay-zs-tidal-for-a-reported-200-million/#33c2eaa51471.

———. "Sprint's Investment in Jay Z's Tidal: Prelude to a Bigger Deal?" *Forbes*. January 24, 2017. http://www.forbes.com/sites/zackomalleygreenburg/2017/01/24/sprints-investment-in-jay-zs-tidal-prelude-to-a-bigger-deal/#6222852470b2. Accessed on February 5, 2017.

Gutman, Herbert. *The Black Family in Slavery and Freedom*. 1750–1925. New York: Vintage, 1977.

Guyjoco, Chiqui. "Erica Campbell: Oprah's Greenleaf TV Drama May Be 'Upsetting' for Some Churchgoers." *Christian Times*. July 10, 2016. Accessed on February 22, 2017. http://christiantimes.com/article/erica-campbell-says-oprahs-greenleaf-tv-drama-may-be-upsetting-for-some-church-people/58587.htm.

Halberstam, Judith. *Female Masculinity*. Durham, NC: Duke University Press, 1998.

Hamm, Nia. "Black Folks and Mental Health: Why Do We Suffer in Silence?" *Ebony*. October 1, 2012. Accessed on June 23, 2016. http://www.ebony.com/wellness-empowerment/black-folks-and-mental-health-610#axzz4CS8uOQT0.

Handley, Lucy. "Jay Z's Latest Ace of Spades Champagne Will Cost $850, Only 2,333 Bottles Available." *CNBC*. April 6, 2017. Accessed on May 11, 2017. http://www.cnbc.com/2017/04/06/jay-zs-latest-ace-of-spades-champagne-will-cost-850.html.

Hannerz, Ulf. "What Ghetto Males Are Like: Another Look," in *Afro-American Anthropology: Contemporary Perspectives*. Edited by Norman E. Whitten, Jr. New York: The Free Press, 1970.

Hansen, Tyler. "Fox Blames Obamacare for Fictional Layoffs at Cleveland Clinic," Blog November 25, 2013. Accessed on January 4, 2014. http://mediamatters.org/blog/2013/11/25/fox-blames-obamacare-for-fictional-layoffs-at-c/197048.

Harris, Aisha. "Why *Scandal's* Ferguson-Themed Episode Was So Frustrating." *Slate*. March 6, 2015. Accessed on July 7, 2016. http://www.slate.com/blogs/browbeat/2015/03/06/scandal_police_brutality_episode_the_lawn_chair_tackles_michael-brown-video.html.

Hartman, Mitchell. "Nielsen TV Ratings Push into Social Media." *Marketplace*. January 20, 2016. Accessed on December 22, 2016. http://www.marketplace.org/2016/01/20/world/media-ratings-agency-pushes-new-ground.

Haverstraw, Jack. "The Making of a Movie Star." *Sepia*. May 1975.

Henson, Tajari P. *Around the Way Girl*. New York: Atria, 2016.

Hernandez, Raymond. "Congresswoman Takes a Whack at 'The Sopranos' Stereotype." *The New York Times*. May 24, 2001. Accessed on August 8, 2016. http://www.nytimes.com/2001/05/24/nyregion/congresswoman-takes-a-whack-at-the-sopranos-stereotype.html.

Higginbotham, Evelyn Brooks. *Righteous Discontent: The Women's Movement in the Black Baptist Church, 1880–1920*. Cambridge, MA: Harvard University Press, 1994.

Hill, Marc Lamont. "Scared Straight: Hip-Hop, Outing, and the Pedagogy of Queerness," in *That's the Joint!: The Hip-Hop Studies Reader* edited by Murray Forman and Mark Anthony Neal. New York: Routledge, 2004.

Hobson, Janell. "Beyoncé's Fierce Feminism." *Ms*. March 7, 2015. Accessed on July 13, 2016. http://msmagazine.com/blog/2015/03/07/beyonces-fierce-feminism/.

Hoo, Fawnia Soo. "How the 'Empire' Costume Designer Is Dressing the Lyon Family in Season 2." *Fashionista*. September 16, 2015. Accessed on December 21, 2016. http://fashionista.com/2015/09/empire-costumes-paolo-nieddu.

hooks, bell. *We Real Cool: Black Men and Masculinity*. New York: Routledge, 2003.

Hope, Clover. "Empire: Jamal Lyon Comes Out, Gives the World a Show." *The Muse*. February 26, 2015. Accessed on June 5, 2017. http://themuse.jezebel.com/empire-jamal-lyon-comes-out-gives-the-world-ashow-1688209305.

Howard, Shenna C. "Dr. Boyce Watkins Charges Lee Daniels with Having a 'Gay Agenda.'" *The*

Huffington Post. May 5, 2015. Accessed on July 21, 2016. http://www.huffingtonpost.com/sheena-c-howard/boyce-watkins-empire-gay_b_6781362.html.

Hudson-Weems, Clenora. *Africana Womanism: Reclaiming Ourselves.* Gordonsville, VA: Bedford/St. Martin's, 2004.

Humphrey, Robert A. "Representing Race, Gender, and Sexuality in Empire: (Counter)Hegemonic Masculinity, Black Fatherhood, and Homosexuality in Primetime Television." Master's thesis, Bowling Green State University, 2016.

Izrael, Jimi. "Tyler Perry Vs. Spike Lee: A Debate Over Class and 'Coonery.'" *NPR.* April 22, 2011. Accessed on August 13, 2017. Http://Www.Npr.Org/Sections/Tellmemore/2011/04/22/135630682/Tyler-Perry-Vs-Spike-Lee-A-Debate-Over-Class-And-Coonery.

J., Miranda. "'Empire' Act and Rapper Yazz Is Being Mentored by Will Smith." *Xxl.* January 22, 2015. Accessed on May 4, 2016. http://www.xxlmag.com/news/2015/01/empire-actor-yazz-will-smith/.

Jacobs, Ben and Murray, Warren. "Donald Trump Under Fire After Failing to Denounce Virginia White Supremacists." *The Guardian.* August 13, 2017. Accessed on August 25, 2017. https://www.theguardian.com/us-news/2017/aug/12/charlottesville-protest-trump-condemns-violence-many-sides.

Jacobson, Mark. "Lords of Dopetown." *New York Magazine.* October 29, 2007. Accessed on June 28, 2016. http://nymag.com/guides/money/2007/39948/.

———. "The Return of Superfly." *New York Magazine.* August 14, 2000. Accessed on June 28, 2016. http//nymag.com/features/3649/

Jaffrey, Zia. "The Salon Interview—Toni Morrison." *Salon.* February 2, 1998. Accessed on February 11, 2017. http://www.salon.com/1998/02/02/cov_si_02int/.

Jefferson, Margo. *Negroland: A Memoir.* New York: Pantheon Books, 2015.

Jeffries, Michael P. "Drake, Childish Gambino, and the Specter of Black Authenticity." *The Atlantic.* November 22, 2011. Accessed on July 26, 2016. http://www.theatlantic.com/entertainment/archive/2011/11/drake-childish-gambino-and-the-specter-of-black-authenticity/248929/.

Jenkins, Nash. "Jay-Z Responds to Pundit Who Called Him a 'Drug Dealer' in New Track." *Time.* May 31, 2016. Accessed on February 6, 2017. Http://Time.Com/4353218/Jay-Z-Drug-Dealers-Anonymous-Pusha-T/.

Jhally, Sut and Justin Lewis. *Enlightened Racism: The Cosby Show, Audiences and the Myth of the American Dream.* Boulder, Colorado: Westview Press, 1992.

Johnson, E. Patrick. *Sweet Tea: Black Gay Men of the South.* Chapel Hill: University of North Carolina Press, 2011.

Jones, Kenneth. "Terrence Howard Shoulders Brick Again, Returning to Broadway's Cat." *Playbill.* May 6, 2008. Accessed on June 16, 2016. http://www.playbill.com/article/terrence-howard-shoulders-brick-again-returning-to-broadways-cat-com-149805.

Kai, Maiysha. "Is *Insecure* Preying on Black Women's Insecurities?" *The Root.* September 28, 2016. Accessed on November 18, 2016. http://www.theroot.com/articles/culture/2016/09/is-insecure-preying-on-black-womens-insecurities/.

Kelly, Jacques. "'Little' Melvin Williams, Baltimore Drug Kingpin Who Appeared on 'The Wire,' Dies." *Baltimore Sun.* July 12, 2016. Accessed on June 28, 2016. Http://Www.Baltimoresun.Com/News/Obituaries/Bs-Md-Ob-Melvin-Williams-20151203-Story.Html.

Kennedy, Lesley. "No Office Scandal Here: How to Get Olivia Pope's Work Look for Less." *USA Today.* September 26, 2014. Accessed on July 7, 2016. http://www.today.com/style/get-olivia-popes-scandal-style-less-2D80176913.

Kerri, Audrey Elisa *The Paper Bag Principles: Class, Colorism, and Rumor and the Case of Black Washington, Part 3.* Knoxville: University Press of Tennessee, 2006.

Kessler, Glenn. "The Stale Statistic That One in Three Black Males 'Born Today' Will End Up in Jail." *The Washington Post.* June 16, 2015. Accessed on October 22, 2016. https://www.washingtonpost.com/news/fact-checker/wp/2015/06/16/the-stale-statistic-that-one-in-three-black-males-has-a-chance-of-ending-up-in-jail/.

Kimble, Lindsay. "Empire's Homophobic Story Line Was Ripped from Co-Creator Lee Daniels' Own Childhood." *Us.* February 26, 2015. Accessed on July 21, 2016. http://www.usmagazine.com/entertainment/news/empires-homophobic-story-line-inspired-by-co-creator-lee-daniels-2015262.

Kiuchi, Yuya. *Struggles for Equal Voice: The History of African American Media Democracy.* Albany: State University of New York Press, 2013.

Kornhaber, Spencer. "Hakeem Mans Up." *The Atlantic.* November 5, 2015. Accessed on July 28, 2016. http://www.theatlantic.com/entertain

ment/archive/2015/11/empire-season-2-episode-6-hakeem-masculinity/414247/.

Leenov, Felecia R. "To Blacks, Precious Is 'Demeaned' or 'Angelic.'" *The New York Times.* February 20, 2009. Accessed on August 8, 2016. http://www.nytimes.com/2009/11/21/movies/21precious.html?_r=0.

Leonard, Scott and Michael McClure. *Myth and Knowing: An Introduction to World Mythology.* New York: McGraw-Hill Education, 2003.

Levin, Josh. "The Welfare Queen." *Slate.* December 19, 2013. Access on October 3, 2016. http://www.slate.com/articles/news_and_politics/history/2013/12/linda_taylor_welfare_queen_ronald_reagan_made_her_a_notorious_american_villain.html.

Levine, Lawrence. *Black Culture and Black Consciousness: African-American Folk Thought from Slavery to Freedom.* United Kingdom: Oxford University Press, 1977.

Levy, Clifford J. "Harlem Protest of Rap Lyrics Draws Debate and Steamroller." *The New York Times.* June 6, 1993. Accessed on August 10, 2016. http://www.nytimes.com/1993/06/06/nyregion/harlem-protest-of-rap-lyrics-draws-debate-and-steamroller.html.

Littlejohn, Cynthia. "TV One Grabs 'Empire' Reruns from Fox." *Variety.* April 13, 2016. Accessed on June 18, 2016. http://variety.com/2016/tv/news/empire-tv-one-fox-rerun-rights-1201753238/.

Long, Colleen. "Former Tennis Player James Blake Agrees Not to Sue New York City." *Chicago Tribune.* June 21, 2017. Accessed on June 23, 2017. http://www.chicagotribune.com/sports/international/ct-tennis-james-blake-nypd-settlement-20170621-story.html.

Love, Bettina L. "Tyler Perry Takes Over TV," in *African Americans on Television: Race-ing for Ratings.* Santa Barbara, CA: Praeger, 2013.

Love, David A. "Beating Our Black Children Furthers the Legacy of Slavery." *The Grio.* September 15, 2014. Accessed on June 23, 2016. http://thegrio.com/2014/09/15/adrian-peterson-child-abuse-slavery/.

Lynch, Jason. "How Fox's Marketing Fanned the Flames of Empire, One of the Biggest New Shows in Years. The Strategy Behind a Breakout Hit." *Adweek.* January 29, 2015. Accessed on June 19, 2016. http://www.adweek.com/news/television/how-foxs-marketing-fanned-flames-empire-one-biggest-new-shows-years-162612.

Magee, Sara. "High School Is Hell: The TV Legacy of *Beverly Hills, 90210* and *Buffy the Vampire Slayer.*" *The Journal of Popular Culture.* 2014. 47.

Majors, Richard and Janet Mancini Billson. *Cool Pose: The Dilemmas of Black Manhood in America.* Lanham, MD: Lexington Books, 1992.

Martin, Nicole. "Women Key in Shaping Black Panther Party." January 6, 2014. Accessed on July 11, 2016. http://gender.stanford.edu/news/2014/women-key-shaping-black-panther-party.

Mathias, Christopher. "Kalief Browder, NYC Teen Jailed for Years with No Conviction, Says Rikers Guard 'Starved' Him." *The Huffington Post.* September 15, 2016. Accessed on October 21, 2016. http://www.huffingtonpost.com/2013/12/02/kalief-browder-n_4373544.html.

Matthews, Nadine. "Lynn Whitfield on Her New Role in Own's 'Greenleaf'" *The Afro-American.* September 2, 2016. C1.

Maxwell, Brandon. "Olivia Pope and the Scandal of Representation." *The Feminist Wire.* February 7, 2013. Accessed on July 7, 2016. http://www.thefeministwire.com/2013/02/olivia-pope-and-the-scandal-of-representation/.

McFadden, Syreeta. "Beyoncé's Lemonade Is #Blackgirlmagic at Its Most Potent." *The Guardian.* April 24, 2016. Accessed on July 13, 2016. http://www.theguardian.com/music/2016/apr/24/beyonce-lemonade-album-video-black-girl-magic-womanhood-america.

McGirt, Ellen. "Netflix's 'Luke Cage': Part of a New, Quiet Revolution in Entertainment." *Fortune.* October 3, 2016. Accessed on November 18, 2016. http://fortune.com/2016/10/03/netflix-luke-cage-black-super-hero/.

Medeiros, Alex and Chandrika Narayan. "Controversial Megachurch Pastor Eddie Long Dies." *CNN.* January 15, 2017. Accessed on January 16, 2017. http://www.cnn.com/2017/01/15/us/bishop-eddie-long-dead/index.html.

Miles, Tiya. "Black Women, Interracial Dating, and Marriage: What's Love Got to Do with It? The *Huffington Post.* November 5, 2013. Accessed on December 1, 2013. Http://Www.Huffingtonpost.Com/Tiya-Miles/Interracial-Dating-And-Marriage_B_4213066.Html.

Miller, Monica L. *Slaves to Fashion: Black Dandyism and the Styling of Black Diasporic Identity.* Durham, NC: Duke University Press, 2009.

Mitchell, Gail. "Timbaland Exits 'Empire' as Rodney Jerkins Signs On: Exclusive." *Billboard.* September 14, 2016. Accessed on October 18, 2016. http://www.billboard.com/articles/columns/hip-hop/7503656/timbaland-exits-eme-rodney-jerkins-ester-dean-exclusive.

Mitchell, Jessica Ann. "Kanye's Frantz Fanon

Complex." December 2, 2013. Accessed on December 18, 2016. https://ourlegaci.com/2013/12/02/kanyes-frantz-fanon-complex/.

Modleski, Tania. *Loving with a Vengeance: Mass Produced Fantasies for Women*. New York: Routledge, 2007.

Morain, Dan. "Garish Oakland Funeral: 1,000 Witness Last Ride of Slain Drug Kingpin." *Los Angeles Times*. August 30, 1986. Accessed on July 17, 2016. http://articles.latimes.com/1986-08-30/news/mn-14145_1_oakland-funeral.

Moynihan, Daniel P. *The Negro Family: The Case for National Action*. Washington, D.C., Office of Policy Planning and Research, U.S. Department of Labor, 1965.

Munoz, Lorenza. "The Hollywood Gospel According to Tyler Perry." *Los Angeles Times*. February 19, 2006. Accessed on June 20, 2016. http://articles.latimes.com/2006/feb/19/business/fi-tylerperry19.

Nama, Adilifi. *Super Black: American Pop Culture and Black Superheroes*. Austin: University of Texas Press, 2011.

Neal, Mark Anthony. *Looking for Leroy: Illegible Black Masculinities*. New York: New York University Press, 2013.

Nestle, Marion. *Soda Politics: Taking on Big Soda (and Winning)*. New York: Oxford University Press, 2015.

Norwin, Alyssa. "'Empire' Stars Taraji P. Henson's Tragic Lover." *Star*. March 26, 2015. Accessed on July 11, 2015. http://starmagazine.com/2015/03/26/taraji-henson-boyfriend-death/.

Nuriddin, Ayah. "'Something Needed to Be Done for the Black Patients': Integrating the Crownsville State Hospital, 1945–1970." (Paper presented at the annual meeting of the Association for the Study of African American Life and History, Atlanta, Georgia, September 24–27, 2015.)

Obie, Brook. "Woman in Viral Photo from Women's March to White Female Allies: 'Listen to Black Woman.'" *The Root*. January 23, 2017. Accessed on January 24, 2017. http://www.theroot.com/woman-in-viral-photo-from-women-s-march-to-white-female-179152461.

Osenlund, R. Kurt. "Lee Daniels on How Empire's Gay Content Is Changing Minds," *Out*. January 23, 2015. Accessed on June 4, 2017. http://www.out.com/entertainment/television/2015/01/23/lee-daniels-howempires-gay-content-changing-minds.

Painia, Brianne A. "My Crown Too Heavy Like the Queen Nefertiti": A Black Feminist Analysis of Erykah Badu, Beyoncé Knowles, Nicki Minaj, and Janelle Monae." Thesis. George Washington University, 2014.

Pearce. Matt. "Kalief Browder, Jailed for Three Years Without a Trial at Rikers Island in New York, Commits Suicide." *Los Angeles Times*. June 7, 2015. Accessed on October 22, 2016. http://www.latimes.com/nation/.

Penrice, Ronda Racha. "Unsung Hollywood: Before Empire, Fox Had New York Undercover, the Original Hip Hop Drama." *The Root*. March 23, 2016. Accessed on August 14, 2017. http://www.theroot.com/unsung-hollywood-before-empire-fox-had-new-york-under-1790854715.

Petkovic, John. "Pam Grier, Queen of 1970s Blaxploitation Films, Speaks in Cleveland on Her Book Tour." *The Plain Dealer*. September 10, 2010. Accessed on October 12, 2016. http://www.cleveland.com/goingout/index.ssf/2010/09/pam_grier_queen_of_1970s_blaxp.html.

Petrozzello, Donna. "'Sopranos' Hits Wrong Note with Italian-Americans." *New York Daily News*. September 8, 1999. Accessed on August 8, 2016. http://articles.chicagotribune.com/1999-09-08/features/9909080134_1_italian-americans-jennifer-melfi-new-series-last-season.

Petski, Denise. "'The New Edition Story' Draws Record Ratings for Bet." *Deadline*. January 31, 2017. Accessed on March 9, 2017. http://deadline.com/2017/01/the-new-edition-story-record-ratings-bet-1201898942/.

Pickens, Josie. "The Respectability Politricks of Ayesha Curry." *Ebony*. December 10, 2015. Accessed on July 13, 2016. http://www.ebony.com/entertainment-culture/the-respectability-politricks-of-ayesha-curry-323#ixzz4CS8Nuodg.

Polan, Dana. *The Sopranos*. Durham, NC: Duke University Press, 2009.

Pols, Mary. "Precious Review: Too Powerful for Tears." *Time*. November 16, 2009. Accessed on December 20, 2016. http://content.time.com/time/magazine/article/0,9171,1935116,00.html.

Ramsey, Donovan X. "The Truth About Black Twitter." *The Atlantic*. April 10, 2015. Accessed on December 22, 2016. http://www.theatlantic.com/technology/archive/2015/04/the-truth-about-black-twitter/390120/

Raymer, Miles. "Jay-Z and the New Age of Rap." *Esquire*. July 8, 2013. Accessed on June 30, 2016. http://www.esquire.com/entertainment/music/a23398/jay-z-magna-carta-holy-grail/.

Read, Jason. "Stringer Bell's Lament: Violence and Legitimacy in Contemporary Capitalism," in *The Wire: Urban Decay and American Television*. Ed. Tiffany Potter and C.W. Marshall. New York: Continuum, 2011.

Richardson, Elaine. "Lil' Kim, Hip-Hop Womanhood and the Naked Truuf," in *Home Girls Make Some Noise! Hip-Hop Feminism Anthology*. Edited by Gwendolyn Pough, Elaine Richardson, Aisha Durham, and Rachel Raimist. Mira Loma, CA: Parker Publishing, 2007.

Roberts, John W. *From Trickster to Badman: The Black Folk Hero in Slavery and Freedom* Philadelphia: University of Pennsylvania Press, 1989.

Roberts, Kamaria and Kenya Downs. "What Beyoncé Teaches Us About the African Diaspora in 'Lemonade.'" *PBS News Hour.* April 29, 2016. Accessed on April 1, 2017. http://www.pbs.org/newshour/art/what-beyonce-teaches-us-about-the-african-diaspora-in-lemonade/.

Robinson, Lisa. "Catch Up with Timbaland, the Man Behind *Empire's* Infectious Beats." *Vanity Fair.* April 2015. Accessed on June 20, 2016. http://www.vanityfair.com/magazine/2015/03/timbaland-empire-music.

Roche, Eddie. "Meet Empire's Costume Designer Paolo Dieddu." November 19, 2015. Accessed on December 21, 2016. https://fashionweekdaily.com/meet-empires-costume-designer-paolo-nieddu/.

Rodulfo, Kristina. "Soon Your Face Can Be Obsessed with 'Empire' Too. Thank You, Covergirl!" *Elle.* March 22, 2016. Accessed on May 1, 2016. http://www.elle.com/beauty/makeup-skin-care/news/a35033/covergirl-empire-collaboration/.

Roig-Franzia, Manuel. "Mistrial Declared in Bill Cosby's Sex-Assault Trial." *The Washington Post.* June 17, 2017. Accessed on June 17, 2017. https://www.washingtonpost.com/lifestyle/style/mistrial-is-declared-in-sexual-assault-trial-of-entertainer-bill-cosby/2017/06/17/6d6d70f2-5114-11e7-be25-3a5193353 81c_story.html?utm_term=.61be6e0639db&wpisrc=nl_most-draw16&wpmm=1.

Rorke, Robert. "How 'Empire' Changed Primetime Diversity for the Better." *New York Post.* October 29, 2015. Accessed on November 29, 2016. http://nypost.com/2015/10/29/how-empire-changed-prime-time-diversity-for-the-better/.

———. "Taraji P. Henson's Rise from the Streets of DC to Hollywood Elite." *New York Post.* October 14, 2016. Accessed on January 26, 2017. http://nypost.com/2016/10/14/taraji-p-hensons-rise-from-the-streets-of-dc-to-hollywood-elite/.

Rovzar, Chris. "Frank Lucas Shouldn't Have Worn That Floor-Length Chinchilla Coat." *New York Magazine.* June 7, 2010. Accessed on May 1, 2017. Accessed on May 1, 2017. http://nymag.com/daily/intelligencer/2010/06/frank_lucas_shouldnt_have_worn.html.

Ryan, Patrick. "Is Kanye West the Greatest Artist of the 21st Century?" *USA Today.* February 9, 2016. Accessed on July 26, 2016. http://www.usatoday.com/story/life/music/2016/02/09/kanye-west-new-album/79814890/#.

Ryan, William. *Blaming the Victim.* New York: Pantheon, 1971.

Satran, Joe. "50 Cent Blames 'Empire' Ratings Dip on 'Gay Stuff.'" *The Huffington Post.* October 6, 2015. Accessed on July 21, 2016. http://www.huffingtonpost.com/entry/50-cent-empire-ratings_us_5612c235e4b0af3706e19b3f.

Sayers, Shoshannay. "Mass Incarceration & People of Color." *Social Coalition for Social Justice.* April 9, 2014. Accessed on December 14, 2016. http://www.southerncoalition.org/mass-incarceration-people-color/.

Schilling, Dave. "Black Gatsbys: Interracial Marriage, Black Social Climbing, and the Rise of Andre on 'Empire.'" *Grantland.* February 26, 2015. Accessed on July 19, 2016. Http://Grantland.Com/Hollywood-Prospectus/Black-Gatsbys-Interracial-Marriage-Black-Social-Climbing-And-The-Rise-Of-Andre-On-Empire/.

Shapiro, Emily. "OJ Simpson Granted Parole for Las Vegas Robbery." *ABC News.* July 20, 2017. Accessed on July 22, 2017. http://abcnews.go.com/US/oj-simpson-granted-parole-las-vegas-robbery/story?id=48689499.

Sherman, Shantella. *In Search of Purity: Popular Eugenics & Racial Uplift Among New Negroes 1915–1935.* Createspace Independent Publishing Platform, 2016.

Silver, Marc. "How 'Empire' Became Social Media's Most Talked-About TV Show." *The Washington Post.* October 26, 2016. Accessed on December 22, 2016. https://www.washingtonpost.com/express/wp/2016/10/26/how-empire-became-social-medias-most-talked-about-tv-show/?utm_term=.d860f458fc91.

Sims, Yvonne D. *Women of Blaxploitation: How the Black Action Film Heroine Changed American Popular Culture.* Jefferson, NC: McFarland, 2006.

Smith, Celia L. "Fashion Flashback: Pam Grier." *Essence.* February 23, 2012. Accessed on July 11, 2016. http://www.essence.com/2012/02/23/fashion-flashback-pam-grier.

Smith, Jada F. "Does Hollywood Still Have a Brown Paper Bag Test?" *The Root.* November 12, 2009. Accessed on January 19, 2016. http://

www.theroot.com/articles/culture/2009/11/all_the_darkskinned_stars_in_precious_are_bad_all_the_lightskinned_stars_in_precious_are_good/.

Stelter, Brian. "Shonda Rhimes Is Leaving ABC for Netflix." *CNN.* August 14, 2017. Accessed on August 15, 2017. http://money.cnn.com/2017/08/14/media/shonda-rhimes-netflix/index.html.

Storrs, Carina. "Suicide Rates Among Young Black Boys on the Rise." *CNN.* May 19, 2005. Accessed on January 14, 2017. http://www.cnn.com/2015/05/19/health/suicide-youth/.

Swearigan, M. Wesley. *FBI Secrets: An Agent's Expose.* Boston, MA: South End Press, 1995.

Taylor, Yuval and Austen, Jane. *Darkest America: Black Minstrelsy from Slavery to Hip-Hop.* New York: W.W. Norton & Company, 2012.

Terrell, Kellee. "Why It's Important to Show Black Female Friendship on Television." *Vogue.* July 21, 2017. Accessed on August 16, 2017. http://www.vogue.com/article/insecure-issa-rae-yvonne-orji-black-female-friendship-onscreen.

Tillet, Salamishah. "What TV Says About Race and Money." *The New York Times.* January 6, 2017. Accessed on January 9, 2017. http://www.nytimes.com/2017/01/06/arts/television/what-tv-says-about-race-and-money.html?src=recg&_r=0.

Toure. "The Book of Jay." *Rolling Stone.* December 11, 2005.

———. *Who's Afraid of Post-Blackness: What It Means to Be Black Now.* New York: Free Press, 2011.

Trebay, Guy. "Homo Thugz Blow Up the Spot." *The Village Voice.* February 8, 2000.

Unger, Laura. "Transgender People Face Alarmingly High Risk of Suicide." *USA Today.* August 16, 2015. Accessed on March 5, 2017. http://www.usatoday.com/story/news/nation/2015/08/16/transgender-individuals-face-high-rates—suicide-attempts/31626633/.

Viola. "Who Needs Hip-Hop Feminism?" *Medium.* April 28, 2015. Accessed on December 28, 2016. https://medium.com/black-feminism/who-needs-hip-hop-feminism-394c40af8f35#.ld08ej60v.

Wallace, Carvell. "Mahershala Ali Thinks We Can Still Make This Country Great." *GQ.* June 19, 2017. Accessed on July 10, 2017. http://www.gq.com/story/mahershala-ali-moonlight-and-america.

Walton, Jonathan L. *Watch This! The Ethics and Aesthetics of Black Televangelism.* New York: New York University Press, 2009.

Ware, Lawrence. "Luke Cage: A Bulletproof Black Man in the Black Lives Matter Era." *The Root.* September 30, 2016. Accessed on November 18, 2016. http://www.theroot.com/articles/culture/2016/09/luke-cage-a-bulletproof-black-man-in-the-black-lives-matter-era/.

Wells, Veronica. "Why the 'Empire' Donnie Mcclurkin Jab Took Things a Little Too Far." *MadameNoire.* September 24, 2015. Accessed on July 22, 2016. http://madamenoire.com/589108/why-the-empire-donnie-mcclurkin-jab-took-things-a-little-too-far/.

White, Kevin. *An Introduction to the Sociology of Health and Mental Illness.* Thousand Oaks, CA: SAGE, 2002.

Wickham, DeWayne. "Bassett Criticism Has Its Merits." *USA Today.* July 8, 2002. Assessed on December 1, 2015. http://usatoday30.usatoday.com/news/comment/columnists/wickham/2002-07-09-wickham.htm.

Wilson, Julee. "The Meaning of #Blackgirlmagic, and How You Can Get Some of It." *The Huffington Post.* January 13, 2016. Accessed on July 8, 2016. http://www.huffingtonpost.com/entry/what-is-black-girl-magic-video_us_5694dad4e4b086bc1cd517f4.

Wilson, William Julius *When Work Disappears: The World of the New Urban Poor.* New York: Vintage, 1997.

Wintz, Cary D. *Harlem Speaks: A Living History of the Harlem Renaissance.* Naperville, IL: Sourcebooks MediaFusion, 2006.

Wong, Curtis M. "Andrew Caldwell, Who Claimed to Have Been 'Delivered' from Homosexuality, Insists Viral Video Is Legitimate." *Huffington Post.* November 14, 2014. Accessed on July 22, 2016. Http://Www.Huffingtonpost.Com/2014/11/14/Andrew-Caldwell-Homosexuality-Video-_N_6159278.Html.

Woods, Kasey. "The Beautiful Face of Mental Illness." *Ebony.* February 18, 2014. Accessed on December 28, 2016. http://www.ebony.com/wellness-empowerment/the-beautiful-face-of-mental-illness-042#axzz4U9IxQ9lf.

Zook, Kristal Brent. *Color by Fox: The Fox Network and the Revolution in Black Television.* United Kingdom: Oxford University Press, 1994.

Index

ABC 13, 17–18, 24, 37, 83–84, 86, 138, 140, 143, 147, 174, 178
Abrahams, Roger 64
Acham, Christine 4, 13, 142
activists 25, 66–67, 98, 101, 113, 146, 166
addiction 22, 39, 52, 91, 100, 142, 171
Africana womanism *see* womanism
Agboh, Courtney Kemp 70
Ailes, Roger 144, 146
Akeelah and the Bee 16
Akil, Mara Brock 14
Alexander, Michelle 45, 96
Ali, Muhammad 15
All in the Family 30
American Cold War propaganda 29
American dream 6, 28, 44, 56–58, 64, 68–69, 73–74, 79–81, 142, 179, 188
American Gangster 61, 63
American Race (docuseries) 165
Amos, Janes 30, 32
The Amos 'n' Andy Show 13, 85, 108, 162
Amsterdam News 60
Ang, Ien 4, 19, 54, 167
Animal Kingdom 6, 83
Another World 2
anti-hero 6, 17, 70, 83, 95
Armwood, George 58
Asante, Molefi Kete 4
athlete 7, 35, 113–114, 166, 174
Atlanta 9, 24, 182–185

bad man 64–67
Baldwin, James 58, 122
Ball in the Family 173
Ballers 9, 173
Barkley, Charles 165
Barnes, Leroy "Nicky" 63
Barris, Kenya 53
Bavity.com 25
A Beautiful Mind 20
Beck, Robert *see* Slim, Iceberg
Being Mary Jane 6, 90
Belafonte, Harry 12, 68
The Bernie Mac Show 5
Berry, Halle 15

Between the World and Me 118
The Beulah Show 13, 84–85, 162
Beyonce 7, 77, 80, 83, 103–106, 108, 131, 185
Billingsley, Andrew 32
bipolar disorder 7, 39, 41, 44, 46–47, 100, 110, 135, 168, 181
The Birth of a Nation 11, 129
The Birth of a Race 12
bitch 43, 63, 83, 97, 103, 106, 108, 134
black bourgeoisie 5, 50, 59
Black Entertainment Television (BET) 14
Black Families in White America (book) 32
Black Feminist Movement 103
Black Lightning 55, 190–191
Black Lives Matter 2, 15, 92, 104–105, 147
black manhood 32, 130, 180, 182, 189
black masculinity 7, 12, 41, 57, 110–111, 114, 122–123, 130–131, 135, 147, 174
Black Nationalism 6, 66, 99
Black Panther (movie) 9, 194
Black Panther Party 2, 62, 66, 99, 104
black pathologies 4, 31, 33
black power 3–4, 13, 30, 50, 99, 104, 107, 113, 188
Black Power Movement 67, 98–99, 115
Black Queer Identity Matrix 121
black Twitter 4, 8, 25, 88
black womanhood 35, 84, 86, 93, 104, 193
Blackbird 123
blackface 12
Black-ish 5, 24, 37, 46, 53–55, 83, 114
blackness 11–14, 24, 30, 36–37, 49–50, 67–68, 92, 112–116, 118, 137, 140, 173, 179, 189, 194
Blaxploitation 2, 6, 67–68, 97, 108, 163
Blige, Mary J. 93
Bogle, Donald 4–5, 12, 67
bootlegger 76, 79, 92
Boston Globe 35
Bowser, Yvette Denise Lee 86
Boyd, Todd 164
Boylorn, Robin 93
Braxton Family Values 55
The Breakfast Club 121, 145
The Breaks 190
Brearley, H.C. 62

Brown, Cecil 6, 62
Brown, Chris 7
Buckley, William F. 58
Buffy the Vampire Slayer 16
Bumpy *see* Johnson, Ellsworth
The Butler 16
Butters, Gerald 12
Byers, Trai 7

Cabin in the Sky 12
Capone, Al 76
Cardi B. 91, 98, 109
Carmen Jones 12
The Carmichael Show 5, 9, 46, 53–55, 166, 173
Carrington, Alexis (*Dynasty*) 17, 94, 109
Carringtons 27, 54
Carroll, Diahann 17, 32, 85
Carter, Shawn *see* Jay-Z
CBS 3, 13, 18, 30, 122, 138, 147–148, 166
Chaiken, Ilene 20, 134
Chained in Silence: Black Women and Convict Labor in the New South (book) 95
Chance the Rapper 20, 169
Chappell's Show 15
The Chi 182
Chicago Defender 12
Chuck D. 14
civil rights 30, 50–51, 80, 84–85, 88, 98–99, 104, 112, 122–123, 162, 166
class *see* social class
Claws 9, 192
Cleopatra Jones 108
Clueless 113
Coates, Ta-Nehisi 58, 118, 162
Cobb, William Jelani 129
cocaine 6, 38, 45, 68–69, 74, 82, 138, 144
Coffy 7, 97, 100, 108
Cole, J. 20 169
Collins, Joan *see* Carrington, Alexis
colonized mind 116
Color by Fox: The Fox Network and the Revolution in Black Television 4, 142
colorism 16, 35, 50, 59, 90, 179, 189, 192
Combs, Sean "Puffy" 17, 78
Complex magazine 23
Cone, James 58
Cool Pose: The Dilemma of Black Manhood in America (book) 130
coon 12, 136–137, 141–142, 163
Coontz, Stephanie 5, 29
Cops 8
corporal punishment 43, 46
Cosby, Bill 33–37, 68, 140, 144, 163
The Cosby Show 1, 14, 23, 45–46, 49, 86, 93, 165–166
criminal (crime) 6, 8, 18, 27, 29, 37–38, 53, 56, 59–61, 66–67, 71–72, 76, 81, 138–139, 168, 193
Crisis magazine 59

Dallas 2, 4, 18, 19, 28, 52–54
Dandridge, Dorothy 12

Daniels, Lee 2, 15, 16, 17, 99, 121–122, 147, 148, 166; survey about *Empire* 148–161, 167–169
Davis, Angela 99, 109
Davis, Viola 89, 166
Days of Our Lives 2
Dean, Ester 20
Dear White People 187
Deep Down in the Jungle: Negro Narrative Folklore from the Streets of Philadelphia 65
Deggans, Eric 165
Detroit 9
Deveraux, Dominique *see* Carroll, Diahann
deviance 47, 62
A Different World 1, 14
disrespectability politics 93
Dobson, Tamara 108
Doubt 170
Drake 7, 111, 130–133
drug dealer 2, 6, 22, 27, 38, 45, 56, 59, 63, 66, 68-69, 70–72, 74–75, 82, 91, 96–97, 112, 126–128, 160, 163, 177
drug trade 5, 22, 27, 75, 167, 189
drugs 39, 40–41, 45, 51, 56, 59, 71, 73, 75, 80, 91, 100, 108, 129, 151, 177, 180, 184, 189, 192
DuBois, W.E.B. 57
Dunn, Stephane 108
DuVernay, Ava 117, 181
Dynasty 2, 4, 17, 18, 19, 28, 54
dysfunction 4–5, 8, 17–19, 27, 31, 38, 48, 54, 133, 137, 143, 151–152, 161, 167, 174, 192
Dyson, Michael Eric 5, 44, 116, 163

Ebony magazine 31, 32, 37, 44, 99
economic marketability 8, 16, 19, 21, 23, 24, 25
Ellison, Ralph 13
Enlightened Racism: The Cosby Show, Audiences and the Myth of the American Dream 44
Esquire magazine 77
Essence magazine 33, 99
The Ethel Waters Show 84
Ewing, J.R. (*Dallas*) 18
Ewing, Sue Ellen (*Dallas*) 6
Ewings 27, 54
ex-convict 66, 82, 92, 95–96

family 1–8, 13–14, 17–19, 21, 23–24, 26–55, 57, 60, 65, 69, 73–74, 80, 84, 89–96, 100, 102, 110—113, 117–119, 121, 131, 134–135, 138–139, 143–144, 166–167, 169, 172–181, 184, 186, 191–193
Family Matters 14
Farrakhan, Minister Louis, Sr. 121
fashion (attire) 17, 18, 20, 21, 24, 61, 70–72, 76, 78–79, 83, 87, 89, 93–95, 99, 104, 106–109, 130
Fat Albert and the Cosby Kids 34
Father Knows Best 29, 30
Female Masculinity 39
feminism 6, 7, 18, 35, 81, 83–84, 98–99, 102, 104, 106, 108–109
The Feminist Wire (magazine) 95, 108

Fences 9, 39, 68
Fire (magazine) 164
The Fire Next Time 118
Flores, Elaine 47–48
Fogel, Jennifer 4, 5, 29
Footnotes to "The Story of O.J." 115
Fox News Channel 8
FOX programming 2, 4, 8, 14, 21–24, 82, 86, 137–148, 167, 170–172, 178
Foxy Brown 7, 97, 108
Franklin, John Hope 4, 65
Frank's Place 14, 166
Frazier, E. Franklin 4, 5, 31, 50, 59
The Fresh Prince of Bel Air 5, 14, 24, 27, 49, 112–113
From Trickster to Badman 6

Gaines, Kevin 50, 162
The Game 86
gangster 67, 70, 73–74
Gates, Henry Louis, Jr. 5, 44, 96, 145
gender 3, 5, 11, 29, 35, 93, 103, 109, 167, 170–171, 173–174, 181
generation Xers 4
Generations 2
Geraghty, Christine 4, 95
Get Christie Love! 86–87
Get Out 9, 116, 194
ghetto 83, 86, 93; *see also* ratchet
Gibson, Ernest L., III 70
Girlfriends 86
Givhan, Robin 78, 87, 93
Glover, Donald 143, 182–185
god-complex 72
The Godfather 119
Goff, Keli 47
Goines, Donald 68
Gone with the Wind 13, 85
Good Times 5, 13, 27, 30–33, 86
Graham, Rev. Danielle 48
Graham, Otis 5, 27, 50–51
Gray, Bryshere 7
Gray, Herman 4, 11, 14, 33, 140
Gray, Linda *see* Ewing, Sue Ellen
Grazer, Brian 19, 61
The Great Gatsby 59, 79
Greek tragedy 19
Greenleaf 5, 9, 24, 53, 55, 123, 175–178
Grier, Pam 7, 83, 97, 99, 109
Griffith, D.W. 11
Growing Up Hip Hop 173
Grown-ish 37
Guerrero, Ed 67–68
Guess Who's Coming to Dinner? 112
Gutman, Herbert 4, 31

Hagman, Larry *see* Ewing, J.R.
Hall, Stuart 4
The Handmaid's Tale 83
Harlem Renaissance 12
Harpo Films 15

The Haves and the Have Nots 5, 52
The Hazel Scott Show 84
HBCUs 59
Hell-Bound 162
Henson, Taraji P. 3, 6, 21, 24, 82–83, 94, 99
heroin abuse 62–63
heroine 7, 68, 83, 86–88, 93, 97, 99, 105, 108–109, 185
Hidden Figures 9
Higginbotham, Evelyn Brooks 162
hip-hop 2, 5, 6, 7, 8, 14, 20, 22, 27, 37, 47, 49, 51, 74, 77, 83, 104, 110–112, 125–131, 136, 173
Hip-Hop: Beyond Beats and Rhymes (documentary) 126
hip-hop feminism 98, 103–104, 109
Hirsch, Arnold 30
Holstein, Casper 59
homophobia 22, 107, 120, 122, 125
homosexuality *see* LGBTQ
hooks, bell 108, 130
Horne, Lena 103
House of Lies 114, 125
How to Get Away with Murder 6, 24, 89, 95
Howard, Terrence 3, 6
Howard University 1, 12, 53
The Huffington Post 102, 113
Humphrey, Robert 7
Hunt, Darnell M. 4, 165
hustler 67–68, 72, 74–75, 93
Huxtable, Clair 35, 52, 93, 109
Huxtables 1, 5, 14, 27, 53, 54, 165
hypermasculinity 132

I Am Not Your Negro 9
I Love Lucy 1
I Spy 13, 34
Imitation of Life 13
In Living Color 8, 140
incarceration 54, 60, 65, 72, 83, 90, 95–96, 105–106, 109, 117–118, 120
initial public offering (IPO) 38, 111
Insecure 15, 24, 107, 185–187
interracial relationships 88, 114

Jackson, Curtis "50 Cent" 70
Jackson, Kenneth A. 69
Jackson family (Joe, Michael, etc.) 5, 27
Jay-Z 6, 17, 26, 74–81, 104, 106, 108, 130, 132–133, 145
Jefferson, Margo 5, 27, 50
The Jeffersons 5, 13, 27, 33, 86
Jerkins, Rodney "Darkchild" 20
Jet 60
Jezebel 107, 109
Jhally, Sut 5, 44
Jim Crow 2, 29, 31, 45, 47, 113
Johnson, Ellsworth 50
Johnson, George 12
Johnson, Pres. Lyndon 31
Johnson, Nobel P. 12
Julia 13, 31, 33, 36, 85

230 Index

Keating, Annalise 6, 83, 87, 109
Kelley, Robin D.G. 5, 67
King, Martin Luther, Jr. 57, 62, 67, 162
King Lear 17
Ku Klux Klan (KKK) 11, 58

The L Word 20
Lamar, Kendrick 20, 169
Lear, Norman 14, 30
Leave It to Beaver 1, 29, 44
Lee, Spike 14, 79, 163
Lemon, Don 25, 136
Lethal Weapon 9, 22
Levittown 29
Lewis, Justin 5, 44
Lewis, Tarika 99
LGBTQ 2, 7, 17, 21, 43, 45, 52, 110, 119–128
Lil' Kim 108–109
Lil Wayne 131
Lilies of the Field 13
The Lincoln Motion Picture Company 12
Lippmann, Walter 57
Living Single 86, 141
Locke, Alain 12, 162
Lost Cause myths 13, 85
Lucas, Frank 60, 62–63
Luke Cage 9, 187–190
lynch mobs 58

machismo or macho 130, 132, 135
The Mack (film) 66–68
maid 107
Making the Second Ghetto (book) 30
Malcolm X 58–59, 79, 104–105, 112, 162
mammie 85
manhood 71, 128–129, 131
marketing strategies 21, 22, 24
Marlon 55
Martin 8, 140–141
mass incarceration 2, 22, 25, 45, 95, 106, 138; see also incarceration
Maude 30
McDaniel, Hattie 84
McDonald, Katrina 89
McGhee, Rita 21, 93
Media 191
Medina, Benny 49
mental Illness 2, 7, 22, 39, 41–42, 44–49, 96, 100, 110–112, 118, 122, 128, 181–183, 193
Michaeux, Oscar 12
Miles, Tiya 88
militants 68
Mill, Meek 133
Millennials 4, 8, 24, 25
Miller, Monica L. 78
The Minds of Marginalized Black Men 69–70
minstrel or minstrelsy 2, 13, 32, 137
misognoir 95
misogyny 20, 107, 122, 128, 136
Modleski, Tania 4
Mo'Nique 15

Monster's Ball 15, 163
Moonlight 9, 126, 164
Morrison, Toni 103
Mosley, Timothy "Timbaland" 20
Moyers, Bill 35–36, 54
Moynihan, Daniel P. 4, 5, 31, 54
The Moynihan Report 4, 5, 28, 31, 85
Mozart's Requiem 20
MTV generation 8
Mudbound 9
murder 63, 65, 71–73, 97, 99, 106, 120
Murdock, Rupert 137, 144, 148
music 3, 20, 22, 24, 27, 36, 38, 40, 41, 43–44, 49–50, 56, 74–76, 100, 103–105, 107–108, 119–121
Music Moguls 173
musician 113, 118
My Wife and Kids 37

Nama, Adilifi 187
Nation of Islam 58
The National Association for the Advancement of Colored People (NAACP) 12, 13, 59, 85, 162
NBC 23–24, 32, 34, 44, 46, 49, 54, 85–86, 103, 138–140, 142, 147–148, 164, 166, 173, 178, 185
Neal, Mark Anthony 6, 70, 77, 78
Negro 12, 57–58
"The Negro Family: The Case for National Action" 31
The Negro Soldier 12
Negro World (magazine) 60
new black programming 173–193
The New Jim Crow (book) 45
New York Post 2
The New York Times 44, 63
Newsweek 14
Nichols, Nichelle 85
Nieddu, Paulo 20, 21
Nielsen Social Content Ratings 25, 36
nightmare 58–59
Nixon, Pres. Richard 62
The Notorious B.I.G. 129, 142

Obama, Pres. Barack 15, 24, 129, 145
Obama, Michelle 21, 109
occupations (new roles) 85–86, 89–90
O'Connor, John J. 30
O.J.: Made in America 115
Opportunity: A Journal of Negro Life 59–60
Oprah 5, 15, 16, 21, 89
Oprah Winfrey Network (OWN) 23, 52–54
Orange Is the New Black 83, 95
outlaw 6, 56–57, 61–63, 68–69, 71, 80–81, 103
overachiever 110

Paul, Mary Jane 6, 83, 87, 90–91, 109
Perry, Lincoln 12
Perry, Tyler 5, 163
Peterson, James 75, 163
Peyton Place 18

Index

Phillips, David Graham 57
pimp 66, 68, 137
Poitier, Sidney 12, 51, 68, 112
police brutality 25, 59, 88, 96, 151, 189
Pope, Olivia 6, 83, 87, 109
popular culture (definition) 4
Poussaint, Alvin 35, 139-140
poverty 45, 54, 76
Powell, Rev. Adam Clayton, Jr. 84, 122-123
Power (TV drama) 6, 69-70, 121, 133
power 3, 4, 6-9, 11, 13, 27, 42, 51-52, 56-57, 59, 67, 78-81, 83, 93, 94, 98-99, 103-104, 108-109, 161, 169, 172, 188, 191, 193
Precious 15, 16, 163
primetime television records 2, 6, 36
prison 25, 38, 42-43, 45, 51, 58, 60-61, 63, 69, 71-73, 76, 80, 82, 91, 93, 95-97, 100-102, 105, 106, 109, 114, 116-120, 139, 147, 168, 171, 180, 182, 185, 187-189
Psychology Today 47
publicly traded enterprise 2, 38, 56, 65, 78
Purple Rain 15

The Quad 190-191
Queen of the South 6, 83
Queen Sugar 9, 24, 55, 178-182

race films 12
racial profiling 25, 88, 112, 116-117, 179, 189
racial uplift 8, 50-51, 162, 168
racism 29, 44, 50, 71, 74, 81, 85, 117, 122, 139, 147, 164-166, 186
A Raisin in the Sun 65
rapper 7, 14, 20, 37, 40, 60, 74-76, 95, 98, 101, 108, 111, 125-128,, 130, 132-133, 139, 141, 145, 168-169, 173, 182, 190
ratchet 83, 91, 93, 95, 109, 175
Reagan, Pres. Ronald 74
The Real Housewives of Atlanta 93, 123
The Reconstruction 11, 58
Reed Between the Lines 37
respectability 3, 5, 7, 8, 12, 22, 35, 39, 44, 50-51, 93, 98, 107-109, 137, 162-163, 194
Revolution Televised: Prime Time and the Struggle for Black Power 4, 13
Rhimes, Shonda 24, 87, 89, 168
Rihanna 109, 172
rivalry 43
Roberts, John 6, 64, 65
Roc (sitcom) 140
Roc Nation 76
Rolle, Esther 32
The Root 16, 47
Rose, Stephany 79-80
Rosewood 22
Run's House 37

Sanford and Son 13
The Saturday Review 32
#SayHerName movement 25
Scandal 6, 24, 87-88

Scarface 74
Scott, Emmett J. 12
Seale, Bobby 62
sex appeal 83, 97
sexism 99, 128-130
sexual abuse or exploitation 107
Sexual Discretion: Black Masculinity and the Politics of Passing (book) 123
Shaft 99
Shakur, Tupac "2Pac" 129, 142
Sharpton, Rev. Al 25, 164
Sherman, Shantella 51
She's Gotta Have It 187
Sims, Yvonne D. 99
single mother 85
sitcom domesticity 29
Slate magazine 88
slavery 4, 31, 45- 47, 62, 64, 89, 107
Slaves to Fashion: Black Dandyism and the Styling of Black Diasporic Identity (book) 78-79
Slim, Iceberg 68
Smiley, Tavis 136
Smith, Jada 16, 147
Smith, Zadie 116
Smollett, Jussie 7
Snowfall 9
soap opera 2, 4, 5, 6, 18, 19, 53, 167
social class status 3, 44, 50-51, 54, 60, 92
social media 2, 8, 24, 25, 83, 172-173
Solange 92, 109
The Sopranos 5, 27
Soul Train 113
soundtrack 3, 20, 23
spirituality 42, 48, 118, 130
Stagolee 61-62
Stagolee Shot Billy 6, 62
Star 123, 170-171
Star Trek 85
Stepin Fetchit *see* Perry, Lincoln
Stormy Weather 12
Straight Outta Compton 126
Strong, Danny 3, 15, 16, 17, 122, 166
substance abuse 22
Super Black: American Pop Culture and Black Superheroes (book) 187
Super Fly 68-70
super woman 94
superhero 111, 121, 128
survey (*Empire*) 148-161, 167-169
Survivor's Remorse 55
Sweet Sweetback's Baadasssss Song 68
Sweet Tea: Black Gay Men of the South (book) 123

Tales 172
Tarantino, Quentin 16
television networks 137
television ratings 24, 25
13th (documentary) 117
This Is Us 9, 54

thug 72, 80, 100, 118, 133
Thurman, Howard 70–71
T.I. & Tiny: The Family Hustle 37
Timbaland *see* Mosley, Timothy
Time (magazine) 15
TIME: The Kalief Browder Story 77, 117
Toure 116
trickster 64–65
True Colors 140
Trump, Pres. Donald 15, 146, 160, 174
Turner Broadcasting Station (TBS) 14
TV One 22
24: Legacy 9

un-freedom 57
United Paramount Network (UPN) 14, 86, 142–143, 172
Universal Negro Improvement Association 59
Uplifting the Race: Black Leadership, Politics and Culture (book) 50

Van Deburg, William 6, 66–67
Van Peebles, Melvin 68
The Village Voice 44, 126
villain 62, 66, 69
violence 38, 44–47, 49, 59, 71–72, 89, 105, 118–119, 129, 133

Walker, Jimmy 32
Wall Street Journal 21
Walt Disney cartoons 1

War on Drugs 45, 62, 69
Warner Brothers Network (WB or WBN) 14, 142, 172
Washington, Booker T. 57
Watching Race: Television and the Struggle for Blackness (book) 4
Watkins, Boyce 60, 121, 136
We Real Cool (book) 130
Welcome to Sweetie Pie's 55
West, Cornel 59
West, Kanye 7, 80, 130, 132
What's Happening!! 33
Which Way Is Up? 62
White, Armond 16
whore 107
Who's Afraid of Post-Blackness? What It Means to Be Black Now (book) 116
Wilson, Flip 15
Wilson, William Julius 76
The Wire 6, 67, 69, 127
womanism 6, 7, 83, 98, 104, 108–109; *see also* feminism
Women of Blaxploitation: How the Black Action Film Heroine Changed Popular Culture (book) 99
Wretched of the Earth 115

Yo' Mama's Disfunktional! 5

Zook, Kristal Brent 8, 95, 142

www.ingramcontent.com/pod-product-compliance
Lightning Source LLC
Chambersburg PA
CBHW051220300426
44116CB00006B/655